CARNEGIE HILL
Architectural Guide

D0710057

For their generous financial support of this Guide,
Carnegie Hill Neighbors wishes to thank the following:

The Helen Shapiro Memorial Donation

The J.M. Kaplan Furthermore Fund

**New York City Department of Youth & Community Development,
office of New York City Councilmember Daniel Garodnick**

Copyright 2008 by Carnegie Hill Neighbors, Inc.
All rights reserved. No portion of this book may be reproduced
or transmitted in any form or by any means without written
permission from the publisher.

Library of Congress Cataloging in Publication Data Pending

ISBN 978-0-615-25001-4

Printed by
Malloy Incorporated

Printed in the United States of America

CARNEGIE HILL NEIGHBORS, INC.
170 East 91st Street New York, New York 10128
www.carnegiehillneighbors.org

CARNEGIE HILL
Architectural Guide

WITHDRAWN

Prepared by
Members of Carnegie Hill Neighbors
Published by
Carnegie Hill Neighbors, Inc.

SPECIAL THANKS

Carnegie Hill Neighbors gratefully acknowledges the
Helen Shapiro Memorial Donation.
Helen Shapiro, who died in 2002, was a stalwart volunteer in the CHN
Landmarks Committee. Her family chose to honor her memory with an
initial and very substantial contribution to the publication of this guide.

Carnegie Hill Neighbors extends a special thank you to these volunteers:
David Balderston, who photographed countless buildings, edited many
entries, and offered expertise on the architectural styles he writes about in
his "Architectural Column" in the *Carnegie Hill News*;
Laura Henkle, for jumpstarting the project, and for her guidance and research;
Gina Morehead, whose design talent enhances all CHN's printed material,
for developing the unique graphic signature of this book;
Bo Niles, who wrote building descriptions and most of the architect
biographies, created the walks, and edited more than a hundred entries; and
Shari Thompson, who created the text style format followed by all writers,
edited several hundred entries and did the final editing of the entire book.

Special thanks from the volunteers who prepared this Guide to
Lo van der Valk, president of Carnegie Hill Neighbors and head of the
CHN Landmarks Committee, for his invaluable knowledge and guidance.

Carnegie Hill Neighbors thanks **Elizabeth Ashby,** President of Carnegie Hill
Neighbors from 1984 to 1997, and her team of volunteers who produced
Carnegie Hill: An Architectural Guide in 1989, for providing the foundation
for this volume.

ACKNOWLEDGMENTS
For their many hours of volunteer contribution,
Carnegie Hill Neighbors wishes to thank the following:

CONTRIBUTING WRITERS
David Balderston, Barbara Coffey, Karen Dubno, Kathleen Fredrick,
Hélène Golay, Laura Henkle, Jennifer Huntley, Renée Klaperman,
Cynthia MacGrath, Bo Niles

CONSULTING ARCHITECTURAL HISTORIAN
Christopher Gray, with Suzanne Braley

RESEARCH AND FACT-CHECKING
Julia Bradford, Elizabeth Davidson, Leslie Garfield, Laura Henkle,
Ethel Holland, Barbara Meltsner, Marion Morey, Bo Niles,
Eve Roshevsky, Samuel Rotrosen, Alicia Svenson, Shari Thompson

EDITING
David Balderston, Barbara Coffey, Simone Kiropoulos,
Bo Niles, Shari Thompson, Lo van der Valk

ART AND PHOTOGRAPHY
David Balderston, Joan Miller, Gina Morehead, Gail Rodney,
Liz Stecher, Lo van der Valk

GRAPHIC DESIGN Gina Morehead

COMPOSITION Cynthia MacGrath

RIGHTS AND REPRODUCTION Suzanne Goldstein

PRODUCTION Melissa Gibbons, Terri Levine

PROJECT EDITOR Cynthia MacGrath

For their professional support,
Carnegie Hill Neighbors wishes to thank the following:

RESEARCH
Sandy Levine, Tony Robins

PRODUCTION Lisa Shafir

CHN OFFICE STAFF
Monica Hirsch, Andre Leith-Tetrault, Jessica O'Hara-Baker

CONTENTS

INTRODUCTION

Andrew Carnegie's Visiting Card

Nearly twenty years have elapsed since the 1989 publication of *Carnegie Hill: An Architectural Guide*. At that time the Carnegie Hill Historic District, designated in 1974, included a handful of mid-block houses in two small, non-contiguous areas. In 1994 the New York City Landmarks Preservation Commission, largely in response to petitions from Carnegie Hill Neighbors led by then-president Elizabeth Ashby, and working closely with our organization, expanded the Carnegie Hill Historic District to include (and thereby protect) approximately half of the Carnegie Hill geographic area. In 1998 a further half-block, the Hardenbergh/Rhinelander Historic District, was added. Carnegie Hill Neighbors is currently working with the Landmarks Preservation Commission and other groups to designate additional deserving building and streets, especially those east of Lexington Avenue.

It was tempting to take the original slim Guide, which focused on the architectural highlights of Carnegie Hill, update it, and plug in some obvious candidates (like much of Park Avenue and all of Fifth Avenue). But where to stop? The more we looked, the more we discovered: a cherub, a dragon, a dolphin, preserved in limestone or terra cotta; Art Deco ziggurats; medieval waterspouts; an Andy Warhol firehouse-studio. We found that almost every building has some feature which sets it apart it from its neighbor. The result: the original 97 entries mushroomed to 400.

As we walked, observed, and wrote, we became increasingly aware that in spite of the overall cohesive character of the neighborhood there are distinct themes, often (but not always) shaped by architectural styles. This prompted us to create a complete new section on self-guided Carnegie Hill Walks, with a map for each.

The entire project has taken more than three years to complete.

The dedicated work of some 30 volunteers has made the publication of this updated Guide possible. The writing, design, editing, fact-checking, and all visuals except for a few historical pictures and architect photographs have been provided by our volunteers. Every building within the 44-square-block area has been researched, mostly by volunteers, using sources ranging from the Landmarks Preservation Commission designation report, residential knowledge, site visits, books, newspapers, magazine articles, Christopher Gray's Office for Metropolitan History and his *New York Times* "Streetscapes," the New York City Department of Buildings, the Society for Architectural Historians, and other reliable on-line sources. We engaged professional researchers to scour the municipal archives and docket books to determine building dates and architects of some of the more elusive addresses.

It is our hope that the publication of this updated Guide will not only intrigue and enlighten residents, visitors, urban historians and architecture buffs of all stripes, but also will provide a catalyst to preserve and protect many of the deserving buildings in historic Carnegie Hill.

Cynthia MacGrath

HOW TO USE THIS GUIDE

The buildings described in this Guide are listed from south to north and from west to east, starting with the avenues and followed by the cross streets. Each building that is a designated landmark or is within the Carnegie Hill Historic District of 1993 is followed by **LM** or **HD** after the entry. Almost all of the 400-plus buildings or rows are discussed, some albeit briefly. A few are simply listed in the building index.

Every effort has been made to ensure that information in this book is factual and as up-to-date as possible at press time. However, inaccuracies or disputed content may exist. Carnegie Hill Neighbors welcomes your comments and will make every attempt to correct errors and incorporate new information in future editions.

ILLUSTRATION CREDITS

HISTORY SECTION

Title page and pages 2 and 10 (Henry Phipps house, street view), courtesy of Museum of the City of New York.

Pages 5, 6, and 9 (street views), pages 7 and 8, courtesy of the New-York Historical Society.

Page 6, Ruppert mansion, courtesy of K. Jacob Ruppert & Family.

Page 6, George Ehret house, courtesy of the New York Public Library, Astor, Lenox and Tilden Foundations.

Page 10, James Speyer house, Michael C. Kathrens, *Great Houses of New York, 1880-1930,* Acanthus Press, 2005.

BUILDINGS

Pages 8, 211, 277, Squadron A (Eighth Regiment) Armory, photograph courtesy of the New-York Historical Society.

Pages 13, 15, 117, 255, Church St. Thomas More, art and photographs courtesy of Margaret Peet, Church of St. Thomas More.

Pages 15, 21, 30, Jewish Museum art, artwork courtesy of the Jewish Museum and of Kevin Roche John Dinkeloo Associates.

Pages 19, 26, Guggenheim Museum, courtesy of The Solomon R. Guggenheim Museum, New York. Photograph by David Heald ©The Solomon R. Guggenheim Foundation, New York.

Pages 136, 253, Otto Kahn Mansion, art courtesy of the Convent of the Sacred Heart.

Pages 137, 250 and back cover flap, Andrew Carnegie Mansion, photograph courtesy of Cooper-Hewitt, National Design Museum, Smithsonian Institution.

Page 149, 70 East 91st Street, art courtesy of Joseph F. Peyronnin.

Page 280, elevation drawing of Francis F. Palmer house by Delano & Aldrich, courtesy of Avery Architectural & Fine Arts Library, Columbia University.

ARCHITECTS, Page 278

William Adams Delano and Chester Holmes Aldrich, courtesy of the Century Association Archives Foundation.

J.E.R. Carpenter, courtesy of Christopher Gray, Office for Metropolitan History.

John Russell Pope, photograph by Alfredo Valente, courtesy of the U.S. National Archives and Records Administration, Group 64.

Henry J. Hardenbergh, Moses King, *Notable New Yorkers of 1896-1899,* a Companion Volume to King's Handbook of New York City, 1899.

Horace Trumbauer, courtesy of Print and Picture Collection, The Free Library of Philadelphia.

Whitney Warren, Warren & Wetmore Collection, courtesy of Avery Architectural and Fine Arts Library, Columbia University.

Charles Delavan Wetmore, Edward Weeks, *My Green Age,* Boston, Little, Brown & Company, 1973.

John Merven Carrère and Thomas Hastings, courtesy of New-York Historical Society.

Frank Lloyd Wright, photograph by Al Ravenna, Library of Congress, Prints and Photographs Division.

Every reasonable attempt has been made to identify the owners of copyright. Errors of omission will be corrected in subsequent printing of this work.

PREFACE

Every neighborhood needs a guide like this one—and every neighborhood needs a group like Carnegie Hill Neighbors, which since 1970 has been looking out for the interests of this unusual plateau, centered around Andrew Carnegie's great house at 91st and Fifth.

The *Carnegie Hill Architectural Guide,* covering over 400 buildings, expertly picks out the individual threads of this tapestry, running from tenements and farmhouses to mansions and fancy co-ops. It will be of service to anyone: from the novice, who can follow the intricately composed walking tours, to the person who "knows everything" about Carnegie Hill (and boy are there lots of those!)

The former group are lucky initiates. Imagine seeing for the first time the stupendous sweep of 91st Street's mansion row, off Fifth Avenue! And to the latter the familiar blocks they have known for years may seem as strangers to them. Who knew how many oriels, triglyphs, dentils, flutes, cartouches, modillions and other arcana lined our streets?

For this guide pays closest attention to the rich architectural detail up and down every block. Have you ever noticed the Dutch girls at 1075 Park? Not me—and I've lived a block away for two decades!

Of course, the *Carnegie Hill Architectural Guide* covers the major monuments. To take just a three block stretch, Frank Lloyd Wright's ornery Guggenheim, then the sublime proto-art deco Church of the Heavenly Rest, and then Andrew Carnegie's mansion, the largest on the hill. My favorite among the big private houses is the often overlooked House of the Redeemer at 7 East 95th Street, a peculiar and wonderful Tuscan-style house of 1917 by Grosvenor Atterbury. It is very unusual in its astonishing integrity, down to the pantry cabinets and top floor maids' rooms. But its most special flavor is an absence of something, an absence of being "preserved" or, sometimes worse, "restored." It just simply is, without melodrama, an Episcopal retreat for half a century almost untouched by time, and which now has concerts, lectures and parties. Whatever the opportunity, go—you will be captivated.

Another unusual residence is the guest house of George F. Baker, Jr., who also had Delano & Aldrich design his mansion at Park Avenue and 93rd Street, now the Russian Orthodox Church Outside of Russia. When Edward Ulmann, the squash champion, diarist and millionaire sportsman lived in the house, at 67 East 93rd Street, he marveled that, "In the dining room, you never had the smell of food because the kitchen was in the basement—in fact, it took me several years to discover we even had a kitchen. There was a bank of freezers that wouldn't have surprised the captain of the QE2."

For me—one of those supposedly "know everything" bores—the best stretches of the guide are those with the more obscure structures, usually east of Park. Who could have imagined the unlikely journey of the otherwise anonymous 1390 Lexington Avenue, which was built on 92nd Street in the 1850s, moved to its present site in 1869, extended upwards in 1871, altered in 1905 and refaced in 1931?

And I have long wondered what a "kolping" was. Turns out, it's really a who—Adolph Kolping, a south German priest who in 1845 dedicated his life to the welfare of young journeymen, a movement which evolved into the present Kolping House at 165 East 88th, a somewhat dour but rich, atmospheric piece of "real Yorkville," created as lodgings for German youth referred by a pastor, school or employer.

Another oddball is the delicious Moderne apartment house of 1937 at 151 East 90th Street by the fascinating Horace Ginsbern, who performed the feat of giving it corner windows despite its inside lot. This gem still has its original steel casement windows—hurry to see them, for they surely cannot last much longer.

Also between Lexington and Third is the garage of Willard and Dorothy Straight, at 162 East 92nd. They had Delano & Aldrich design not only their impeccably tailored house at Fifth and 94th but also this chaste little building, despite some clunky alterations in the past. These pairings of mansions and carriage houses could make an interesting little study: Otto Kahn built his own giant house at Fifth and 91st and his garage still stands at 424 East 89th Street. And Carnegie's "automobile house" (as it was called when designed) still stands at 55 East 90th Street, although nearly squashed to death by a later, quite uninspired addition.

Like me, everyone has their own personal take on the history of Carnegie Hill. The doorman at the recently-named "Gatsby" told a guidebook researcher that his building is so named because F. Scott Fitzgerald's son lived there. Indeed Scott and Zelda did have a child, also named Scott, but better known as Scottie—a girl. It would be riveting to do another history of Carnegie Hill, just from the accounts of doormen.

Many of these entries are outside existing historic districts, and that sets this remarkable guide apart from similar efforts all over the city. Carnegie Hill Neighbors take as their text not just the buildings within existing historic districts—as if everything beyond those boundaries were irrelevant—but the entire area, the good, the bad and the so-so. That is a completely different kind of vision for a preservation organization, and one which bestows honor upon both this remarkable neighborhood, and upon its protectors.

To both strangers and veterans, this book says, "Welcome to Carnegie Hill."

Christopher Gray

A BRIEF HISTORY

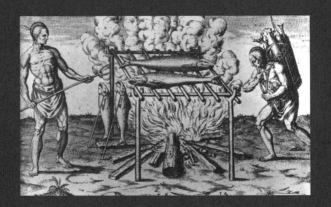

The neighborhood called Carnegie Hill has not always been known for its historical architecture. The history has been in the making for centuries. The name Carnegie Hill was first used in the early 1900s to describe a few blocks surrounding Andrew Carnegie's mansion at 91st Street and Fifth Avenue. Today it extends from Fifth Avenue to Third Avenue, from 86th Street to 96th Street, and from Fifth Avenue to Park Avenue up to 98th Street, and is home to 28 individually landmarked buildings. The original Carnegie Hill Historic District, designated by the New York City Landmarks Preservation Commission in 1974, was comprised of two non-contiguous areas west of Park Avenue and was expanded in 1994 to include 40 percent of Carnegie Hill. The small Hardenbergh/ Rhinelander Historic District (1340-1350 Lexington Avenue and 121 East 89th Street) was added in 1998. Carnegie Hill Neighbors is working to have several blocks east of Lexington Avenue, lined with some of the oldest row houses in the area, as well as all of Park Avenue in Carnegie Hill, designated.

When Andrew Carnegie moved his family into their new Fifth Avenue residence in 1902, the Carnegie mansion, now the Cooper-Hewitt, National Design Museum, Smithsonian Institution, established Carnegie Hill as one of the finest residential sections of Manhattan. The history of Carnegie Hill, both before Andrew Carnegie and after him, is clearly shown in its streets and especially in its architecture, which represents styles typical of several eras in the history of New York City. Because of this history and CHN's efforts to preserve it, Carnegie Hill is a unique section of the city.

In the beginning, there were Indians

Before Henry Hudson sailed up the Hudson River in 1609, the Carnegie Hill landscape rose and dipped with hills and valleys and was intersected by several streams. It was the hilliest part of the island called Manhatta (literally, "hilly island") by the Indians who inhabited its upper portion. Near what is now the intersection of East 98th Street and Park Avenue stood the Indian village of Konaande Kongh, meaning "the place near the sand." Overlooking the Hell Gate Bay and the sandy point that then extended along the mouth of the Harlem Creek into the East River, it was home to roughly 60 Wickquasgeck Indians, who lived in bark-covered houses, each with a single center hole to ventilate the smoke of fires. The holes did not ventilate very effectively, but the fumes were useful as a sort of insecticide to keep out the "muskettas," which hatched in the nearby river flats. The village bordered on a spring-fed brook and was positioned on a branch of a footpath that went down to what is now East 96th Street and across into

An early view with local residents.

what is now Central Park. It connected with the Manhattan Path, which then continued down the island to the territory of the Canarsie Indians. The Wickquasgeck hunted, trapped, fished, gathered clams and oysters, and picked blueberries. They also cultivated beans, pumpkins, and corn and tapped syrup from the maple trees for their corn bread.

With the sale of Manhattan to the Dutch in 1624, white settlers began to cultivate the flat land alongside the East River in the area now called East Harlem. This was considered the choicest location on the island for farming because it was protected from icy blasts off the Hudson River, the soil was rich, and it was clear of trees.

Although the Wickquasgeck were gentle by nature, the Dutch and later the English regarded them with suspicion. Eventually, this mistrust resulted in several Indian wars. The consequence of one of these wars was the formation by settlers of New Harlem, a fortified and neatly laid-out village, in an area above the Indian path that ran diagonally between what are now 125th and 110th streets before crossing what is now Central Park to connect the Hudson and East rivers. Its boundaries, which separated New Harlem from New York, were fixed in 1664 by the first British Governor, Colonel Nichols, to run from the Hudson River at what is now 129th Street to the East River at what is now 74th Street. A portion of Carnegie Hill fell within the boundaries of what was known as the Common Lands of New Harlem and was owned by the freeholders of that growing community. Too hilly for farming, too far inland for river traffic, and too far from lower Manhattan for building speculation, this land remained unfenced, untilled, and uninhabited, and it was not divided into lots until the 19th century.

On Waldron Farm

What today is Carnegie Hill and its surrounding area became part of a large tract of farmland that can be traced back to at least 1677, when it belonged to one Peter Van Ogliensis. The farm extended from about what is now 82nd Street to 94th Street, and from Harlem Commons (Fifth Avenue) to the East River. The area was known as Waldron Farm after a Dutch patent conveyed the land to Baron Resolved Waldron, who owned it until he died in 1705. His son Samuel and, in turn, his grandson William became owners of the farm. The farm underwent no material change for more than 50 years until it was divided by William Waldron's heirs after his death in December, 1769.

One of Waldron's sons, Adolph Waldron, gained the bulk of the property and, apparently, lost it all as well. Abraham Duryea, a merchant of the City of New York, bought the farm at auction for 800 pounds. The borders of the farm were described for the transaction in detail, following the style of the time, as "all that piece or parcel of land situated lying and being in Harlem division of the outward of the City of New York aforesaid on which William Waldron deceased lately lived beginning at a cleft in a large rock at the waterside, hence running south . . . to a stone marked W thence south . . . to the stump of a large chestnut tree . . . etc. etc. along the waterside to the beginning bounded northerly and westerly by the land late of the said William Waldron deceased and easterly by the sound at Hell Gate Cove or Horn's Hook containing thirty four acres . . ." There is no documentation regarding further distribution of the original Waldron Farm, although an 1880 map shows extinct borders of smaller farm parcels and is evidence that sections of Waldron Farm were eventually sold to a number of people.

In 1807, in anticipation of heavy immigration to the United States through the port of New York, three commissioners were appointed by the state to lay out streets north of the tip of Manhattan in a grid pattern of identical rectangular boxes suitable for similarly-shaped buildings. This plan, which was issued in 1811, set up the familiar grid of streets and avenues of Manhattan. Speculators who expected the value of land to rise in the years following publication of the grid map invested in East Harlem real estate. In 1825 the Common Lands of New Harlem were surveyed by Charles Clinton and divided into lots, which were put up for sale. They were bought by a man named Selden, who sold off single-owner parcels. However, since there were as yet no people to live in these streets, the area remained semi-rural until the 1880s.

At that time there were only two major thoroughfares in upper Manhattan: the Boston Post Road (Third Avenue) and the Bloomingdale Road (Broadway). Fifth and Park avenues were dirt roads, the former used by drovers to reach the Bowery Market in lower Manhattan, the latter crossing the hilly uptown wilderness to the village of Harlem. The great country estates of the old New York families on both rivers were served by long lanes intersecting the two main arteries. Lexington Avenue (named for the famous Revolutionary War battle of 1775) and Madison Avenue (named for James Madison) were not part of the 1811 grid plan. They were created at the urging of lawyer and real-estate developer Samuel Ruggles (the founder of Gramercy Park) in 1832 and 1833, respectively; in fact, Lexington Avenue was opened through his own property. The road that became 86th Street led west from Hell Gate Ferry, connecting the two coasts of the island.

Observatory Place and the railroads link Yorkville to lower Manhattan
The growth of Carnegie Hill was to a great extent precipitated by the New York and Harlem Railroad, chartered in 1831 to link the lower end of Manhattan with Harlem, seven miles to the north. The object of the railroad was to attract commuters and shoppers away from the riverboats they normally used for the long trip downtown. The line ran along the Bowery and then along Fourth Avenue (now Park Avenue) via a double track of horse-drawn cars from Prince Street. By 1834 there was a stop in Yorkville (the area around 86th Street east of Lexington Avenue) near Observatory Place, a section of open land at 93rd Street that was the highest point on the east side of Manhattan Island. According to a magazine account published that year, the cars ran every half-hour, and for 12 1/2 cents one could travel a five-mile route that afforded "no beautiful view of cultivated fields and gardens, but conveys an idea of the great amount of labor bestowed in cutting the track through hills of solid rock." Upon disembarking, the traveler would find a splendid hotel, Prospect Hall, run by one George Nowlan, and built by the railroad on ten acres of Observatory Place located between 89th and 94th streets and Fourth and Fifth avenues. It was "a spacious two-story building with a piazza round both stories . . . commanding the view of the surrounding country, Hellgate and the East River that has no equal on the island." (In 1865 the state legislature ordered 90th, 91st, 92nd, and 93rd streets opened from Fifth Avenue to Fourth Avenue, abolishing Observatory Place.) In 1837 a deep tunnel was dug through the hard rock of Mount Pleasant, from 92nd to 94th streets, allowing the railroad to progress into the Harlem flatlands and eventually beyond. Locomotives replaced horse-drawn cars in 1839.

Over the next twenty years unemployed Irish immigrants established squatter settlements along the hilly wilderness of Fourth Avenue, eking out a meager existence by milking goats and slaughtering pigs, and scavenging the coal dumped by the locomotives. By the early 1860s, breweries and piano factories appeared among the trackside hovels in response to population growth east and west of the railroad line. As the railroad expanded under the entrepreneurial leadership of Commodore Cornelius Vanderbilt, who housed his extensive train yards and the Grand Central

View southwest from 93rd Street and Park Avenue in 1882. In the foreground stands Prospect Hall, now the site of the Russian Orthodox Church Outside of Russia. The spire of the Church of St. Thomas More on 89th Street is visible in the background.

Depot at street level at Fourth Avenue and 42nd Street, there was a public outcry over coach and pedestrian safety as well as appearance. Under the influence of the newly formed Fourth Avenue Improvement Committee, by 1875 most of the Grand Central tracks had been lowered and spanned with iron bridges, and the remaining tracks to 96th Street had been expanded to four and sunk in cuts and channels. From 56th Street to the 90s the two outer tracks were roofed over; the center ones were topped by fenced-in but bare malls with large open ventilation slots that conveyed the thunderous noise and the polluting cinders and smoke of the locomotives onto Fourth Avenue. Nevertheless, the improved appearance of the avenue eventually attracted hospitals, armories, and schools, and the occasional elegant house on Lenox Hill and in the hilly 93rd Street area, where the cuts were completely roofed over. By the end of the 1880s it was optimistically renamed Park Avenue. The pollution and noise were eventually overcome when the railroad switched from coal to electricity for power after the turn of the 20th century.

Carnegie Hill retained its essentially rural character throughout the 19th century. At about the time of the Civil War (1861-1865), the majority of houses in the area were of frame construction, the work of carpenter-builders, intended for families of moderate means. Because of fire hazards, an overall ban on such buildings was eventually implemented. In any case, these houses were so easily demolished that very few of them have survived in Manhattan intact. Among the few are the landmarked houses at 120, 122, and 160 East 92nd Street and 128 East 93rd Street.

The most notable buildings in Carnegie Hill in the late 19th century were churches and charitable institutions—the New York Magdalen

View west from 95th Street in 1882 with frame construction of the Eagle Hotel at Fifth Avenue and the Ruppert mansion at Fifth Avenue and 93rd Street. Below, the Ruppert mansion, left, and the George Ehret house at 94th Street and Park Avenue.

Asylum, "affording an asylum to erring females," at Fifth Avenue and 88th Street (1850); the St. Luke's Home for Indigent Christian Females at Madison Avenue and East 89th Street (1870); the Protestant Episcopal Church of the Beloved Disciples, subsequently the Reformed Church of Harlem and now the Roman Catholic Church of St. Thomas More, on 89th Street between Madison and Park avenues (1870s); the New York Christian Home for Intemperate Men on 86th Street between Madison and Park avenues; and the Immanuel Lutheran Church on the southwest corner of 88th Street and Lexington Avenue (1885), which was erected by German immigrants for a growing Yorkville congregation.

The first mansions
Among the earliest large residences in Carnegie Hill were those built for nearby breweries. George Ehret, who by 1877 owned the largest brewing

business in the Untied States, built a house on the southeast corner of Park Avenue and 94th Street in 1879. He was followed by Jacob Ruppert, whose mansion on a lot at Fifth Avenue and 93rd Street was an isolated structure surrounded by small farms when it was built in 1881. Neither building now exists. Scattered frame houses, two-story brick buildings, and a few rows of brownstones erected by developers were interspersed with squatters' shacks, which also lined the edges of Central Park.

In 1868 plans for a new elevated railroad to replace the horse-drawn line on Third Avenue that was begun in 1853 and eventually ran up to 125th Street set off a speculative boom in residential construction on the East Side. Some lots are known to have changed hands as often as four times in 60 days, doubling the cost. However, the Panic of 1873, a severe national economic crisis, led to many real-estate foreclosures and brought a temporary halt to construction on the Third Avenue elevated line and another elevated line parallel to it on Second Avenue.

The age of row houses

By the fall of 1891, with both of these elevated lines in operation along with East River ferries, there was a resurgence of building activity. From the mid-1880s through the 1890s, the side streets between Madison and Third avenues, as well as Madison, Park and Lexington avenues, were developed on speculation with small brownstone row houses intended for people of "modest fortune." This building boom constitutes the first of three major periods of development in Carnegie Hill. Because the determining factor in the architectural design of these small houses was not necessarily quality but speed and economy, the houses followed a fairly standard set of plans aiming for uniformity and making the services of a professionally trained architect an unnecessary extravagance. The ornamentation used was dependent on the whim of the architect-builder and his notion of what would sell.

Among these new houses in Carnegie Hill were twelve on the south side of 95th Street and twelve on the north side of 94th Street east of Lexington Avenue, all of which survive, though many have lost their stoops and several have had their facades altered substantially. There were more than a dozen other rows throughout Carnegie Hill, though few survive today. Carnegie

Queen Anne row houses built for William C. Rhinelander on the southeast corner of 89th Street and Lexington Avenue in the late 1880s.

7

The Squadron A (Eighth Regiment) Armory at Madison Avenue at 94th-95th Streets, completed in 1895.

Hill is unique, however, in having many groups of row houses that were designed by professionally trained architects and that are distinguished by their attention to detail. Among these are six brownstones on the north side of 93rd Street between Fifth and Madison avenues and five red-brick houses on the east side of Madison Avenue between 91st and 92nd streets. At this time, too, a few large townhouses were built in uniform rows on Fifth Avenue on a speculative basis, but they lacked individuality.

The Carnegie Hill row houses represent many of the new styles popular in New York City during the last decades of the 19th century: neo-Grec, Queen Anne, Romanesque Revival, and Renaissance Revival.

The most imposing structure erected in this period was an armory, built in 1888, fronting on Park Avenue and extending west for part of the block between 94th and 95th streets. After the social military group called the New York Hussars that used the space became a mounted New York State National Guard Unit in 1889, they commissioned a larger building—the Squadron A Armory—to be built in 1895 in the same castellated style in the remaining block facing Madison Avenue. In 1920 the two interior spaces were combined to create a riding ring encompassing most of the block. Some long-term Carnegie Hill residents remember the polo games and dances that were held in the space. They also recall the clop of hooves as the horses returned at night to the stables within the armory.

Although much of Carnegie Hill was developed in the 1880s and 1890s, squatters still occupied shanties on unimproved lots. Fifth Avenue remained largely the territory of squatters who had moved their animals and gardens out of the recently developed Central Park (1857-1877) onto the still undeveloped east side of Fifth Avenue. Thus when Andrew Carnegie purchased his land between 90th and 91st streets in 1898, squatters were on it. A riding academy was on the 90th Street corner.

Andrew Carnegie's mansion makes uptown upscale

Carnegie built what he called "the most modest, plainest and most roomy house in New York" on a big open lot that provided the air and sunshine that his doctor recommended. He was 65 in 1902, when he moved into the new house on the so-called Highlands of New York. With the construction of the Carnegie mansion, upper Fifth Avenue took on a new appeal. The formerly elite residential section of the avenue from 23rd to 57th streets was rapidly becoming commercial, and wealthy New Yorkers who wanted a fashionable address had to move north. Carnegie's presence established the fine character of upper Fifth Avenue, extending "Millionaire's Row" along the stretch of the avenue facing Central Park. To further ensure the residential character of the neighborhood, Carnegie purchased most of the property on the blocks to the north and south of his lot, selling off parcels only when he was satisfied with the quality of a buyer's plans. Carnegie's land north of 91st Street was sold to such prominent New Yorkers as James A. Burden, John Henry Hammond, Otto Kahn, Charles M. MacNeil, and John B. Trevor. The Kahn, Burden, Hammond, and Trevor houses are now landmarked.

The Carnegie mansion initiated a change in building trends, and the second major period of development in Carnegie Hill. The construction of row houses virtually stopped, to be replaced by larger, elegant townhouses

Looking east on 93rd Street from Lexington Avenue, about 1915.

Two great early mansions: the Henry Phipps house (1905) at 1063 Fifth Avenue, and the James Speyer house (1914) at 1056 Fifth Avenue. Both have been demolished.

for the wealthy who began to pour into the area. In many cases, these residences rivaled the townhouses in other parts of the city. They were designed in revival styles popular at the time: Beaux-Arts, neo-Classical, and neo-Renaissance. Neo-Georgian and neo-Federal styles appeared in the second and third decades of the 20th century. (The term Beaux-Arts is sometimes loosely applied to these gracious townhouses because they represent a particular manner of execution and finish characteristic of professionally trained architects—rather than architect-builders—whose training was based on the model of the Ecole Nationale Superieure des Beaux-Arts in Paris.) Ornamental detail and individuality were far more important than cost, and many resemble French chateaux, Italian palazzi, and English castles. Construction of these fine houses continued until the Depression, although the last large residence, the William Goadby Loew house at 56 East 93rd Street, was completed as late as 1932.

Apartment buildings rise on the avenues
The third major period of development in Carnegie Hill, the construction of luxury apartment buildings, began shortly after the Carnegie mansion was built and burgeoned after World War I. While tenements were standard housing in the 1880s for the largely immigrant

Modest frame houses survived as late as 1915 at the corner of Park Avenue and 86th Street.

population living between Third Avenue and the East River on the Upper East Side, the luxury apartment building with one or two apartments to a floor, high ceilings, wood-paneled rooms, and other amenities normally found in private houses, signaled a new way of life for upper-income families. At the turn of the century the great majority of the well-to-do in Manhattan lived in private residences; by 1935 most lived in luxury apartments.

At first Fifth Avenue saw the most building activity. However, once it had been demonstrated that tall buildings could be built on stilts free from the vibration of the railroad under Park Avenue, elevator apartment living on Park Avenue became fashionable, catching up to Fifth Avenue in popularity. Frame houses, brownstones and vacant lots gave way to what has become the standard living arrangement in Manhattan.

Since the era of the luxury apartment building in Manhattan (1900-1930) corresponds to the eclectic period in American architecture, it is not surprising that the popular revival styles were adapted to apartment buildings in Carnegie Hill. French and Italian styles predominated. In general, the features of these styles were expanded by several stories in order to fit the greater height of apartment buildings. Toward the end of the 1920s sleek Art Deco buildings began to appear, followed by apartment houses with more austere Moderne styling. After World War II a few Modern apartment towers punctuated the skyline.

Over time, major alterations have changed the facades of some of the houses in Carnegie Hill, particularly those dating from the 19th century. Stoops have been removed to provide basement entrances, ornamental details have yielded to smooth stucco refacings, and in a number of cases two row houses have been combined behind an entirely new facade. The lower floors of most of the row houses on Madison and Lexington avenues have been converted into stores. Many of the larger townhouses have been converted into apartments and institutions; Carnegie Hill probably has the largest concentration of private schools in the city today. Nevertheless, these changes have for the most part been done attractively, and the neighborhood retains its residential and historic character.

While evidence of the earliest settlers of Carnegie Hill, the Wickquasgeck Indians, is long gone and Waldron Farm is visible only on a yellowed map, reminders of the era of wooden houses, late-19th-century row houses, and early-20th-century mansions have been preserved and enrich this neighborhood. It is hoped that when the history of Carnegie Hill is revised at the turn of the 22nd century, the landmarks we appreciate today will still give testament to the architectural heritage of this unique part of New York City.

ARCHITECTURAL STYLES
IN CARNEGIE HILL

ITALIANATE (1840-1865) Borrowed from the rural architecture of northern Italy, this style is characterized by overhanging cornices with decorative brackets, round-arched forms, foliate carving, recessed entrances, ornate door and window designs, and high stoops with robust cast-iron railings. 120 and 122 East 92nd Street are among the very few examples of the Italianate style in Carnegie Hill.

NEO-GOTHIC, GOTHIC REVIVAL (1865-1930) This style originated in Europe between the twelfth and sixteenth centuries. It is characterized by rib vaults, battlements, lancet-arched windows, diamond-pane casement windows, hood moldings, tracery arches, buttresses and pinnacles. Neo-Gothic was widely used in the design of churches from the mid-19th through the first quarter of the 20th centuries; the Church of St. Thomas More, at 59-65 East 89th Street, is one of several Northern European Gothic examples in Carnegie Hill. References can be seen in some apartment buildings—notably the Venetian Gothic 1185 Park Avenue.

SECOND EMPIRE (1870-1880) Taking its inspiration from the French Second Empire of Napoleon III (1852-1870), the chief architectural features of this style are the signature high mansard roof with slate shingles and a curb around the top of visible slopes. The style often includes ornate iron cresting and dormer windows with segmental pediments. One of the few Carnegie Hill examples is 1388 Lexington Avenue, near 91st Street.

NEO-GREC (1875-1890) This is the most ubiquitous of the early row house styles in Carnegie Hill because many of the elements could be mass-produced. Houses exhibit boldly protruding wood or galvanized iron cornices and high stoops with railings. The lines are straight and angular; doors and windows are framed with prominent moldings and feature modestly curved brackets under lintels and sills. Doors are often topped by triangular pediments. Decorations are limited to stylized classical and foliate motifs—rosettes, an incised single-line flower, narrow parallel channels, a string of dots. Facades are predominantly brownstone, but a few are brick with brownstone trim. Some houses feature oriels, like those at 115-121 East 91st Street.

QUEEN ANNE (1880-1890) The name comes from the use of Gothic and Renaissance elements revived during the reign of Queen Anne (1702-1714). The style was introduced just before 1870 in England, where its most notable architect was Richard Norman Shaw (1831-1912). As seen in Carnegie Hill, Queen Anne combines neo-Grec and Romanesque Revival elements. Buildings are characterized by asymmetry, eccentric detail, a playful contrast of materials, colors and textures, and use of terra-cotta ornament and colored-glass insets. Details include Tudor roses, sunflowers, molded faces, multi-paneled wood doors, gabled dormers and roof lines, flared chimneys and finials. A charming Queen Anne row may be viewed at 146-156 East 89th Street.

ROMANESQUE REVIVAL (1885-1895) With origins in the ninth-century architecture of France and Italy, this style is robust and masculine. In America its most notable architect was Henry Hobson Richardson (1838-1886). Its characteristic features are asymmetry, rough-faced stonework, broad round arches with voussoirs, stout dwarf columns, and massive, often L-shaped stoops. The fortress-like appearance is offset by stained-glass ornaments, Byzantine-

style carving, carved heads, and foliate ornamentation on friezes, panels, capitals and the walls and newel posts of the stoops. The finest example in Carnegie Hill is 22 East 89th Street, originally the Hotel Graham.

RENAISSANCE REVIVAL (1890-1910) This style marked the return to the classical forms that originated in ancient Greece and Rome and were revived in Italy, spreading throughout Europe during the fifteenth and sixteenth centuries. In Carnegie Hill it brought an end to the eccentric detours of the fanciful Queen Anne and massive Romanesque Revival periods, providing formality, balance and dignity. Characteristics include classical columns supporting entablatures, triangular and segmental pediments, finely molded window enframements, scroll decorations, medallions and carved floral motifs. 1326 and 1350 Madison Avenue and 1240 Park Avenue are good examples of Renaissance Revival apartment buildings.

FRANCOIS I, CHATEAUESQUE (1900-1920) This style is loosely based on chateaux of the Loire valley, built during the reign of Francois I (1515-1547). The castle-like buildings featured steeply pitched hipped roofs, round turrets, wall dormers, gabled parapets, spires and elaborate Gothic detailing. Windows are arched with a "basket handle" at the apex, and often add hood moldings and tracery. Favorite embellishments include cherubs, gargoyles, dragons and griffins. The only examples in Carnegie Hill are 1067 Fifth Avenue and 1109 Fifth Avenue, the Jewish Museum.

BEAUX-ARTS (1900-1928) This style is derived from the same European model as Renaissance Revival architecture but is more ornate, and is seen mostly in townhouses of the wealthy and in grand public buildings. Facades are usually of deeply rusticated limestone or marble and may include bow fronts with large brackets to support shallow balconies, often with fine iron railings or balustrades. Ornamentation includes swags, scrolls and cartouches. The second floor, often termed the *piano nobile,* is emphasized by its unusual height and dominant windows or French doors with elegant enframements. The National Design Academy, at 1083 Fifth Avenue, is an outstanding example.

NEO-CLASSICAL (1905-1925) This term refers to a mid-18th-century movement in France and England that was a reaction to the excesses of the late Baroque and Rococo styles; it is rooted in the Greek and Roman classical orders. Houses are flat-roofed, subdued and dignified; facades are of stone and are symmetrically designed, punctuated with rhythmic rows of columns, windows or French doors. 1 East 94th Street and the Andrew Carnegie public library at 112 East 96th Street are the neighborhood's prime examples.

NEO-RENAISSANCE (1910-1930) Similar to the earlier Renaissance Revival and Beaux-Arts styles, details are executed with less flamboyance and more sophistication and restraint. Characteristics include subdued classical motifs such as fluted pilasters and swags, spandrels, urns, quoins, and segmentally-arched windows with carved tympana. The style is seen in some townhouses but primarily in medium-height and tall apartment houses like many of those lining Fifth and Park avenues.

NEO-GEORGIAN, NEO-FEDERAL

(1915-1930) These very similar styles refer to the period in America from 1700 through the Revolution, and represent a British interpretation of classical elements by designers such as Christopher Wren and Robert Adam. The facades are characteristically of red brick with contrasting white trim. Window lintels are often a single white stone, sometimes splayed at the corner or with a slight peak. The Georgian entrance often used rectangular panes in a transom, while Federal doors added sidelights and a fanlight. The Georgian facade was a flat plane, while the Federal front might add bay windows and a small portico. In Carnegie Hill the styles are seen in townhouses and mansions of the wealthy, notably the Delano & Aldrich complex at 67-75 East 93rd Street, now the Russian Orthodox Church Outside of Russia.

NEO-REGENCY (1920-1930)

A variation of neo-Classical, this style derives from a style popular during George IV's regency as Prince of Wales from 1811 to 1820. Characteristics include scrollwork, curves, and strict balance and proportion. The Loew mansion at 56 East 93rd Street, now the Spence School, is an excellent example.

NEO-MEDIEVAL, NEO-TUDOR (1920-1930)

This style combines neo-Gothic and Romanesque Revival elements. Facades are usually of brick and include fortress-like details: crenelations, battlements, turrets, trefoils, escutcheons and crossed swords. The style was often favored by the architect George F. Pelham (1866-1937), as at 51 East 90th Street.

MEDITERRANEAN REVIVAL

(1925-1930) The characteristic features of this style are stuccoed facades, pitched tiled roofs and gabled towers, reflecting Moorish and Spanish influences. A curious example can be seen at 140 East 95th Street.

ART DECO (1925-1935) The fashionable Jazz Age style was first presented at the Exposition Internationale des Arts Décoratifs et Industriels Modernes held in Paris in 1925. The style strove for sleekness and modernity to communicate strength, speed and energy. Art Deco is characterized by geometric ornament (parallel straight lines, zigzags, chevrons, and circles), streamlined floral motifs and the curves of ocean liners. An important motif is the ziggurat, used both as a structural and an ornamental form, sometimes designed in a series of arcs. Emphasis was on verticality, expressed by small flare-ups at the termination of a column on a roof line, and in windows designed in vertical strips. Materials included stainless steel, chrome, glass, mosaic and marble, often in black and white. An exuberant Art Deco building can be seen at 19 East 88th Street.

MODERNE (1930-1940)

This style is similar to Art Deco, with streamlined geometrical elements and stylized classical detailing. Ornament is held to a minimum except for horizontal or vertical grooves designed as "speed lines." A striking Art Moderne structure in Carnegie Hill is 2 East 88th Street, with its goddess-like stone heads atop tall brick piers.

MODERN (1935-1970)

Slow to find a footing in America, Modernism was an outgrowth of the International Style developed by Bauhaus architects such as Mies van der Rohe (1886-1969) and Walter Gropius (1883-1969). The style is best characterized by the phrase "less is more." Modernists rejected historical

references in favor of clean lines and volumetric form devoid of superfluous ornament. The use of steel and concrete made it possible to eliminate load-bearing walls, which encouraged the use of wide expanses of glass, free-flowing exterior walls and interior space. Frank Lloyd Wright was America's most famous Modernist architect; his last and crowning achievement was the Guggenheim Museum at 1071 Fifth Avenue.

POSTMODERN (1970–1990) This trend emerged as a reaction to the starkness of the International Style, breaking the uniformity of the brick or glass box and employing contemporary interpretations of classical ornament. Like Modernism, however, Postmodern architecture fell out of favor through inexpensive and slapdash interpretations—peaked roof lines, garish colors, "cute" details—and was mostly abandoned by the end of the century. A handsome Postmodern building can be seen at 60 East 88th Street.

FRANCOIS I, CHATEAUESQUE
1900-1920

NEO-GREC
1875-1890

ARCHITECTURAL STYLES

ITALIANATE
1840-1865

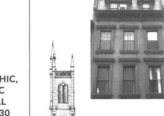

QUEEN ANNE
1880-1890

| | 1860 | | 1880 | | 1900 |
| 1850 | | 1870 | | 1890 | |

SECOND EMPIRE
1870-1880

NEO-GOTHIC, GOTHIC REVIVAL
1865-1930

ROMANESQUE REVIVAL
1885-1895

RENAISSANCE REVIVAL
1890-1910

**NEO-CLASSICAL
1905-1925**

**NEO-GEORGIAN,
NEO-FEDERAL 1915-1930**

The 50-year period between 1880 and 1930 saw a surge of building in Carnegie Hill, from simple pattern-book row houses to grand private residences and elegant apartment houses. The Great Depression marked the abrupt end of classically-inspired architecture—not only in Carnegie Hill but across America.

N CARNEGIE HILL

**NEO-REGENCY
1920-1930**

**BEAUX-ARTS
1900-1928**

1920   1940   1980

1910   1930   1960   2000

**MEDITERRANEAN
REVIVAL
1925-1930**

MODERN 1935-1970

**NEO-RENAISSANCE
1910-1930**

**MODERNE
1930-1940**

**NEO-MEDIEVAL,
NEO-TUDOR
1920-1930**

**ART DECO
1925-1935**

**POSTMODERN
1970-1990**

21

THE BUILDINGS:
AVENUES

1048 Fifth Avenue (86th Street)
Neue Galerie New York
ARCHITECTS: Carrère & Hastings
DATE: 1914

We begin our Guide with this extraordinary landmarked building. (Strictly speaking, 1048 Fifth Avenue marks the northern border of the Metropolitan Museum Historic District, which merges seamlessly with the Carnegie Hill Historic District at 86th Street). Carrère & Hastings, famed architects of the New York Public Library and the Frick mansion, were commissioned by industrialist William Starr Miller in 1914 to build his Beaux-Arts-style mansion. Miller (1857-1935), a Harvard graduate, married the former Edith Warren in 1886. Together with their one child, Edith Starr Miller, they divided their time between the opulent Fifth Avenue residence and their "cottage" in Newport, "High Tide." In 1944 Grace Wilson Vanderbilt, the widow of Cornelius Vanderbilt III, bought the Miller house, moving from her larger mansion on 51st Street to what she called "the gardener's cottage." She entertained there relentlessly until her death in 1953. YIVO Institute for Jewish Research purchased the building and converted the rooms into offices, covering the elaborate oak paneling and interior details with sheetrock.

The building was in disrepair when Ronald Lauder purchased it in 1994. Under the direction of architect Annabelle Seldorf, it was thoughtfully transformed into a modern museum of early 20th-century Austrian and German Expressionist art. The original classical interior details, from polished marble moldings and floors to gilded plaster friezes, were uncovered and restored while necessary contemporary features, such as a frosted-glass enclosed elevator, were added.

The exterior is best viewed from the north side of 86th Street. The reticulated limestone base, red-brick facade, floor-length windows with segmentally-arched pediments, bold keystones and voussoirs, and steep mansard roof are reminiscent of a Louis XIII country chateau. The classical facade features a projecting central mass that is three bays wide, defined by double-story Ionic pilasters. Running the width of the mansion between the base and parlor floor is a wide stone band course pierced with oval forms. Second- and third-story windows are trimmed with stone quoins contrasting the red brick. Below the modillioned roof cornice is a frieze embellished with widely spaced rosettes; a limestone balustrade crowns the facade. At the attic story, four small oculus windows and three dormers, each elegantly framed with pilasters and capped with pediments, pierce the high slate roof. **HD LM**

1050 Fifth Avenue (86th Street)
ARCHITECTS: Wechsler & Schimenti   DATE: 1958

Sunshine pours through the large picture windows of 1050's corner lobby, gardens adorn its exterior, and a fountain trickles faintly within, helping viewers and residents alike to forget that it sits on the busy northern corner of Fifth Avenue and 86th Street. This buff-brick building has nineteen stories and a tiered "wedding cake" effect from terracing which begins on the fourteenth floor. Considered innovative in its day, 1050 boasts an in-house garage (with, thankfully, an 86th Street entrance) and built-in air conditioners. Reflecting the requisite unadorned functionalism of the '50s and '60s, the only note of exterior decoration is its marble ground-floor facade. The developer was Bernard Spitzer, father of Eliot Spitzer, New York State Attorney General from 1998 to 2006 and Governor from 2007 to 2008. Previously there were two mansions on the site, owned by George Leary and William H. Erhart. **HD**

1056 Fifth Avenue (87th Street)
ARCHITECT: George F. Pelham, Jr.   DATE: 1948-49

The Fifth Avenue block between 86th and 87th streets was once the site of three side-by-side lavish mansions owned by Morton Plant (1050), James Speyer (1056) and Henry Phipps (1063). Speyer, a banker and philanthropist, willed his residence, which was designed by architect Horace Trumbauer, to the Museum of the City of New York, an institution he had helped found in 1923. (In 1930 the museum moved into its neo-Georgian building at Fifth Avenue and 103rd Street.)

The nineteen-story Modern apartment house that fills the space of the Speyer mansion rises from a granite base; smooth limestone blocks define the first two stories. The remainder is of buff brick. Many of the balconies have been enclosed. The sides of the building step back gradually above the sixteenth story to form terraces, creating the effect of a free-standing tower. A single-story garage on 87th Street provides light and air to the rear of the building. The primary Fifth Avenue entrance is framed by richly grained black-and-white marble in a repeated square pattern. The bronze-and-glass double doors have sidelights and a transom. The lobby was designed by Beryl Austrian, credited with developing the field of lobby decoration, to suggest "the spirit and character" of the demolished Speyer mansion. It has since been redone, but the original marble walls remain. **HD**

1060 Fifth Avenue (87th Street)
ARCHITECT: J.E.R. Carpenter   DATE: 1927-28

With many newer buildings defining Fifth Avenue near 86th Street, the neo-Renaissance 1060 Fifth stands out like a bastion of quiet, old-guard elegance. J.E.R. Carpenter, who designed twelve apartment houses in Carnegie Hill, was famous not only for classical facades but also for his lavish interiors: 1060 once claimed to contain one of the largest apartments in the city—a forty-one room, sixteen-bath duplex owned by John Markle, a retired coal operator and philanthropist. The three-story limestone base is topped with a cornice, as are alternating stories on the remainder of the brick facade. Limestone quoins accent the building extremes. Two-story pilasters support round arches above third-story windows; arches with carved spandrels grace fifth- and twelfth-story windows. Juliet balconies front several third-story windows. The double-height arch motif is repeated at the main entrance. **HD**

1067 Fifth Avenue (87th-88th Streets)
ARCHITECT: C.P.H. Gilbert   DATE: 1917

The style of this thirteen-story apartment house is French Gothic, sometimes referred to as Francois I or Chateauesque. It was favored by its prolific architect, who also designed mansions for Otto Kahn (now the Convent of the Sacred Heart) and Felix Warburg (now the Jewish Museum). 1067 was the second luxury apartment building to be built on Fifth Avenue (McKim, Mead & White designed the first, at 998), with just one apartment per floor. The facade is of Indiana limestone; decorative detail is concentrated at the two-story base and the slate mansard roof, from which project crested dormers with finials. Small balustraded balconies can be seen at the sixth and tenth stories; a balustraded cornice runs above. Lively ornamentation includes drip moldings terminating with putti heads; leaf moldings around the door and ground-level windows; a child's head; fleur-de-lis; and winged putti. Of particular interest are pairs of dolphins, which appear to be kissing, and four dragons breathing fire over the entrance. The spacious apartments attracted such early residents as conductor Leopold Stokowski, editor Robert Collier, former New York State Governor W. Averell Harriman, and actress Polly Bergen. **HD**

1071 Fifth Avenue (89th Street)
The Solomon R. Guggenheim Museum

ARCHITECTS:
Frank Lloyd Wright DATE: 1956-59
Gwathmey Siegel   1992

The iconic Frank Lloyd Wright masterpiece is one of the most recognizable buildings in the world. From the beginning its unique design generated sharply mixed reactions, with comparisons ranging from a nautilus shell to a toilet bowl. In 1943 Solomon R. Guggenheim (1861-1949), a member of a prominent family and a noted philanthropist, chose Wright to build a museum to showcase his growing collection of modern art. It took sixteen years for the idea to become a reality and neither Guggenheim nor Wright lived to witness the opening in 1959.

The concrete spiral, likened to an inverted ziggurat, expands upward from a low base. Wright used primary shapes—circles, rectangles and triangles—throughout the structure. Stainless-steel rings set in concrete distinguish the surrounding sidewalk, a design that is repeated on the terrazzo floor of the lobby rotunda. The solid six-inch exterior walls were created using the same method as that applied to in-ground swimming pools: Plywood forms and steel rods were filled with layers of sprayed Gunite, and the resulting form was painted with a vinyl plastic skin Wright called "the Cocoon."

The interior reveals Wright's use of light, from the opaque glass section of wall in the rotunda to the giant spiderweb-like dome. He envisioned visitors taking the elevator to the top level and descending the quarter-mile-long poured-concrete ramp, which he likened to a "quiet, unbroken wave." He used rectangular windows on the highest levels of the spire, while on the ground floor round portholes and dome skylights repeat the circle theme. Triangle shapes are found in recessed ceiling lights. The enclosed interior stairway viewed from above is a series of cascading triangles.

In 1990 the building was the youngest to receive landmark status from the New York City Landmarks Preservation Commission. Two years later, the spotlight focused on Gwathmey Siegel's ten-story tower addition, which the architects based on one of Wright's early draft designs. Their use of limestone blocks creates a Mondrian-like grid on the tower's exterior walls. A ladder of inset glass-block rows and a massive, recessed rectangular window wall punctuate the 89th Street side. Four rows of more discreet windows face Fifth Avenue and Central Park. The firm repeated Wright's Art Deco elements of circles and triangles on the double-height steel, brass-and-glass service doors on 89th Street and the large circular air vents on the 89th Street wall. The tower created three two-story galleries and a one-story gallery with a glass wall connecting to Wright's original building. A terrace was added on the rotunda roof and a sculpture terrace on the fifth-floor roof. The Guggenheim Museum was added to the National Register of Historic Places in 2005. Cracks in the concrete structure plagued the building since its opening in 1959. Wright was notoriously indifferent to such practical matters and in 2005 the museum removed twelve layers of paint and spent a year analyzing the damage. For the next two-and-one-half years the building was encased in scaffolding as repairs continued at a cost of $29 million, more than ten times the cost of the original back in 1959. A subject of debate was the restoration painting of the facade: The building was originally coated with a light brownish-yellow, but since the 1960s had been clad in various shades of pale gray. After a lively public meeting late in 2007, the Landmarks Preservation Commission voted to maintain the off-white to which people had become accustomed. **HD LM**

1080 Fifth Avenue (89th Street)
ARCHITECTS: Wechsler & Schimenti   DATE: 1961
This 21-story Modern apartment house replaced three townhouses. Designed by the architects responsible for 1050 Fifth Avenue just three years earlier, this glazed-white-brick building is distinguished primarily by its upper-story setbacks creating cascading terraces. Its real beauty comes from the inside, looking out. To the south, its apartments tower over the Guggenheim Museum's striking sculptural curves; to the north the National Academy Museum's low stature affords 1080 plenty of light and air; and to the west stretches the city's grandest front yard. **HD**

1083 Fifth Avenue (89th-90th Streets) and 3 East 89th Street
Originally Archer M. Huntington houses, now National Academy Museum
ARCHITECTS: Turner & Kilian   DATE: 1902
              Ogden Codman, Jr.   1913-15
One of three houses built on speculation by George C. Edgar & Sons, 1083 was bought in 1902 by Archer Milton Huntington. In 1913 he commissioned Ogden Codman, Jr. to remodel and enlarge it, in conjunction with the addition of a new wing at 3 East 89th Street.

Huntington was born Archer Worsham in 1870. He was given his stepfather's name when his mother married railroad tycoon Collis P. Huntington in 1884. The elder Huntington was one of the "Big Four"

who built the Union Pacific, Southern Pacific, and Chesapeake and Ohio railroads. By the time Archer Huntington was twelve, he had developed a fascination with Spanish culture, and went on to found the Hispanic Society of America in 1904. He long served as its president, and built the Audubon Terrace museum complex at Broadway and 155th Street.

The Beaux-Arts-style Fifth Avenue house has six stories with a bow-fronted facade. Codman replaced most of the original brick-and-stone elements with a cooler Indiana limestone, inspired by late-18th-century French design. Rising above a rusticated limestone base, a second-story balustrade is supported by fluted brackets. The central window is capped with a carved panel and segmental arch. Topping the bow front is a modillioned cornice and balustrade. Above the flat-fronted fifth story is a slate mansard roof with three classically pedimented dormer windows.

Codman designed the adjoining wing at 3 East 89th Street, creating an L-shaped residence. The *pièce de resistance* was a circular marble hallway and sweeping spiral staircase. Two points of controversy have arisen, however, from his use of false rusticated stone for the stairwell and inexpensive yellow-brick facing for the upper floors of the refined No. 3. Perhaps the answer can be found in the book *The Decoration of Houses,* in which Codman and Edith Wharton wrote, "If the effect is satisfactory to the eye, the substance used is a matter of indifference." In the early 1920s Huntington married his second wife, the sculptress Anna Hyatt, and created a studio for her on top of No. 3; the easternmost staircase still contains the block-and-tackle system used to haul her materials. A fine example of her work is the life-size statue of Diana which can be seen by the stairway of 1083.

3 East 89th Street is a neo-Renaissance building faced with rusticated limestone at the base, above which is a bracketed limestone balcony. Three high round-arched windows are separated with simple brick pilasters and capped with scrolled keystones. The facade is terminated with a modillioned cornice, capped with a balustraded parapet. Not visible from the street are three additional stories. The building originally housed the kitchen, a formal dining salon on the second level, and bedrooms above.

In 1943 Huntington donated both 1083 and 3 East 89th Street, along with the vacant lot at the corner, to the National Academy of Design (now the National Academy Museum), whose former house had been destroyed by fire. The interiors were renovated by William A. Delano in 1941. The organization opened its National Academy School of Fine Arts at 3 and 5 East 89th Street [see 5 East 89th Street]. **HD**

1084-1089 Fifth Avenue (90th Street)
See 2 East 90th Street, Church of the Heavenly Rest

1107 Fifth Avenue (92nd Street)
Triplex penthouse originally
Post-Hutton residence
ARCHITECTS: Rouse & Goldstone
DATE: 1925

The distinctive architecture of this thirteen-story-plus-penthouse building reflects the involvement of its premier tenants: Marjorie Merriweather Post, heiress to the Post cereal fortune, and her then-husband, E.F. Hutton, founder of the eponymous brokerage house. To get above the din of ever-increasing street traffic, they commissioned this apartment house to be built on the site of their previous mansion and included for themselves a specially designed 54-room triplex penthouse (with a guaranteed fifteen-year lease). That dwelling is reputed to be the largest apartment ever built in New York City, a veritable "mansion in the sky." The Huttons had their own entrance, which can be seen on the south side of 92nd Street. Here, a *porte cochère* was built so that the family could proceed directly into a private vestibule and up to the apartment by private elevator.

Above the three-story rusticated limestone base, double-height pilasters with Ionic capitals support a terra-cotta entablature. Fourth-story windows are balustraded, and are topped with alternating segmental and triangular pediments. (Note the similarity to the design of the Otto Kahn mansion just to the south.) For a grand view of the elegance of this neo-Renaissance building, stand on the west side of Fifth Avenue and look up at the enormous Palladian window at the twelfth story. This window opened into the Huttons' foyer and served as a focal point of the apartment's first floor (the penthouse is set back from the brick facade). After World War II the apartment was subdivided into half-a-dozen still-luxurious apartments. Actress Dina Merrill, the Huttons' daughter, grew up in the penthouse. **HD**

1109 Fifth Avenue (92nd Street)
Originally Felix and Frieda Schiff Warburg house, now the Jewish Museum
ARCHITECTS: C.P.H. Gilbert   DATE: 1908
Kevin Roche/Kevin Roche John Dinkeloo and Associates 1993

This mansion was designed in the French Renaissance Chateau style of Francois I for Felix Warburg, a partner in the Wall Street investment banking firm of Kuhn, Loeb and Company, and his wife, Frieda. Originally from Hamburg, Germany, Warburg gained a reputation as an art collector and philanthropist; he organized the Federation of Jewish Philanthropies and the Julliard School of Music. Gilbert modeled his "Millionaires Row" six-story residence after the Fletcher house at Fifth Avenue and 79th Street (now the Ukrainian Institute of America), which he also designed.

Faced with Indiana limestone, the building is richly decorated throughout with ornate carvings. The immense arched doorway on 92nd Street is surrounded by detailed reliefs and balanced on either side by set-back windowed alcoves. Above the entrance is a lavishly carved cornice and balcony. Look closely at the supporting brackets: A string of small faces and mythical creatures guards the portico. The parlor floor features over-scaled bay windows with tall window segments, including a richly carved three-sided projecting bay above the entrance. Balconies project beneath all windows at the fourth story. The steeply pitched roof, dormers, spires and finials of the mansion are representative of the French Gothic Chateau style. Behind the 92nd Street entrance stands an enormous staircase with a Gothic-style oak balustrade that takes up almost a quarter of the space on each floor. Warburg kept a squash court on the fifth floor.

The Warburg family lived in the house until 1944, when Frieda Warburg donated it to the Jewish Theological Seminary to be the home of the Jewish Museum. In 1963 the List Building, a low modern structure, was added on the Fifth Avenue side.

In 1989 the museum bought a townhouse adjacent to the List

Building and announced plans for a 30,000-square-foot enlargement
to the north, which allowed the museum to double its gallery space and
add an auditorium, an education center, and an on-site conservation
laboratory. Rather than build another modern addition, the architect,
Kevin Roche, designed the facade to sensitively echo the original mansion.
Indiana limestone was quarried from the same site that provided the
original limestone, and the stonework was crafted by Cathedral Stoneworks,
the masons for the Cathedral of St. John the Divine. The addition is so
close a match that you must examine it carefully to detect any difference.
On the Fifth Avenue windows, compare the squirrels at the base of the
hood moldings: The newer ones have a slightly sharper relief than the 1908
originals. The museum also purchased the brownstone at 1 East 92nd
Street for offices and an ancillary museum shop. **HD LM**

1115 and 1120 Fifth Avenue (93rd Street)
ARCHITECT: J.E.R. Carpenter DATE: 1924-26

These neo-Renaissance buildings were developed by Naples-born Anthony Campagna, who
became a successful New York apartment-house
builder. Campagna was also a philanthropist;
he contributed funds for the restoration of
Virgil's Tomb at Naples, the excavation of
Herculaneum, and the construction of Casa
Italiana at Columbia University.

1115 and 1120 stand across 93rd Street
from each other and are commonly referred to
as twins. In reality, they are more like fraternal
twins. 1120, completed in 1925, is considerably wider, with a Fifth Avenue
frontage of 150 feet, compared with 100 feet for its "twin." The molded,
eared window enframements embellishing the second, fifth and twelfth
stories of 1120 are rectangular, with carved terra-cotta panels
separating fourth-story windows. Arches and curves appear at the Fifth
Avenue main entrance: Wood-framed round-arched windows flank the
arched doorway and wrought-iron fanlight. 1115, completed in 1926,
announces its distinct personality at the main entry, which is on 93rd
Street: The rectangular door is framed with double pilasters supporting a
carved entablature and a broken triangular pediment. Contrasting with its
"twin," second-, fifth- and twelfth-story windows have arched pediments
decorated with keystones and carved lunettes.

Fraternal bonds between the two fourteen-story buildings include
three-story limestone bases, brick facades articulated by horizontal
divisions, and stone quoining at the corners. **HD**

1125 Fifth Avenue (94th Street)
ARCHITECT: Emery Roth   DATE: 1925-26

A modest 1890 row house once occupied this narrow site. In its place stands this slender, fourteen-story-plus-penthouse apartment building, rising from a three-story rusticated limestone base. Designed in neo-Renaissance style, there is a flurry of street-level interest: at the entry, stone pilasters support a broken pediment, which embraces a second-story window with carved reveals. Large limestone blocks line the building's corners. Step back to view the fourth-story central window, fronted with a pseudo balcony and embellished with carved classical motifs. The best vantage point, however, is from the park side of Fifth Avenue. Stone pilasters applied to the brick facade soar from the fourth to the eleventh story, above which Roth pulls out all the architectural stops. At the twelfth story the three center bays are arched with carved surrounds; fourteenth-story windows alternate with decorative panels. Above the modillioned, balustraded cornice rises the penthouse tower, with three double-height arches, a carved cornice and a huge central cartouche. **HD**

1130 Fifth Avenue (94th Street)
Originally Willard and Dorothy Payne Whitney Straight house
ARCHITECTS: Delano & Aldrich
DATE: 1914-15

A refined merger of neo-Federal and neo-Georgian design, this gracious mansion is considered one of the finest works by venerable architects Delano & Aldrich. It was built for the socially prominent diplomat, financier and publicist Willard Straight and his wife, the daughter of financier and Secretary of the Navy William C. Whitney. It was here that the Straights launched *The New Republic* magazine and the large-format picture magazine *Asia,* as well as the club India House to encourage foreign trade. Mrs. Straight, a leading suffragist, pioneer in progressive education, and philanthropist, was widowed in 1918 and remarried; she lived in the house until 1926. After that it was privately owned until the National Audubon Society bought it in In 1953. The mansion was landmarked in 1968, and sold to the International Center for Photography in 1974. In 1999 the ICP announced that it would relocate to new quarters in midtown. The house was sold to Bruce Kovner, a private investor and chairman of the board of trustees of the Julliard School of Music. Mr. Kovner commissioned the architects Swanke Hayden Connell to restore the interior to its original grandeur as a private residence.

The four-story-plus-penthouse exterior is faced with a pleasing color combination of red brick, white-marble trim, and black shutters. Resting on a stone water table, the main mass is divided by marble band courses into a one-story base, two-story midsection and one-story crown. The Fifth Avenue facade incorporates three window bays; the 94th Street side is seven bays wide. Tuscan columns flank an arched, paneled central doorway; the wrought-iron grille over the fanlight is in the form of a peacock. The bird motif is echoed in the triangular pediment above the center second-story window. All square-headed windows have incised marble lintels. Particularly noteworthy are the oculus windows on the fourth story, similar to those on Hampton Court Palace designed by Christopher Wren. The facade is topped with a marble cornice and balustrade. Above the shallow slate roof is a penthouse and conservatory.

Set back behind a historic wrought-iron fence, a recessed wing to the east features a curved metal oriel that compresses three levels of windows into two stories; the wing is capped with a balustraded cornice. The overall impression of the building is one of architectural sophistication combined with great dignity. **HD LM**

1133 Fifth Avenue (94th Street)
ARCHITECT: Emery Roth   DATE: 1927-28

This fourteen-story-plus-penthouse building was built by Bing & Bing and is ornamented in a neo-Federal style. One of its earliest residents was Thomas. E. Mitten, a traction magnate and banker from Philadelphia who occupied what was then a sixteen-room triplex penthouse that extended into the tower.

A wave-carved band course separates the two-story limestone base from the brick facade. An incised Greek key motif embellishes lintels above the windows on the third through fifth floors, and on the thirteenth and fourteenth floors. Classical urns punctuate the dentiled cornice. The front entrance has a stunning broken segmental pediment rising above fluted pilasters. Step across Fifth Avenue to view the grand water-tower enclosure rising proudly above the penthouse: The design echoes the entrance, with each side bearing double-tiered openings framed by pairs of terra-cotta fluted pilasters, a segmental arch and scrolled keystone. **HD**

**1136 Fifth Avenue
(95th Street)**
ARCHITECT: George F. Pelham
DATE: 1926

The three-story rusticated limestone base of this fifteen-story neo-Renaissance building is capped by an acanthus-leaf-and-rosette frieze and a modillioned cornice. Carved bas-relief designs frame the centered main entrance, which is topped by a dentiled cornice. The wood-and-glass doors and some first-story windows are decorated with crossed-arrow black-and-gold iron grilles, which appear to be later additions. Carved lunettes further embellish the street-level windows. Above a dentiled string course, the beige-brick midsection is framed by rusticated bands flanking the end windows. Swags adorn the fourth-story windows. The crown section gains importance from windows framed with terra-cotta pilasters which support molded arches ornamented with keystones and lunettes. A grand terra-cotta cornice makes a strong finishing statement. In 1928 Pelham was hired to replace a large cornice section with a much smaller one and an iron railing, presumably to provide a better view of Central Park from a rooftop garden. The removal of damaged ornamental balconies in 1962 left residual scars. A historic wrought-iron gate remains, spanning the alley of the east elevation. **HD**

1140 Fifth Avenue (95th Street)
ARCHITECTS: Fred F. French Co.   DATE: 1921
What seems like a restrained neo-Renaissance tan-brick building bursts with detail at its upper reaches. It is best viewed when the late-afternoon sun slants across Central Park and spotlights the central bays at the twelfth and thirteenth stories. Here, two-story columns support arches over windows accented with medallions and spandrels. (Unfortunately, enlarged windows on the fourteenth floor have altered the original fenestration.) Above, dentil and egg-and-dart moldings are capped with a band of anthemia medallions alternating with foliate brackets supporting a wide cornice. More upper-facade detailing can be seen in the arched and balustraded windows at the end bays. This fourteen-story-plus-penthouse apartment house was built for the estate of the late Lloyd S. Bryce, a socialite, former congressman, diplomat, novelist and editor of the *North American Review*. His wife, Edith Cooper, was the daughter of New York City Mayor Edward Cooper and granddaughter of iron magnate Peter Cooper, founder of Cooper Union. **HD**

1143 Fifth Avenue (95th-96th Streets)
ARCHITECT: J.E.R. Carpenter   DATE: 1923

A David surrounded by Goliaths, this slim neo-Federal building was originally designed with six one-floor apartments and one story containing two apartments. The two-story limestone base is topped with red brick, framed with brick quoins. Stone band courses define the second story; windows have recessed brick arches with rosettes. Slender fluted pilasters flank the wood-and-glass main entrance, which has an iron grille and transom. An egg-and-dart molding and brick parapet cap the seventh, once terminal, story.

   In 1953 the building was taken over by the Posners, a real-estate family, who converted the floor-through apartments into medical offices. Family discord ensued, and the building was vacated in 1989 and allowed to deteriorate. In 1993 it was purchased by the French government as a residence for its consular and cultural services staff. Extensive renovations, both inside and out, included the addition of another floor, set back and visible at street level only from Central Park; a tasteful replication of the original six-over-six windows; and a return to the three-bedroom layouts envisioned by the architect some 70 years earlier. **HD**

1148 Fifth Avenue (96th Street)
ARCHITECT: J.E.R. Carpenter with Walter B. Chambers   DATE: 1922-23

There is some uncertainty as to the lead architect of this thirteen-story neo-Georgian apartment house. Experts view the role of Walter B. Chambers, often listed as architect, as secondary. Its characteristics make it similar to—almost indistinguishable from—neighboring buildings by J.E.R. Carpenter; architectural historian Christopher Gray pairs it with 1150 Fifth, across 96th Street, as a "sibling structure." The smooth-faced limestone base is topped with red brick; above the fourth story, brick quoins accent the corners. Double-height fluted pilasters frame the second- and third-story windows, which are separated by spandrels carved with classical motifs. Echoing vertical panels punctuate fourth-story windows. There are cornices above the third, fourth and twelfth stories and string courses above the remaining odd-numbered stories, creating an overall horizontal emphasis. A balustraded parapet caps the building. The main entrance is on 96th Street. Iron-and-glass doors and transom are flanked by molded limestone; four carved, foliate brackets support a shallow balcony. On either side of the door, panels carved with garlands, urns and fleurs-de-lis complete the classical design. **HD**

1150 Fifth Avenue (96th Street)
ARCHITECT: J.E.R. Carpenter   DATE: 1923-24

One of eight buildings on Fifth Avenue designed by J.E.R. Carpenter, this U-shaped apartment house was built for the owners of the Lion Brewery of New York City. The plan called for fourteen stories with five apartments per floor, each of six or nine rooms. It surely did not envision the demolition of the then-requisite maids' rooms on the roof level, and in their place the construction in 1997 of three duplex penthouses, wrapped in glass, with nineteen-foot-high living rooms.

Rooftop additions notwithstanding, 1150 retains its dignified neo-Georgian facade. The central entrance on 96th Street has sidelights and a molded acanthus-leaf surround, embellished with fleur-de-lis and garlands. The first four stories are of rusticated limestone capped with a cornice; the remaining facade is of dark-red ironspot brick with brick quoins at the corners. Balusters front fifth-story windows, which are flanked with fluted pilasters and topped by brick arches with keystones and carved panels. At the crown story, window surrounds are of limestone; a classical balustraded parapet gives no hint of the modern penthouse trio above. **HD**

1158 Fifth Avenue (97th Street)
ARCHITECTS: C. Howard Crane & Kenneth Franzheim   DATE: 1924

Noted for its eight-sided Adamesque lobby with large vaulted ceilings and sculptural niches, this fifteen-story neo-Renaissance building was among the first in New York City to be built as a cooperative apartment house. The ground level is richly ornamented. Above the three entrances on 97th Street are round-headed relieving arches topped with scrolled keystones and garlands of fruit and leaves; in the tympana, look for carvings of rams' heads, men fighting lions, arrows, suits of armor and menacing masques. Decorative ironwork can be seen on the secondary entrance doors as well as on gold-accented window grilles and on the Fifth Avenue service gate with "1158" entwined in its design. Above the three-story limestone base, the tan-brick facade is relieved by rusticated brick quoins at the corners,

and stone balconies with wrought-iron railings on the tenth and fourteenth floors. Simplified detailing appears around fourteenth- and crown-story windows. The ornately designed facade may reflect the influence of Crane, whose architectural specialty was theaters; he was responsible for more than 250 in the United States, including the Music Box in New York City, which also opened in 1924. Fittingly, the actor Sidney Poitier and his family once occupied an apartment in this building. **HD**

1160 Fifth Avenue (97th Street)
ARCHITECT: Fred F. French Co.

DATE: 1922-23

Although only six stories high, this neo-Georgian building announces its architectural stature immediately by its deeply recessed entrance court. Framing the door are triple pilasters and a broken pediment with dentils and a classical urn. Rising from the two-story limestone base are enormous three-story pilasters with elongated acanthus-leaf capitals, leading the eye upward to a decorative entablature and one-story brick crown section. Stone urns, echoing the entryway ornamentation, punctuate the corners of the parapet. Wrought-iron Juliet balconies front third-story windows, which are embellished with scrolled keystones and garland swags. **HD**

1165 and 1170 Fifth Avenue (98th Street)
ARCHITECT: J.E.R. Carpenter   DATE: 1925, 1926

These twin tan-brick-and-limestone apartment houses tip their J.E.R. Carpenter hats to each other across 98th Street. Both buildings rise fifteen stories plus a penthouse; both are neo-Renaissance in style, with medieval accents. In design they are almost identical, with the exception that 1165 crowds in an extra window on the Fifth Avenue side, making nine bays instead of eight, and also on the 98th Street facade, creating fourteen bays instead of thirteen. Their complementary entrances have richly carved surrounds and are topped with broad metal-and-glass canopies. Pilasters framing the windows on the second, fifth, ninth and thirteenth stories support brick Gothic arches; in the tympana are cast-stone rabbits, birds and dolphins. Further ornamentation is seen in the brick and terra-cotta panels separating fourth-story windows. Vertical cable moldings applied to the quoined corners rise above the lightly rusticated three-story limestone base. Five spiral string courses span the facades at various levels. Both buildings terminate with molded cornices and balustraded parapets. **HD**

1232 and 1234 Madison Avenue (88th-89th Streets)
ARCHITECT/DEVELOPER: Edward Kilpatrick   DATE: 1887

This pair of neo-Grec brownstones has more or less survived for some 120 years. Edward Kilpatrick, who had come from Ireland to the United States around 1830, worked his way up from carpenter to contractor to New York City developer. He built four speculative brownstones at 1228-1234 Madison Avenue, at the time an area of frame houses with few modern amenities. Nos. 1232 and 1234 went through a succession of owners and eventually became boarding houses. In 1921 the architects Gronenberg & Leuchtag removed the stoops; in 1923 the houses were converted to apartments and stores. The second story of No. 1234 was the office of Carnegie Hill Neighbors from 1994 to 1998.

1261 Madison Avenue (90th Street)
ARCHITECTS: Buchman & Fox
DATE: 1900-01

The generous proportions and exuberant detailing of this seven-story Beaux Arts building reflect the desire of luxury apartment dwellers at the turn of the 20th century to display the grandeur of private mansions. The two-story rusticated limestone base, rising from a granite water table, is surmounted by a three-story midsection; the central bays are framed with limestone quoins and separated vertically by spandrels. Above the fifth story, scrolled brackets support a heavy modillioned cornice which serves as a base for a wrought-iron balcony coursing the entire facade. Sixth-story windows are keyed and capped with a rondel frieze. A string course forms a sill for seventh-story windows, which are set off with volutes and segmentally-arched pediments. The red-tiled mansard roof is trimmed with copper exhibiting verdigris.

Punctuating the Madison Avenue facade are slightly projecting end bays with tripartite windows; those at the second and fifth stories are arched and embellished with shells, scrolls and voussoirs, while openings at the top two stories are flanked by pilasters topped with cartouches and arched pediments. The central entrance has a magnificent portico composed of rusticated piers and garlanded console brackets supporting a swan's neck pediment, above which is a framed marble medallion. **HD LM**

1281 and 1283 Madison Avenue (91st-92nd Streets)

ARCHITECT: Frederick T. Camp   DATE: 1885-86

In 1885 developer Alexander Duff engaged architect Frederick T. Camp to design a half-dozen four-story Queen Anne-style Victorian houses on the east side of Madison Avenue. Duff himself moved into No. 1283. Early in the 20th century the ground floors of the houses were extended and converted to storefronts. In 1950 Nos. 1273 to 1279 were demolished for a one-story bank; this building was replaced in 2003 by an apartment building.

This surviving pair of picturesque Queen Anne buildings attests to Carnegie Hill's rich architectural heritage. Although the widths vary—No. 1281 is seventeen feet wide and Duff's former home, No. 1283, fifteen feet—the upper two stories are almost identical. No. 1281's facade is red brick, while No. 1282 is painted; both have brownstone trim. Above the stores, north windows in each building are framed by brick pilasters which support bracketed cornices; those to the south have fluted stone pilasters, underscored by dentils and capped pediments. The tops of both buildings are all quirky Queen Anne: spiky pointed gables with wide dentils pierce the roof line; their triangular shapes splay at the bottom to frame the north windows. South windows have eared and carved lintels, bracketed pediments and dentils. Stone copings ornamented with shields, rosettes and finials further punctuate the parapet. **HD**

1285-1293 Madison Avenue (92nd Street)

ARCHITECT: James Edward Ware   DATE: 1889-90

These five buildings with their repeating round arches constitute one of the last Romanesque Revival rows of distinction on Madison Avenue. They were built for Dr. James V. S. Woolley, an East Side developer who was also a physician. The architect, James Edward Ware, bought No. 1285 where he lived with his wife, Edith, and their five children. The houses remain relatively unaltered at the upper stories. The original basements at ground level have been converted into shops, as have the former parlor floors in Nos. 1285, 1287 and 1289. The northernmost houses, Nos. 1291 and 1293, have the best-preserved exteriors, although they have been combined internally. The group is best viewed in the afternoon sun, when the smooth-surfaced deep-red brickwork contrasts with the cocoa-colored sandstone trim, sparked with small-pane windows.

The first series of arches appears at the original parlor-story entries of Nos. 1285 and 1291-1293: Engaged columns topped by carved brown-

stone impost blocks support round-arched openings, accented with carved spandrels. Above, each house features a three-sided bay—note the oval window panes—topped by a small balcony with a delicate wrought-iron railing, which fronts a great round-arched window trimmed with radial brickwork. The final story of the quintet alternates three round-arched windows and three square-headed openings, separated by stone colonettes with foliate capitals. Contributing to the overall design is a continuous band course that sets apart the brownstone parlor floor from the brick upper stories; additional band courses define the top story, and a molded brick checkerboard frieze runs beneath the dentiled roof cornice. Adding verticality—and drama—are six engaged stone shafts resting on corbels, crowned with elongated foliate impost blocks that punctuate the roof line. **HD**

1290 Madison Avenue (92nd Street)
The Wellington
ARCHITECT: A.B. Ogden & Co.   DATE: 1898

Designed in the Renaissance Revival style, this six-story building is faced in cream brick with a limestone base and limestone-and-terra-cotta trim. Although the stoop was removed in 1931, the main entrance remains quite elaborate. Flanking the door are double pilasters with decorative capitals and carvings: Look carefully at the pair on the left, and your stare will be returned by mustached terra-cotta guards. The entrance surround has been altered, but a surviving acanthus molding is echoed in the etched glass of the door panels. Above, a shell is centered in a leafy entablature. Storefronts (five were provided for in the original building design) are separated by banded piers with decorative capitals, two of which sport whimsical faces.

The third- and fourth-story windows have finely carved surrounds; splayed lintels top the second- and fifth-story windows. Of particular note are the end bays: Three-sided oriel, supported by carved corbeled bases, are separated by foliate spandrels. An elaborate enframement surrounds the two center windows at the third and fourth stories. Terra-cotta banding with Vitruvian scrolls distinguishes the sixth story. The cornice has been removed; a one-story penthouse perches at the center of the roof. **HD**

1295 Madison Avenue (92nd Street)
Hotel Wales

ARCHITECT: Louis Korn   DATE: 1900
Designed in an early interpretation of neo-
Renaissance style, this nine-story building has
undergone many name changes. Originally the
Hotel Chastaignary, it reputedly was renamed
the Bibo, the Bon Ray, the Berkshire, and the
Carnegie Hill Hotel; since the 1940s it has
been called the Hotel Wales. Little remains of
the original ground story, now occupied by
restaurants, except for the Madison Avenue
entryway, with its polished-granite pilasters,
foliate capitals and entablature, and multiple carved moldings. Above the
first-story cornice the facade is of brick with horizontal banding (now
painted gray and white). Fluted keystones top second-story windows, above
which runs a band course embellished with a Vitruvian scroll. Eclectic
decoration enlivens the remaining facade. End bays are quoined; windows
are capped with triangular pediments and dentils, cornices and lintels carved
with ferns and leaves, and round arches at the crown section. Balustraded
stone balconies project from the fourth, sixth and seventh stories. Now
shorn of its cornice, the parapet is of uneven heights, suggesting work-in-
progress; behind it is a newly added roof terrace. **HD**

1296-1304 Madison Avenue (92nd Street)

ARCHITECTS: A.B. Ogden & Son   DATE: 1889
This row of three-story brownstones was built for Walter Reid, a developer
responsible for at least seven other rows in Carnegie Hill. The first four
buildings have storefronts replacing the original stoops. Glancing upward,
the viewer will note that all retain characteristics of Queen Anne and
Romanesque Revival styles. The upper stories of the three center buildings
retain their original metal cornices—modillioned and bracketed, with
carved panels—and share similar window patterns, providing both a
coherent and varied streetscape.

No. 1296 had a faux mansard roof of slate and tin, which was
removed in 1901 when a fourth story was added. Its entire Madison
Avenue facade was replaced in 1955 with a Modern brick bulkhead and
ribbon windows. However, the 92nd Street side retains much historical
interest: the brick facade (now painted) has round-arched windows
trimmed with curved projecting lintels and bowed sills. Stone quoins line
the building's original corners, the square-headed windows on the second
and fourth stories, and the carved and corbeled chimneys.

The color differences between Nos. 1298 and 1302—red and white vs. brown and black—disguise the similar openings on the upper two stories. Second-story double windows display pilasters and cornices; those above have cornices and surrounds that flare at the bottom. Between the stories are incised spandrels. At No. 1298, note the remaining arched, rope-molded entry over what was once the stoop, and the arched double window with quoins and foliate keystone. No. 1300 has rough-faced quoins framing an arched, tripartite window and door on the second story, and corniced windows on the third story. No. 1304, originally part of the group, was annexed by the Hotel Ashton [see 1306-1313 Madison Avenue] in 1917 and was subsequently used as a solarium. In 1935 it was reduced to a one-story building for commercial use. **HD**

1305-1309 Madison Avenue (92nd-93rd Streets)
ARCHITECTS: A.B. Ogden & Son   DATE: 1890
These three buildings were originally part of a row extending to 93rd Street, designed for the developer Walter Reid. Changes to Nos. 1305 and 1309 started as early as 1899 and 1902, when fourth stories and new mansard roofs were added. In 1930 Robert Louis Houget, president and chairman of the board of Emigrant Savings Bank and owner-resident of nearby 45-47 East 92nd Street, commissioned the firm of Moore & Landsiedel to remove the stoops from all three buildings and convert the parlor-story entrances to windows. In 1933 the architect, George Victor Harvey, added a story to No. 1307, making its height consistent with that of its neighbors. At approximately the same time, two levels of stores were created for the buildings, and the top two stories were turned into apartments. The resulting neo-Georgian facade, now stuccoed, is symmetrical; alternating third-story windows are set within shallow arches capped with diamond shapes. A pedimented cornice projects over the center building. **HD**

1306-1312 Madison Avenue (26 East 93rd Street)
The Ashton
ARCHITECT: George W. Spitzer   DATE: 1897
The Ashton, a ten-story Renaissance Revival building, was originally an apartment hotel, a popular living option at the time. The name derives from that of the original hotel owner, Frederica Ashton Benneche. The kitchen was in the basement, the first story was for offices and living/dining rooms, and the remaining floors had four apartments each. The building is now a co-op, with shops and restaurants lining the Madison Avenue side. Above the cast-stone base, arched and keyed window openings are intersected with tan-brick bands and stone coursing, topped with a frieze and cornice.

The original entrance on Madison Avenue had engaged columns, an entablature and, later, an iron marquee; all have been removed. Today, the more restrained but still elegant entrance is on 93rd Street. An arched green-marble entryway frames double wood- and glass doors; preening above is a green wrought-iron-and-brass fanlight. **HD**

1311 Madison Avenue (92nd-93rd Streets)
ARCHITECT: Henri Fouchaux   DATE: 1901

The single-family A.B. Ogden design of 1890 was substantially altered in 1901 to accommodate an office for the new owner, Emanuel Hochheimer, a physician. The architect added a fourth story, a four-story rear addition, and a new fireproof facade with metal piers framing a bay window (removed in the 1960s.) All windows were arched with molded surrounds, and a bracketed cornice was added. In 1929 the stoop and facade up to the second story were replaced with an extended two-story shop front, faced in quarry tile. During the 1970s the tenants painted the tile a bright yellow. In 1983 Joan and Jay McLaughlin took ownership and renovated the entire building. They added a cornice and metal railing to the first story, replaced the quarry tile with stucco to match the rest of the building, and installed a projecting curved steel-and-glass storefront with a two-story window. The retail space has been the home of one of the J. McLaughlin clothing stores; the McLaughlins live on the top three stories. **HD**

1313 Madison Avenue (93rd Street)
ARCHITECTS: A.B. Ogden & Son   DATE: 1890

This brick-and-brownstone townhouse was designed for the developer Walter Reid as one of five row houses that included 1305-1311 Madison Avenue. Only No. 1313 retains a semblance of its original appearance. However, across 93rd Street on both the northeast and northwest corners of Madison Avenue are two buildings of very similar style, which make for a unique trio in Manhattan.

The two upper stories of the Madison Avenue brownstone facade include an incised three-sided bay window and single-window openings, a carved panel and a pediment. The main attraction of this Renaissance Revival building is the East 93rd Street facade with its many decorative elements—stylized leaves and flowers, egg-and-dart moldings, arched windows with curved sills and hood moldings, and arches in the chimney projections. The red brick is very fine and is said to have come from Pennsylvania. Topping the facade is the original metal cornice. The small yard at the rear is enclosed by the original iron fence and gate, and contains fragments of neighborhood buildings razed to build the high-rise at 40 East 94th Street.

In 1927 the owner, Henry L. Moses (1879-1961), commissioned the architect Louis A. Sheinart to transform the single-family residence to accommodate a store, an office and two apartments. Work included removing the stoop and the front of the basement and first story, raising

the levels of those two floors, installing a ground-floor entrance on Madison Avenue, and erecting new show windows. On the 93rd Street side, a fire escape and a new residential entrance were provided.

The building was sold in 1976 to Raymond Sherman and Hélène Golay, who reverted the building above the store to a one-family residence and restored the original brick-and-brownstone facade. The commercial space, which had been a pharmacy since the 1927 renovation, was adapted by the owner-residents to become The Corner Bookstore. The 1927 wood cabinetry and terrazzo floor were preserved and the tin ceiling was restored. Sherman also designed, built and installed the bookstore facade and made the gilded lettering from lumber found in the basement. **HD**

1316-1320 Madison Avenue See 25-33 East 93rd Street

1321 and 1323-1325 Madison Avenue (93rd Street)
ARCHITECT: James Edward Ware   DATE: 1890-91
No. 1321 was once the bastion of a quintet of Queen Anne row houses marching up Madison Avenue; today, only its attached neighbor to the north survives. The group was built for the developer/physician James V. S. Woolley; one year earlier Woolley and Ware had collaborated on the Romanesque Revival row houses down the street, at 1285-1293 Madison.

No. 1321 is an individual landmark. Above the Madison Avenue parlor stories, which were converted to shops in the late 1920s, three-sided bay windows are capped with paneled balconies. The sandstone-fronted third stories display additional Queen Anne characteristics—molded round-headed windows with engaged colonnettes and anthemion keystones, and swag-and-scallop-shell friezes below modillioned metal cornices. The peaked round-arched dormer, dwarf columns and slate-covered pyramidal roof of No. 1321 are unique in Carnegie Hill.

Stone quoins mark the corner of the red-brick 93rd Street facade. Here, the entrance is both charming and striking: A brownstone stoop

with curved balusters and fluted newel posts leads to an arched doorway embellished with carved spandrels and flanked by foliate pilasters. Their capitals support a dentiled cornice with balusters echoing those lining the stoop. A small adjacent round-arched window, also flanked with pilasters, is accented with leaded glass. Second-story windows rest on corbels; their stone surrounds are eared. A corbeled string course forms the sill of third-story windows, which are neatly bonneted with larger shells from the frieze. Tall narrow chimneys project above the roof and corner tower. Back at ground level, note the historic grillwork beneath the stoop and the sunburst motif in the sidewalk fence. **HD LM**

1326 Madison Avenue (94th Street)
ARCHITECTS: Neville & Bagge   DATE: 1899-1900
Dominant limestone banding and projecting cornices on the first three floors of this seven-story Renaissance Revival building create a bold horizontal impression. This changes to vertical from the fourth to seventh stories, due in part to windows elongated by arches, segmental and triangular pediments, keystones, and other ornamentation. At the center of the tan-brick facade on Madison Avenue, double pairs of brownstone pilasters flank the main entrance and a window to the north; between them is a carved terra-cotta wreath and shell. Directly above, note the voussoirs and keystones on the third story connecting the stone banding; the carved window surrounds on the fourth and fifth stories; and the cartouches at the seventh story. The crowning modillioned cornice has a dentil course and paneled frieze. **HD**

1339-1351 Madison Avenue / Squadron A (Eighth Regiment) Armory
See 71 East 94th Street.

1340 Madison Avenue (94th Street)
ARCHITECTS: A.B. Ogden & Son   DATE: 1894
This five-story-and-basement apartment building stands as a typical example of the Renaissance Revival style, much favored in New York City in the 1890s, that recalls (in a somewhat heavy-handed manner) the classical forms of Greece and Rome. Capping the rough-cut limestone basement and first story is a wide stone band course that wraps around the chamfered corners on 94th Street. The remaining stories are faced with dark-cream brick. Two arches supported by low pilasters frame the

Madison Avenue entrance (altered in 1931 to remove the stoop and enclose the porch). Intricate brickwork surrounding recessed second- and third-story windows creates a pleasant vertical relief. The building's horizontal thrust resumes above the string course: Brick is layered with terra cotta carved in Vitruvian scrolls, alternating with raised brick bands. A quick glance at the fourth and fifth stories would suggest that all windows are round-arched; note, however, that square-headed windows at the attic story are enlivened with lunettes, like raised eyebrows weighing the classical elements below. The building terminates in a bracketed metal cornice. **HD**

1350 Madison Avenue (30 East 95th Street)
ARCHITECT: John C. Burne DATE: 1892-94

Above the nondescript ground story rises a seven-story Renaissance Revival building deserving some scrutiny. This tan-brick apartment house is trimmed in brownstone, with terra-cotta bandings that vary on each story. Two full-height projecting bays on Madison Avenue create an undulating facade, playing against the flat center section with squared stone quoins and flush banding. The contrasts continue: Square-headed windows have bowed railings; round-arched openings are framed by shell-encrusted bands and corbeled pilaster segments. Other details include sunburst lunettes, corbeled sills, and geometric panels carved with shells and leaves. Step across the street for a final treat: Above the seventh-story windows a horizontal string course explodes into a bell shape at the center, crowning a devilish masked keystone. A metal cornice reinforces the building's undulating design. **HD**

1356 Madison Avenue See 27 and 29 East 95th Street

1361 Madison Avenue (95th Street)
Madison Court
ARCHITECT: Harry B. Mulliken DATE: 1900-01

This handsome red-brick-and-stone apartment house rises seven stories from a widely rusticated limestone base (now painted). Early neo-Renaissance details include limestone voussoirs and keystones over windows on the first two stories, pilasters and columns flanking the main entrance, and a wide entablature with a dentiled cornice. The four-story midsection is defined by a limestone cornice that extends to form balconettes fronting window bays. Note the Beaux-Arts-style cartouches marking the base of tall brick pilasters, which support broken limestone pediments punctuating the crown story. Central windows, separated by carved spandrels, are protected with wrought-iron Juliet balconies; those on the sixth story are segmentally arched and embellished with more elaborate cartouches. Outer window bays have eared lintels and keystones and are flanked with stone quoins, further emphasizing the verticality of the midsection. A secondary cornice sets off the top story, which features limestone window surrounds and a wide frieze. The building terminates in a prominent sheet-metal cornice, accented with modillions and dentils and supported by ornate pairs of stone brackets. **HD**

1391 Madison Avenue (97th Street)
ARCHITECTS: Neville & Bagge   DATE: 1904

Rising from a rusticated (painted) limestone base, this imposing six-story Renaissance Revival building is of red-and-blue brick laid in Flemish bond. The second- and sixth-story facades are predominantly limestone, creating a strong horizontal emphasis. At the three-story midsection, limestone quoins define not only the corners but also the double bays on both the avenue and the 97th Street side. These bays are indeed grand: molded pilasters with scrolled, foliate brackets support balustraded balconettes; above the fourth story windows are cornices with broken segmented pediments enclosing ornamental relief carvings. The outer bays have splayed limestone lintels. A Vitruvian scroll pattern adorns the third-story band course. Topping the classical facade is a green-metal cornice with carved panels, mutules, brackets and a dentil course. Tucked between Madison Avenue shops is the main entrance, clearly a later design.

1392-94 and 1396-98 Madison Avenue (24 East 97th Street)
ARCHITECT: George F. Pelham   DATE:1906

These identical six-story buildings have striking similarities to 55-59 East 96th Street and 150-152 East 91st Street, both designed by the prolific George F. Pelham. The entry to No. 1396-98, on 97th Street, has a rusticated limestone base. The segmentally-arched door is framed by an acanthus-leaf molding; over it are a cartouche, voussoirs, and scrolled brackets which support a modillioned and dentiled cornice. A similar entry-way to Nos. 1392-94 is sandwiched between Madison Avenue storefronts. The remaining facades are of red brick laid in Flemish bond. Neo-Federal and Renaissance Revival references embellish the second and crown stories: Windows have blocked-limestone enframements connected by horizontal chain ornamentation; scrolled keystones lap egg-and-dart band courses. Midsection windows are capped with eared lintels and decorative keystones; under each limestone sill are small leafy brackets. The buildings terminate with metal cornices projecting over modillions and dentil moldings.

1040 Park Avenue (86th Street)
ARCHITECTS: Delano & Aldrich   DATE: 1924

The tortoises and hares racing along the third-story frieze of this building share their fame with the fabled first occupant of the penthouse, Conde Nast. The 30-room penthouse, one of the first in the city, was then the neighborhood's largest apartment (although it would soon be surpassed by Marjorie Meriweather Post's 54-room triplex at 1107 Fifth Avenue). The entire apartment was decorated by Elsie de Wolfe. A glass-enclosed ballroom and dining terrace overlooked Park Avenue. It was the frequent scene of luminaries including George Gershwin, Jascha Heifitz, George Grosz, Mary Pickford, Fannie Hurst, Fred Astaire, Bernard Baruch, Katherine Cornell, Rube Goldberg, Cecil Beaton, Edward Steichen and Clare Booth Luce. At Nast's death in 1942 the apartment was broken into smaller units.

The date of the building would suggest neo-Renaissance styling, although some of its ornamentation is so unusual as to defy categorization. The facade is of beige brick over a three-story limestone base; a massive scrolled keystone bracket tops the arched marble entry. There are Art Deco hints in its projecting piers and bull's-eye windows flanking the upper corners. The fourteenth story, just below the penthouse, has an elegant wrought-iron balcony beneath stately rounded windows. The building has no cornice; a frieze of triglyphs and shells is divided by scrolled brackets, with three guttae under each.

1045 Park Avenue (86th Street)
ARCHITECTS: Schwartz & Gross
DATE: 1923

Designed by the architectural team responsible for no fewer than ten buildings in Carnegie Hill, this understated Renaissance Revival building is of reddish-brown brick with limestone accents. Fluted pilasters and a marble entablature with a rosette-and-triglyph frieze flank the doorway. Rising above the entrance is a cast-iron balconette, and a colonnade of four more pilasters topped with a segmentally-arched pediment. Band courses above the third, twelfth and fourteenth floors echo the frieze design. The elaborately ornamented top three stories display limestone window surrounds with urn-and-swag friezes and round-arched pediments, all capped with a dentiled and modillioned cornice.

1049 Park Avenue (86th-87th Streets)
ARCHITECTS: Mills & Bottomley   DATE: 1919

The steep grade up Park Avenue offers immediate rewards with this handsome, thirteen-story-plus-penthouse neo-Renaissance apartment building. The brown-brick facade has rosette-carved quoins on its lower two floors at its corners, echoed in four columns of carved plaques. Limestone window surrounds have carved keystones. Of special note is the classical, three-story entrance design: Double pilasters with composite capitals flank the foliate door surround and balconied window. The entablature is capped with a dentiled cornice, a broken pediment and a triangular pediment. Four classical heads above third-story windows eye passersby serenely. The top three stories offer more visual rewards: Six vertical terra-cotta plaques between the windows are carved with cartouches and garlands. One of the first post-World War I buildings to be completed on Park Avenue, in 1922 the building received a Gold Medal from the American Institute of Architects for the "Best designed Apartment Hotel erected during the past three years."

1050 Park Avenue (87th Street)
ARCHITECT: J.E.R. Carpenter   DATE: 1923

Two fourteen-story apartment houses, 1050 and 1060 Park Avenue, designed by the same architect in the neo-Renaissance style, act as book-ends on the western corners of 87th Street. 1050 sits on a base of rough marble blocks capped with a band course. Italianate urns and swags are the primary decorative motif throughout the building facade. Above the third story a glazed-terra-cotta frieze is topped with an egg-and-dart molding and a small cornice. Arched surrounds with prominent keystones set off the third-story windows. The unadorned midsection is of red brick, broken at the twelfth story by a band course below and a medallion frieze.

The primary entrance on Park Avenue was renovated in 2004. New black-metal-and-glass doors have brass-medallion detailing. The transom has been painted black. Carved rough marble and egg-and-dart moldings frame the doors, which are topped with a small cornice supporting an iron balconette. Carpenter gives the entrance importance by framing the second-story window with paired stone pilasters that support three rows of header bricks, creating an arch with keystone. The tympanum displays swags cascading from an upright urn. The grandest treatment is reserved for the final two stories: Brick patterns create double-height arches surrounding windows; spandrels with urns and swags appear beneath. Arched lintels with a similar motif add large rosettes to top the fourteenth-floor windows. A brick parapet and stone balustrades finish the building.

1055 Park Avenue (87th Street)
ARCHITECT: H. Thomas O'Hara   DATE: 2009 (projected)
Plans call for a twelve-story condominium with a glass curtain wall.

1060 Park Avenue (87th Street)
ARCHITECT: J.E.R. Carpenter   DATE: 1924
The grand entrance to this otherwise relatively modest J.E.R. Carpenter apartment house is on 87th Street. Wood double doors with wrought-iron-and-glass inserts are flanked by carved stone panels. Paired foliate brackets support a cornice forming a narrow balcony. Above, a carved panel is centered between windows framed with pilasters and capped with a rosette-accented entablature. Second-story windows are fronted with iron balconettes and topped with terra-cotta lintels embellished with urns and garlands.

The ground level of the eighteen-story building is clad in smooth limestone. The remainder is red brick; few details distract from the impression of a solid mass. Brick quoins define the corners. Bricks laid vertically form bands between paired floors above the fourth story; more decorative brickwork can be seen in squares between the third- and thirteenth-story windows. Below the crown section is a large stone cornice. There was once an on-premise restaurant, Maison de Lion, to serve the needs of the original housekeeping apartments; it has since been converted into doctors' offices.

1065 Park Avenue (87th Street)
ARCHITECT: Stephen C. Lyras   DATE: 1974
A deeply arcaded white-marble entry with green awnings and double wood-and-glass doors dramatizes the facade of this 30-story beige-brick building. However, it is the abundantly landscaped gardens with their seasonal plantings that give this structure its visual appeal. Not visible from the street, nestled between the plantings and the pathway to 87th Street doctors' offices, is an attractive fountain constructed of informally stacked stones of varying sizes and colors.

1067 Park Avenue (87th-88th Streets)
ARCHITECT: Gilbert A. Schellenger   DATE: 1885

Nestled between substantial apartment buildings, densely shaded, is a 25-foot wide, five-story brick building. It is now painted white and has two street-level commercial establishments—grandfathered, one presumes. There is no cornice. The remaining details reflect Renaissance Revival and Queen Anne styling: Brick piers define the building's corners, dogtooth and beaded bands connect windows, and decorative brickwork tops the fourth story. Partially obscured by fire escapes are eight terra-cotta panels; their egg-and-dart moldings frame finely carved vines encircling mythical winged creatures.

1070 Park Avenue (88th Street)
ARCHITECTS: Schwartz & Gross
DATE: 1928

The exuberant detailing of this sixteen-story building can be broadly characterized as neo-Venetian Gothic. There are similarities to its neighbor five blocks north, 1185 Park Avenue, which was designed by the same architectural team. Presiding over the entryway, between the corbeled hood moldings and double-ogee arch, is a mythical creature spewing vines. More vines are seen in the glass-and-wrought-iron doors. Flanking the entry are pinnacled iron lanterns, niches and pinnacled piers. Above the doorway is a corbeled frieze of mini-lancet arches. More friezes, each bearing a variation of an arch shape, can be seen above the third, twelfth and thirteenth stories.

Perhaps the most dramatic facade features are the three-story-high window bays at the fifth and ninth stories, echoed in two-story versions at the crown. Triple-ogee arches of carved stone enclose trefoil arches; brick pilasters flanking the nine windows are topped with stone pinnacles and rest on carved brackets. Carved limestone plaques separate windows vertically at each story.

Not to be overlooked are the limestone quoins edged with rope moldings, and the water tower with ogee-arched windows, lancet-arched brickwork and a shaped parapet.

1075 Park Avenue (88th Street)
ARCHITECTS: George and Edward Blum   DATE: 1923

The inventive Blum brothers combine classical motifs with enough design quirks to warrant close scrutiny. Paired round-arched windows on the third, sixth, ninth and twelfth floors give the fifteen-story red-brick apartment house a soaring, regal quality. The window surrounds are leafy and spiral; within the arched lintels terra-cotta urns spill flowers and vines. A row of decorative circles underscores the metal modillioned cornice. Returning to ground level, the limestone base over granite has geometric grilles guarding the basement windows. The classical entryway is capped with a flat cornice over rows of egg-and-dart and dentil moldings, above a floral carved entablature. Look closely at the door surround: In the center of the leafy terra-cotta carvings are small Dutch-girl heads.

1080 Park Avenue (88th Street)
ARCHITECTS: Frederick T. Camp   DATE: 1887
              Harry Hurwit   1927

This corner building was the first of eight five-story brick row houses erected in 1887, when steam billowing from the railroad beneath Park Avenue made the area less desirable for residential use. The owner withstood pressures to sell to developers, and in 1927 engaged the architect Harry Hurwit to redesign and stucco the facade. In 1928 David Bogen established the Boghen Pharmacy on the ground story (the name variation is due to a mix-up in licensing); today it is one of a handful of commercial survivors on the avenue.

On 88th Street, the residential entrance is segmentally arched, flanked with pairs of cinched, partially engaged columns with foliate capitals. The carved entablature supports a balconette onto which open windows with pilasters and swan's neck pediments. Third-story window surrounds have engaged columns, echoing those at the entrance, and round-arched pediments. Peaked chimney flues and a hip-roofed enclosure with three arched openings and quoins break the roof line. The entire roof is slightly pitched; under the center section is a series of small blind arches.

1082 Park Avenue (88th-89th Streets)
ARCHITECTS: Frederick T. Camp   DATE: 1887
              Augustus N. Allen   1925

This once-brick, now brightly-colored-tile building was bought in 1902 by Simon Ginsberg, an upholsterer with a shop across the street. Ginsberg opened his store on the ground floor, expanding his business to the fourth

story in 1911. Meanwhile, in 1907 the railroad below was electrified and Park Avenue was being redeveloped with large luxury apartment houses. The 1916 zoning law established this section of the avenue as residential, but Ginsberg's commercial operation was grandfathered. In 1924 the developers of 1088 Park tried to buy No. 1082: Ginsberg was a holdout, and the co-op syndicate acquired an L-shaped plot surrounding both 1080 and 1082.

Not to be outdone, in 1925 Ginsberg hired Augustus N. Allen, designer of the 13-century Florentine-palazzo-style office in Grand Central Terminal for financier John W. Campbell, to create a "neo-Florentine" look. The resulting facade is of glazed-white-and -poly-chromed terra cotta above a ground floor of rusticated blocks. Originally there was lettering reading "Ginsberg" at the attic level and "Furniture & Decoration" at the third story. Over the entrance is an escutcheon with a lion, fleur-de-lis and crescent moon. Seven rosettes decorate the ceiling of the shallow-vault portico, supported by pilasters depicting winged female figures and leaf-and-fruit motifs. At the second story the openings (originally show windows) are framed by spiral columns capped with flattened foliate capitals. The third and fourth floors are joined with double-height panels, punctuated with carved shields and rosettes. The attic story has round-arched windows under a tiled, projecting roof.

An A&P took over the ground floor in 1935. By the 1940s the upper stories were used for medical offices; today they are apartments. The store is occupied by the Dutch Girl Cleaners. In 1997 one of the owners, Evelyn Alvarez, was murdered as she opened her shop early one June morning. In front of the store a tree, with a plaque, is dedicated to her memory.

1085 Park Avenue (88th Street)
ARCHITECTS: Schwartz & Gross   DATE: 1926
The entrance to this understated neo-Renaissance building is flanked with pairs of Corinthian pilasters supporting a simple entablature. Above the door is a double window with a scrolled enframement and keystone. The first three stories are of limestone; the band course under the third floor is detailed with an edge roll and a dentil course. The remaining twelve stories are of buff brick, with the edges marked by stone quoins. Two band courses define the three-story crown section. Visual interest focuses on the thirteenth and fourteenth stories: Window pairs are framed by rope moldings and topped with a dentiled cornice and an escutcheon. Two single windows have scrolled enframements. A row of dentils, an egg-and-dart band and modillions comprise the ornate building cornice.

1088 Park Avenue (88th-89th Streets)
ARCHITECT: Mott B. Schmidt
DATE: 1925

Known for its large yet charming garden courtyard, this fifteen-story apartment house is among Park Avenue's most distinguished buildings. Schmidt intended for his neo-Classical building to encompass the entire block, but a real-estate holdout on the corner of 88th Street necessitated modifying his U-shaped plan while still allowing all apartments a view of the interior garden. The austere limestone-and-gray-brick facade is devoid of ornamentation except for the gargoyle keystone above the main entrance and a giant modillioned cornice framing the roof line. The double-height entrance beneath a great arched glass window leads to a spacious vaulted lobby. The building surrounds a landscaped courtyard on three sides; from the brick terrace the arched glass doorways of the lobby hallways are reminiscent of a Roman aqueduct. At the far end of the courtyard an Italian Mannerist fountain and loggia built above a shallow rectangular pool form the focal point of this hidden city garden.

Robert J. Cuddihy, publisher of *The Literary Digest,* is said to have financed the construction of the building because in 1925, as a Roman Catholic, he was unable to get into another Fifth or Park Avenue co-op. Always an elegant address, the building is favored by families. The courtyard and main vestibule were used as a set in the film *Six Degrees of Separation.*

1095 Park Avenue (89th Street)
ARCHITECTS: Schwartz & Gross   DATE: 1929-30

Rising from a two-level limestone base, this eighteen-story red-brick building was designed for the Tishman family by their longtime architects. The entryway has a rope-coiled limestone surround flanked with multiple panels and hexagonal lanterns. Above the wood-paneled door is a fanlight and keystone. Foliate brackets support a cornice carved in a leaf pattern, above which are decorative limestone window surrounds topped with garlands and a cartouche.

In addition to classical details, the building provides a few surprises in deference to a growing taste for simplified ornamentation. In place of conventional Greek triglyphs, the fifth-story band course is decorated with streamlined indentations. The only major additional decoration is concentrated at the twelfth story: Step back and note the elaborately carved terra-cotta swags and escutcheons. The corners have brick quoins blending with the facade, with an unexpected contrast of limestone against brick at the third and fourth stories. The upper four stories are set back to form terraces.

1100 Park Avenue (89th Street)
ARCHITECTS: DePace & Juster   DATE: 1929-30

A mixture of Venetian, Gothic and Romanesque references lends this architecturally eclectic building its pronounced medieval character. Above a pink-granite base, the first three stories are of ruddy sandstone; the fifteen stories above are reddish brick. Three double-story flattened arches with composite-style capitals and dentils announce the entrance, which is guarded by gargoyles. Within the larger arches, decorative wreaths separate pairs of multi-paned casement windows; the upper windows are also round-arched. More arches are visible immediately above the entrance. At the third story, foliate brackets support two balconies with arched balustrades. Topping the base section is a cornice with Gothic arches and carved shells; an abstract rope detail accents the corners.

The brickwork is also curious: individual bricks project erratically, and brick headers flank many of the windows. At the fourteenth and fifteenth stories are double-height, triple-arched window surrounds, echoed at the water-tank enclosure. Another Gothic-arched cornice tops the seventeenth story. Carved stonework wraps around the building corners.

1105 Park Avenue (89th Street)
ARCHITECT: Rosario Candela   DATE: 1923

One of the earliest designs by the legendary architect Rosario Candela, this reserved fourteen-story building rises from a rusticated limestone base. Limestone brackets support first-level window sills. The midsection and crown are of lightly variegated brick, punctuated by four string courses and capped with a modillioned copper cornice. Evenly spaced brick quoins line the facade extremes. Especially noteworthy is the three-level entry surround. Limestone voussoirs frame the arched doorway; double

pilasters and Ionic capitals rise to a dentiled cornice below the third story. A surprise is just above: The center window is flanked with carved panels and profiles of two classical female figures, suggestive of expectant caryatids. The women support a broken pediment, in the center of which is a shield bearing the letter P, for Michael Paterno, the developer.

1108 and 1110 Park Avenue (89th-90th Streets)
ARCHITECTS: unknown   DATE: 1856

These modest brick houses are among the oldest buildings in Carnegie Hill. Erected as private residences, by 1880 they had stores on the ground level. According to Christopher Gray in a *New York Times* article, "The 1910 census shows them occupied as two-family dwellings; the tenants included a policeman, a Parks Department driver and a department store saleslady in 1108 and an artist and music teacher in 1110." By the 1930s the store tenants were the Baldwin Fish Market and the Bristol Market—"Choice Meats." At this writing the ground-floor occupants of No. 1108 are Marta Salon de Coiffeur and Park Avenue Nutrition Spa; No. 1110 is vacant. Each house was originally three stories. Both retain their bracketed metal cornices, although a bulky modern top-floor art studio was added to No. 1110 in 1985. Note the Victorian doors with colored Minton tiles.

1111 Park Avenue (90th Street)
ARCHITECTS: Schwartz & Gross   DATE: 1926

This fifteen-story red-brick building rises from a low granite base; the first two stories are faced with limestone. Although similar in feeling to its neighbor across 90th Street, 1125 Park, it combines classical motifs with Art Deco geometric elements. Pilasters with flattened foliate capitals rise severely to the notched band course below the third story; window lintels are carved in simple geometric shapes. Above the notched pedimented entrance a large elliptical window is flanked by cornucopias. Third-, thirteenth- and fourteenth-story windows have stone enframements

embellished with curved, fan-carved lintels and flat keystones. Stone quoins and a modillioned, notched cornice define the building's extremities.

1112 Park Avenue (90th Street)
ARCHITECT: Emery Roth   DATE: 1927
Viewed from street level on Park Avenue, this building's most striking feature is a modest second-story window topped with a broken pediment; a small curved balcony is supported with modillions. On either side are flat wrought-iron balconies. Above the three-story base section are a wide band course and stone quoins. A glance upward, however, is rewarded with elaborate terra-cotta window surrounds on the twelfth story, including a larger bracketed balcony and a swan's neck pediment; these elements are repeated on the 90th Street facade. From across the street one can glimpse the attractive water-tower enclosure with broken pediment.

Perhaps the best view of this fourteen-story neo-Italian Renaissance building is from 90th Street. Flanking the main entrance are double pilasters, an entablature carved with ellipses, and a broken pediment and urn, all of which are capped with a dentiled cornice, a balcony and wrought-iron railings. Note the decorative grilles, garlands, more ellipses, and the brickwork around the arched doorway to the service entrance. A final treat is reserved for bird watchers: Over fourth-story windows one can spot medallions bearing terra-cotta eagles.

1120 Park Avenue (90th Street)
ARCHITECT: George F. Pelham   DATE: 1929-30
The entrance to this twenty-story neo-Georgian apartment building is on 90th Street. Glass double-doors and a transom light are framed by carved limestone. Foliate brackets support a cornice capped with feathery scrolls, suggestive of a swan's neck pediment, and a centered cartouche.

Above the limestone base the facade is red brick. The third story is topped with a bas-relief frieze of fruit-garland swags and urns and a band course with a wave-scroll pattern. A thin string course runs above the thirteenth story. The frieze is repeated above the fourteenth floor, adding a diamond pattern beneath a large modillioned cornice. These elaborate details of stone and glazed white terra cotta stand out against the red brick and harmonize with the adjacent red-brick buildings.

Pelham used a variation of the newly-popular "wedding cake" style to draw attention to the center section of the upper floors. Two-story tiers are outlined with white terra cotta across the top and quoins on each side, like cake frosting. The unadorned penthouse extensions are stepped back to create terraces.

1125 Park Avenue (90th Street)
ARCHITECTS: Schwartz & Gross   DATE: 1925-26
A sister to its neighbor at IIII Park (also designed by Schwartz & Gross), this fourteen-story red-brick building rises from a low limestone base sporting a pronounced bullnose; stone quoins line the corners. The elegant two-story entrance surround has extended foliate brackets supporting a carved entablature and projecting cornices. Above, double windows are topped with a broken pediment and urn. There is a garland plaque and cartouche under two second-story windows. The garland-and-urn motif is repeated on the band course above the third story, on fourth-story lintels, and on the two-story crown section, providing a grand view as one looks upward.

1130 Park Avenue (91st Street)
ARCHITECT: George F. Pelham   DATE: 1927
This simple but elegant building is of red brick, rising fifteen stories plus a penthouse from a low marble base. The double-story entrance surround is graced with a flowery carved entablature, foliate brackets and a dentiled cornice. A single window above the door is framed with marble carved in a scroll pattern. Egg-and-dart string courses span the second and thirteenth stories, and more elaborate band courses, each with a garland frieze and dentils, traverse the third and thirteenth stories. Projecting from the eighth floor on both Park Avenue and 91st Street are narrow balconies with marble balustrades.

1133 Park Avenue (91st Street)
ARCHITECT: Nathan Korn   DATE: 1924
Address notwithstanding, the entrance to this sixteen-story red-brick apartment house is around the corner on 91st Street. The building is designed in neo-Italian Renaissance style, much favored by the architect. (The builder was Harris H. Uris, a Latvian immigrant, whose family would become a significant name in post-World War II office developments.) Glass double-doors piercing the two-story limestone base feature ornate wrought-iron motifs, which are echoed in ground-floor window grilles. Delicate terra-cotta carvings of urns and vines embellish the entry surround; above is a cornice composed of a dentil course and two courses with egg-and-dart details. Terra-cotta reveals surround the third-story windows and sections of ornamental brickwork. Balconettes with wrought-iron rails project under windows on the ninth and twelfth stories, and a patinated cornice tops off the building.

1140-1144 Park Avenue
(91st Street)
Brick Presbyterian Church
ARCHITECTS: York & Sawyer
DATE: 1938

The name of the church comes from the material used for the congregation's first church, constructed in 1767, at Beekman and Nassau streets. In 1858 it moved to its second home, on Fifth Avenue and 37th Street. The cornerstone of the present neo-Georgian-style building was laid in 1938, with the dedication in 1940. The architect was William Louis Ayers, of York & Sawyer, the firm that also designed the New-York Historical Society on Central Park West and the Academy of Medicine at 103rd Street and Fifth Avenue.

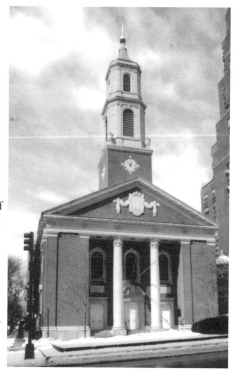

The entire church complex consists of four buildings: the sanctuary, chapel, and old and new parish houses [see 62-64 and 66-70 East 92nd Street]. In 1962 a garden loggia was built to provide a covered passageway between the buildings.

Approach the church along 91st Street and you will best sense that combination of monumentality and human scale that marks this handsome structure. Since the north side of 91st Street is lined with low buildings, the four-story-high brick facade, pierced by tall arched windows, gives both dignity and continuity to the street wall. Turn up Park Avenue, and the facade assumes a more imposing stature. The porch is set within soft red-brick walls laid in Flemish bond, cornered with brick pilasters. The temple front is divided into three bays by two great unfluted columns with Corinthian capitals. The central doorway, surmounted by a double-scroll motif, would make a Salem merchant proud. The pediment above the porch assembly bears a great cartouche containing the Tablets of the Law, a stern reminder of the Old Testament foundation of the Calvinist tradition.

From ground to golden weather vane, the Brick Presbyterian Church rises 149 feet. The square brick tower base, clock faces and gently curved turret are of a size which would seem overbearing in a country setting, but here they help the body of the church stand tall amid the bulk of the neighboring apartment buildings. The small octagonal structure inserted between the church proper and one of those apartment towers is a charming surprise— a bit of *quattrocento* Florence, serving as the entrance to the baptistry and chapel. The otherwise austere facade of the chapel has a pedimented limestone entrance and an oculus window.

In 2005 a four-year restoration program was completed, returning the sanctuary to its original glory. Red-leather doors open to reveal the interior. Its Georgian-style design is the work of Barnet Phillips, whose use of soft light and color reflects the influence of Georgian-era Scottish architect Robert Adam. A flat barrel vault rises on both sides from five transverse barrel vaults, which in turn are supported by great fluted Corinthian columns on pentagonal piers. The coloring is in tones of soft gray with touches of crimson in moldings; details are accented with extensive gilding. The chandeliers were designed by Edward F. Caldwell, whose Art Deco influence can also be found in St. Patrick's Cathedral and the Waldorf Astoria. Observers will spot cherubs, animals, and florals among the neo-Classical motifs of the ceiling and arches. The detailing of the architectural elements is illuminated by natural light pouring through the glass windows, diffusing the sanctuary with subtle amber-and-amethyst tones.

The organ in the sanctuary was built by Casavant Frères of St-Hyacinthe, Québec, and was installed in the summer of 2005. Designed in the French symphonic style, it is modeled after those instruments built in the latter part of the 19th century by the renowned Parisian organ builder Aristide Cavaillé-Coll. The ornately carved console is constructed of red oak and mahogany. The facade consists of twin carved, painted and gilded cases with polished tin pipes, whose sixteen-foot heights flank the chancel. **HD**

1141-1149 Park Avenue (91st Street)
ARCHITECT John Sullivan   DATE: 1885-86
These five adjoining buildings, together with a similar grouping between 94th and 95th streets, are the only remaining clusters of 19th-century row houses on all of Park Avenue. All were originally brownstones, designed in the neo-Grec style. Together, their low-lying symmetry creates a sense of rare open space on Park Avenue, although in 2006 rooftop additions raised the heights of Nos. 1145, 1147 and 1149. Let's look at each building separately, beginning with the northernmost and first to be redesigned, No. 1149.

No. 1149. In 1917 architect Emery Roth redesigned this one-family dwelling, giving the three-story-and-basement row house a Modern

From north to south: Nos. 1149, 1147, 1145, 1143, and 1141 Park Avenue.

Classical limestone facade. The new design called for removal of the stoop and addition of a rear extension, as well as reconstruction of the front wall. A service entrance and a window, both with metal grilles, flank the first-story, classically inspired entrance. Band courses divide the facade above the first and third stories. Each of the upper stories has a large central window with tripartite multi-pane casement sash with transoms. At the fourth story, scrolled brackets support a balconette with decorative ironwork. Rectangular panels flank the window and articulate the parapet.

No. 1147. Although the original stoop was removed sometime after 1929, this house is the only one to retain much of its original character. Each story has its original square-headed window openings. At this writing the cornices and sills are being restored to the first story windows, together with neo-Grec ornamentation to windows, panels, door cornice and door jamb casing. The historic metal roof cornice with large molded brackets and decorative panels caps the building.

No. 1145. Following a plan very similar to the one he used at No. 1149, Emery Roth redesigned this one-family dwelling in the Modern Classical style in 1920-21. The first story has a classically inspired entrance with sidelights and a transom. It is flanked by a service entrance and a window, both with metal grilles. Each of the upper stories has a large central window opening with tripartite windows. Two-story pilasters flank the second- and third-story bays. Balconettes with decorative ironwork adorn the second and fourth stories; the upper balconette is supported by scrolled brackets. A simple stone cornice and a parapet wall surmount the facade.

No. 1143. By the early 1920s the basement and first story of this row house had been converted to commercial use. Extra-large first-story window enframements were installed. In 1924 Emery Roth added project-ing sills to the three windows at each of the upper stories and painted the facade to match the limestone below. (In the late 1980s classically inspired pediments were installed over the windows.) The plate-glass display win-dows and pivoting transoms at the center of each commercial story appear in Roth's plans. The second-story casements and ground-story shop door are later replacements. A small cornice caps the facade.

No. 1141. John Sullivan designed this four-story building with flats for three families, one per story, and stores at ground level. In 1921 the architect Bernard E. James removed the storefronts and converted the space into a doctor's office. At the same time he installed round-arched openings separated by flat pilasters on the Park Avenue facade, and continued the arches along the 100-foot-long 91st Street side. By 1928 the original neo-Grec ornamentation, including window surrounds and the cornice, had been removed. Today the building has a painted-stucco facade. A simple parapet, above which is an iron railing fronting a set-back penthouse, caps the building. **HD**

1150 Park Avenue (92nd Street)
ARCHITECT: George F. Pelham, Jr.   DATE: 1940

Constructed in the Moderne style, this eighteen-story apartment house is an example of evolving architecture on Park Avenue. George F. Pelham, Jr., son of the prolific architect of the same name, used an understated design of red brick and symmetrical vertical lines to complement rather than compete with neighboring classical buildings. Viewed from the south, the building rises from a granite base and provides a seamless backdrop for the Brick Presbyterian Church. The first-story facade consists of white-limestone blocks defined by vertical patterns of striated lines, topped with a half-round molding above a carved scalloped band. This simplicity allows the entryway—of clear-finish aluminum doors, geometrically etched glass and transom, and carved address—to shine.

Above the first-story entrance the building is set back, creating the impression of two asymmetrical towers clad in red brick. Angled windows on each corner reinforce the effect. The pattern of single-and-triple metal-frame windows forms vertical bands emphasizing height. Terraces of varying sizes are stepped back erratically on upper floors, with the largest occurring on the west side of the building. Streamlined metal railings are reminiscent of an ocean liner.

One wonders whether George Jr. felt any competitive pressure in the design process, since his father's building, 1160 Park Avenue, is directly across 92nd Street. **HD**

1155 Park Avenue (92nd Street)
ARCHITECT: Robert T. Lyons   DATE: 1914
This imposing thirteen-story brown-brick apartment house is one of the earliest designed in the neo-Renaissance style. Above a rusticated two-story limestone base, brick quoins frame the building extremes. Applied bricks form vertical piers rising the full height of the building. The three-bay entry projects slightly, framed by double-story pairs of pilasters with egg-and-dart moldings. Capping the entablature is a dentil course and a decorative iron railing. The midsection is unadorned: Ornamental interest is reasserted above the eleventh-story band course, where there are bracketed stone balconies at the end bays, and double-height limestone window surrounds are arched at the top, with diamond spandrels between stories. The modillioned cornice runs above the twelfth story; fortress-like arched parapets frame the top-story end bays. Set-back penthouses were added by architect Emery Roth in 1915 and 1922. **HD**

Park Avenue Mall at 92nd Street "Night Presence IV"
ARTIST: Louise Nevelson DATE: 1972

"Night Presence IV" is among the very few public sculptures cited in this book devoted to architecture. Indeed, the piece has a structural feeling; its 22 1/2-foot height and four-and-one-half tons of bolted steel plates have the visual impact of a small building. The sculpture had previously been located at the southeast entrance to Central Park, a site specifically for temporary displays of artwork. "Night Presence IV" was a gift to the city by the artist; she supervised the installation of the work on the Park Avenue mall at 92nd Street in 1973. Ms. Nevelson created at least six sculptures in her "Night Presence" series, the smallest of which is eleven inches high. A native of Kiev, Louise Nevelson was born in 1899 as Leah Berliawsky and was raised in Rockland, Maine. She married Charles Nevelson in 1920. Eleven years later she separated from him and their nine-year-old son and devoted herself to art. She lived in Carnegie Hill for some years prior to her death in 1988. Today Louise Nevelson is one of America's most recognized artists, with works exhibited at the Whitney Museum, MoMA, and museums throughout the world. **HD**

1160 Park Avenue (93rd Street)
ARCHITECT: George F. Pelham   DATE: 1926

This handsome fourteen-story-plus-penthouse apartment house replaced three smaller buildings known as Holland Court. Pelham's monochromatic design of limestone and beige brick is neo-Renaissance. The smooth limestone base features paired pilasters with elongated acanthus-leaf capitals framing the corner windows and a centered entrance that rises three full stories, giving an impression of sleekness and height. Double wood-and-glass doors with matching transom are framed with a full-swag entablature and a dentil band under a cornice. Above an unadorned entablature and cornice, the nine-story midsection is clad in beige brick. What appear to be balustrade balconies beneath thirteenth-story windows are, in fact, decorative elements of a wide band course. The crown section echoes the pattern of paired pilasters and capitals, using stone blocks surmounted by a wreath-embellished frieze and projecting finishing cornice. The penthouse is set back, providing a glimpse of terraced gardens. **HD**

1165 Park Avenue (93rd Street)
ARCHITECTS: Schwartz & Gross   DATE: 1925-26

Designed in the classic red brick and white limestone of the neo-Georgian style, this fourteen-story apartment house replaced seven residential buildings and a synagogue. Rising from a low stone base on Park Avenue, the basement increases in height with the steep downhill grade on 93rd Street. The entryway is elaborate; fluted pilasters frame wood-and-glass doors topped by a fanlight transom and an entablature with rosettes and dentils. The embellishment continues to the second story. Here, carved limestone reveals and a broken segmental pediment with a cartouche frame the double windows. Limestone quoins line the building extremes. Windows on the second and third stories have splayed limestone lintels and keystones; fourth-story lintels are eared. Above the third story there is a garland frieze and rows of dentils and acanthus leaves. The view of the crown section is very grand indeed: Double- and triple-window bays are framed with two-story terra-cotta surrounds and spandrels. A cornice with dentils and modillions caps the building. **HD**

1172 Park Avenue (93rd Street)
ARCHITECT: Rosario Candela   DATE: 1925-26

Built in the era of grand apartment buildings for developer Michael Paterno, this was one of the earliest cooperative residences in the city, and

among the most luxurious. Many apartments had eleven or twelve rooms. Candela's neo-Renaissance design starts with a three-story limestone base and an appropriately impressive main entry. Rope-coiled moldings surround wood-paneled doors with iron grilles; above is a molded archway with a floral carved tympanum and projecting scrolled keystone. Flanking the doorway are elaborate iron lamps. Secondary entrances echo the arched tympana. A band course of rosettes tops the second story.

The ten-story brick midsection is relatively unadorned. However, ornamentation resumes at the fourteenth-story crown section, with garlanded spandrels beneath windows and a modillioned cornice above. Close inspection—binoculars are suggested—reveals spouts with alternating lions' and rams' heads, guarding their turf and, perhaps, keeping an eye on Candela's bears which adorn his building just up Park Avenue at 1192. **HD**

1175 Park Avenue (93rd Street)
ARCHITECT: Emery Roth   DATE: 1924-25

Rising majestically at the peak of Park Avenue, this fourteen-story-plus-penthouse apartment building exhibits rich classical detailing at the lower

sections and crown story. On the Park Avenue side, eleven double-story pilasters with Corinthian capitals rise from the rusticated limestone base, framing second- and third-story windows and supporting an entablature carved with rosettes. Quartets of pilasters echo the design on 93rd Street. Limestone quoins embellish the corners. The red-brick midsection is relatively unadorned, except for stone balconettes at the twelfth story. The crown section is framed with dentil and rosette-embellished courses; between window bays are panels with terra-cotta shields. The neo-Renaissance building is topped with a cornice supported by scrolled foliate brackets.

Around the entrance are multiple moldings carved with acanthus leaves and flowers, and panels with garlands, ribbons, shields, vases and—look closely—rams' heads terminating with talons. The entryway is capped with modillions supporting an acanthus-carved cornice and a shallow iron rail. **HD**

1185 Park Avenue (93rd-94th Streets)
ARCHITECTS: Schwartz & Gross   DATE: 1929

This sixteen-story apartment house, encompassing an entire block front, is a fine example of Venetian Renaissance style, drawing inspiration more from the Gothic than from classical antecedents. Built by Bricken Construction, it was the last of the large apartment buildings designed in the shape of a quadrangle, in the tradition of the Belnord, the Dakota, and the Apthorp on the Upper West Side.

Centered on Park Avenue is a triple-ogee-arched portal framed by multiple engaged columns with foliate capitals. A wide central driveway is flanked with pedestrian walkways with lanterns suspended from the vaulted arches, leading to an interior courtyard. Within are six separate apartment units (connected only through their basements); individual lobbied entrances are set around a raised, sun-filled oval garden with a fountain in the center. The facade is of red brick, richly ornamented with limestone and terra cotta. The base and first two stories are faced with limestone ashlar, topped with a leafy frieze. Third-story windows are flanked with spiral columns, above which runs a wide frieze carved with overlapping arches and trefoils. Cornices, some accented with foliate corbels, intersect the facade every third story. Five-bay vertical sections are defined by quoined corners and three-story-high spiral engaged columns; connecting spandrels are carved with ogee arches, quatrefoils and shields. Even the brickwork is embellished with lancet-arch designs. The building terminates with a grand, open-arched frieze and a water tower that echoes the Venetian Gothic elements below.

A subject of frequent comment are the "police" uniforms of the doormen. Reports from the building staff indicate that the uniforms are specially made and originated during the controversial trial of Ethel and Julius Rosenberg in 1951. The judge, Irving Kaufman, was a resident of 1185 Park Avenue at the time, and the building asked the New York City Police Department to furnish the doormen with police uniforms—caps included—to appear as if the judge had round-the-clock protection, should anyone wish him harm. **HD**

1192 Park Avenue (94th Street)
ARCHITECT: Rosario Candela   DATE: 1926

Considered one of the country's greatest designers of luxury apartment buildings, Candela was responsible for seven buildings in Carnegie Hill, four of which are on Park Avenue. Rising from a rough-hewn gray-stone base, this fifteen-story brown-brick building has ornate wrought-iron grilles over the first-level windows. Much attention was paid to decoration on the facade. Above the central third-story window is a carved plaque. On both Park Avenue and 94th Street, window pairs on the fourth story have elaborate ornamentation adding carved projections, finials and corbels. Third- and thirteenth-story windows have spiral surrounds; under string courses and every sill are a row of dentils. The double-crown section terminates with an arched banding and a Mediterranean red-tile roof line.

The round-arched entry surround was originally constructed of pre-cast concrete to emulate limestone. Over the years the concrete deteriorated. In a major renovation in 2006, the entire decorative entry and second-story window surround were removed and replaced with carved limestone, replicating the crisp detail in Candela's original design. Carved escutcheons, corbels and a row of Mediterranean arches are topped with a curved cornice and finials resembling chess pieces. Above the window is an architrave and segmental pediment with a carved tympanum. A surprise awaits beneath the entrance canopy: a newly designed fanlight, framed in wood with amber-hued leaded glass. At the building base, the concrete bull-nosed string course was replaced with limestone, and concrete blocks were replaced with granite. Candela would have been proud.

1199 Park Avenue (94th Street)
ARCHITECTS: Sylvan & Robert L. Bien   DATE: 1961

Rising near the peak of Carnegie Hill, this eighteen-story red-brick apartment house features a reddish-brown marble entry surround and projecting balconies. A landscaped perimeter garden wraps around Park Avenue and slopes gently down 94th Street.

1209 Park Avenue (94th-95th Streets)

ARCHITECTS: Flemer & Koehler   DATE: 1889-90
    Lucien David   1960-62

This three-story building was once a part of a group of seven Renaissance
Revival row houses that included Nos. 1209 through 1217 on the avenue
and Nos. 112 and 114 on 95th Street. Shortly after its original construction
an addition was made in the rear; the stoop was removed in 1930 to
accommodate the widening of Park Avenue. In 1960 the residence was
redesigned in the Modern style by French architect Lucien David (his work
was interrupted and later completed by two other architects) for the Ecole
Francaise. The facade is stark and executed in tan brick with a recessed
southern bay and steel sash window openings. Since 1976 the building has
been occupied by the Town House International School. **HD**

1211 Park Avenue (94th-95th Streets)

ARCHITECTS: Flemer & Koehler   DATE: 1899-90
    William L. Bottomley 1922

Like its neighbors on either side and around the corner, this townhouse
saw its Renaissance Revival row-house beginnings in 1889. Some 35 years
later, the stoop was removed and the entire facade was stuccoed and
redesigned in a neo-Georgian style. The basement level was extended, with
two paneled-wood doors and a pair of windows added; above it is a Juliet
balcony with wrought-iron railings. The grand first story, treated as a *piano
nobile*, has three full-length windows with transoms; the center window is
topped with a broken pediment and urn, flanked with rondels. A dentil
course caps the second story. Third-story windows are round-arched with
flattened keystones, framed with pilasters. A classical balustrade terminates
the roof line. **HD**

1213, 1215, and 1217 Park Avenue; 112 and 114 East 95th Street

ARCHITECTS: Flemer & Koehler   DATE: 1889-90

These row houses were originally part of a group of seven. (Nos. 1209 and
1211 have been substantially altered, so we have given them individual
descriptions.) The houses on Park Avenue retain their original Renaissance
Revival character, and as such are unique survivors on a two-mile stretch
of imposing apartment buildings. The paired brownstones on 95th Street
have typical Queen Anne elements, as do their companions down the
block known as Goat Hill. The Park Avenue buildings display metal cornices with brackets and swags. All five buildings include brownstone basement and parlor floors; the upper stories are red brick.

  Below the cornice of No. 1213 are three floral carved panels. Brick
pilasters with foliate capitals unify the upper two stories. Smaller pilasters

frame third-story windows, which are capped with egg-and-dart moldings.
A three-sided sheet-metal oriel is elaborately decorated with moldings and
panels. The stoop was removed in 1930; in 1958 a curved iron staircase
and parlor-floor entrance were installed. The three round-arched openings have hood moldings; there are foliate keystones over the windows and
an unusual double-masque keystone over the door. Below the windows are

North to south on Park Avenue:
Nos. 1217, 1215, 1213, 1211, and 1209

panels carved with fruit and flowers. The lower facade is scored stucco.

No. 1215 adds rosettes to its cornice and echoes the carved panels
below the roof line. The top-story windows are round-arched, separated
by brick pilasters; an acanthus frieze runs below. A swelled bay rises from
the basement through the second story. The original red brick is now
mottled; the lower facade is of rock-faced brownstone. The stoop was
removed in 1958 and a basement entrance was created. Historic iron
grilles protect ground-level windows.

No. 1217 underwent extensive restoration and facade resurfacing in
2006. Except for the absence of carved panels, the upper two stories on
Park Avenue are identical to those at No. 1213. Under the oriel a corbeled
brick facing was added. Round-arched windows on the parlor floor have
hood moldings; a trio of whimsical creatures eye passersby. On either side
are terra-cotta escutcheons, incised to suggest tiny bearded faces. On 95th
Street, a wide three-step stoop is flanked with newel posts and iron
railings. Gas-burning lanterns hang on either side of the door. Only the
lowest portion on 95th Street is brownstone; the top three stories are red
brick, with brownstone quoins defining the corners. Centered over the
entrance, brick pilasters flank the second- and third-story windows,

between which is a carved spandrel (including, perhaps, another face). The upper round-arched window has a hood molding. Narrow arched niches shelter foliate carvings. Also in 2006 a garage was re-introduced and two stories were added above it, plus a third, set-back story behind an iron railing.

112 and 114 East 95th Street are mirror-image Queen Anne row houses, and both have been well preserved. Newel posts highlight their shared eleven-step stoop; two of the three stair rails are historic, as are both basement window grilles. The main entryways vary: No. 112 has a glass-and-iron door and grilled transom, while No. 114 has a painted wood-paneled door. The center pilaster features a carved diamond motif. Look carefully: The outer pilasters framing each door are topped with impish faces. More scrutiny will reveal panels carved with leaves and—dragons? Both doors and parlor-story windows have projecting cornices with dentil rows. Upper-story windows are framed with terra-cotta blocks carved with acanthus leaves. Beneath the cornice are dentils, geometric brickwork and an egg-and-dart string course. **HD**

1220 Park Avenue (95th Street)

ARCHITECT: Rosario Candela DATE: 1929

This sixteen-story-plus-penthouse building was designed by one of the city's leading architects of luxury apartments. A three-story limestone base with granite footing is capped by a band course with rosettes; the remaining facade is of brown brick with neo-Classical ornamentation. The main entrance on Park Avenue has a one-step-up entrance framed with rosettes and surmounted by a scrollwork cartouche. Two secondary entrances are set within deep arches, framed by columns with rosette-decorated Doric capitals that support a cornice of triglyphs and raised disks. Second-story windows directly above have balconettes and form a unit with the doors below: both windows and entrances are set within shallow arches with scrolled cartouches. All first- and second-story windows have grilles. Openings directly above are connected visually by limestone swags. At the fifth story are three windows with decorated pediments and limestone surrounds and balustrades; two similar windows continue the theme on the 95th Street facade. Above the thirteenth story are corner setbacks with terraces.

Crowning an arched double-height penthouse is a balustraded parapet and eight neo-Classical urns. The highly visible (and much photographed) water-tank enclosure has pedimented openings within arches with scrolled keystones, all capped with a modillioned cornice.

Former New York State Governor Hugh Carey was a resident.

1225 Park Avenue (95th Street)
ARCHITECT: George F. Pelham   DATE: 1926

This apartment house may well have been designed to complement the original Squadron A (Eighth Regiment) castellated armory that was diagonally across the street (now replaced with a modernistic interpretation, designed in 1971 to house a public school). Its style is neo-Tudor Gothic, with turrets framing the entrance, and battlements at the cornice and on the penthouse and water tower. Rising sixteen stories plus a penthouse, the facade is of smooth beige brick. Trefoil banding above the third story and Tudor-style molding above the entrance and windows of the first and second stories complete the fortress-like impression.

1230 Park Avenue (96th Street)
ARCHITECTS: Gronenberg & Leuchtag   DATE 1928

This sixteen-story neo-Renaissance building is more elaborate than its neighbor across the street (1235 Park Avenue), designed by the same architects. Details are concentrated in the two-story base and three-story crown section; the thirteen-story midsection is unadorned brown brick.

The double-height central section on Park Avenue is faced in limestone, which frames the main entrance and a similar-sized window. Both openings are capped with five mini-arches, each filled with a shell motif. Flanking the door and window are pairs of engaged columns carved with flowers and spirals, and topped with mischievous faces. Above are pairs of arched windows with decorative moldings; Corinthian capitals top the dividing columns. On either side, square-headed windows are ornamented with winged horses and lions. A carved band course supported by small brackets tops the second story.

Double string courses run above the thirteenth story. At the fourteenth and fifteenth stories, groups of paired windows are separated vertically with rosette panels, and unified with double-story brick pilasters and decorative limestone arches. A frieze of mini-arches and a shallow limestone cornice cap the building.

1235 Park Avenue (96th Street)
ARCHITECTS: Gronenberg & Leuchtag   DATE: 1929
This fifteen-story-plus-penthouse building is designed in a similar neo-Renaissance style as its sister building (1230 Park) across the avenue. The facade is of rough-textured brown brick. Flanking the entrance, which is framed by two finely carved moldings, are large iron lanterns. Above the third floor are pairs of windows framed by foliate engaged columns topped by arches with finials; there are rosettes in the central panels. Cable molding appears above the second and twelfth stories, and more foliate arches are visible above the top-story windows. The cornice is roofed with round tiles. Note the panels of twin birds at the second story.

1240 Park Avenue (96th Street)
The Van Cortlandt
ARCHITECT: George F. Pelham   DATE: 1905

Four buildings by the same architect—53-55, 57-59, and 65 East 96th Street, and 1240 Park Avenue—create a pattern and balance on the north side of 96th Street between Madison and Park avenues. Perhaps it was the Park Avenue address that prompted George F. Pelham to incorporate so many Renaissance Revival embellishments on the six-story Van Cortlandt.

The off-center entrance on 96th Street is flanked with iron lanterns on elaborate iron stands, and paired polished-granite columns with stylized Ionic capitals. Identical pilasters and a carved ribbon-and-leaf molding frame the doors and transom. "The Van Cortlandt" is carved in the entablature, above which is a balustraded balcony. Ground-level windows have carved stone plaques below and are capped with voussoirs and keystones. Horizontal bands of rusticated limestone define the first story; the red-brick remainder of the building sets off the extensive stone carvings. Quoins frame paired windows in the center and on end bays from the second to the fifth stories; embellishments include segmented and pointed pediments with carved tympana, keystones, shells and carved plaques. Small windows are framed with horn-and-fruit carvings and mythical mascarons. The fifth story is topped with a band course with cartouches and a cornice. A stylized frieze of swags and triglyphs, dentils and a modillioned cornice caps the building.

1245 Park Avenue (96th Street)
ARCHITECTS: Pomerance & Brienes   DATE: 1967
This nineteen-story buff brick building has a recessed bi-level entrance on 96th Street, and terraced setbacks above the thirteenth and fifteenth stories. It was taken over in 1977 by Mount Sinai Hospital as a staff residence.

1293-1301 Lexington Avenue (87th Street)
ARCHITECT: Edward W. Gayle   DATE: 1896-97

The centered residential entrance (No. 1297) of this five-story flats building displays Renaissance Revival elements typical of the period. The doorway is framed with multiple moldings carved with egg-and-dart motifs, acanthus leaves and coiled vines; birds can be spotted in the pilasters flanking the steps. Above, however, the style is closer to Romanesque Revival: Rough-cut brownstone quoins and band courses connect lintels and sills, accenting the (painted) creamy-brick facade. Triple bays over the entrance are edged with stone quoins, separated at each floor with sturdy stone panels. Fifth-story windows are round-arched, crowned with more rough stones. The building terminates with a molded metal cornice embellished with dentils, modillions and vines.

1311-1329 Lexington Avenue (141 East 88th Street)
ARCHITECTS: Sugarman & Berger
DATE: 1928

The architectural features of this neo-Renaissance building are easy to overlook due to the bustling commercial space on the street level. In the center of the full-block facade is a double entry; the entablature over each of the doors bears a wreath and the Lexington Avenue address (however, the awning reads "141 East 88th Street"). Identical projecting cornices are carried by foliate brackets. Three pilasters with Corinthian capitals support a second-story entablature; under the double-width cornice is a small dentil course. Even the service entrances have pilasters with Doric capitals.

Rising from a three-story limestone base, the remaining eight stories are of red brick. Limestone quoins accent the corners. Wrought-iron balconettes project above the entrance and at various stories on all three sides of the building. A wide limestone frieze at the eleventh story is capped with a modillioned cornice.

Visible from several blocks away (and worth the walk) are the building's most striking features: its twin water towers. Each side has a molded Roman arch supported by Doric pillars and pilasters, with a full classical entablature above. The corners are graced with urns festooned with garlands. Topping the red-brick towers are molded limestone cornices with notched corners.

1324 Lexington Avenue (88th Street)
ARCHITECTS: Bernstein & Bernstein   DATE: 1904

This exuberant example of Renaissance Revival architecture rises to six stories above Lexington Avenue's busy shop fronts. The facade is of beige brick. Paired and symmetrically grouped windows offer varying surrounds, including triangular and segmental pediments embellished with cartouches, carved tympana, foliate brackets, and stone facing extending to the sills above. Windows on the fourth to sixth stories are capped with carved keystones and splayed lintels. In the center of the building, pairs of oculus windows are framed with lushly carved oval wreaths. Band courses accent the second and fifth stories. A bracketed, modillioned cornice with a garland frieze crowns the facade.

1340-1350 Lexington Avenue (89th Street)
ARCHITECT: Henry J. Hardenbergh   DATE: 1889

In the early 1800s William C. Rhinelander owned real estate both in downtown New York City and uptown, including an irregularly shaped thirteen-block Yorkville tract. At this time, plans were announced for elevated trains to replace the Third Avenue horse-drawn line, causing a speculative boom. The Rhinelander family descendants erected more than 100 row houses and flats between 86th Street and 91st Street, from Lexington Avenue to First Avenue.

These six houses are the only survivors on Lexington Avenue. They

1STECHER

are quality buildings, designed in an a-b-c-c-b-a pattern as single-family residences for people of "modest fortune." Queen Anne in style and three stories tall, all are of brick trimmed with dark or buff-colored brownstone. Stoops have been removed, but original hooded doorways and arched parlor-story windows display inventive use of splayed stonework and carved spandrels. Decorative panels, peaked pediments over jaunty projecting bays, and cornices topped with bull's-eye stone railings and newel caps are some of the whimsical features. Each house has its own tiny garden. Andy Warhol moved into No. 1342 in 1959 with his mother and, by the early 1960s, they reportedly housed 25 cats, all named Sam. He used the ground floor as a studio and lived there until 1974.

In 1991 the corner building, No. 1340, was totally renovated to create a commercial space with a large picture window. Construction was undertaken without the required work permit, prompting Carnegie Hill Neighbors to protest. However, work was not stopped because the building did not have landmark status. To protect this unique group of buildings from future changes and to insure their architectural integrity, CHN led a vigorous campaign to designate the six buildings, together with the contiguous 121 East 89th Street [which see], as the Hardenbergh/Rhinelander Historic District. The designation was granted by the New York City Landmarks Preservation Commission in 1998. **HD**

1349 Lexington Avenue (90th Street)
ARCHITECTS: Maynicke & Franke
DATE: 1921
The plot of ground on which this ten-story building stands originally belonged to the Rhinelanders; at the time it opened it was called the Paulding, an old family name of the Rhinelanders. A cursory glance would characterize the style as neo-Renaissance. Classical design elements abound: The three-story base (now stuccoed) is topped with a five-story midsection and a two-story crown. Guarding the entryway, double-height  engaged columns and pilasters with acanthus capitals support an entablature with rosettes. Directly above are a dentil course, cornice and balconette. Fourth-story windows have brick voussoirs and limestone keystones; fifth- and seventh-story windows have curved balconettes. Over the eighth story is a band course with triglyphs and more rosettes. At the ninth story, pairs of windows are capped with round-arched limestone carved sunbursts. A modillioned cornice terminates the building's classical design. Around the

corner on 90th Street, the apartment house recesses, providing light for upper-floor residents and a shady planted courtyard.

But wait! (as they say in commercials)—The Lexington Avenue entry surround is of black marble, leading to a brass-and-glass door; there are geometric brass grilles over small street-level windows; balcony railings throughout the facade are of stylized wrought iron; and the brass address number, 1349, is in Futura, a popular typeface of the '30s and '40s . . . all characteristics of Art Deco style. Presumably, these modifications were made after the building changed hands in 1944.

1361 Lexington Avenue (90th Street)
ARCHITECT: Brandt & Co.   DATE: 1885
This four-story red-brick flats building is designed in a simplified Queen Anne style. Multiple stone bands (painted) connect windows and lintels, creating a horizontal emphasis. Second-story windows have stone cornices and sills; those in the center are divided by pilasters, which are incised to resemble fluting. Wide brick piers with stone corbels stop just short of the band course above the shop fronts. Terminating the facade (and worth noting) is a row of geometric brickwork and a metal cornice with brackets and sunburst carvings.

1364 Lexington Avenue (90th-91st Streets)
ARCHITECT: Weber & Drosser   DATE: 1892
Acanthus-bearded lions atop fluted pilasters guard the entryway of this weathered five-story Renaissance Revival building. Above street-level shops, the midsection is of beige brick; windows, corners and the slightly projecting central facade are faintly quoined with a lighter shade of brick, while darker bricks provide horizontal accents. Window pediments are richly carved and of varying forms: Those on the second story alternate triangular and segmental shapes, while those above display jaunty curves and peaks. Terra-cotta carvings cap fourth-story windows.

Step across Lexington Avenue to view the elaborate crown section: Horizontal bands of dark brick connect windows, which are flanked with paired brick pilasters and capped with terra-cotta shells, sunbursts and floral motifs. The heavily-bracketed molded metal roof cornice peaks over the center of the building. A once-ornate dentiled frieze below the attic story has been removed from all but a tiny section of the 90th Street facade, which also rewards the viewer with another surprise—a palmette-crowned, flowered-and-beribboned goddess peering down serenely.

1372-1378 Lexington Avenue (128 East 91st Street)
ARCHITECT: Schuman & Lichtenstein   DATE: 1953

Stores line the street level of this four-story building, which replaced four neo-Grec brownstones. Only the Lexington Avenue facade exhibits architectural detailing: Six horizontal bands of brick alternate ocher and light brown, with every third row of brown bricks projecting slightly to reinforce the "streaming" effect reminiscent of Art Deco design of several decades earlier. Four pairs of windows interrupt the brown-brick sections at each floor. A simple stone molding caps the building. The residential entrance is through a courtyard on 91st Street.

1377-1379 Lexington Avenue (91st Street)
The Weber
ARCHITECTS: Weber & Drosser   DATE: 1889-90

This five-story brown-brick structure is surely among the more curious survivors of 19th-century Yorkville. Few surface areas have escaped the designers' relentless Renaissance Revival hand. At the street level run seven rows of horizontal brick-and-stone bands, before even reaching the first dentiled and beaded string course. Presiding over the two projecting entryways are terra-cotta laughing creatures—mascarons—flanked with voussoirs, bracketed skew-backs, flowers, and fish.

Window surrounds on each story display an amazing assortment of ornamentation: panels carved with urns and vines; lapped stone moldings; lintels with garlands and small faces; foliate keystones; and carved reveals. At the third story, segmentally-arched pediments and shells alternate with heavily corniced windows, below which are fluted pilasters, spandrels, and—count them—ten stone goddesses. Above the fourth story are bands of wave scrolls, wide dentils and a cornice; fifth-story windows have brick pilasters and foliate keystones. Finally, above the heavily detailed metal cornice perches a pedimented roof house, inscribed—lest we forget—WEBER.

1380-1386 Lexington Avenue (91st Street)
ARCHITECT: Adam Weber   DATE: 1885

These four row houses were designed in the neo-Grec style for builders John and Louis Weber. Viewed in the morning sun, the red brick with brownstone trim, crisply incised pilasters, bracketed metal cornices and lush wisteria vines paint a visually arresting architectural streetscape. Nos. 1380 and 1382, which are the most intact, share a double masonry stoop parallel with the buildings. Both have historic double-leaf wood-and-glass

doors. On the avenue facade of No. 1380, stone brackets support a second-story iron balcony. Around the corner on 91st Street, a parlor-story oriel is capped with a wood cornice; above and below are paired windows with stained glass. An original wrought-iron fence encloses a moat-like passageway. A freestanding clapboard garage was added in 1922.

Brownstone quoins edge the windows of Nos. 1384 and 1386. In the mid-20th century, stoops were removed and projecting storefronts were added to both buildings. **HD**

1388 Lexington Avenue (91st-92nd Streets)
ARCHITECT: John B. Snook   DATE: 1871-72

This five-story brownstone is one of the few in Carnegie Hill designed in Second Empire style, characterized by a high, slate-covered mansard roof with a top curb and pedimented dormers. A metal cornice tops the fourth story, beneath which are two stories of flat-hooded windows. Parlor-story windows are pedimented, and all sills have small neo-Grec-style brackets. The building was originally a one-family residence and included such amenities as nine wood-burning fireplaces, a wood-paneled library, and oak parquet flooring with teak-and-mahogany borders. Extensive renovations in 1928 created one apartment per floor. In 1950 the parallel stoop was removed and a ground-level projection was added for commercial use. **HD**

1390 Lexington Avenue (91st-92nd Streets)
OWNER/DEVELOPER: D.M. Smith   DATES: 1855(?), 1871, 1905, 1931

Originally a small frame house on East 92nd Street, possibly built by Albro Howell, this building was moved around the corner In 1869 when Lexington Avenue was cut through. It was expanded upwards in 1871 and in 1905 architect A.B. Ogden installed storefronts. A brick extension and stepped parapet were added in 1931, and the facade was stuccoed. Today, the only reminders of its 19th-century character are the upper windows with projecting lintels. **HD**

1395 Lexington Avenue (91st-92nd Streets)
The 92nd Street Y
ARCHITECTS: Necarsulmer & Lehlbach—Gehron & Ross   DATE: 1929-30
            Gilbert Seltzer 1968

Formally known as the Young Men's and Young Women's Hebrew
Association, the 92nd Street Y has been a unique cultural landmark for
the city—and indeed the entire country—for more than 100 years. Founded
in 1874, by 1900 the organization had outgrown its quarters at 861
Lexington Avenue. Banker-philanthropist Jacob Schiff (father-in-law of
Felix Warburg, who built the mansion now occupied by the Jewish Museum)
bought the property on the corner of 92nd Street and Lexington Avenue,
and then financed the construction of a stately four-story building
designed by architect Arnold Brunner in the Beaux-Arts style. Just 28
years later it was demolished to make way for the larger present-day facility.

Architecturally, the twelve-story building is eclectic, with pronounced
Art Deco references. Variegated red brick is laid in the common bond
style (five rows of stretchers followed by a row of headers). On 92nd Street
a band of limestone blind arches can be glimpsed above the ninth story;
full-height brick arches are visible on the setback above the eleventh story.
Sections of herringbone-patterned brick appear above the fourth and
sixth stories. Vertical bricks form window lintels; above the double-height
ground story, corner brick piers rise six stories to frame the central section.
Stone balconies with whimsical carved figures project from corner windows
on the seventh story. On both 92nd Street and Lexington Avenue, street-
level window surrounds display keyed
enframements, with the upper blocks
carved to remind viewers of the institution's cultural mission: art, music,
literature, biblical study, physical fitness.
A limestone band course bears quotes
from Ecclesiastes: "Rejoice, O Young
Man, in thy Youth" and "Remember thy
Creator in the Days of thy Youth."

Most striking is the vertical design
of the central portion above the
Lexington Avenue entrance. Limestone
bands rise uninterrupted through the
tenth story, framing three pairs of windows
at each story. The outer bands are quoined.
Stonework diamonds above the third
story frame leaded-glass windows; directly
above is a row of stone balconettes.

Between each of the higher stories is an interplay of stone and brick, forming a variety of geometric designs leading the eye upward.

In 1968 the Henry Kaufmann Building, a residential, office, music and art studio facility designed by Gilbert Seltzer, was added to the south, extending the footprint to 91st Street. Rising from a brown-marble base, the second and third stories are of stone, with projecting vertical window dividers; the remaining eight stories are of white brick.

1402 Lexington Avenue (92nd Street)
ARCHITECTS: C. Abbott French & Co.   DATE: 1886-87

Austere and gleaming in the morning sun, this five-story red-brick building is designed primarily in Romanesque Revival-style on the Lexington Avenue facade. However, its 92nd Street side has a full brownstone facing (now painted) with neo-Grec molded lintels and brackets, presumably to blend with the adjoining row houses. The most dramatic features are tall chimney flues, articulated with brick channels and carved stone panels. There is decorative brickwork above second-story windows, and carved spandrels below the fourth story. A continuous stone band connects fourth-story lintels. Top-story windows are round-arched with keystones and flush stone imposts. **HD**

1413 Lexington Avenue (92nd-93rd Streets)
ARCHITECT: George Mort Pollard   DATE: 1924

There are no records of the original construction of this freestanding four-story building. The facade dates from a 1924 alteration, when the basement was removed to create two projecting stories of commercial space. At the top two floors, white shutters accent the red brick, which rises uninterrupted to a parapet and fence.

1428 Lexington Avenue (93rd Street)
The Summit
ARCHITECT: Edward Wenz   DATE: 1889-90

Most flats buildings of this era were designed for builders who developed large tracts of land. The Summit was designed for a local grocer, Theodore Cordler, with eight apartments and ground-story stores. (The architect also designed the adjacent building in a similar Queen Anne style.) The red-brick facade has projecting central bays and decorative chimney flues. Horizontal stone bands connect sills and lintels. Softening the grid are foliate panels, foliate arches topped by extended keystones, elliptical double arches with spandrels, and small incised pediments. A metal cornice with scrolled brackets caps the facade. The main entrance on Lexington Avenue has been remodeled in a jarringly Art Deco style. Note the small address stone at the corner. **HD**

1432 Lexington Avenue (92nd-93rd Streets)

ARCHITECT: Edward Wenz   DATE: 1889-90

This four-story Queen Anne-style building shares many decorative details with its adjacent neighbor to the south, designed by the same architect. The brown-brick facade is divided into three slightly recessed bays, accented with stone bands and continuous sill courses. Windows exhibit an amusing variety of trims: projecting hoods with small brackets; pediments, and foliate spandrels. Over the center window is a foliate arch and keystone. A sunburst radiates from in the center of the three-section modillioned cornice. **HD**

1434-1440 Lexington Avenue (93rd-94th Streets)

ARCHITECT: Frederick T. Camp   DATE: 1882-83

These four-story brownstones were originally part of a row of six buildings; the two northernmost were demolished in 1901 for the construction of 138 East 94th Street. All were built to accommodate one family per floor. The original triangular pediments and other ornamental details have been removed. A storefront was added to Nos. 1436 and 1438 in 1905 and to No. 1434 in 1908; the earlier buildings were joined internally in 1947. No. 1440 had its first floor lowered and a storefront added in 1931. **HD**

1435 Lexington Avenue (94th Street)

ARCHITECTS: George & Edward Blum   DATE: 1925

The fourth and final building in Carnegie Hill to be designed by the innovative Blum team, this eleven-story brown-brick apartment house rises from a two-story limestone base. Its decor fuses Gothic elements, seen in the lancet-arched windows trimmed with carved terra cotta, with traditional themes. Engaged columns with floral capitals divide round-arched window pairs. The entry surround combines geometrics and leafy terra-cotta carvings; cherub-like figures frolic above the canopy. The glass-iron-and-brass door is embellished with leafy patterns; and just above, two griffins guard an urn. Decorative brickwork enlivens the window sills. The building is best viewed in the late-afternoon sun, when the textured facade is studded with brick crosses and diamonds. Above the eleventh floor is a slightly projecting cornice—more like a frieze—composed

of squares and circles. These are interrupted by three sets of whimsical creatures, each nestled in its own peaked brick niche, protected from the elements.

1449 Lexington Avenue (94th Street)
ARCHITECT: Raymond J. Beech   DATE: 1989

Originally part of the neo-Grec brownstone row designed in 1878 by Thom & Wilson [see below], this building was reclad in blue brick in 1955 and allowed to deteriorate. When the owner went into bankruptcy in 1989, Beech Associates, a tenant and design firm specializing in brownstone renovations, purchased the property and made its own restoration and renovation, partly to showcase the firm's abilities. Beech rebuilt the rear garden, covered the facade with a stucco-like material scored to resemble limestone, and recreated a two-story mahogany bay window on 94th Street.

1451-1457 Lexington Avenue (94th-95th Streets)
ARCHITECTS: Thom & Wilson   DATE: 1878-79

Like honor guards of a Victorian regiment, this quartet of neo-Grec brownstones has stood tall, defying developers and take-out counters. The buildings were part of a square block of 40 nearly identical brownstones erected for Michael Duffy. Remarkably, 29 still stand. [See 157-179 East 94th Street and 158-180 East 95th Street, Hellgate Hill.) In the 1950s, with the widening of Lexington Avenue, the stoops were removed. In 1981 a developer filed plans for a 33-story "sliver" building on the eighteen-foot-wide site of No. 1451. The building was to be named the Empyrean, meaning "highest heaven." The plan so outraged the neighborhood that it joined with local groups opposing other slivers, which resulted in the enactment in 1983 of New York City's "sliver law," limiting narrow mid-block buildings to the height of adjacent buildings. In the ensuing years, the individual owners of the four brownstones cooperated on a stunningly authentic and cohesive facade restoration. No. 1453 had the best-preserved exterior and served as a guide for recreating the flower medallions, cornices, window ledges, wrought-iron grillwork, and iron fencing topped with classic English spears, and matching ironwork around the tree wells.

   No. 1451: The first occupant was Orren Hutchinson, an agent for Poland Spring Water, who remained only until 1881. The second family was that of German immigrant Raphael Ettinger, who worked in the worsted goods business. Ettinger died in 1904, and his family moved to an

North to south on Lexington Avenue: Nos. 1457, 1455, 1453, and 1451

apartment building on East 97th Street. By 1922 No. 1451 was converted to apartments; one tenant was Dustin Rice, who ran an art gallery. Fifty years later the building was an abandoned shell. It was purchased in 1989 by Douglas and Anne Young, who rebuilt the house from the inside out, with interior detailing appropriate to the original period.

No. 1453: This was once the home of Leo Lerman, the writer/critic. In 1979 the building was purchased by John and Jenseen Payne (together with the Park Avenue Christian Church, where John Payne was minister). They made extensive interior renovations, adhering closely to the original plans. During the mid-1980s numerous developers tried to purchase the four buildings; the Paynes, having led the fight against the proposed sliver, refused to sell the building air rights, thus preserving the integrity of the entire row of brownstones.

No. 1455: At one time this house was owned by a plumber, who leased the ground floor to a real estate business. Eventually it became a series of small studios. It was bought in 1980 by Elise Frick, who over the next eleven years restored the building interior as tenants moved out.

No. 1457 has a colorful past. During the 1960s it was reputedly owned by Xavier Hollander, author of *The Happy Hooker*. Beyond the red door with a modest plaque saying "Daphne's Gifts" was a swimming pool that occupied much of the ground floor. After a highly publicized police raid, No. 1457 became temporary headquarters for New York City Councilman Carter Burden, after which it was sold to Rona Deme, a neighborhood caterer. Elise Frick purchased the building in 1987.

**1459 Lexington Avenue
(94th-95th Streets)
Congregation Orach Chaim**
ARCHITECTS:
Schwartz & Gross DATE: 1906-07
David Mood   1956

In 1906 the Jewish Orthodox congregation of Orach Chaim ("path of life"), founded in 1878 and previously established at 221 East 51st Street, bought two houses at 1461-1463 Lexington Avenue. The buildings were part of a square block of 40 nearly identical brownstones built by the prodigious developer Michael Duffy in 1878-79. The front and rear walls were torn down and internal walls removed to provide an auditorium, offices and classrooms. When the new building was completed in 1907 it was an intimate house of worship in the style of German synagogues of the 1800s. The entrance was via a flight of exterior stairs leading to the sanctuary on the second story, which receives light through original Tiffany windows representing the twelve tribes of Israel. In 1923 the congregation purchased 1459 Lexington Avenue for use as a community house.

Concurrent with the widening of Lexington Avenue in 1955-56, the cream-colored brick-and-stone building was remodeled by removing the exterior stairway and installing two stained-glass windows over street-level wooden doors with carvings of open Torah scrolls. David Mood, architect of the remodeling, also designed the two windows. The larger window depicts emblems of the Sabbath and major Jewish holidays, interspersed with such religious symbols as the Tablets of the Ten Commandments, the Torah, and the Eternal Light that hangs in every synagogue. The smaller window above, with a central design of grapes and Kiddush cups symbolic of the Sabbath celebration, marks the women's gallery.

A second major restoration project was completed in 2000. The adjacent brownstone, No. 1459, was incorporated to include an expanded entrance with a skylight, new offices and reception facilities, as well as apartments for the cantor and caretaker. Interior work included installation of a new heating system and restoration of the gilded ceiling in the sanctuary. At that time the address was changed to 1459 Lexington Avenue.

1460-1464 Lexington Avenue (94th-95th Streets)
ARCHITECT: Michael Duffy   DATE: 1878
Once a uniform row of neo-Grec brownstones similar to those at 121-137
East 94th Street, these buildings have been substantially altered. No. 1460
retains its upper-story neo-Grec windows and cornice. In 1931, when the
building was used as a funeral parlor, a two-story stone extension was
added. The arched quintet of second-story windows has special leaded and
tinted glass, with recesses below filled with balusters. No. 1462 lost its top
two stories in 1937; a mezzanine with casement windows was added in
1951. No. 1464 had its facade stripped of ornament and resurfaced in
1931 and a red-brick two-story extension was added, with an iron railing
and brick piers at the top edge. **HD**

1469 Lexington Avenue (95th Street)
ARCHITECTS: Bernstein & Bernstein
DATE: 1900
With its once-commanding vistas north and
down the slopes toward the East River, this
seven-story Renaissance Revival building appears
as imposing as a castle. The best view of the
facade is from the northwest corner of 95th
Street and Lexington Avenue. Bulbous bays
project from all corners and from the mid-95th
Street side. Each level displays design variations:
At the corners, first- and second-story bays are
flanked with carved, engaged columns with com-

posite capitals. Third-story windows boast elaborate cartouches; second-
and fourth-story windows on 95th Street have raised splayed lintels and
foliate keystones. Strange faces peer from fifth-story keystones; sixth-story
round-arched windows add drip moldings and shields.

Flanking the Lexington Avenue entrance, two pairs of reddish-brown
marble columns are each divided by a niche in which nestles a carved shell.
Iron-and-glass doors with lace grillwork are capped with a carved panel;
a cornice over the entablature is supported with foliate brackets. Window
pairs above the entrance receive different decorative details at each level,
including what appear to be upside-down swags (!) at the third story.
A stone band course with an egg-and-dart molding runs above the fourth
story. The fifth story explodes with a flurry of ornamentation: Brackets
support a shallow balcony, from which rise pairs of ornate columns
capped with carved segmental pediments. Above the unadorned attic story
is a double-height modillioned metal cornice, embellished with a frieze of
swags and rosettes.

THE BUILDINGS:
CROSS STREETS

7 East 86th Street
ARCHITECTS: Schuman & Lichtenstein   DATE: 1960

Over a base of polished granite, this seventeen-story red-brick apartment tower (originally glazed) has set-back terraces above the fourteenth story. The eastern section of the building is recessed; at the entrance, glazed doors are framed by sidelights and a transom. The building replaced a five-story brick-and-limestone mansion designed by Warren & Wetmore for Francis K. Pendelton, the grandson of Francis Scott Key, author of *The Star Spangled Banner*. **HD**

9 East 86th Street
Originally William and Elsie Woodward house
ARCHITECTS: Delano & Aldrich   DATE: 1916-18
Sandwiched between two modern buildings, this neo-Classical townhouse rises grandly from its marble-faced base. Although Delano & Aldrich worked in the red-brick neo-Federal style elsewhere in Carnegie Hill, here they created an elegant facade faced in smooth limestone and trimmed in marble. Highlights include first-floor windows with eared marble surrounds; pediment-capped second-story windows, accented with a classical anthemion; and a steeply pitched slate mansard roof with dormers, which rises behind a third-story balustrade. A one-story entrance pavilion extends westward; here, three steps lead to the front door, which is flanked by fluted pilasters topped by an arched segmental pediment. Behind a balustrade just above the entry, a narrow terrace extends back into the recessed fourth bay of the building.

Born in New York, William Woodward was an attorney who held high posts in banking and business, including that of president of the Hanover National Bank. In 1957 ownership of the house passed to the Town Club. In 2005 the building was sold to a private investor and reverted to a private residence. **HD**

11 East 86th Street
ARCHITECTS: Sylvan and Robert L. Bien   DATE: 1961
This white-brick, twenty-story-plus-penthouse building re-clad its base with cream-colored stone in 1999. Above the fourteenth story are terraced setbacks. Sylvan Bien and his son, Robert Bien, were responsible for three Modern-style apartment buildings in Carnegie Hill.

25 East 86th Street
(1178-1188 Madison Avenue and 20 East 87th Street)
ARCHITECTS: Sugarman & Berger   Date: 1929

Rising fifteen stories from a two-story limestone base, this large dark-brown-brick building spans the entire block on Madison Avenue between 86th and 87th streets. The primary residential entrance is on 86th Street. Because of the steep incline on Madison Avenue, the first two stories on the 86th Street side are extremely high, resulting in a large vaulted lobby. A small wrought-iron balcony is placed asymmetrically over the entry. Shops line the Madison Avenue street front. The 87th Street residential entrance is topped with a charming wrought-iron balcony and oval canopy.

Between band courses above the second and third stories runs a continuous row of windows capped with arched lintels; in the center of each is a diamond-shaped floral design. Many of the features of the upper portions of the building are visible from across Madison Avenue, where one can see small decorative balconies projecting from the ninth and fourteenth stories. Additional string courses set off the two-story crown. Decorative brickwork at the corners is suggestive of quoins. Note the large cartouches on the 87th Street facade.

49 East 86th Street
ARCHITECTS: Pennington & Lewis   DATE: 1931

A string course with a Greek key design runs above the three-story limestone base and sets the tone for this understated seventeen-story Moderne apartment house. (The architects also designed 2 East 88th Street, famous for its serene stone faces on rooftop piers.) At the street level, polished

green marble frames the upscale merchandise in the shop windows. The arched residential entryway on 86th Street has a geometric marble surround with an inverted lintel, echoing the neo-Classical string-course design. The remaining facade is a soft reddish-brown brick; terrace setbacks start at the fifteenth story. Crowning the building is an elegant chimney surround and a buttressed water-tower enclosure; limestone caps the setbacks and both top structures. For a better view, walk up Madison Avenue a block or two.

55 East 86th Street
ARCHITECTS: Schwartz & Gross   DATE: 1924

Rising from a three-story limestone base, this neo-Renaissance brown-brick apartment building has a ten-story midsection and a two-story crown, terminating with a modillioned cornice. Above the brass double doors is a dentiled cornice supported by scrolled brackets. Four festoons accent the limestone between the second-story windows. Fluted pilasters frame the third-story windows, which are capped with round arches or pediments with decorative infill—a treatment echoed over windows at the crown. A simple limestone course runs beneath the lower crown-story windows; terra-cotta spandrels and rosettes set off the upper row. Panels between window pairs are adorned with an urn-and-vine motif.

61 East 86th Street
ARCHITECTS: Neville & Bagge
DATE: 1900

The ubiquitous Renaissance Revival style achieves monumental qualities in this handsome seven-story apartment house. The two-story rusticated limestone base is broken by two large arched openings—one serving as the main entrance, the other a window to balance it. Each is crowned with a stone cartouche, an egg-and-dart molding, and a balustraded balcony supported by large decorated consoles. A low stone wall fronts the shallow planted areaway; globe lamps on wrought-iron stands flank the doorway.

The buff-brick facade is broken vertically into three parts. The central section is four bays wide with double windows; openings on the third story are capped with elaborately carved stone swags and escutcheons. Fifth-story windows display alternating segmental and triangular pediments, and are united with fourth-story windows by carved plaques. The side bays are capped with triangular pediments and splayed lintels punctuated with scrolled keystones. Above the sixth-story band course and cornice is a series of carved plaques with shield motifs. Stone quoins accent the building corners and delineate the central section.

103 East 86th Street
ARCHITECTS: Schwartz & Gross   DATE: 1913-14

Designed in the Renaissance Revival style, the facade of this fifteen-story building is of yellowish-brown narrow brick rising from a low limestone base. Carved limestone window boxes project from the second story. There are no fewer than six string courses, although the two widest ones appear to have had decorative elements removed. Patches of light-brick coloration on the sixth, ninth and twelfth stories suggest that balconettes or window boxes have also been removed. Of interest is the double-height limestone entry surround. Carved vertical panels alternate floral and shield motifs. Above the wood-and-glass-paneled doors runs a leafy frieze; French doors open to a balconette and wrought-iron railing on the second level. Capping the entryway are multiple carved bands, a cartouche, a dentil course, and foliate brackets supporting a projecting cornice.

115 East 86th Street
ARCHITECT: George F. Pelham, Jr.   DATE: 1927

Set mid-block, this fifteen-story-plus-penthouse building is neo-Georgian in style. The tripartite design divides the red-brick facade using classical details. Above the third story runs a festooned garland frieze topped by egg-and-dart and dentil moldings beneath a cornice. The center section of the building features prominent balconies with stone balustrades, supported by paired foliate brackets placed symmetrically beneath two ninth-story windows. A narrower and simpler band course and cornice run above the thirteenth story. The building is finished at the fifteenth story with a swag-and-rosette medallion frieze, a small dentil band, and a heavy dentiled cornice. Stone pilasters with elongated acanthus-leaf capitals, topped with a swan's neck pediment and urn, frame the entrance. Two sets of French doors and matching tall transom lights lead to the lobby and its attractive plaster ceiling carved in a rectangular pattern of rosettes, dentils and egg-and-dart moldings.

123 East 86th Street
Citibank
ARCHITECTS: Walker & Gillette   DATE: 1927

At any time of day there is a line-up at the westbound bus stop at 86th Street and Lexington Avenue. How many glance above the Citibank sign to take in the Art Deco eagle sculptures? The understated linear door enframement is echoed in the window surrounds on the third and final

story. This modest limestone building was designed by none other than Walker & Gillette, who also designed the Fuller Building at 57 East 57th Street and the Loew mansion, now part of the Spence School, at 56 East 93rd Street.

151-155 East 86th Street

ARCHITECTS: William Whitehall   DATE 1926
Copelin, Lee & Chen   1978

Constructed as a "taxpayer," (a basic structure, usually below the height allowed by zoning laws, designed and built for rental income to cover property taxes), this multi-level commercial building has undergone myriad changes to accommodate tenants and use. Starting with storage and showrooms, it was modified to include "physical culture, limited to squash courts" in 1977 and, later, a gym above a street-level women's specialty store. Its current facade is a modification of a 1970s Postmodern design by architects Copelin, Lee & Chen. Vertical ribbed concrete and right-angled windows contrast with 45°-angled concrete blocks and colorful accent striping.

157 East 86th Street

ARCHITECTS: Howells & Stokes DATE: 1903
William I. Hohauser   1928

This brick-and-stone "taxpayer" was originally designed as a three-story theater. In 1928 the architect William I. Hohauser added two stories and converted the ground level to stores; the upper floors accommodated a restaurant, dance halls and meeting rooms, later replaced by offices. The commercial building is four bays wide with narrow extensions on both sides. The decorative limestone elements, in Art Deco style, consist of five triangular piers rising from a string course above the first story and culminating in framed female busts crowned with stylized sunbursts. Capping the top-level windows are wide lintels with angled corners—streamlined versions of skew-backs used half a century earlier. Above are brick panels with rosettes; a cornice decorated with a row of small blossoms rises to a shallow peak in the center.

6 East 87th Street
Originally Henry and Annie Phipps house, now the Liederkranz Club

ARCHITECT: Grosvenor Atterbury
DATE: 1902
Designed in a neo-Venetian Renaissance style, this five-story limestone building was designed for Philadelphia-born Henry Phipps, a metal manufacturer and philanthropist and long-time friend and partner of Andrew Carnegie. Phipps also owned a mansion, now demolished, around the corner at 1063 Fifth Avenue. In 1916 he sold the elegant Grosvenor Atterbury building to Walter P. Bliss. The Liederkranz Club bought the property in 1949. Founded in 1847 as the Deutscher Liederkranz—metal shields flanking the door bear the initials D and L, and a plaque affirms the date—the focus of the group is to sponsor German classical music performances, musical scholarships, and other cultural activities in New York City.

A highlight of the building is the exuberant ironwork at the entryway: Ornate fences top a low stone wall, echoed in matching door grilles and a sunburst fanlight. The door is trimmed with rope moldings and topped with a detailed cornice. Foliate brackets support a balcony and carved balustrade fronting three round-arched windows, also with rope-coiled surrounds, surmounted by decorative spandrels and cornices. Third- and fourth-story windows are square-headed and rest on small corbels. More exuberant design returns at the fifth story: Bowed wrought-iron balconies front round-arched windows inset with Venetian-style rondels. Large decorative brackets support the terminal cornice and pantile-design (alternating arcs) roof tiles. To the east of the building is a bronze statue of a lyre-bearing goddess and child sculpted in 1896 by Giuseppe Moretti. It once stood in the association's earlier clubhouse (since demolished) on East 58th Street. **HD**

10 East 87th Street
ARCHITECTS: Felix Augenfeld and Jan Hird Pokorny   DATE: 1955-58
                    Lichten Craig   2002
The site of this Modern townhouse was an empty lot until 1955, when Muriel Buttinger, a writer and book collector, commissioned architect/designer Felix Augenfeld to build her a private residence with a research library large enough to hold 50,000 volumes, plus a collection of

Cambodian sculpture. Augenfeld collaborated on the project with architect Jan Hird Pokorny, a longtime commissioner of the New York City Landmarks Preservation Commission. The two created the six-story house so that the library would be accessible to students and visitors without intruding on the upper-floor duplex of Ms. Buttinger and her husband, Joseph. The library itself overlooked a central patio through a wall of glass.

The facade of the building was originally composed of glass-mosaic tile above a travertine-sheathed base. Much of the tile subsequently deteriorated and was replaced by buff-colored brick. When the Phelps Stokes Fund, an educational foundation, purchased the building in 1981, a set-back seventh story was added.

In 2002 the townhouse reverted to private ownership, with renovation and restoration executed by the architectural firm of Lichten Craig. The brick was replaced with mosaic tiling that closely resembles the original; slender bands of stainless steel demarcate sections of the mosaic and play off the sashes of ribbon windows at every level to create a subtle, pale, Mondrian-like grid. Steel is elsewhere employed to harmonious effect: as a band running up the northwest corner of the house; as window boxes under the second-story windows; and for the service and parking-garage doors. The entrance, recessed at an angle, is highlighted by a paneled-wood door. **HD**

11 East 87th Street
ARCHITECT: Tito di Vincenzo DATE: 1953
This modern, twelve-story red-brick building has a gray-and-white marble projecting entryway flanked by an attractive street-level garden. In typical "wedding cake" style, the upper floors become narrower, revealing balconies and terraces.

12 East 87th Street
The Capitol
ARCHITECTS: George & Edward Blum DATE: 1911
During the course of its construction, this idiosyncratic building first achieved publicity because of its luxurious space: Each of its eight floors housed a single apartment with fourteen rooms and four bathrooms.

(Mary Pickford, the actress, once rented one of these apartments.) Further press coverage followed after several workers died when part of the floor system collapsed.

The stylized neo-Renaissance design dates from the Blums' early and most creative period. The Capitol is one of the best examples of the firm's combination of traditional forms, such as egg-and-dart moldings, with innovative geometric and organic features. Much of the facade is of white brick and glazed terra cotta with an "eggshell" finish. A boldly rusticated base is textured to resemble corrugated cardboard. The entrance, windows and spandrels are framed with decorative tiles in a circle-and-triglyph pattern. Above the first story runs a four-part frieze of shells and rosettes, anthemions, circular motifs and triglyphs, all capped with a modillioned cornice. A multi-patterned frieze tops the second story. At the seventh story, yet another frieze intersects three-sided balconies at the outer windows. A final frieze alternates diamonds and triglyphs. The upper portion of the cornice was removed in 1980, presumably for safety reasons; what remains consists of modillions and foliate brackets silhouetted bizarrely against the sky. **HD**

21 East 87th Street
ARCHITECT: Emery Roth   DATE: 1927

This beige-brick, thirteen-story building is typical of many restrained neo-Renaissance apartment houses of the era. The first story has a rusticated limestone base. Over the entry, foliate brackets support a limestone cornice; the address is carved in the entablature. Stone quoins accent the second-story. Window surrounds on the second and eleventh stories feature extended lintels embellished with rosettes and garlands. A handsome enclosed water tower displays three "windows" on each side, embellished with brick pilasters topped with carved capitals. Thanks to the building management's concern for an attractive streetscape, the Madison Avenue shops display trim awnings with uniform signage and color.

47 East 87th Street
ARCHITECT: Leonard Schultze & Associates   DATE: 1945-47
Rising from a two-story rusticated stone base, the facade of this fourteen-story building is pale-gray brick; there are set-back terraces above the eleventh story, and a penthouse above the fourteenth story. Although built just after World War II, there are some nice Art Deco touches: Pairs of stone piers flank the entrance, and the glass door has bronze-colored metal grillwork in a geometric pattern, echoed in grilles over the windows on either side.

50 East 87th Street
Park Avenue Synagogue
ARCHITECTS: Walter S. Schneider   DATE: 1926
James Rush Jarrett/Schuman Lichtenstein Claman & Efron 1980
The older building of this complex, a synagogue faced in buff-colored cast stone, chosen because it most closely resembles Jerusalem stone, has an entrance on the side street framed by a soaring arch. As it curves

toward its apex, the arch is bordered by scalloped cutouts reminiscent on a grand scale of the decorations of the buildings of medieval Granada or Seville. Above, fourteen engaged columns rise to blind arches. All these elements are set off by a richly carved trim of acanthus leaves, flowers and geometrics. Note the gold mosaics surrounding rondels with the Star of David directly above the entrance doors. The facade is a wonderful exercise in a Moorish style that was thought appropriate for synagogue design from the mid-19th century through the early decades of the 20th century.

In 1955 the architects Kelly & Gruzen designed an adjacent addition for offices and activities. Rising from a windowless one-story base, the 87th Street facade consisted of a curtain wall of stained-glass panels created by the noted Abstract Expressionist painter Adolph Gottlieb. However, in 1980 the Conservative congregation, which dates its beginnings to 1882, contracted the architect James Rush Jarrett to design a new five-story administration and school building fronting on Madison Avenue and adjoining the original synagogue, replacing the 1955 structure. The addition is of rusticated Mankato limestone from Minnesota. The style, which today might be identified as Postmodern, displays strong classical elements: Large bays on both Madison Avenue and 87th Street rise to the structure's full height, topped by arched windows. A two-story arcade is cut into the northeast Madison Avenue facade; over the entrance is a bittersweet set of sculptural panels by Nathan Rapoport dedicated to the memory of the Jewish children killed in the Holocaust. The original Gottlieb panels of stained glass can now be viewed inside in the entrance gallery.

Ask at the main desk for entry into the great sanctuary, designed as a theatre centered on the Bimah (pulpit) standing in front of the Ark. Set into the ceiling is a stained-glass dome depicting the Star of David radiating golden rays. Go up into the balcony and you will see that the dome is supported on a short drum of pierced screens (the Moorish influence, again). The auditorium roof slopes gently upward, creating the illusion that the drum and dome float above the congregational space below.

55 East 87th Street
The Parc
ARCHITECT: Schuman & Lichtenstein   DATE: 1961

Polished-black granite and large iron lamps define the entrance of this fifteen-story beige-brick building. The design is symmetrical; covered balconies line the bays up to the tenth story, above which are set-back terraces.

56 East 87th Street
ARCHITECT: George F. Pelham
DATE: 1904-05

Subtle classical details are evident throughout the facade of this early neo-Renaissance building. The first two stories consist of rusticated limestone; the remaining four are of cream-colored brick. Engaged columns with foliate capitals separate paired lower-level windows. Some of the upper windows are ornamented with carved keystones and splayed voussoirs; others display carved terra-cotta surrounds and garlands. Cartouches and delicate green-metal lanterns flank the door. The arched entryway is surmounted by a keystone and foliate brackets supporting a cornice. The entire center portion of the facade is recessed, edged with limestone quoins, and culminates in a basket-handle arch with egg-and-dart molding. More classical details—modillions, dentils, wreath-and-garland scrolls, and foliate brackets—are evident in the elaborate cornice.

62 East 87th Street
ARCHITECT: Edward Wenz   DATE: 1891

This five-story stuccoed building was probably neo-Grec. Its original ornamentation has been stripped; extensive renovations were made in 1940. The facade is neo-Classical: Fluted pilasters flank the entry, above which is a triangular pediment. A multi-layered cornice separates the first and second stories, echoed at outer bay windows and at the roof line.

110 East 87th Street
ARCHITECTS: Boak & Paris   DATE: 1927

This handsome mid-block apartment building steps back above the tenth story to accommodate two stories with wrap-around terraces to the east and west, and a two-story penthouse tower. The facade is of rosy brick with tinted stone detailing above a rusticated limestone base. There are casement windows throughout. Its style mixes Art Deco verticality with neo-Tudor Gothic references.

In the three-bay central section, the entry, second- and tenth-story windows have square Tudor-style hood moldings above the quoined stone surrounds. This section also displays convex stone panels with framed, raised escutcheons in a modified fleur-de-lis design, filling all of the spaces between the third- through tenth-story windows, and in the tower. The parapets at the twelfth and penthouse stories have stone battlements, while cream-toned metal railings at the eleventh and twelfth stories have modern elements. The building's symmetrical form (only the entrance is off-center) is emphasized by triangular brick piers rising to the tenth story beside the center windows, decorative stonework centered at the top two parapets, and a central stone peak atop the tower.

111 East 87th Street
Church of the Advent Hope
ARCHITECT: Alfred B. Heiser   DATE: 1956

This diminutive neo-Gothic church was built by a German Seventh-Day Adventist congregation after their Bronx-based building was damaged by fire. Forced to relocate, they chose an area close to German-speaking Yorkville; here they purchased a lot originally occupied by two brownstones. The architect for the church, Alfred B. Heiser, was actively involved with the Seventh-Day Adventists in Newburg, New York, and built their

first home for the aged there. The minister of the East 87th Street church, Elder Zucker, held the first service on March 16. 1957.

The masonry streetfront facade is inset with simple, rough-hewn fieldstones, placed as if into a hearth or chimney. The double-arched doors into the church are contained within a larger Gothic arch; this motif is repeated at the top of four vertical pilasters that rise through the peaked roof line. Today's congregation is no longer exclusively German-speaking; indeed, it is a diverse body of worshippers, who meet to pray on Saturdays.

115 East 87th Street / 110 East 88th Street
Carnegie Towers / Robert F. Kennedy School, P.S. 169
ARCHITECTS: Feldman-Misthopoulos   DATE: 1973

With a double-level parking garage, gym and auditorium, four stories of classrooms, and 198 residential apartments, this 38-story block-through tower may truly be called mixed-use. Residents enter through the lushly landscaped 87th Street side; four street lamps in Art Nouveau style illuminate the second-level esplanade. Nine steps under a double-height canopy lead to a green-marble-and-mahogany lobby. The facade is of beige-and-brown brick; a granite promenade for residents projects from the fifth story. Students enter through a simple side portal on 88th Street. The building is a project of the New York City Educational Construction Fund that owns the land and leases the air rights over the school.

120 East 87th Street
Park Avenue Court
ARCHITECTS: Skidmore Owings & Merrill   DATE: 1990

In its current form, this imposing red-brick building wraps around the corners of East 86th Street, Lexington Avenue, and East 87th Street. The first two stories include chain stores, a movie theater marquee (a bone of contention among neighborhood groups, as the theater is long since gone), the entrance to the Downtown 4, 5, and 6 trains, and a luxury condominium with seventeen stories. The complex has seen many reincarnations. The earliest date for which records are available is 1924, although undoubtedly there were buildings on the lot prior to that time. Architect Thomas Lamb, who also designed 49 East 96th Street and Madison Square Garden, designed a three-story office building with a two-level theater at the northwest corner of 87th Street and Lexington Avenue. In

1951 a six-story apartment building was erected, abutting the theater on 87th Street. By 1971 the theater extended through to 86th Street and included a marquee. The following year Gimbels, the Herald Square department store, built a satellite store over the existing buildings and theaters. (The blasting needed for the taller building's foundations was strong enough to cause the collapse of many stained-glass windows in the Immanuel Lutheran Church one block north.) The windowless structure, designed by Abbott, Merkt & Co., was twelve stories high. The new store was not a success and the chain dissolved in 1986. William Zeckendorf, Jr. and Partners then commissioned architects Skidmore Owings & Merrill to convert the abandoned store into a condominium, adding five stories with set-back terraces. Its high ceilings, detailed facade in a restrained Modern idiom, unusual six-pane windows, and quiet 87th Street entrance have assured its continuing popularity as a residence.

125 East 87th Street
Sherry House
ARCHITECTS: Sugarman & Berger   DATE: 1962

Rising fifteen stories plus a penthouse, multiple shades of marble accent this beige-brick apartment building. The base is red marble with recessed white-marble vertical inserts; the black-marble entry opens to a rounded lobby finished in light-brown marble. Above the twelfth floor the massing sets back between three bays with chamfered corners. The triple-bay pattern is repeated in two more setbacks forming a series of terraces. There are stores on the corner and along the Lexington Avenue side of the building.

150 East 87th Street
ARCHITECT: Albert Huttira   DATE: 1890-91

Originally a modest apartment house, this five-story brown-brick structure was built for Cavinato Natate, probably a carpenter, and was identified as "the Cavinato." Its style can be characterized as Renaissance Revival, although there are Romanesque Revival and Queen Anne references. Its many eccentricities are above the ground-level commercial distractions, best appreciated from across the street. Rather than a continuing surface, the facade has a series of projecting piers that continue to the cornice, delineating window bays and forming an erratic roof line. The corners of the building feature three-sided projections with narrow windows and carved panels between each story. Although all

windows are square-headed and most are paired, there are a variety of toppings: carved segmental arches, Gothic arches, carved lintels, and peaked connecting moldings. Centered at the top story on Lexington Avenue is a wide segmental arch with voussoirs and a masqued keystone, below which are round moldings and a carved spandrel. More embellishments can be seen in the projecting metal cornice, including foliate panels and brackets, dentils, and garlands. The 87th Street facade offers a surprise treat: Between the second-story windows is a statue carved in brownstone of a young woman wearing a plumed headdress.

153 East 87th Street
Morgan House
ARCHITECT: Richard Deeves & Sons   DATE: 1926
With its humble beginnings as a warehouse with several offices, by 1986 this beige-brick structure had added three stories; it is now a fourteen-story residential building. The two-story base is of painted limestone; four rows of applied brick quoins front the facade, which sets back above the tenth story.

154-164 East 87th Street
The Alan Garage and The
Franklin Hotel
ARCHITECT: Frank J. Schefcik
DATE: 1930
Although dissimilar in appearance, the hotel and garage share a common birthright. After the stock-market crash of 1929, Emanuel Ornstein, a local

developer, took over the plans of the Stanhope Estates to build a garage and hotel on the empty lot. At the time, in response to neighborhood zoning protests, a Board of Standards variance required that the "front elevation shall be designed in attractive architectural treatment . . . with face brick and architectural terra cotta." The resulting garage has a flamboyant Art Deco facade (with a nod to Arts and Crafts geometrics of a decade earlier). Vertical white strips run up the facade, intersected with yellow and green terra cotta shapes, playful lions' heads and garlands. The words UP, DOWN, and THE ALAN GARAGE are in two-foot-high red-terra-cotta relief letters, circumventing restrictions on signage because they were considered architectural detailing. Two terra-cotta automobile tires adorn the top floor, and the elevator headhouse is covered in terra cotta with a diaper pattern.

The Franklin Hotel is a narrow, nine-story red-brick building with a far more conventional design. Above the second-, eighth- and ninth-story windows are plaques with garlands; the top two stories have six stone pilasters. A lighted marquis projects over the door.

And the names? Says architectural historian Christopher Gray, "According to J. Alan Ornstein, born in 1928, the garage was named for him — he was his grandfather's first grandson. The hotel was named for his brother [Franklin Ornstein], born in 1930."

159 East 87th Street
"13 Hook & Ladder 13"
ARCHITECT: William Williams (?)
DATE:1859/1863 (?)

Early land-use maps indicate that the Cornelius V. Anderson Hook and Ladder Company was located at this address, serving Yorkville and the vicinity. The ladder company is shown as #10, rather than #13; but fire companies changed numbers from time to time. From the earliest days until 1865, this was a volunteer fire department. In 1907 Hook & Ladder Company #13 helped douse a dramatic fire at P.S. 86, then located at the southeast corner of Lexington Avenue and 96th Street; the school continued to serve the Carnegie Hill area for the next 53 years.

The style of the (painted) red-brick firehouse is Italianate/Romanesque Revival. Round-arched moldings with keystones and an eared lintel and cornice embellish tripartite second-story windows, which are fronted with a simple iron balcony. At the ground level are bricked-up round-arched openings with vestigial keystones; paneled double doors mark the entry. The building is currently used for storage.

Its real fifteen minutes of fame came in the 1960s, not as a firehouse but as a studio for none other than pop artist Andy Warhol. A 1962 photo shows Warhol with a Campbell's Soup print in his 87th Street firehouse gallery. The New York City Buildings Department records from 1966 show a Certificate of Occupancy for the building for use in loading, unloading and storing art, and as an art gallery. Warhol himself lived just a few blocks away, at 1342 Lexington Avenue.

169 East 87th Street
ARCHITECTS: Richard Berger   DATE: 1895-96
            J.M. Felson   1930-31

Neon arrows, in themselves Art Deco phenomena, point to this relatively obscure building from which they project. The structure was originally a stable. In 1931 it was enlarged, resurfaced, and converted to the Yorkville Garage "for storage of pleasure cars only," and included a chauffeur's locker room. (The garage is now under different management.) The Art Deco facade is of tan brick, with design interest starting above the mezzanine band course. There are five bays of windows; the lower center window has an arched brick surround. Outer windows display decorative brickwork and continuous framing, creating a vertical emphasis. At the seventh story, in place of openings runs a row of small geometric brick "windows." Under a flat cornice is a row of brick arches, echoed at the top of the rooftop enclosure rising from the center of the parapet.

170 East 87th Street
The Gotham
ARCHITECTS: Frank Williams & Partners
DATE: 1994

This Postmodern, 27-story condominium tower has a beige-brick facade with white-stone horizontal bandings. The windows of the ground-floor commercial spaces are flanked with austere stone pilasters echoing the two-story travertine entrance. Below grade are seven movie theaters that are accessed from Third Avenue. Above the fifteenth floor are two stories to reinforce the cornice line; the next eleven stories step back in a gentle slope, creating terraces and a ziggurat-like profile. Of particular note, and best viewed from several blocks south, is the octagonal water-tower enclosure with a pale modillioned cornice.

175 East 87th Street
Doyle Galleries
ARCHITECT: Charles Stegmayer   DATE: 1909

Constructed of red brick with stone trim, this six-story commercial building has long been used for storage, offices, light manufacturing, and as a public auction showroom and gallery. The base is of painted, paneled wood; the remaining stories have horizontal windows running the width of the building. Stone band courses above each story connect to decorative blocks with guttae. A row of wide dentils runs below the fifth story.

2 East 88th Street
ARCHITECTS: Pennington & Lewis
DATE: 1929-30

The workaday water tank soars to architectural heights when enclosed by inventive designers like Pennington and Lewis. Atop this Moderne apartment house, several enormous stone heads on tall brick piers gaze serenely at Central Park and Carnegie Hill. The architects may have taken their inspiration from depictions of Greek kourioi (freestanding figures of young men) or from the goddess-like caryatids supporting the Erectheion on Athens's Acropolis. The effect here is one of the most striking in New York City.

The thirteen-story-and penthouse building stands on the site of two Fifth Avenue mansions owned by Walter Douglas and Lewis Nixon, prominent manufacturers and capitalists. Its triplex penthouse, overlooking the Guggenheim Museum and the reservoir, was once the home of media magnate Rupert Murdoch. The building's design mixes bold massing and stylized classical detailing. The limestone facade features belt courses carved in wave and guilloche designs above the second and third stories, and iron balconettes at the fifth story. A cornice supported by shallow blocks separates the twelfth and thirteenth stories; rosettes and triglyphs adorn the uppermost elements. The entrance, flanked by brass lamps and stylized piers, is topped with a uniquely enframed window and balconette that is supported by shallow fluting, an Art Moderne characteristic. **HD**

4 East 88th Street
ARCHITECTS: Electus Litchfield & Rogers
DATE: 1921-22

With its balanced proportions and subtle details, this nine-story building is perhaps the finest example of Federal-inspired apartment houses in New York City. Surfaced with red brick laid in traditional Flemish bond, the white trim is of stone and terra cotta. Square-headed windows at the ground level are set in brick arches accented with limestone keystones and rondels; second-story windows feature flat keystones and splayed brick lintels. All windows retain their original eight-over-eight sash with raised wooden mullions, nowadays a rarity. Eighth-story windows are crowned with alternating triangular and segmental-arched pediments. Dentiled cornices top the second and seventh stories. Above the molded roof cornice is a limestone balustrade. Centered within the broken segmental-arched entry pediment is a unique detail—a whimsical terra-cotta sculpture of three heads, presumably depicting American patriots: The one peering towards Central Park bears a strong resemblance to George Washington. **HD**

5, 7 and 9 East 88th Street
ARCHITECTS: Turner & Kilian   DATE: 1902-03

These three elaborate Beaux-Arts-style townhouses were erected not for a discerning and wealthy patron but on speculation. Porticoed entrances, cartouches, and lavish stone-and-marble trim mark the architectural grandeur of the five-story buildings. Nos. 5 and 9 are similar: Each is faced with red brick and stone, with pairs of Doric columns with guttae flanking iron-and-glass doors. Above the entry, heavy foliate brackets support a marble balustrade fronting the bowed, three-story midsection.

Stone quoins define the buildings' extremes and windows, which are square-headed on the second and fifth stories. Windows are round-arched with cartouches at the third story, and segmentally-arched with key-stones at the fourth. Wrought-iron railings and balustrades are prominent at each level and cap the projecting bays. Both buildings terminate with balustraded parapets. No. 7 is completely faced in limestone. An arched transom surmounts elaborate iron-and-glass doors. The portico is supported with engaged columns and piers; an elaborate cartouche is centered on the entablature. A two-story projecting oriel is footed and capped with marble balustrades. Paneled piers separate windows that are flat at the front and curved at the sides. Above the fourth story runs a modillioned cornice; large dormers with eared, segmentally-arched pediments project from the mansard slate roof. Together, the trio comprises an elegant mid-block streetscape. **HD**

11 East 88th Street
ARCHITECT: Leo Stillman   DATE: 1954

This eight-story Modern apartment building features a brown-brick facade with contrasting white window reveals. Blocks of white marble frame the off-center entry and wood-and-glass doors. End bays with tripartite windows are set back; the projecting central section is topped with a fluted stone parapet. **HD**

12 East 88th Street
ARCHITECT: Rosario Candela DATE: 1931

Capping the two-story rusticated limestone base of this neo-Georgian twelve-story apartment building is a wide band course with set-in marble balustrades. The remaining stories are of red brick; brick quoins define the corners. Carved lintels adorn windows on the central section of the third story; segmentally-arched lintels cap the double windows at the building extremes. A simple string course underscores fourth-story sills. Above the tenth story, three sections of the facade are set back; central windows are ornamented with balustrades, curved iron balconettes and broken pediments.

15 East 88th Street
Originally Robert Fulton Cutting, Jr. house
ARCHITECTS: Delano & Aldrich   DATE: 1920-22

Robert Fulton Cutting, Jr., a descendent of Robert Fulton, inventor of the steamboat, was known in his time as "the first mayor of New York" for his philanthropy and leadership of several civic groups. He helped found the Citizens Union. His six-story red-brick townhouse, designed in the neo-Federal style, was one of several Cutting residences built by the architects Delano & Aldrich [see 12-16 East 89th Street]. The ground level features a loggia with three tall arches accented with keystones, enclosed with wrought-iron fences and connected by stone impost blocks. An iron-framed fanlight tops the double-leaf paneled-wood door. At the parlor story, a stone balcony with iron grillwork spans three extraordinarily high windows with carved stone lintels. Above the fifth story runs a dentiled stone frieze ornamented with palmettes. The pitched slate roof is pierced by five copper-fronted dormers and framed with stone cheek walls. **HD**

19 East 88th Street
ARCHITECT: William M. Dowling
DATE: 1935-36

Combining vertical and horizontal elements, this sixteen-story-plus penthouse
apartment building is a late—and unusual—
example of Art Deco style. Light-tan bands
of brick between stories contrast with the
darker-brick bands connecting windows,
speeding the eye outward to the chamfered
windows at the corners. The central section
of the building projects a powerful vertical
emphasis: Tall fluted pilasters flank the
entrance, and subtle facade variations
delineate bays and form piers above the thirteenth story. (Many projecting
air conditioners, however, distract from the design's integrity.)

Three-story-high geometric and sculptural forms frame the main
entry, terminating in stylized scallops; slender bronze-and-glass lanterns
reinforce the linear motif. Above the second story is a stone frieze in a
leaf-rosette and geometric pattern; note its subtle design transformation
into the number 19 above the entryway. A characteristic style note can be
seen in the rounded metal balconies and rails, suggesting a streamlined
ocean liner. Near the top of the facade are panels of sawtooth-patterned
brickwork. A final surprise awaits the viewer from across Madison Avenue
at 89th Street: Two flying buttresses at the rear of the building are used
not to support the structure, but to conceal vents as they rise along the
facade and zoom across terraced setbacks.

20 East 88th Street
ARCHITECT: Unknown   DATE: 1894 (?)
Although city records indicate this five-story co-op to be of 19th-century
origin, the current facade would suggest otherwise. The entry surround is
of polished-green marble; a multi-pane wood door was recently installed.
Limestone string courses above each story punctuate the red brick.

40 East 88th Street
ARCHITECTS: Sugarman & Berger   DATE: 1930
Triple limestone moldings capped with a stylized floral keystone define the
entrance of this subtly designed Art Deco apartment house. Double doors
display wrought-iron grilles with bronze floral motifs. The fifteen-story,
beige-brick building rises from a three-story limestone base; the name of
the builder, Joseph E. Gilbert, Inc., is carved into the corner block. Of

particular note are the fluted limestone panels between third-story windows, echoed at the thirteenth and fifteenth stories and on the enclosed water tower. The terraced upper stories have decorative wrought-iron railings.

47 East 88th Street
ARCHITECT: George F. Pelham   DATE: 1930

This traditional sixteen-story apartment house has a smooth limestone base, which is topped at the third story with a small cornice over a dentil and modillion course, a detail that is repeated above the eleventh story. The remainder of the neo-Renaissance facade is clad in brown brick, finished with a coiled-rope design on each corner. Mirror-image white-marble quoins rise above the fourth story and descend from the twelfth story to bracket the midsection. A large cornice with foliate brackets appears to finish the building; however, three additional stories are stepped back, providing wrap-around terraces. The building is topped with two penthouses set back so as to be nearly invisible from the street.

The limestone arched entry is decorated with carved and floral motifs on the keystone, medallions and pilasters. Above the main entrance the building is recessed, creating the impression of two towers. The Madison Avenue facade features a pair of limestone balustraded balconies at the tenth story.

60 East 88th Street
ARCHITECTS: Beyer Blinder Belle
DATE: 1985

Circles, spheres and half-rounds enliven this handsome fifteen-story Postmodern building. With just one apartment per floor, the condominium offers a luxury of space not seen since the 1920s. The red-brick facade has a two-story limestone base and limestone banding above each succeeding story. Pairs of stone columns flank secondary doors at the east and west ends of the building. A low stone wall defines a curved driveway leading to cylindrical planters and to the main entrance. Walls and columns are topped with stone spheres, echoed in the large oculus window over the half-round portico and the rondel above the limestone cornice. Curved wrought-iron rails project from lower windows and balconies. The carved address number—60—completes the circular design pattern.

111 East 88th Street
ARCHITECT:
George G. Miller
DATE: 1930
Nine stories tall, plus a penthouse, this modest mid-block brick apartment building calls attention to its Art Deco elements in unobtrusive ways. Exceptions are the swirling purplish-gray marble in a step-up pattern that surrounds the entryway, and a playful blue-and-yellow ceramic sunburst plaque centered over the door. The base of the building is created from dark-toned, purplish bricks set on end; similar brickwork rises on either side of the marble surround. Six stone-and-brick panels rising serenely to the top of the building create a toothy crenelated roof line, emphasizing the Art Deco flavor. Stacked brick masonry (punctuated with striations set in straight-bond style) between the two triple-window bays at the center of the building reinforces the verticality of the facade. Centered at the very top is a second playful geometric design, framed with stones echoing the ground-floor step-up pattern.

120 East 88th Street
ARCHITECT: Erwin Rossbach   DATE: 1908
A five-step stoop flanked with curved, carved cheek walls leads to double wood-and-glass doors and a leaded-glass transom. Fluted pilasters and scrolled brackets support a simple entablature. Above the rusticated stone base (now painted) is a cornice. The remaining four stories have four bays of identical windows; scrolled keystones connect to bracketed sills above. A metal cornice with a geometric frieze and dentils terminates this modest Renaissance Revival structure.

121-123 East 88th Street
ARCHITECTS: A.B. Ogden & Son   DATE: 1884-85
Sparkling in the afternoon sunlight, the top four stories of these neo-Grec/Queen Anne buildings (now joined) are of bright red brick accented with white-stone lintels and sills. The end bays are recessed, effectively creating a series of vertical piers; corbeled brickwork below windows and above the fifth story articulates the facade. Transversing both buildings is a corbeled brick parapet. The painted-stone ground story is modern; an oval, notched opening is cut above the off-center doorway.

122 East 88th Street
Immanuel Lutheran Church
ARCHITECT: Arthur Crooks   DATE: 1886

Even with the use of Maine granite, limestone and massive buttresses, the exterior of this neo-Gothic church presents a lovely, almost delicate impression. The church was erected by German immigrants for a growing Yorkville congregation. The cornerstone was laid on November 1, 1885; within a cavity in the stone were placed German and English bibles. The church was dedicated on Thanksgiving Day, 1886. The bell tower rises 200 feet and houses three bells inscribed *"Glaube, Hoffnung,* and *Liebe"*

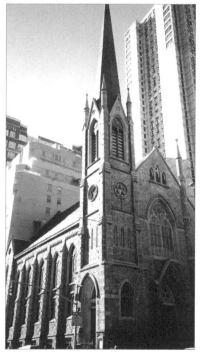

(Faith, Hope, and Love), a gift to the new congregation from the Empress of Germany. The church is designed in a Gothic style prevalent in northern Europe at the time. Lancet-arched stained-glass windows alternate with slender stone buttresses. The octagonal steeple is flanked by peaked gables and conical pinnacles. Of particular note in the interior, which soars 75 feet to the rafters, are the ornate chancel woodcarvings, which were hand-carved in the Black Forest of Germany.

Adjacent to the church on 88th Street is the parish house. The five-story neo-Grec building, now painted, retains some original details including window cornices and bracketed sills, and a cast-metal roof cornice with modillions and a decorative frieze.

125 East 88th Street
ARCHITECT: Charles Stegmayer   DATE: 1898

In spite of drab-gray paint, the upper stories of this Renaissance Revival brick building retain a certain elegance. Windows are nearly identical: stone enframements are embellished with beading and acanthus moldings and topped with a cartouche trailing vines. Fourth- and fifth-story sills are supported with small foliate brackets; all but the attic-story windows have cornices. A foliate frieze can be glimpsed behind street-level commercial signs.

153 East 88th Street

ARCHITECTS: John P. Leo   DATE: 1887
           Hubert, Pirsson & Hoddick   1890

Completed in 1887, the building was altered substantially three years later by Hubert, Pirsson & Hoddick for William Rhinelander. The round-arched openings, brick voussoirs and decorative impost bands of this four-story house combine Romanesque Revival and Renaissance Revival elements. There are subtle color variations in the buff brick of the facade, tan-brick and pale-stone trim, and warm wood-paneled doors, creating a pleasingly mellow effect. Diamond-shaped glass openings in the door are echoed in the diamond-patterned stained-glass windows. Above, horizontal brick channels define stories; brick panels separate windows. The building projects slightly at the fourth story; brick pilasters with carved capitals flank windows, above which is a dentiled cornice. More decorative brickwork can be glimpsed at the parapet.

155 East 88th Street

ARCHITECT: Stephen B. Jacobs
DATE: 1973-74

The lobby of this six-story modernistic building is three steps below street level, forming a base for duplex apartments rising to mid-story mezzanines. The visual effect of verticality created by one-and-one-half-story windows is offset by square mid-level windows. The red-brick facade is unrelieved by trim. Angular openings at the entry are echoed in the fire stairs which, unlike many buildings, are clearly part of the unusual and rhythmic design.

160 East 88th Street

ARCHITECTS: Kavy & Kavovitt   DATE: 1964

Typical of design during the "white brick" era, this fifteen-story building includes stores on the commercial street (Lexington Avenue), a garage, a modest green-marble entryway, and a front garden behind a retaining wall. The building sets back irregularly above the tenth and twelfth stories, creating terraces of varying sizes.

161 East 88th Street

ARCHITECT: J.M. Felson   DATE: 1936-37

Designed by the architect responsible for the Yorkville Garage [see 169 East 87th Street], this six-story Art Deco apartment building is of buff-and-beige brick. The entry surround is of white-painted lapped stone; the

brick base of the facade is also painted white. Although the building is
more than 50 feet wide, its verticality is emphasized by windows connected
with decorative spandrels of vertical bricks between stories. Fire escapes,
painted to match the building facade, have rounded railings with geometric
grille patterns. There is no cornice; above the top story, brick piers of
varying heights create a series of rhythmic flare-ups.

162 and 164 East 88th Street
ARCHITECT: John W. Marshall
DATE: 1871

These sturdy survivors embody an odd
combination of Italianate and Queen
Anne styles. Each building is five stories high, constructed of beige brick
with stone trim; each retains its modillioned sheet-metal cornice. Brick
piers, intersected with decorative brickwork, define the building extremes
and separate window pairs. The ground level of No. 164 is commercial, but
No. 162 has a four-step winged stoop and residential entrance, with a stone
surround and segmental arch over the door. The lower facade is painted
dark brown with beige trim, a counterpoint to the upper surface coloration. Note the paired windows: Each has a slightly arched lintel with a
curved keystone. At the corners are skew-backs incised with curlicues,
which connect to tiles between windows embellished with rosettes arranged
in sets of four; each set is unique. These are echoed in panels below
third-story windows. Decorative iron balconies adjoining the fire escape
add to the ornamentation.

165 East 88th Street
Kolping House
ARCHITECT: Nast & Springsteen   DATE: 1912

Rising austerely from a low granite base, this
seven-story building is constructed of dark-tan
brick accented with stone sills and band courses.
Above the entry is a painted entablature carved
with the words KOLPING HOUSE. Flanking the
three window bays on the second and third
stories are double brick pilasters topped with
egg-and-dart moldings and flat capitals.
Throughout the facade there is much decorative
brickwork, seen in panels between windows,
diamond motifs between string courses, window
lintels, and panels below the brick cornice. The
building is topped with a low crenelated parapet.

Adolph Kolping was born in 1813 in a small village near Cologne, Germany. He was ordained a priest in 1845 and vowed to dedicate his life to improving the welfare of young journeymen. The Kolping Society has since grown to 370,000 members worldwide. This building is one of two constructed in the city by the Catholic Kolping Society of New York; the other is a co-ed facility in the Bronx. (There is also a 50-acre estate on the Hudson River in Montrose, New York.) Kolping House is a nonsectarian residence for young men who come from all over the world to study and gain experience in New York City. They must be referred by an employer, a school, or a pastor. The society retains much of its German heritage; social activities include evenings in the building's Rathskeller, and an Oktoberfest outing at the Hudson facility.

166 East 88th Street
ARCHITECT: Richard Buckley(?)   DATE: 1870
The upper floors of this four-story brownstone have been stripped of ornamentation; only a trace of stone trim remains at the parapet corners. At ground level, the brick base and wood facing may date from a 1938 modernization. Stone steps and a ramp lead to wood-paneled doors. A dentiled wood cornice runs above the first story.

169 East 88th Street
ARCHITECT: Charles Houghton   DATE: 1875
White-stone lintels and sills accent the red-brick facade of this three-story neo-Grec/Queen Anne building. Above the ground-level stores runs a limestone band course; the horizontal ridges are echoed in the corbeled brickwork under the metal cornice. Indented vertical channels with limestone bases and corbeled tops articulate the building extremes. More corbels define the brackets supporting third-story curved sills.

3 East 89th Street
See 1083 Fifth Avenue, National Academy Museum

4 East 89th Street
ARCHITECTS: Eggers & Higgins; H.I. Feldman   DATE: 1953-54
Displaying a post-war Modern style, this thirteen-story building is of buff brick over a one-story stone base; a white-marble central section frames the entrance. The overall design consists of two mirror-image masses; concrete balconies with sleek metal railings cantilever from a chamfered recessed section over the entryway. Above the ninth floor are set-back terraces. H.I. Feldman replaced the original architects in 1950 before construction began, making slight alterations, primarily to the interior configuration. **HD**

5 East 89th Street
The National Academy School of Fine Arts
ARCHITECTS: William and Geoffrey Platt   DATE: 1959
This four-story Modern building was designed as an extension of the
school that it adjoins at 3 East 89th Street. Rising from a granite water
table and limestone base, the austere facade in shades of buff ironspot
brick blends with the hue and texture of the parent building. The
asymmetrical composition of the base is punctuated with four windows
and a door; diagonal grillwork echoes the diamond-patterned raised brick
headers on the upper facade. A limestone band course is inscribed with
the name of the school. **HD**

9 East 89th Street
ARCHITECT: Oscar Bluemner   DATE: 1903
At first glance, this five-story building seems
to be a vernacular version of the Beaux-Arts
style. Close examination, however, will
reveal an idiosyncratic use of detail. Oscar
Bluemner, a German-born Expressionist
painter and architect, must have been
conscious of the Art Nouveau movement and
its further development into geometrics.
This building is the only Bluemner

architectural work in Manhattan. (He also designed No. 7 East 89th Street,
but it is no longer standing.) Like his artwork, it is highly individualistic.

The most noticeable feature of this building is the designer's persistent
use of detail and openings to underline the structure's verticality. Tall
wrought-iron fences surround the basement areaway. The windows
flanking the central bay are tall and narrow. Over the entrance is a
geometrically shaped keystone so attenuated that it runs from the door to
the balcony above. The stone consoles supporting the second-floor
balcony, while of generous length, are insignificant when compared with
those supporting the fifth-story balcony. Despite the building's vertical
emphasis, the horizontal balance is maintained by the two balconies and
the cornice of the fifth-story tripartite window. Between the second and
third stories are ovals trimmed with garlands. These seem to be a classical
touch, but they are shallow and contrast sharply with the long wedge-
shaped keystones above the third-story windows.

Since 1981 the building has been the headquarters of the New York
Road Runners Club. Note the addition "Frank Lebow Place" to the street
sign. Lebow was the founder and long-time president. His statue can be
seen at the entry to Central Park at Fifth Avenue and 90th Street. **HD**

11 East 89th Street
Originally Lawrence L. Gillespie house, now the Trevor Day School
ARCHITECT: Arthur C. Jackson   DATE: 1912
Proportion, classical detail, and rich materials characterize this low-key,
neo-Renaissance six-story townhouse, which was designed for Lawrence L.
Gillespie, a banker. The facade is of American marble; decorative
wrought-iron gates contrast with the simple architrave trim of the two
doors and the small paired consoles on the ground story. The *piano nobile*
is spanned by an ornate iron balcony supported by a bracketed stone base.
Arched French doors with fanlights have simple surrounds and nicely
detailed keystones. Upper-story square-headed windows have molded surrounds; a band course separates the third story from the fourth, forming
its sills. A balustraded balcony and modillioned cornice underscore the
fifth-story windows. The mansard roof of the attic story is faced with
verdigris copper; two ogee-hooded dormers peer beneath the cornice.

In 1990 the building was acquired by the Trevor Day School, at
4 East 90th Street, to house the school's nursery, kindergarten and
administrative offices. Founded in 1930 by the Church of the Heavenly Rest,
the Day School, which has been independent since 1967, is connected at
the rear with the parish house. **HD**

12-16 East 89th Street
**Originally Cutting houses, now
Saint David's School**
ARCHITECTS: Delano & Aldrich
DATE: 1919-20
Simultaneous to building his own
house at 15 East 88th Street, Robert
Fulton Cutting, Jr. commissioned
the same architects to build these
three contiguous—and nearly identical—
six-story houses for three of his six
children. Because they have an
unbroken facade and a continuous roof line, the three Cutting houses
appear to be a single mansion. The effect is heightened by the seven-bay
ground-floor arcade, the stone balcony with wrought-iron railings on the
second floor running the length of the buildings, and the uniform pitch
of the slate-covered roofs, underlining the unity of the buildings. The
nine-bay facade is accented with lintels carved with bellflowers and
profiled heads over the three tall central windows on the second story.
The terminal cornices are ornamented with dentils and palmettes.

Although the neo-Federal ensemble was built earlier, there is no record of their being occupied until 1922, when the New York Social Register lists Helen Cutting (Mrs. Lucius) Wilmerding at No. 12, Charles Suydam Cutting at No. 14, and Ruth Cutting (Mrs. Reginald) Auchincloss at No. 16. There was a 50-foot garden extending from the three houses all the way back to Cutting's house on East 88th Street.

In 1950 Mrs. Wilmerding sold No. 12 for $95,000 to Saint David's School for boys. Founded in 1951 in the Catholic tradition, the school originally had one teacher and four students. In 1953 the Suydam Cutting house at No. 14 became available to Saint David's for $100,000. The adjoining garden was also on the market for an additional $60,000, but at the time the school could not afford to make both purchases. The third Cutting house, which was previously converted to a nursing home, was added to Saint David's in 1963. 22 East 89th Street [which see], originally the Hotel Graham, was added in 1972. The school today, which includes 385 students and more than 100 faculty and staff, is lay-run and independent. Although extensive renovations have been made to the interiors, the Cutting house facades remain exactly as created. **HD**

17 East 89th Street
ARCHITECTS: Gaetan Ajello   DATE: 1925
The primary entrance to this neo-Renaissance beige-brick-and-limestone building has a two-story classical enframement; double-leaf iron-and-glass doors are protected with wrought-iron grilles. A pair of lanterns flanks the entry; one is repeated at the Madison Avenue corner. Windows display carved lintels and double-height terra-cotta surrounds on several upper stories. Terra-cotta band courses underscore the building's horizontal appearance. Juliet balconies project from seventh-, ninth- and eleventh-story windows. The twelve-story apartment house is capped with a terra-cotta cornice, above which rises a penthouse. **HD**

22 East 89th Street
Originally Hotel Graham
ARCHITECT:
Thomas Graham
DATE: 1891-93
The apartment hotel, which offered multi-room suites with private bath but no kitchen, was once a popular concept in multi-family living in New York. Architect/developer

Thomas Graham promoted the Hotel Graham as "the East Side's first apartment hotel." The seven-story building provided a handsomely appointed central dining room with separate tables for each of the 31 apartments, and a ladies' reception area and private dining room for parties. Other amenities included electricity, steam heat, an elevator, and a choice of furnished or unfurnished suites. Graham maintained his practice in a front basement office but soon ran into financial difficulties; after foreclosure proceedings, one of the early owners was Victor Loew. His son, William Goadby Loew, would build the stately Loew mansion at 56 East 93rd Street, now part of the Spence School. The Hotel Graham saw a steady decline and was converted to an apartment house in the 1930s. It is currently owned by Saint David's School.

The Romanesque Revival-style building is distinguished by its grand arched entry, framed with rock-faced voussoirs and flanked by stout engaged columns and sweeping wings. The Indiana limestone base is articulated by a series of round-arched windows on 89th Street (shop fronts occupy the Madison Avenue street level). The remaining six stories are of limestone-trimmed ironspot brick. Window treatments vary at each floor, and include eared, carved and corniced lintels, embellished with peaks, triangular pediments, dentils, keystones, swags, faces, spandrels and brick arches. Pilasters with carved stone capitals flank sixth-story windows. At the corner of the seventh story a fluted engaged column, footed with a carved corbel, rises to meet the bracketed and modillioned terminal cornice that echoes the column's curve. Two corbeled chimney flues on 89th Street add exclamation points to this extraordinary structure. **HD**

40 East 89th Street
ARCHITECTS: Sylvan and Robert L. Bien   DATE: 1958
An angled black-marble entryway and low stone planters lead to recessed glass doors; just to the east a stone cherub fountain stands guard. Constructed of red brick, this eighteen-story building has three sets of projecting bay windows that relieve it of its otherwise boxy appearance. Above the thirteenth story are a series of set-back terraces.

45 East 89th Street
ARCHITECT: Thomas Lehrecke/Oppenheimer, Brady & Lehrecke   DATE: 1969
With 40 stories looming above the relatively low-scale Madison Avenue buildings, this red ironspot brick apartment tower has been a subject of controversy among its neighbors (and continues to incur wrath on windy days). Full-walled cantilevered terraces project from three of its four

sides; string courses define each floor. The surrounding street plazas, a bonus of a 1961 zoning resolution permitting additional building height and bulk, are paved in red brick and include truncated pyramidal brick planters. The building's side-street address notwithstanding, the entrance is actually on Madison Avenue. A wide driveway leads to bronze framed doors which open onto a double-height mahogany-and-brick lobby.

50 East 89th Street
ARCHITECTS: Emery Roth & Sons   DATE: 1973-74
This soaring Modern apartment house has a facade of brown brick with stone banding delineating each of its 33 stories. The 89th Street entrance is recessed through a *porte cochere* driveway that extends to 88th Street. The two lower stories are comprised of four duplex residences with individual entrances. All apartments from the seventh to the 32nd floor have large balconies. Three penthouses cap the building.

59-65 East 89th Street
Church of St. Thomas More

ARCHITECTS: Hubert, Pirsson & Co.
DATE: 1870
Built of gray sandstone like that used in the nearby walls of Central Park, this Gothic-style church appears to be closely modeled on Edward B. Lamb's Church of St. Martin, Gospel Oak, in London, which surprisingly was not a medieval church at all but a five-year-old Gothic Revival interpretation. The architects, Philip Hubert and James Pirsson, also designed the eclectic Queen Anne row houses at 145-156 East 89th Street.
Since its cornerstone was laid, the church has undergone three reincarnations. Originally the Episcopal Church of the Beloved Disciple, it was constructed to serve residents of St. Luke's Home for Indigent Christian Women next door. It merged in 1925 with the Church of the Heavenly Rest, which was located on Fifth Avenue and 45th Street but decided to relocate several years later to 90th Street and Fifth Avenue. In 1929 the vacant 89th Street complex was bought by the Dutch Reformed Church of Harlem; over the next two decades there was a steady decline in membership. The Catholic Archdiocese of New York acquired the building in 1950 and

the new parish was rededicated as the Church of St. Thomas More.

The church complex consists of four parts, giving the exterior some rambling facade planes. Walking east from Madison Avenue to Park Avenue you encounter first the smooth-stone octagonal chapel—note the stylized angel wings over the pilasters flanking the entry. Between the chapel and the church is a curious, turret-like pinnacle. Next is the church proper (1870) with its chamfered, square bell tower topped with four pinnacles; the Gothic-arched entrance bears a large stone eagle and is flanked with pairs of engaged columns topped with rosettes, leaves and lilies. To the east is the rough-stone rectory with steep hipped roof, and finally the brick, stone-quoined parish house (dated 1897, according to the apex carving). The Gothic embellishments of the facade are subdued and include square-headed windows with hood moldings and lancet-arched windows with drip moldings. In 1994 a new oak pulpit designed and carved by Hugh Harrison of England was installed in the church chancery. The pulpit is composed of five sides of an octagon, decorated with ogee arches and a Tudor rose—the design of a pendant worn by Sir Thomas More when he was speaker of the House of Commons during the reign of Henry VIII. The Tudor rose is a popular design element found in many late 1800's buildings in Carnegie Hill.

108 East 89th Street
The Dalton School
ARCHITECT: Richard Henry Dana IV
DATE: 1929

When the Dalton School—which had been housed in a Georgian town-house on the west side of Manhattan—needed to expand, they hired Richard Henry Dana IV to design their new quarters. The result was a handsome ten-story neo-Classical brick build-ing. Entry into the school is through a great arch flanked with Ionic-capped engaged columns. The recently refurbished French-style double doors are multi-pane, as are sidelights and a transom; the arch, too, is filled in with a multi-pane window. On the second story, four oriels supported by plain brackets are striking in their simplicity. Above the fourth floor, window bays are grouped in threes, giving the building a light and open feeling. The original crown story, at the tenth floor, is framed by limestone band courses; "phantom" courses turn the corners of the building. At this level, window bays are separated by stone pilasters; below each window a stone half-round or triangle is set into the brick facade. In 1969 a gymnasium was added to the top of the building and in 1995, as the school expanded, this was converted to classrooms and yet another floor was added, along with a rooftop play area.

115 East 89th Street
ARCHITECT: George F. Pelham   DATE: 1923
Red brick, restrained white ornamentation, and clean symmetrical lines characterize this nine-story neo-Georgian apartment building. Brick is laid in Flemish-bond style; above the second story a band of header bricks is framed by bands of white-glazed terra-cotta cornices. All windows have stone sills and are arranged in a pattern of twos and threes. Triple windows at the third story have brick relieving arches and terra-cotta surrounds. The banding pattern is repeated above the eighth story, as are the arch surrounds on the crown-section triple windows. The building is finished with a large terra-cotta cornice over dentil and egg-and-dart bands. The centered entrance of wood-and-glass double doors and matching transom is enframed by Ionic limestone pilasters and a dentiled cornice over a carved swag-and-urn entablature.

120 East 89th Street
ARCHITECT: Irving Margon   DATE: 1936
A keyed enframement accents the entry of this six-story red-brick apartment building; above the door a simple cartouche bears the address. Stained-glass lobby windows open onto a landscaped rear courtyard. The building had its "fifteen minutes of fame" when Ascot Realty bought it in 1999 and filed plans to erect an additional four stories over half of the building, and one story over the rest. In spite of receiving approval from the Department of Buildings, the owner was defeated, the result of vigorous opposition by residents.

121 East 89th Street
ARCHITECT: Henry J. Hardenbergh   DATE: 1888
This charming Queen Anne building is part of the Hardenbergh-Rhinelander Historic District, designated in 1998, which includes the group of six houses just around the corner at 1340-1350 Lexington Avenue [which see]. The rough-stone street-level facade is without interest; but a glance

upward rewards the viewer, floor by floor. Between the second- and third-story windows runs a checkerboard of stone-and-plaster carvings; the window mullions are fluted pilasters. Over the third story a garland frieze is topped with an exuberantly scrolled broken pediment. In its center a single window is framed with another set of pilasters. This in turn is capped with a Queen Anne pediment flanked by a pair of rosettes. **HD**

146-156 East 89th Street
ARCHITECTS: Hubert, Pirsson & Co.   DATE: 1886-87
This row of wondrously picturesque Queen Anne houses is a part of a proposed group of ten commissioned by William Rhinelander. Materials, size and design subtly unite the six houses, but remarkable variety has been achieved with myriad details and their placement. (Sixteen years earlier the same architects designed the rambling Gothic Revival Church of St. Thomas More two blocks to the west, whose buildings also display unexpected aberrations within a cohesive architectural style.) The houses are of dark-red brick and stone with terra-cotta trim. Each has a partially raised basement, retains its wrought-iron fence and low stoop, and is connected to its neighbor (somewhat erratically) by stone banding. Each is four stories high, with an overlapping, bracketed and tiled mansard roof pierced with dormers. When viewed from the street, their perky triangular pediments and chimneys of varying heights and shapes punctuate the roof line.

No. 146, the westernmost of the row, is the widest—20 1/2 feet, while

Looking east to west: 156, 154, 152, 150, 148, and 146 East 89th Street

the others are a diminutive 12 1/2 feet, half a standard New York City lot. No. 146 varies the most, particularly its L-shaped plan that sets the door facing west rather than the street. Ground-story windows are keyed and segmentally arched; and the asymmetrical third story displays curious brick channeling. Both Nos. 146 and 150 have bracketed second-story balconies, although the wrought-iron railings and central windows vary. The entries of Nos. 148 and 154 are recessed behind wide arches with voussoirs; one archway is of heavily rusticated stone, while the other is smoother and carried on imposts. Second-story window pairs are connected with decorative terra-cotta bands, although their lintels vary. Third-story oriels have whimsically decorated (but not identical) corbels and balconies. The oriels of Nos. 152 and 156 are on the second story; their corbels offer yet more decorative motifs. The attic dormer of No. 152 has a particularly graceful surround. The more one looks, the more variations are evident—in plaques, rondels, floral and geometric motifs, splayed and eared lintels, incised pediments—all characteristic of the Queen Anne style. Much care and creativity went into the design of this fascinating row that might have been just six small houses. The group was designated an individual landmark in 1979. **LM**

157 East 89th Street
ARCHITECTS: Barney & Chapman   DATE: 1905

Classical elements abound in this gracious Renaissance Revival building. Six steps and winged railings on limestone cheek walls lead to double wood-and-glass doors and transom. Flanking the entry are fluted pilasters with composite capitals, supporting a carved limestone entablature. Above, a segmentally-arched pediment displays floral carvings and a cartouche; the central second-story windows are ornamented with carved reveals and a keystone. The facade, which projects in the four-bay center section, is an unusual combination of red-brick stretchers and tan headers. This subtly dappled appearance is a pleasing contrast to the splayed limestone lintels. Band courses run above the first and fourth stories. A modillioned metal cornice and a set-back penthouse cap the building.

160 East 89th Street
ARCHITECTS: Boak & Paris
DATE: 1938

Art Deco elements enliven the red-brick facade of this eight-story-plus-penthouse building, designed by the innovative team that broke away from the sedate firm of Emery Roth in 1927. A reeded horizontal limestone band course above the first story is punctuated with vertical carved geometrics, which are echoed at the parapet. The entry is framed with curved, reed-type pilasters and a classical Greek key motif intersected with a carved abstract floral design. More Art Deco elements are evident in the brass-crossed spears on the glass doors, and in the lighting fixtures and wall decorations in the black-and-white lobby. Most of the multi-pane steel casement windows are still intact. Chamfered corner windows frame the recessed bay above the building's entrance.

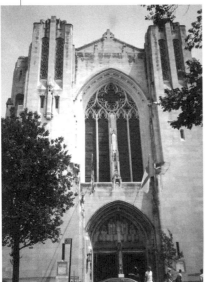

2 East 90th Street
(1084-1089 Fifth Avenue)
Church of the Heavenly Rest
ARCHITECTS: Mayers, Murray & Phillip/ Hardie Phillip, principal and architect-in-charge   DATE: 1927-30
POST-FIRE RESTORATION: Gerald Allen and Jeffrey Harbinson 1993-98

The original Protestant Episcopal Church of the Heavenly Rest, founded by veterans of the Civil War seeking a "restful life," stood at the corner of Fifth Avenue and 45th Street. Its move to its present site on the corner of 90th Street occurred with the purchase of land from Mrs. Andrew Carnegie, who reserved the right to approve the architecture.

Heavenly Rest, which merged with the nearby Church of the Beloved Disciple (now Church of St. Thomas More), retained the renowned church architect Bertram Grosvenor Goodhue, architect of St. Bartholomew's Church and Temple Emanu-El, to design the new building. He died, leaving the task to Hardie Phillip, one of the partners who took over Goodhue's firm.

The design, conforming to a rather narrow rectangular footprint (which incorporates a six-story parish house at its eastern end and the relocated Church of the Beloved Disciple to the south), has been variously described as "Stripped Gothic," "American Gothic," and "Gothic Deco." In reality, the restrained, rather austere silhouette of the limestone-faced structure ably combines elements of both the Gothic (in its verticality and stained-glass windows) and period Art Deco (in its sculptural massing and details). Twin towers flank the arched portal, which contains oak doors with embossed strap hinges. Sculptures of Moses and St. John the Baptist and two angels, the work of Ulrich Ellerhausen and Lee Lawrie, also flank the doorway. Two pairs of lancet-arched windows separated by a block of miniature Gothic elements rise to a rose window; stained-glass windows adorn the sides of the church.

These windows, the work of J.H. Hogan of the British firm of James Powell (Whitefriars) Ltd., were cleaned and restored—as was the interior of the church—after a fire in 1993 that consumed the organ console. More than 150 firefighters fought the blaze, which reached temperatures of 1,000 degrees Fahrenheit, bringing it under control mere minutes before the windows would have imploded and destroyed the entire church. Today a new, movable console by the Quebec firm of Guilbault-Therien (and restored pipes re-voiced by Konzelman Organs of New York), and new choir stalls designed by architect Gerald Allen and constructed in England under the supervision of Master Carver Hugh Harrison, stand in the chancel, under a still-spalled archway, as eloquent reminders of human frailty and supplication of divine intervention. **HD**

9 East 90th Street
Originally McAlpin-Miller house, now part of the Cooper-Hewitt, National Design Museum
ARCHITECT: George Keister   DATE: 1903

In 1876 David H. McAlpin, a former cigar-store owner who had developed a successful tobacco business (later bought out by the American Tobacco Company), purchased a plot on the east side of 90th Street off Fifth Avenue. Twelve years later he built three row houses for his sons, George, Charles and William. McAlpin died in 1901, leaving an estate of $3.5 million. The family promptly demolished the row houses and built two very substantial houses on the property: No. 9, designed for George McAlpin, the treasurer of D.H. McAlpin & Co., and No. 11 [which see], designed for William McAlpin. In 1919, at the age of 84 and shortly before he died, Andrew Carnegie bought No. 9 as a wedding present for his daughter, Margaret, and her husband, Roswell Miller. A rear wing that projects into the Carnegie mansion's garden was added in 1928. When the

mansion was transferred to the Smithsonian in 1972, the McAlpin-Miller house was included. It is now used as offices for the Cooper-Hewitt, National Design Museum.

Rising from a rusticated white-marble base, the five-story townhouse is robustly neo-Georgian. A grand portico at the ground floor is supported by Ionic columns and surmounted by a pediment and a balustraded balcony that extends the width of the building. The red-brick facade is trimmed in stone; marble quoins accent the corners. The second and third stories are bowfronted, surmounted with a marble-and-iron balustrade. The round-arched, second-story windows are framed with channeled voussoirs, while those at the third and fourth stories are topped with splayed lintels. Capping the fourth story is a marble modillioned cornice, above which rises a sloped roof with pedimented dormers and high sidewalls. The rear wing has an attractive arched doorway leading onto the rear terrace of the Carnegie mansion. **HD LM**

11 East 90th Street
Originally McAlpin-Minot house, now part of the Cooper-Hewitt, National Design Museum
ARCHITECTS : Barney & Chapman DATE: 1902-03
                    A. Wallace McCrea   1929-30

This handsome, four-and-one-half-story house of restrained architectural detail was built for M. Louise McAlpin and her husband William McAlpin, the tobacco heir [see 9 East 90th Street]. Inspired by the Beaux-Arts traditions of the French 18th-century townhouse, it originally featured a brick-and-limestone bowfronted facade and columned portico. The facade and interior were redesigned in 1930 at the behest of the owner Grafton W. Minot, a member of a prominent Boston banking company, with the resulting neo-Renaissance details. As with No. 9, the mansion is currently owned by the Cooper-Hewitt, National Design Museum.

The building, now of smooth-faced limestone ashlar, features a band course separating the ground level from the parlor floor and a string course below the fourth story, effectively dividing the facade into three sections. On the ground floor, tall round-arched window and door openings with deep reveals and festooned keystones contrast with square-headed French casement windows at the upper stories. Elongated console brackets ornamented with bellflowers distinguish the balustraded parlor-floor windows. The square-headed third- and fourth-story windows display eared enframements. A dentiled roof cornice crowns the facade, above which rises a balustraded parapet of similar design to the parlor-floor balustrades. Three dormer windows with segmentally-arched pediments, survivors of the 1903 design, project from the slate mansard roof. **HD LM**

14 East 90th Street (1246-1254 Madison Avenue)
ARCHITECT: J.E.R. Carpenter   DATE: 1928-29
Constructed as a co-op just before the Great Depression, from the outset this twelve-story-plus-penthouse apartment house attracted prestigious tenants. The Church of the Heavenly Rest bought an apartment to be used as its rectory; Drs. W.W. Harrick and Thomas T. Mackie, noted New York City practitioners, were also early occupants.

Like many of Carpenter's buildings, No. 14 was designed in an understated neo-Renaissance style. The one-story limestone base is topped by a dentiled cornice and a tan-ironspot brick facade, accented with brick quoins. Looking up, one sees that the third-story windows are ornamented with round-arched hoods with foliate panels; carved rectangular panels top flat-headed windows. A dentiled stone cornice with a frieze of anthemions

sets off the final story. Capping the building is a brick parapet with balusters.

The street and avenue entrances are noticeably different. Lighting the main entrance on East 90th Street are elongated colored-glass lanterns bearing the number "14." Egg-and-dart and rope moldings surround wood-and-glass doors and transom. Around the corner on Madison Avenue, the storefronts sport painted-masonry piers and business-like granite bulkheads. Much to the credit of the building's board, all store awnings are of a uniform design and color. **HD**

15 East 90th Street
Originally Emily Trevor house
ARCHITECT: Mott B. Schmidt   DATE: 1928
Designed by the architect responsible for the
"baby Dalton" school at 57-61 East 91st Street,
this four-story, neo-Federal building displays
elements identified with the Georgian Revival
style. Emily Trevor's brother, John B. Trevor,
had moved to 11 East 91st Street in 1909. Miss
Trevor acquired the 90th Street property in
1926 and demolished the existing house on the
site, a three-story brick building dating from
the 1880s. She lived at No. 15 until her death
in 1943 at the age of 70.

The red-orange brick is contrasted with white-marble-and-limestone
detailing. Corinthian columns and fluted pilasters support the well-
proportioned portico; the entablature is embellished with a frieze of
rosettes and triglyphs, above which runs a dentiled cornice and iron
railing. The building fenestration is symmetrical, with high nine-over-
nine sash at the second story; a marble surround and triangular pediment
distinguish the central window. Other windows are crowned with simple
stone lintels balanced by shutters. Below the cornice are square mutules—
large, widely spaced dentil-like flat projections. Set behind a brick
parapet is a steeply pitched attic story with dormer windows. The restraint
shown by the architect has produced a simple yet elegant house. **HD LM**

17 East 90th Street
Formerly Wanamaker Munn house, now part of
the Spence School
ARCHITECT: F. Burrall Hoffman, Jr.   DATE: 1917-19

A few years after this house was completed, the original owner sold it to Fernanda Wanamaker de Heeren
Munn. Her daughter-in-law, the international
socialite Aimée de Heeren (who died in 2006 at the
age of 103), and other members of the Munn family
occupied the distinguished neo-Georgian house for
four generations. It was acquired by the Spence School in 2008.

One of the most-photographed landmarks in Carnegie Hill, this five-
story, 29-foot-wide townhouse rises majestically from a rusticated limestone
base. An arcaded loggia pierced with high, round-arched openings spans
the front; from the keystones, a pair of goddess-like masks gaze intently at
passersby. Behind the recessed entrance are niches; the one to the west

displays a classical urn and bouquet. Marble balusters flank the elaborately carved double doors, which are adorned with a medallion, swags, and egg-and-dart molding. A wrought-iron railing fronts the eastern bay.

A projecting cornice with a decorative iron railing separates the ashlar base from the brick upper facade. Parlor-story windows are capped with splayed lintels and festooned keystones; balconettes and scrolled keystones embellish upper-story windows. The contrasting band course and stone cornice unite the building above the fourth story, while the high, small-pane French windows counter the horizontal elements. The attic story is set back behind the balustraded parapet. **HD LM**

21 East 90th Street
ARCHITECT: George F. Pelham   DATE: 1927

Much of the charm of this seventeen-story Art Deco building is well above the cast-stone ground story. A careful observer will spot splashes of color throughout its yellow-brick facade—in the polychrome terra-cotta corbel table with stylized trefoils above the third floor, and in terra-cotta arcades above the thirteenth- and fourteenth-story windows. Rising from the third-floor corbels are slender angled piers, terminating in colored finials; piers also flank the octagonal water tower. The blind arcades and crenelated parapet with terra-cotta coping add unexpected medieval touches. **HD**

51 East 90th Street
ARCHITECT: George F. Pelham   DATE: 1926

George F. Pelham often used medieval castle details in his architectural designs. This nine-story apartment house features a base of smooth limestone with a deep hood drip molding over the windows and the Tudor-arched main entrance. Above the stone cornice the remaining facade is clad in beige brick, with pairs of windows arranged symmetrically. Two sets of rusticated brick bands rise parallel to the end windows, creating the impression of flattened castle towers with triangular pediments. A crenelated stone-coped parapet adds to the fortress-like appearance and serves as an interesting wall for the penthouse rooftop gardens.

The main entrance consists of paired wood-and-beveled-glass French doors capped by a fanlight. A second set of glass doors leads to the intimate, multi-level lobby. Here the design is classical, with a black-and-beige diamond-patterned stone floor and the recent addition of gold leaf to accentuate the details of historic plaster moldings. **HD**

55 East 90th Street
Horace Mann School for Nursery Years
ARCHITECTS: Whitfield & King   DATE: 1904

Shortly after Andrew Carnegie had completed his Fifth Avenue mansion, he needed an "automobile house" for his cars, footman, and several chauffeurs; Carnegie tapped his brother-in-law's newly formed architectural firm to do the design. It was reported to be one of only two private

garages in the city at the time. Originally three stories high, it was designed in a neo-Federal style; a fourth story was added in 1914, also by Whitfield. Margaret Carnegie Miller, the Carnegies' daughter, used the building as an office into the 1960s. Two additional stories were added in 1964, when the garage was purchased by the New York (now Horace Mann) School for Nursery Years. The architect, Ferdinand Gottlieb, redesigned the upper facade but left the grand first level intact.

The marble-trimmed red-brick building features a Palladian opening with divided fanlight and marble keystone, and heavy glazed oak doors with strapwork hinges. Two side openings, also of wood, are topped with flat marble bands extending to the facade extremes, which are slightly recessed. Above each side door is an oculus window with marble voussoirs and radiating brickwork. **HD**

57-65 East 90th Street
ARCHITECT: J.C. Cady & Co.   DATE: 1886-87

Built as part of a row of eight brownstone-fronted houses, Nos. 57 to 63 were originally a left-hand set, mirrored by Nos. 65 to 71. Of the five houses that remain, the facades of Nos. 57, 59 and 61 retain their sturdy Romanesque Revival character. A unifying horizontal emphasis is achieved by means of a continuing modillioned and dentiled cornice, and alternating bands of smooth-cut and rough-cut stone which extend across the parlor floors and projecting round-cornered bays.

Only No. 57 remains in the original brownstone finish; at the basement entrance, a large arched door has a wrought-iron gate. Both Nos. 57 and 59 retain their original stoops; at No. 59, the handsome curved cheek wall is ornamented with balustrades and a curious half-moon iron grille. In 1955 architect Miles A. Gordon removed the stoop of No. 61 and added a classical enframement to the lowered entrance. In 2008 the owner

Looking west to east: Nos. 57, 59, 61, 63, and 65 East 90th Street

of No. 57, having acquired Nos. 59 and 61, obtained approvals to combine all three houses into a single residence and add one story set back from the streetwall. A balustraded parapet would also be re-introduced.

Architects Treanor & Fatio remodeled No. 63 in 1924. After removal of the stoop, the front was extended with a neo-Georgian red-brick facade. Details include windows with stone lintels, stone band courses forming sills below the second and fourth stories, and a brick parapet.

No. 65 was returned to a single-family residence in 1964 by architect Michael Maas; the stoop and parlor-floor arched-window openings were removed and a stucco finish was applied to the surface. In 2007 the facade was once again redone using smooth and rough-cut stone designed to resemble the 1887 original. **HD**

113 East 90th Street
Allan Stone Gallery
ARCHITECT: George E. Harney   DATE: 1878
Under the aegis of the New York Board of Fire Underwriters, this red-brick structure was built as a private firehouse station. The site included a rear building originally used as a stable. In 1946 the property was bought by Dr. William S. Ladd. Two years later he donated it to the American Alpine Club, of which he later served as president; the rear building was the club's museum of mountaineering. In 1994 the property was purchased by the Allan Stone Gallery. The rear building, accessed through a landscaped garden, is often used as

additional exhibition space and for showing films.

Designed in a playful combination of Queen Anne and Romanesque Revival styles, the three-story building is trimmed with white stone. The first story has a fire-engine-size arched entryway, surrounded by white quoins and voussoirs, capped with an incised keystone. Flanking the curved paneled doors are narrow doorways, over which are small windows with brick hood moldings. Textural brickwork occurs throughout the facade—between double string courses above the first and third stories, and over second-story windows. Third-story round-arched windows echo the narrow-wide-narrow street-level pattern, and are capped with hood moldings. The white fascia board near the top probably displayed the fire-station number. Like a Victorian bonnet, the roof line is capped with iron railings and a dentiled peaked parapet.

114 East 90th Street
ARCHITECT: Emery Roth DATE: 1924-25
A low marble base anchors this handsome nine-story, neo-Georgian building. The entrance is framed with marble pilasters capped with carved capitals and medallions, and a slightly curved entablature. Partially obscured by an awning is a graceful swan's neck pediment, above which is a carved foliate window surround.

Contrasting the red brick are clearly defined window enframements on the first three stories; each has slight variations. On the ground level, white marble-framed openings have intricately designed wrought-iron grilles with swags, arrows, and geometric elements. Extended keystones connect to a marble string course. On the second story, double-window bays have center pilasters; carved entablatures and aprons meet the upper and lower courses. All nine of the center windows are fronted with curved wrought-iron balconettes. Third-story bays have eared lintels embellished with urns and swags. The center nine windows have round-arched lintels with keystones extending to fourth-story sills. A carved plaque is centered above the fourth story. The building sets back slightly at the ninth story; window surrounds and railing echo the architectural details of the lower floors. A dentil course and cornice complete the classical design.

115 East 90th Street
ARCHITECT: George F. Pelham   DATE: 1917
This classical red-brick building rises nine stories from a low limestone base. The entryway has a simple limestone surround and entablature, topped with a dentil row. Carved brackets support a segmented pediment and a second row of dentils. Of interest are the fish-scale wrought-iron grilles over ground-level windows, echoed in curved railings projecting from second-story windows. Six-over-six double-hung sash windows are mostly intact throughout the facade.

120 East 90th Street
Trafalgar House
ARCHITECT: H. I. Feldman   DATE: 1963
Typical of the "white brick" style popular at the time, this fifteen-story building rises from a low black-marble base. Rusticated limestone flanks the wood-and-glass doors, over which projects a simple keystone. Above the tenth floor are set-back terraces.

121 East 90th Street
ARCHITECT: unknown   DATE: 1875
This charming five-story building displays Romanesque Revival characteristics seen in the round-arched windows with voussoirs, and Renaissance Revival detailing in the elaborate carvings. Posts with pyramidal tops lead up five steps to double wood-and-glass doors with a transom. Square engaged columns of white limestone have foliate panels and fluting, capped with leafy capitals and cherub heads. Delicately carved acanthus leaves and flowers adorn brackets and the entablature. Note the mischievous faces in keystones over the first-level windows. Above the rusticated limestone base, the facade is of buff brick. Rows of horizontal stone banding between windows and floors have egg-and-dart moldings. Brick pilasters frame and separate the four window bays; those at the top level have acanthus capitals. Capping the building is a metal cornice with swags, wreaths, brackets and modillions.

123 and 125 East 90th Street
BUILDERS: Loonie & Parker   DATE: 1888
As the only remaining neo-Grecs in this short block between Park and Lexington avenues, these modest five-story buildings retain much of their historic character. Windows have incised surrounds with rosettes at the

upper corners and shallow brackets beneath. Deep incised brackets support window pairs at ground level, which are narrowed to include a centered entryway. Iron-and-glass double doors with transom are just two steps above the sidewalk: Although the ironwork appears historic, it is possible that the original stoops were removed. The building is capped with a metal bracketed and modillioned cornice.

127 and 129 East 90th Street
ARCHITECT: Frank Wennemer
DATE: 1890

Designed in the Romanesque Revival style, these sturdy five-story row houses are survivors of the architect's prolific output in Carnegie Hill, which includes 168-172 East 90th Street, 49 and 51 East 92nd Street, and 129-143 East 95th Street. The facades mix smooth and rock-faced sandstone with beige brick. Horizontal stone banding connects openings on the first two stories. Five-step stoops of stone and red brick lead to glazed wood-and-glass paneled doors with transoms. Foliate brackets support first-level windows which, like the doors, are topped with keystones. Above is a limestone band course with rosettes, a dentil course and a cornice; string courses provide sills at upper stories. Second-story windows are square-headed; all other openings have segmental surrounds accented with ornamental moldings (archivolts). Capping both buildings is a floral frieze; the cornices have been removed.

151 East 90th Street
ARCHITECT: Horace Ginsbern   DATE: 1937
Alternating beige- and red-brick vertical planes characterize this six-story Moderne building. The recessed center section provides for corner window bays while minimizing the visibility of fire escapes. The entry surround is of brown granite; large multi-pane casement windows with metal frames are slightly recessed.

161 East 90th Street
Trafalgar Court
ARCHITECTS: Warren & Wetmore DATE: 1923-25
There is little in the plain facade of this nine-story, red-brick building to suggest the work of Warren & Wetmore, designers of the Beaux-Arts Burden mansion at 7 East 91st Street. Yet these are the architects of record,

according to the New York City Department of Buildings. Originally constructed as a hospital in 1923, the 145-bed Trafalgar Hospital complex succumbed some 56 years later to the financial pressures put upon small proprietary hospitals and was converted to an apartment building in 1979. Limestone keystones and segmental brick arches over several lower-story windows are among the few details of architectural interest.

162 East 90th Street
ARCHITECTS: Bernstein & Bernstein
DATE: 1901

This five-story-plus-basement beige-brick building retains much of its original Renaissance Revival flavor—with a sense of humor. Flanking the wood-and-glass doors are stone pilasters incised with bell-like flowers; above the incised entablature are modillions carved with acanthus leaves. Keystones over parlor-story windows have dragon-like profiles. Second-story outer windows feature formal triangular pediments, but look closely at the tympanum: A small face nestles in the foliage, while just below another face peers from the cartouche centered in the egg-and-dart molding. Elaborate foliate keystones top third-story windows, while those above have carved hood lintels. Even attic-story windows introduce new design elements, with eared stone lintels and cartouches. Wrought-iron fire escapes have gracefully turned railings. The building terminates with a garland-and-wreath frieze and bracketed metal cornice.

164 and 166 East 90th Street
ARCHITECT: Jacob H. Valentine (?)   DATE: 1879

Designed as a pair, these five-story-plus-basement buildings now bear little resemblance to each other except for their winged stoops and chunky beveled newel posts. Above the stripped parlor story, No. 164 retains much of its neo-Grec flavor. The brownstone facade has been painted; four bays of windows exhibit typical enframements—modest brackets under the sills, vertical pilasters topped with small incised lines and dots, and overhanging lintels. (Identical windows can be viewed just to the east, on Nos. 168–172.) A bracketed, dentiled metal cornice terminates the building. By contrast, No. 166 has been resurfaced in beige brick; all ornamentation, including the cornice, has been removed. A small shield in a brick frame is centered just below the parapet.

165 and 167 East 90th Street

ARCHITECTS: unknown   DATE: 1890 (est.)

These Romanesque Revival/neo-Grec row houses differ in detail but share stylistic similarities. Both have retained their splayed brownstone stoops and modillioned metal cornices. Facades are of shades of tan-brown brick, with stone trim and band courses creating sills at each of their five stories.

At the entrance to No. 165, fluted pilasters with composite capitals flank double wood-and-glass doors and a transom. Round-arched windows have splayed keystones; underneath are stone panels carved with garlands and rosettes. There is diversity in window treatments: Those at the second story have segmentally-arched pediments; third- and fourth-story windows are square-headed with incised hood moldings and beaded cornices; fifth-story windows are round-arched with stone voussoirs and narrow keystones that extend to the cornice. Stone banding connects all windows.

The entry to No. 167 has a carved entablature and projecting cornice supported by large incised brackets. Ground-level windows are round-arched with decorative iron grilles; hoods are connected with egg-and-dart moldings. The left keystone still bears a mischievous face. Windows on the upper stories have identical cornices and are connected with multiple rough-stone bands. The central section of the building projects slightly. Just beneath the cornice is a band of dogtooth brickwork.

168-172 East 90th Street

ARCHITECT: Frank Wennemer   DATE: 1890

These three identical row houses, now a single co-op unit, retain their sprightly neo-Grec detailing. The stone facades have been painted a pale yellow, contrasting nicely with the natural brownstone entryways. Chunky stone newel posts with large rosettes and mush-

room caps guard the five-step stoops. Freestanding brownstone columns, fluted at the upper portion and topped with floral capitals, support pedimented entablatures. Rosettes bloom in profusion! Fluted pilasters flank carved wood-and-glass double doors. The basement facades of rubblework masonry yield to rusticated stone at the parlor floors. Windows enframements are supported with modest brackets under the sills and topped with stone cornices; on the sides, moldings are lightly incised and scalloped. Dentil rows and bracketed metal cornices complete each of these historic buildings.

171-175 East 90th Street
ARCHITECTS: A.B. Ogden & Son   DATE: 1890-91
Little remains here of the inventive output of the architect responsible for many row houses in Carnegie Hill. These three buildings were five stories high, constructed of brick. Today there are no cornices; stoops have been removed and doorways lowered to street level. No. 175 has been stripped of all ornamentation. Nos. 171 and 173 are of yellow-painted brick rising from a stone base. String courses separate the stories. Simple eared lintels cap windows.

181 East 90th Street
The Metropolitan
ARCHITECTS:
Philip Johnson and Alan Ritchie
DATE: 2004

The exterior of this 32-story condominium tower is perhaps the last project by the renowned architect Philip Johnson, who was 97 at the time of the commission. Among the building's distinctive characteristics is its highly unusual cantilevered massing that projects fifteen to twenty-one feet over adjoining buildings. The horizontal striping effect created with two-tone beige brick contrasting with ribbon windows of dark, glare-resistant glass is purely Modern. Topping its seven slightly rounded bays is a banded crown that is softly illuminated at night.

1 East 91st Street
Originally Otto and Addie Kahn house,
now Convent of the Sacred Heart

ARCHITECTS: J. Armstrong Stenhouse with C.P.H. Gilbert   DATE: 1914-18

Home to German-born Otto Kahn, a noted philanthropist, art collector, and partner in the banking firm of Kuhn, Loeb & Co., and his wife and two children, the mansion at the corner of 91st Street and Fifth Avenue was at its completion one of the largest private dwellings in the city. Andrew Carnegie, who lived across the street, was said to have been "mad as hell" that Kahn's house was taller than his.

Modeled on the Cancellaria, a government building in Rome, the Kahn mansion is one of the finest examples of neo-Italian Renaissance style in New York City. Clad entirely in limestone, the exquisitely restrained mansion rests on a rusticated base, which opens inward via two arched doorways to an enclosed vehicular *porte-cochere* devised to drop off early-20th-century automobiles at the protected entryway underneath. The symmetrical facade can be read in three distinct sections: the rusticated base; the second-story rusticated *piano nobile* featuring balustraded windows topped with alternating segmental and triangular pediments, and flanked by paired pilasters with Tuscan capitals supporting an entablature; and a smooth-faced section comprising the third and fourth stories. Cornices cap third-floor windows; those above rise from a string course at the sill line and display simple eared enframements. A series of simple rosettes accents the space between the third and fourth stories. The north and east facades echo the more visible exteriors facing 91st Street and the park. A deep modillioned cornice topped by a balustrade partially conceals the recessed fifth story. A contemporary glass breezeway, added in 2002, connects the mansion with the Burden house next door without totally obscuring the massive staircase "drums." [See 7 East 91st Street].

Shortly after her husband's death in 1934, Addie Kahn transferred the house to the Roman Catholic Convent of the Sacred Heart, which uses it (together with 7 East 91st Street) as a school for girls. The building was restored in 1994. Several of its luxurious spaces may be rented for parties, including a first-floor parlor; Kahn's music room, once a recital hall for Enrico Caruso; and a Renaissance-style terrace/courtyard with a balustrade overlooking Central Park. The terrace wraps a second-floor foyer with a massive carved stone fireplace, coffered ceiling, and tapestries. **HD LM**

2 East 91st Street
Originally Andrew and Louise Whitfield Carnegie house;
then the Columbia University School of Social Work; now the
Cooper-Hewitt, National Design Museum, Smithsonian Institution
ARCHITECTS: Babb, Cook & Willard   DATE: 1899-1903
                  Polshek Partnership   1998

In 1902, a year after he retired from business, Scottish-born Andrew
Carnegie—then 67 years old and, with a net worth of some $300 million,
one of the richest men in the world—moved into what he termed "the
most modest, plainest and most roomy house in New York." With 64
rooms, the house was, indeed, roomy, but it was hardly modest—or plain,
especially on its robust exterior. Here, the mansion vigorously elucidates a
wealth of architectural details such as festoons, corbels, brackets and
cartouches with ebullient élan. It is not for nothing that our neighborhood is called Carnegie Hill.

Now a designated landmark that includes a commodious garden facing
East 90th Street, the Beaux-Arts-meets-neo-Georgian mansion, which was
loosely modeled after a stately British house, took four years to build.
Planned primarily as a residence for Carnegie, his wife, Louise, and their
daughter, Margaret, the house was also the locus from which the coal, iron
and steel magnate could oversee the myriad philanthropic projects he
undertook in his retirement—including the vast network of free public
libraries and the creation of institutions to foster world peace.

At its completion, the four-story-plus-basement, brick-and-limestone house boasted a number of innovations. Its floor system—spanning
steel beam to steel beam with arches, a patented wire-mesh, concrete-slab

system developed by the engineer for the Brooklyn Bridge—was the first example of a structural steel frame used for a private residence in the United States. The house was also one of the first to have its own private elevator and both central heating and a rudimentary cooling system; its boilers were fed by coal that traveled from bin to furnace via a scaled-down railroad track. The house also had an artesian well with two purification systems, one for drinking water and one for bathing.

Each of the three public facades of the mansion bristles with limestone ornament. The 90th Street entrance, a grand bronze-and-glass assembly with fanlight, sits within an arch outlined by a beribboned-and-foliate rope under a swelling glass canopy. Above hangs a heavy balcony supported by massive brackets. On the Fifth Avenue side, the basement level becomes visible; it is distinguished by heavy rusticated granite, while the first floor wears a lighter rusticated Indiana limestone facing. First-story windows on the Fifth Avenue and garden facades are arched; those above are plainer, though completely enframed in limestone. The servants' quarters at the top of the house have arched dormers highlighted by exaggerated keystones. The garden (designed by Schermerhorn & Foulks) is reached by a wide double stair from the house; there is also a gate into the garden from 90th Street.

Carnegie mansion, 90th Street facade and garden

The mansion is surrounded by a tall wrought-iron fence punctuated by posts topped with finials, and by a sidewalk of massive pink-granite slabs, unique in the city.

The sumptuous interiors (expertly converted to museum use by architect Hugh Hardy) include the first-floor parlor, with musical instruments painted on the ceiling, and the former bedrooms, sitting rooms and library (now galleries) on the second floor. Many of the rooms are paneled in Scottish oak, recalling Carnegie's ancestry. Adjoining the main house is a charming conservatory entered by a Tiffany portico. A two-story compatible addition designed by Polshek Partnership Architects in 1998 includes the Link Cafe and links the mansion to museum offices in the former McAlpin-Miller house at 9 East 90th Street [which see].

Andrew and Louise Carnegie lived in the mansion until his death in 1919. Mrs. Carnegie stayed on until her own death in 1946, following which the house was used by the Columbia University School of Social Work. In 1968 it became the Cooper-Hewitt, National Design Museum, Smithsonian Institution. **HD LM**

7 East 91st Street
Originally James A. and Florence Sloane Burden, Jr. house,
now part of Convent of the Sacred Heart
ARCHITECTS: Warren & Wetmore   DATE: 1902-05

Cited by the New York City Landmarks Preservation Commission as having "the finest Beaux-Art townhouse rooms in the City," the Burden mansion was commissioned by William D. Sloane and his wife, Emily Vanderbilt Sloane, a daughter of William K. Vanderbilt and a granddaughter of Commodore Cornelius Vanderbilt. The building was a wedding present for their daughter, Florence, and James A. Burden, Jr., scion of an ironworks family from Troy, New York. This house and No. 9 (designated for their other daughter) occupy part of a parcel of land the Sloanes purchased from Andrew Carnegie; at its sale, Carnegie stipulated that seventeen feet of undeveloped land remain between any two structures. (That gap, a former side court, is now set off by a modern metal gate and used as a carpark by No. 9, the Russian Consulate.) After James Burden's death in 1932, his widow moved into River House on East 52nd Street, and No.7 was sold to John Jacob Astor VI, who lived there from 1934 until 1939. Astor sold the house the following year to the Convent of the Sacred Heart.

The five-story Beaux-Arts mansion features a boldly articulated limestone facade on a two-story rusticated granite base. A segmentally-arched doorway at ground level was designed to be wide enough to accept a carriage, which could then exit to the street through the side of the build-ing and court. Originally the sides of the house were to be rendered in brick, but Mrs. Sloane insisted they be as imposing as the facade. To that end, limestone-clad side elevations exhibit arched windows (some are blind) to match the dramatic trio of arched windows set within deep concave enframements on the third floor, or *piano nobile*—a motif the architects may have consciously replicated in their design for the massive triple portals on the southern facade of Grand Central Terminal. The *piano nobile* windows are fronted by a balcony accented with wrought-iron railings and carried by four sturdy brackets; a second set of smaller, square windows is tucked underneath. Windows at the top story are separated by wide incised spandrels and underscored by egg-and-dart moldings. A deep modillioned cornice accented by dentils runs along the roof line; a parapet interrupted by balustrades completes the ensemble, and hides the recessed attic.

Upon entering the mansion (with its interiors credited, it is believed, to the firm of J.H. Morgan), a sweeping marble staircase rises from a handsome rotunda which is crowned by a cupola painted by the French artist Hector d'Espouy. The rooms on the *piano nobile,* which may be rented for parties, consist of a reception room, banquet hall, and 65-foot ballroom with mirrored walls and a vaulted ceiling festooned with elaborate plasterwork. **HD LM**

9 East 91st Street
Originally John Henry and Emily Vanderbilt Sloane Hammond house, now the Consulate of the Russian Federation in New York
ARCHITECTS: Carrère & Hastings   DATE: 1903

When the second Sloane daughter, Emily, was married to John Henry Hammond in 1899, Mrs. Sloane commissioned Carrère & Hastings to design a Beaux-Arts mansion based on a 16th-century Italian Renaissance palazzo on the lot adjacent to that of her elder daughter, Florence. The Hammonds moved into the lavish five-story structure with limestone facade and boldly rusticated base with some apprehension. The entry in Mrs. Hammond's diary for November 30, 1903 reads in part: "Today John and I moved into our new house. It is huge, and there is no getting away from its size. Perhaps in time we shall feel at home in it, but alas! we both long for a small house where we can lead the simple life we both love." Despite their misgivings, the Hammonds raised five children there while employing sixteen live-in servants.

The facade offers an interesting counterpoint to its neighbor at No. 7. No. 9 is more austere and has a symmetrical progression of windows from floor to floor. The upper portion of the building is framed with heavy quoins, above which is an elaborate frieze and modillioned cornice. The three high French windows of the *piano nobile* are framed with pilasters with Ionic capitals topped with segmentally-arched pediments and dentils. The central window is fronted with a wrought-iron balcony supported with heavy carved brackets. Just behind there is a ballroom large enough to accommodate 250 guests, and the adjoining music room can hold another hundred. It was in this room that the Hammonds' son, John, who went on to become a major producer of jazz and popular music, was first introduced to music; it was also in this room that Benny Goodman, who would become the Hammonds' son-in-law in 1942, performed the Mozart Clarinet Quintet.

In 1952 the mansion was bought for use as a 31-bed privately-owned eye hospital. It changed hands again in 1975 when the U.S.S.R. bought it, together with 11 East 91st Street, planning to open a consulate. Their plans went awry after the invasion of Afghanistan in 1980. President Carter ordered the Russian officials to leave the country and the house was shuttered until 1992. After twelve years of neglect, extensive repairs were needed and a crew of sixteen skilled Russian artisans spent two years restoring the mansion to its original splendor. The building was initially opened to the public in January, 1995, with an exhibition of photographs of the expertly done restorations provided by Random House for its newly published book, *The Russian Century*. **HD LM**

11 East 91st Street
Originally John B. and Caroline Wilmerding Trevor house, now Consulate of the Russian Federation in New York
ARCHITECTS: Trowbridge & Livingston   DATE: 1909-11

After observing the great palaces to the west, one might overlook this small exquisite townhouse. Before he married in 1909, John B. Trevor bought the lot from Andrew Carnegie. The architects designed a dignified, five-story residence in a restrained Beaux-Arts style for the newly-wed couple. Trevor, a politically controversial figure, died in 1956; Caroline Trevor continued to reside in the house until 1974. It was purchased in 1975 by the U.S.S.R., together with No. 9 next door, and today is used as offices for the Russian Consulate.

Above the rusticated base of the ground story are three floors set in smoothly finished limestone; string courses surmount the ground and third stories. Foliate brackets support the cornice slab over the molded entrance surround. The areaway is enclosed by a wrought-iron fence with urn-topped posts. The importance of the *piano nobile* is emphasized by the height and depth of recess of the round-arched openings, into which are set French casement windows with protective wrought-iron grilles. A slate mansard roof pierced with three copper-clad dormer windows rises behind a limestone balustrade that rests on the dentiled modillioned cornice. **HD LM**

15 East 91st Street
ARCHITECTS: Leonard Schultze & Associates   DATE: 1946-47
Although this Modern buff-colored brick building is on the corner of the block, there are no stores on the Madison Avenue side. A low granite base and granite planters flank the two-story entrance. Decorative chrome-and-glass double doors, a fluted limestone entrance surround and geometrics on the entablature give a late nod to Art Deco styling. Slightly cantilevered corner balconies, many of which have been enclosed, rise to set-back terraces above the tenth story. **HD**

22 East 91st Street
The Spence School
ARCHITECTS: John Russell Pope   DATE: 1929
       Fox & Fowle   1985-87
This handsome red-brick-and-limestone building housed boarding as well as day students when it was opened in 1929. Today all girls from the fifth to twelfth grades are day students. Younger students attend the lower school in the former Loew mansion at 56 East 93rd Street [which see], acquired by Spence in 1999.

  The restrained eight-story neo-Georgian facade is marked by limestone facing of smooth-cut ashlar at the ground level. Tall second-story windows display bracketed hoods and iron railings; the center window is pedimented. Directly above runs a limestone course with a Greek key motif. A narrow balcony with a wrought-iron railing projects from the sixth story, which is defined by high windows with limestone surrounds. A limestone cornice and balustrade cap the seventh floor; the terminal story is set back.

  Noteworthy is the contextual three-story west wing housing a gymnasium, added in 1987. The architects designed a building respectful of the original school structure; subtleties include three-sided projecting bays dipping slightly below the second-story string course, and an oculus window piercing the enclosure rising above the roof line. **HD**

26 East 91st Street
(1268-1272 Madison Avenue)
ARCHITECT: A.B. Ogden & Son
DATE: 1890-91

Although the brick facade of this six-
story Renaissance Revival building
has been painted, many original
design elements remain. Corbeled
band courses separate each story; a
pressed-metal cornice divides the fifth
from the sixth story. On the second
through fifth stories, windows have
flat and segmentally-arched heads;
round-arched windows connected with banding distinguish the crown story.
Capping the building is a bracketed metal cornice with a decorative frieze.
Other original elements include rounded balconettes at the fifth story,
slightly projecting paired bays and a rounded corner bay. The round-arched
second-story surround on Madison Avenue was originally the upper portion
of the entrance to the building. In 1930 the residential entrance was moved
around the corner and the Madison Avenue storefronts were created. The
building also received a new address: 26 East 91st Street. **HD**

46 East 91 Street
ARCHITECT: George F. Pelham   DATE: 1929-30

The unpretentious lines of George F. Pelham's Art Deco apartment house
are well suited to the fashionable shops along Madison Avenue. Rusticated
stone flanked by pilasters on the corners visually link the progression of
shop windows and retail entrances, as does a modest cornice just above the
window line. The building is clad in beige brick. Above the third-story
cornice, vertical bands in a lively red-and-buff checkerboard pattern on
brick headers delineate window openings and end bays. This creates an
impression of rising towers, an ornamental device used in various ways by
Pelham in his apartment house designs. The thirteen-story building
includes a multi-level penthouse with a third-story crown and a pointed-
arch window. Painted white, the penthouse is a small version of the
"wedding cake" style that came into fashion at the end of the Jazz Age. **HD**

47 East 91st Street
ARCHITECTS: Platt Byard Dovell White   DATE: 2003-04

Few buildings in Carnegie Hill have been subjected to such a vociferous
hue-and-cry as the Postmodern ten-story condominium that now
dominates the northeast corner of 91st Street and Madison Avenue. The

site originally contained a row of six Queen Anne-style houses designed in 1885 by architect Frederick T. Camp for developer Alexander Duff. Four of these were demolished in 1950 to make way for a one-story bank.

In 1999 the Tamarkin Corporation, owners of the building housing the branch of the bank as well as one of the two surviving Camp buildings that adjoin it [see 1281-1283 Madison Avenue], filed plans for a seventeen-story luxury apartment building. The neighborhood mobilized under CitiNeighbors and Carnegie Hill Neighbors, decrying the height and scale of the condominium as inappropriate. After multiple hearings the height of the building was reduced to ten stories and approved by the New York City Landmarks Preservation Commission.

The one-story rusticated limestone-and-sandstone base, housing the bank and the residential entry on 91st Street, is topped with multi-colored sand-toned brick. As a result of the height reduction, the facade design underwent a radical overhaul; the only significant feature retained from the elevations as originally planned is the fenestration. Echoing an Arts-and-Crafts prototype, windows are defined by grids enclosing pairs of casements. Room-high windows at the southwest corner are recessed into the brick surround; bronzed metal panels link them, top to bottom. **HD**

48-54 East 91st Street
ARCHITECTS: A.B. Ogden & Son   Date: 1885-86
                Peter Pennoyer Architects   2007

All four of these brownstones share some original neo-Grec/Queen Anne detailing. Most window surrounds are fluted at the sides, with slightly curved, center-peaked upper moldings carved with acanthus leaves. The bracketed roof cornices are intact: Those on the wider, outside buildings feature dentils, lapped brackets and rosette-embellished friezes, while the center cornices display simple panels contrasted with foliate brackets.

No. 48 has been stripped of window detailing. The stoop was removed in 1951, and at the basement level, centered double doors with iron grilles flanked with lanterns and small openings were introduced. A cornice inset with decorative ironwork runs below parlor-story windows.

No. 50 lost its stoop in 1931. Peter Pennoyer Architects restored the building in 2007: At the entry floor, one door was removed and a cornice was added. The areaway was enclosed by a low wall with an iron railing. The front facade brownstone was refinished, and the the parlor windows were widened and accentuated. The rear facade was altered in neo-Federal style using red brick and stone trim, all visible from a 90th Street alley.

When the stoop was removed from No. 52 in 1930, a bay window was created at the basement level, fronted with a small garden. Fluted pilasters, a bracketed cornice and entablature frame the wood-and-glass door and sidelights. The eastern parlor-story window was widened; a wide fluted molding runs under third-level openings.

Only No. 54 remains essentially unaltered. Historic curved newels and iron railings carved with Tudor roses guard the ten-step stoop. At the parlor-level entrance, wood-paneled doors and transom are flanked with beaded pilasters and rose-embellished brackets; above is a foliate entablature and a heavily projecting cornice. Corbeled blocks support window sills; those at the parlor story extend to include incised geometrics and more roses. Alone among the quartet, the basement facade retains its rock-faced banding. **HD**

49 and 51 East 91st Street
ARCHITECT: A.B. Ogden & Son   DATE: 1884-87
Of these brownstone row houses, No. 49 retains considerably more of its neo-Grec integrity. Both were designed for Emeline and Elizabeth Johnston. Under the parlor-floor windows of No. 49 are three carved plaques, the outer ones each bearing an initial—E and C. Full window surrounds remain on the second and third stories, including small brackets under sills, and larger incised brackets supporting cornices. The stoop was removed in 1931; the surround of the newly created ground-level entrance echoes those of the windows. A penthouse and small terrace were added above the bracketed metal cornice. Basement windows retain their historic grilles.

All that remain of the original facade of No. 51, built in 1884, are the bracketed window hoods on the second and third stories, the paneled metal cornice and the basement grilles. In 1950 the stoop was removed and decorative details were stripped from the brownstone front, which was then resurfaced and painted. Wrought-iron newel posts flank the steps leading into the areaway and the relocated main entrance. **HD**

53-55 East 91st Street
The Dalton School
ARCHITECT: Edward I. Shire
DATE: 1907-08
This grand red-brick townhouse, nearly 33 feet wide, was the result of substantial alterations to two row houses built by A.B. Ogden & Son in 1884. Today, with Nos. 57-61, the building houses "baby Dalton," as neighbors refer to the First Program of the Dalton School. Prototypical of the neo-Federal/neo-Georgian style, it

was designed to unite the two previously existing buildings and now forms part of the casual mix that makes up the harmonious ensemble of 91st Street. The entranceway features a round-arched door with fanlight and wood frieze, capped with a double keystone. It is flanked by high multi-pane French windows with wrought-iron guards and modified Federal lintels. Four limestone panels separate the parlor floor from the second story. A three-sided oriel supported by curved brackets interrupts the four-opening scheme of the first and third stories. A limestone band course forms the sills of the third-floor windows, which retain their eight-over-eight sash. Above them is a modillioned and dentiled limestone cornice topped with a balustraded parapet. The slate-roof attic story with round-arched dormers and set-back penthouse were added by the Dalton School in 1979. **HD**

57-61 East 91st Street
Originally Guy and Cynthia Roche Burden Cary house, now the Dalton School
ARCHITECT: Mott B. Schmidt DATE: 1923-24

This stately neo-Federal building was designed as a one-family residence for Guy and Cynthia Cary. Guy Cary was an attorney and served on the board of many large corporations. Cynthia Roche Burden Cary, the daughter of Emily Vanderbilt Sloane White and the Third Lord Fermoy of Sandringham, was first married to Arthur Scott Burden, a prominent philanthropist. After Guy Cary's death in 1950, the house became a nursing home. It was sold to the Dalton School in 1965 and became part of the adjacent "baby Dalton" at 53-55 East 91st Street.

The soft-pink tones of the brick are in contrast to the red-orange of No. 53-55, yet the two buildings are united by their similar scale, common detailing and decoration, and a continuous heavy modillioned cornice above the third story. The facade of this five-story building is dominated by a central three-bay projection framed by brick quoins at the second and third stories. The full-length windows at the *piano nobile* are accented with keystones, splayed lintels and projecting half-round balconies. The focal point is a portico with a segmentally-arched roof, supported by two sets of Ionic columns and pilasters, sheltering the entryway with its wood-and-glass door and fanlight. Other features of note are the windows at the ground story set within blind arches, and the wrought-iron fence with ornamental posts and boot-scrapers. **HD**

56-62 East 91st Street

ARCHITECT: Gilbert A. Schellenger   DATE: 1887-89

Designed in subdued Romanesque/Renaissance Revival style, these four
brownstones contribute much to the pleasant character of the streetscape.
Nos. 56 and 58 are narrower than Nos. 60 and 62 to the east, but the
similarity of the two upper floors of the four houses establishes that the
same hand was at work. Second-story windows are square-headed,
trimmed and connected with stone moldings; round-arched openings at
the third story are embellished, Romanesque-style, with archivolts—wide
block moldings springing from corbeled horizontal impost bands. The
two upper stories are divided by a wide band course with rectangular
panels. Bracketed and modillioned metal cornices are similar, with some
variation in the design on frieze panels. All four houses lost their stoops—
Nos. 56 and 58 in 1949, and their neighbors to the east some 25 years
earlier—with entrances relocated at the basement level. Ornamentation has
been removed from the parlor and basement floors of Nos. 56 and 58,
and the facades have been painted a pale green.

The round-headed windows and original entrance of the parlor
floor of No. 60 are set into rock-faced ashlar, contrasting nicely with the square-headed openings and
smooth facing of the parlor floor of No. 62. Of special
interest are the carved panels set below parlor- and
second-story windows of both eastern buildings, the
vertical panels on No. 60, and even the tiny round
plaques capping the scrolled brackets of No. 62: Here,
the observant viewer can spot putti, benign and devilish
creatures, winged dragons, birds, urns and shells, all
embraced with vines and flowers. **HD**

63 and 65 East 91st Street

ARCHITECTS: Wray & Bussell   DATE: 1888-89

These brownstones, each three stories high plus a basement, were designed
as a pair, although both have been substantially altered. The stoop,
railings and newel posts of No. 63 remain, as does the handsome
wrought-iron door; the cast-iron enframement is of a later date. Now
stuccoed and stripped of most of the original detailing, the building still
displays a three-sided oriel on the second story. The original cornice has
been replaced with a simple dentil course. Since 1990 No. 63 has been
owned by the adjoining Dalton School. The facade (now painted) of No.
65 retains much of its original Renaissance Revival detailing. The stoop
has been removed and the original door with fluted pilasters has been
replaced with a large second-story window, topped with an entablature

supported by floral-carved brackets. Multiple band courses and other horizontal elements span the facade, and the bracketed sheet-metal cornice is ornamented with Tudor roses set within a frieze. Also worth noting is the panel below the parlor-story windows, carved to depict two swans sipping from an urn. **HD**

64-68 East 91st Street

ARCHITECTS: James Henderson DATE: 1887-89 John P. Volker 1927
            Snelling & Potter 1909   William A. Boring 1910

Although these three row houses bear little resemblance to each other today, they share a common grandparent: the architect James Henderson, who designed them for developers Sigmund Warshing and James Palmer. At that time the 22-foot-wide brownstones, designed in Renaissance Revival style, had stoops, iron grilles protecting basement windows and doors, and metal cornices.

With the removal of the stoop by architect John P. Volker, No. 64 relocated its entrance to the basement level; protective ironwork may be original. Volker deleted all embellishment; only the new entryway received a simplified neo-Classical stone surround consisting of pilasters supporting an entablature and curved pediment. On the third story, a larger window opening was recut and fitted with multi-pane steel casements.

At No. 66, results of the 1909 Snelling & Potter facelift include removing the stoop and adding a neo-Classical surround and wrought-iron grille to the basement-level entry (the brass address shield may be a later addition). A year later, architect William A. Boring added a single-story, slate-covered mansard roof with a skylight. Today a metal fascia replaces the cornice, and the roof, now asphalt-shingled, has a metal-framed dormer.

No. 68 underwent the fewest alterations, except for the installation of single-pane windows—and a coat of bright white paint. The parlor-floor entrance (reached by the row's only remaining stoop) and window surrounds exhibit intricate carvings of flowers, fruit, birds and mythical creatures. A deep cornice supported by foliate brackets projects three feet over the entryway; its entablature is classically carved with an urn flanked by putti. A rounded foliate base distinguishes the pedimented center window; all other windows are set on corbel blocks. A frieze of Vitruvian waves runs under the modillioned cornice. **HD**

67 and 69 East 91st Street
ARCHITECTS: Gilbert A. Schellenger   DATE: 1891-92
              Delano & Aldrich   1915
              James E. Casale/Smith & Leo   1925-1928

Conceived as a pair, these three-story-and-basement brownstones were designed in the ubiquitous Renaissance Revival style. Little remains of the original architectural details except the basic fenestration pattern. In both cases, once the stoops were removed, the entries were relocated to the basement level, ornamentation was stripped, facades were resurfaced, and one story was added.

Delano & Aldrich's 1915 redesign of No. 67 deleted a second-story oriel window; in 1942 the homeowners installed a set of elongated parlor-story windows protected with decorative ironwork. Today the facade is seasonally covered with ivy.

No. 69 underwent three updates, including one in 1925 registered by architect James E. Casale. Smith & Leo subsequently added a brick-faced penthouse, which was extended in 1964 to align with the facade. At the same time a copper cornice was added, the surface was stuccoed and a garage entrance was created in the former basement. **HD**

70 East 91st Street
Formerly Frederick W. Marks house
ARCHITECTS: Schwarzmann & Buchman
DATE: 1885-86   Robert T. Lyons   1905

Once part of a row of four brick and brownstone houses, this elegant Beaux-Arts residence was commissioned by developer Frederick W. Marks for his own use in 1905. Designed in the style of the west garden of the Palace of Versaille (Louis XIV), the facade is clad in smoothly rusticated limestone. A low stoop with wingwalls leads to a narrow entrance of wrought-iron and glass, crowned with a garlanded keystone. The parlor story French windows are set beneath multi-pane transoms. Arched French windows with fanlights mark the second story; these are protected by wrought-iron balconies typical of Parisian apartments and are surmounted by scrolled keystones and cartouches. Scrolled keystones also accent the windows at the top story. A metal modillioned and bracketed cornice projects beyond a stone balustrade enclosing a roof-top garden. **HD**

72 East 91st Street
Formerly John Foster Dulles house
ARCHITECTS: Schwarzmann & Buchman   DATE: 1885-86
Walter Haefeli   1927

Like its elegant neighbor to the west, No. 72 was originally part of a row of brownstone-fronted houses. It received its neo-Classical facade in 1927 at the behest of owner John Foster Dulles, who lived there for more then 30 years. Educated at Princeton, Dulles earned an international reputation as chairman of the Rockefeller Foundation and the Carnegie Endowment for International Peace. He also served as United States delegate to the United Nations, and as United States Secretary of State.

Clad in limestone, No. 72 features twin, subtly arched doorways at ground level. The entry is shielded by delicately tendriled wrought-iron grillwork—a motif repeated on rounded balconies fronting the tall second-story windows, which are surmounted by bas-relief panels displaying urns spilling over with flowers. A rosette-embellished dentiled cornice furnishes the remaining ornament. **HD**

103 East 91st Street
ARCHITECTS: John Sullivan
DATE: 1884-85
C. Dale Badgeley 1950-51

Originally designed—with its neighbor, No. 105—as a pair of brownstones in the ubiquitous neo-Grec style, No. 103 underwent a severe overhaul in 1950-51, which resulted in a stark neo-Georgian interpretation. Once the stoop was removed, the architect extended the lower half of the house to create a terrace off the third floor; he also veneered the lower facade with limestone.

At one time the home of Edward Everett Tanner III, a.k.a. Patrick Dennis, author of the spirited novel *Auntie Mame* (a character interpreted on the stage by the ebullient Ethel Merman), the house wears a coat of powder-pink paint that completely obscures the limestone. A mock-Palladian-style window with voussoirs rises almost the full two stories at the center of the house; this multi-pane window is flanked by mahogany-hued wooden doors, each of which is surmounted by a scrolled bracket and an oculus window. (Note that the circular door panels echo the shape of windows above.) A delicate wrought-iron railing in a lozenge-inspired geometric design accents the setback; a second railing runs across the front of the roof line. Both railings are painted gray, as are the narrow shutters, added in the late 1980s, which flank the French doors and six-over-six windows on the third and fourth stories of the house. **HD**

105 and 107 East 91st Street
ARCHITECT: Wilfred E. Anthony   DATE: 1927

These two buildings, constructed as neo-Grec row houses in 1884-85, were redesigned with neo-Georgian facades some 40 years later. The ground stories are almost identical: Paneled doors are flanked by multi-pane windows protected by decorative wrought-iron grilles. Red brick, laid in a Flemish bond pattern, visually unifies the facades, as does an uninterrupted terra-cotta cornice above the fourth stories. The fifth stories, set back from the floors beneath, are barely visible behind a brick parapet capped with stone.

A four-bay casement window with a centered fanlight spans the facade of No. 105; the window is traversed by a wrought-iron railing. In contrast, the parlor floor of No. 107 features two tall round-arched windows accented with fanlight transoms and keystones. The third stories of both buildings are similar, with pairs of six-over-six double-hung wood sash; No. 105 added black paneled shutters. The roof terrace of No. 105 is accented by a wrought-iron railing. **HD**

108 East 91st Street
ARCHITECTS: Gronenberg & Leuchtag   DATE: 1927

The ground story of this understated neo-Renaissance building is of buff-colored painted limestone; a band course of acanthus leaves and dentils separates the base from the remaining eight stories of variegated light-brown brick. Panels of geometric brickwork separate second-story windows.

Foliate engaged columns topped by acanthus capitals frame the round-arched entrance; twin pairs of arched windows on the third and ninth stories echo the design. The outer-window enframements are of brick set in a stacked bond pattern; each pair is separated by a ribbon-and-rosette carved engaged column. Arches are outlined in dentils; above, impish faces peer from decorative medallions. The third-story window pairs feature Juliet balconies with decorative wrought-iron railings. Windows at the ninth story are fronted by rope-coiled balustrades supported by foliate brackets. Arches are filled in with medallions and leafy carvings. Below the cornice are more medallions—two round, two square—and a row of dentils. The scalloped rim of Mediterranean-style roof tiles is barely visible from the street.

109 East 91st Street
ARCHITECT: Frederick J. Sterner
DATE: 1916-17

This elegant red-brick-and-limestone house, designed in neo-Georgian style, was built for Mrs. I. Townsend Burden, Jr. Upon its completion, it was sold to Egerton Winthrop, Jr., a partner in the law firm of Winthrop & Simpson. It replaced two of a group of four row houses built by John Sullivan in 1885.

Its simplicity and restrained ornamentation make it particularly striking. A handsome arched window and doorway, both framed in limestone, grace the first floor. Glass double-doors and transom are protected with ornate iron grillwork. Above the limestone band course, double rows of bricks surround arched multi-pane casement windows and fanlight transoms (which were meticulously restored in 1990). All windows are accented with decorative iron railings. A simple limestone cornice separates the fourth from the fifth floor; the building is capped with a projecting stone cornice with wide modillions. Of particular interest is the ornamental brickwork: Note the projecting horizontal bands on the ground story, and the brick quoins framing the midsection and upper facade. **HD**

112 East 91st Street
ARCHITECT: John Lambeer, Jr.   DATE: 1906

Originally a stable and carriage house designed for a Mrs. T.W. Shannon, No. 112 was purchased in 1924 by Louis Gordon Hamerslay, who lived at Fifth Avenue and 84th Street, for use as his private five-car garage. Completely renovated in the late 1990s, the prim, neo-Federal facade is in restrained colors of buff textured brick with black trim, contrasting with the earth tones of its neighbors. The building retains its original black carriage doors featuring beadboard panels set beneath multi-pane windows protected by wrought-iron grilles. The delicate traceries of the grillwork are repeated in the outer pedestrian entrance. All three round-arched openings are edged with voussoirs alternating stone and brick. A pedimented central section sets off the second story, which projects slightly; a continuous lintel unites four windows. Behind the pediment is a corbeled brick section and cornice. **HD**

113 East 91st Street

ARCHITECT: John Sullivan   DATE: 1884-85

This three-story-and-basement brownstone is a neo-Grec survivor in a string of row houses (Nos. 107-113). Just fifteen feet wide and set back from its brick-faced neighbor, the recently remodeled dwelling is easy to miss; the building is further obscured by a maple tree and lushly planted forecourt. The stoop has been removed and windows have simple boxy surrounds. Crowning the otherwise unassuming facade is a run of dentils and a deep wooden cornice supported by three large fluted brackets. HD

114-122 East 91st Street

ARCHITECTS:
Brandt & Co.   DATE: 1889
Oswald Wirz   1890

The camaraderie of these four (originally five) buildings is not readily evident, but they were all commissioned by the same developer, William McNabb—Nos. 120 and 122 from Brandt & Co., and in the following year, Nos. 116 and 118 from Oswald Wirz. No. 114 was also designed by Wirz. Featuring a facade in the playful Renaissance Revival style with Queen Anne elements, its brownstone trim resembles quoins; round-arched window openings have foliate keystones and corbels. Flanking the entrance are suspended foliate columns terminating with whimsical faces. Plaques carved with putti, birds and fish run beneath the ground-level windows; additional plaques are set below the windows on the fourth story, which is topped with a modillioned stone cornice. Fluted pilasters flank fifth-story windows. A metal cornice embellished with dentils and modillions extends along the roof line.

Mirror images of each other, Nos. 116 and 122 appear more staid than No. 114. Their facades are of rusticated stone at the basement level, a brownstone first story, and red brick with brownstone trim above. Entrances, framed with pilasters topped with foliate capitals, are capped with elaborate friezes accented with urns, lions' heads and vines. Pedimented window bays project slightly; enframements are incised with Queen Anne elements. Horizontal bands and cornices connect windows, except for two on the fourth story which are united by a wide curved and carved window head. Bracketed metal cornices complete the facades of these Victorian twins.

In 1936, Nos. 118 and 120 were stripped of their stoops and combined into a single building. Today this 40-foot-wide flats building stands out for its lack of ornament and for its heavily-troweled stucco veneer. Only the height and location of the window openings suggest the original Brandt/Wirz design. **HD**

115–121 East 91st Street
ARCHITECT: Arthur B. Jennings
DATE: 1876-77

This handsome row of virtually identical neo-Grec brownstones has survived remarkably intact— ensured, in part, by sensitive maintenance (and restoration) of their facades. All four feature three-sided oriels at the second story; those at either end of the row are distinguished by pairs of narrow colonettes inset at protruding angles, by sawtoothed bezant trim running under their cornices, and by panel inserts centered with round button-like motifs. Uniting the quartet are arched entry doors and windows at the parlor level; the houses on either end of the row are accented with repeating bezants set within the arches. All four houses feature pronounced architraves, scrolled keystones, and delicate incisions between their entrances and the parlor windows, and all have decorative molding above the parlor- and third-floor windows. The cornices, supported by scrolled brackets, are identical as well. The differences are minimal: The door to No. 121 is protected by an iron grille, and No. 119 no longer has a stoop; No. 119 also wears festoons of ivy. **HD**

123-133 East 91st Street
ARCHITECTS: Schwarzmann & Buchman
DATE: 1885-86

This row of six buildings was originally built in the neo-Grec style for developer John Weber. The facades were identical, forming a pattern of three mirror-image designs.

No. 123 has been substantially altered. Sometime in the mid-20th century the stoop was removed and the facade was refaced with stucco. About 1988 an attic with a slate-covered mansard roof was added; perched in the center is a pedimented dormer.

Nos. 125-133 retain their brick facades

131 and 133 East 91st Street

with windows framed in brownstone. Original stoops and decorative iron railings remain at Nos. 129 and 133, and a matching stoop and stained-glass transom have been recreated at No. 131. Of particular interest are the diamond-point brick spandrels between the second and third floors and the keystones atop the third-story lintels. All buildings except No. 125 retain their cornices with scrolled brackets and paneled friezes. **HD**

124 East 91st Street
The Trent
ARCHITECT: John P. Leo   DATE: 1899-1900

Spanning more than 40 feet, this six-story neo-Georgian building is faced with limestone on the first two stories and red brick on the remaining four. The wide entryway is flanked with double pilasters supporting an entablature with rosettes and garlands. Above the glass-and-wrought-iron door and transom is a cartouche. Each story has a parade of six windows, under which extend string courses doubling as sills. Window surrounds vary: Those on the first and second stories have cornices, while stories three through five have splayed lintels and keystones, and carved arched headers over the center pairs. Sixth-story openings have molded voussoirs, keystones, and merged stone bands. There is a high parapet from which the cornice has been removed. **HD**

135 East 91st Street
See 1380-1386 Lexington Avenue

150-152 East 91st Street
ARCHITECT: George F. Pelham   DATE: 1906

This six-story neo-Federal and Renaissance Revival-style building is a near duplicate of the matched pair of Pelham buildings at 53-55 and 57-59 East 96th Street, built in the same year. A historic wrought-iron fence encloses the street-level stairs; short square pillars lead to a low stoop. Flanking the entryway, foliate brackets support a carved entablature and cornice. The first story is of smooth limestone; the remainder of the facade is of red brick laid in Flemish bond. Windows on the second and sixth stories have blocked and carved limestone enframements; those on the second story are  topped with keystones and a belt course with an anthemion molding. Mid-section windows have eared limestone lintels with decorative key-stones, and eared sills. A black-metal cornice with modillions and dentils caps the parapet.

155 East 91st Street
ARCHITECT: J.M. Felson   DATE: 1929

Limestone pilasters, a keystone and rosettes embellish the arched entryway
of this nine-story brown-brick apartment house. Above the door, paired
windows have a foliate limestone enframement. Band courses define the
base and five-story midsection; rising from the center of the crown
section is a limestone arch topped with a curved plaque and escutcheon.
A roof line with a central peak lends verticality to the overall design.

160 East 91st Street
The Hillhurst
ARCHITECT: Bernstein & Bernstein
DATE: 1903

According to architectural historian
Christopher Gray, in a *New York Times* article
(10.02.05), the building was first known as
The Highlands, a sly reference to both the
Scottish birthplace of steel magnate Andrew
Carnegie, whose new mansion further west
on 91st Street would elevate the social tone of
the neighborhood, and to its elevated land
area, later to be called Carnegie Hill. The
Highlands was actually two separate red-brick
structures combined as one, with an unusual
undulating facade. Rough-hewn stones form the ground-floor base. Lintels
above the second-tory windows have splayed voussoirs. Stone bandings above
the remaining six stories further emphasize the bowed design; even the
cornice undulates. Like the Hotel Graham [see 22 East 89th Street] and
other apartment hotels of the era, the 400-room Highlands had telephones,
an all-night elevator, a central dining room, and an elaborate roof garden.
In 1907 it was renamed The Hillhurst and remarketed as a residence for
nurses, advertising its unfurnished housekeeping apartments as "lovely suites
for refined tenants." The building was converted to a co-op in 1985.

161 East 91st Street
ARCHITECT: Charles Kreymbourg   DATE: 1940

Resembling more a suburban residence than a city apartment house, this
six-story building is of red brick with painted-white trim. Four Doric-style
columns and two engaged columns support a wood entablature flanking
the entryway. A six-foot recessed porch, paved with brick, leads to a
doorway with sidelights and a fanlight; French doors flank the main entry.
All openings are topped with flat keystones and splayed bricks.

162 East 91st Street
ARCHITECT: George F. Pelham   DATE: 1899-1900

Hugging the imposing Hillhurst is this smaller but more elaborately ornamented Romanesque Revival building. The first level, of rusticated limestone, is surmounted with four stories of tan brick. Pilasters ornamented with bellflowers and foliate capitals flank the spiral-framed entry. The egg-and-dart motif under the carved entablature is echoed in the string courses above. Second- and fourth-story round-arched windows display carved keystones; above the first- and third-story windows are carved stones plaques.

164 East 91st Street
ARCHITECTS: Jacob H. Valentine   DATE: 1879
Rosenberg Kolb Architects   2008

The original four-story house was set back some eight feet; the facade was reportedly of cast iron. During the 1950s the building was extended and the facade was stuccoed. In 1995 a tripartite window was introduced at the second story. An extensive renovation in 2008 included a new scored and rusticated limestone facade, a segmental arch uniting the windows of the upper two stories, and a classically inspired cornice.

166 East 91st Street
ARCHITECT: John Sullivan   DATE: 1884

Simplified neo-Grec details characterize this modest brownstone. Iron railings and newel posts flank the three-step stoop. Pointed window lintels are embellished with rosettes and incised curlicues. Capping the fifth story is a bracketed copper cornice.

168 East 91st Street
ARCHITECT: Charles Stegmayer   DATE: 1884

This is surely one of the more perplexing buildings in Carnegie Hill. The vintage storefront was originally a wagon access to a rear building, filled in 1906. Above, three square-headed windows are connected horizontally by rough-stone banding and punctuate the (now painted) red-brick facade. Windows have brownstone sills and bracketed cornices, in neo-Grec style; however, the carved spandrels uniting the second- and third-story windows are characteristic of Renaissance Revival design. The dominant projecting cornice is ornamented with a floral frieze and modillions; a Queen Anne peaked pediment and cartouche break the floor line. But look—the cornice rises above the third, not the fifth and final story! Was it dropped intentionally? A clue to its lowly location may be found in the slightly projecting facade above the doorway. Above the cornice, the facade is flat all the way to the roof parapet. So one might conclude—correctly—that this 19th-century three-story building acquired two additional stories many years later—in fact, in 2005—created as an almost perfect match to the eclectic facade.

169 East 91st Street
ARCHITECTS: Wechsler, Grasso & Menziuso   DATE: 1980-85
Rising twelve stories from a 50-foot width, the western half of this red-brick apartment building is recessed, allowing space for narrow projecting balconies. The building sets back at the seventh and ninth stories, creating terraces of varying sizes.

170 East 91st Street
ARCHITECT: John Hauser   DATE: 1901
In spite of patched spandrels and many coats of paint, the facade of this five-story Renaissance Revival building displays both wit and variety. A historic wrought-iron fence with curved grillwork protects the descending stairways; bowed and decorative grilles guard first-level windows. Horizontal foliate panels above the lower-level windows are echoed (but not duplicated) in vertical panels flanking the main entrance and in spandrels between upper-level windows. Short columns at either side of the stairs have bird-and-leaf carved moldings and pyramid-shaped tops. Engaged columns by the carved wood-and-glass doors are capped with—*mythical creatures? frogs?* Above the round-

arched transom are multiple moldings. There are also a scrolled and foliate keystone, round portraits—*husband and wife?*—and a cornice.

A fruit-and-garland frieze and dentil molding separate the stone first level from the remaining brick facade. Stone banding connects second-story windows, which have carved keystones. At the outer bays, vertical brick pilasters join third- and fourth-story windows. Each window has a segmented pediment, but lest the viewer becomes bored, the arch shapes and carvings vary. Fifth-story outer-bay windows are framed with pilasters with foliate capitals. Center windows have both splayed lintels and scrolled keystones. Finally, at the roof line, another floral frieze and dentil molding is capped with a tripartite modillioned metal cornice.

Since 1998 the lower level has been the office of Carnegie Hill Neighbors.

1-3, 9, and 15-25 East 92nd Street
ARCHITECT: A.B. Ogden & Son   DATE: 1890-91

Most of the buildings on the north side of 92nd Street between Fifth and Madison avenues were designed by A.B. Ogden & Son for developer Walter Reid. The unity of this block is preserved by bracketed metal roof cornices, relatively uniform four-story height, arched windows, second-story oriels, string courses to emphasize floor divisions, and delicate Renaissance Revival details. No two buildings are exactly alike, and all deserve close scrutiny. Nos. 1, 3 and 9 were designed with input from the developer's son, Walter Reid, Jr., who was associated with the Ogden firm. All except Nos. 23 and 25 had stoops replaced with basement-level entrances. No. 11 was built some six years earlier, and Nos. 5 and 7 were replaced by a townhouse in 1934; these three are covered separately.

Above the somewhat Spartan parlor floor of No. 1 is an oriel with unusual transom bars over its four windows; the delicately carved floral frieze is echoed over third-story windows and in the spandrels of round-arched attic-story openings. All windows have cornices. The Jewish Museum, which owns the building, houses its ancillary museum store in the basement level. No. 3 lost its cornice, facade detailing and bay window in the 1930s; in 1964 the French government, which had bought the house as a residence for its United Nations representative, installed a basement garage.

With full-height curved bays and roof cornices, Nos. 9 and 15 seem to bow to each other, framing the pre-existing No. 11. Arched parlor-story windows with keystones and molded surrounds distinguish each building. No. 9 has a pedimented entryway with guttae; the house was once the home of actor Basil Rathbone. From 1928 to 1985 No. 15 was owned by the Clarence

West to east on 92nd Street: Nos .9 and 11; Nos. 15 and 17

H. Mackey family: His father, John W. Mackey, was one of the richest men in America, thanks to his two-fifths share in the "Bonanza" mines of the Comstock Lode, and his daughter, Ellin, married songwriter Irving Berlin.

No. 19 was probably similar to No. 25, but the projecting facade has been refaced and substantially altered. The ground-level entrance was centered and framed by classically inspired pilasters. Seated on the entablature are two stone lions. Delicately carved panels punctuate the new mullioned windows; at the parlor story, a string course is arched at the central section, completing the formal facade.

The best preserved of the group are Nos. 17, 21, 23 and 25. Their many original details include rough-faced basements, round-arched windows at the parlor and fourth stories, corbeled oriels with foliate friezes, and stylized key motifs over third-story windows. Note the splayed window

hoods, quoin-like window surrounds and the paired bracketed roof cornices. Under the corniced second-story window of No. 21 are deep scrolls and a delicately carved spandrel. Note the curiously shaped panes in the parlor-story window of No. 23. All windows of No. 25 exhibit unusually fine details: fluted pilasters, friezes ornamented with birds and vines, bellflowers at the fourth story. At the top of Nos. 23 and 25's tall stoops, lions and putti (shown at left) gaze down from embellished pilasters while keeping an eye on the fire-breathing dragons below. **HD**

5-7 East 92nd Street
Originally Garrard Winston house
ARCHITECT: William J. Creighton   DATE: 1934-35

The site was originally occupied by two brownstones in a row that ran from Nos. 1-9, and 15-25, designed with input from Walter Reid, Jr., an

architect associated with A.B. Ogden & Son. William J. Creighton designed this three-story neo-Federal townhouse for Garrard Winston, an attorney who held a number of corporate and public positions, including that of Under Secretary of the United States Treasury.

The surface is of red brick laid in Flemish bond and trimmed in limestone. Over time the facade has softened in color and detailing, giving the impression of a far older building—which perfectly suits its elegant demeanor. Two square-headed windows capped with lintels carved with a Greek fret motif flank the entrance. Above the paneled-wood door is a limestone band course embellished with four bellflowers. The second story is exceptionally high: Long narrow brick quoins emphasize the midsection, and three arched multi-pane windows are set off by foliate keystones. A second band course serves as a sill for the flat-arched third-story windows. A wide frieze and a low pedimented roof line complete the facade. **HD**

11 East 92nd Street
Untermyer-Clarkson house
ARCHITECTS: Hugo Kafka & Co.   DATE: 1884-85
              William Adams   1924

Isaac and Samuel Untermyer were sons of a prosperous Virginia tobacco planter. They came to New York early and formed a law partnership that handled prominent cases, later organizing syndicates of investors. Their house was extensively altered in 1924 by Helen S. Clarkson, an amateur horticulturist, and her husband Banyer Clarkson, a descendant of Supreme Court Chief Justice John Jay.

The original four-story structure was brownstone with Renaissance Revival details. Architect William Adams removed the stoop, stripped and stuccoed the facade and changed the top story to a mansard roof with pedimented dormers. The windows of the three-sided, full-height bay rest on string courses. The ground-level entry is flanked by stone piers and capped with a modillioned cornice and iron railing. **HD**

6-14 East 92nd Street
ARCHITECT: Thomas Graham   DATE: 1890-92

Originally, eight row houses designed in a mirror image, a-b-c-d-d-c-b-a pattern, occupied the west half of the block from Fifth to Madison avenues. In 1925 No. 4 was replaced by 1107 Fifth Avenue, famous for its 54-room Marjorie Meriweather Post penthouse triplex, and Nos. 16 and 18 were demolished in 1989 to make way for the expanded Nightingale-Bamford School. The remaining five houses have a west-to-east b-c-d-d-c pattern, which is best understood when viewed from across the street: Nos. 10 and 12, the two "d's," form the centerpiece, and a delicious one it is indeed.

The style of the group is generally classified as Renaissance Revival, but there are strong Romanesque elements—in the rough-cut rusticated stone surfaces at the basement and parlor stories, and in the heavy voussoirs radiating from parlor-story windows. The buildings are unified by modillioned metal cornices which alternate paneled and floral friezes, by round-arched windows at the fourth and parlor stories, and by double string courses under oriels spanning the facades (at all but No. 6). All buildings retain their upper-story window cornices; those at Nos. 6 and 8 are pedimented.

East to west on 92nd Street: No. 14; Nos. 12 and 10; No. 10.

It is easy to speculate that Nos. 10 and 12 were built as one house (they were not): Their cornices run together; their shared three-story, four-bay projecting window terminates in a richly carved bracketed base; and the round-arched basement entrance appears to be shared as well. Note especially the panels carved with shells, flowers, swags, ribbons and fruit, and the god and goddess masks (for whom the riches were proffered?) between parlor-story windows. No. 10 displays the sole surviving stoop, which is box-shaped with carved panels and delicate ironwork. No. 14, originally the mirror image of No. 8, retains spiral-carved engaged columns flanking the original entry, and foliate keystones over carved window surrounds. **HD**

16-26 East 92nd Street
The Nightingale-Bamford School
ARCHITECTS: Delano & Aldrich (Nos. 20-24)   DATE: 1929
                  Adams & Woodbridge (No. 26)   1967-68
                  Jack L. Gordon Architects/JLGA (Nos. 16-18) 1989-91

The Nightingale-Bamford School dates its beginnings to 1903, when Miss Frances Nightingale and Miss Maya Bamford began teaching small groups of young ladies in a private house. By 1920 the school had moved to Carnegie Hill; nine years later it engaged the distinguished firm of Delano & Aldrich to construct a five-story-plus-basement building at 20-24 East 92nd Street. The schoolhouse was designed in the neo-Federal style, faced in red brick laid in Flemish bond with limestone trim. The facade is dominated by four double-height arched windows with multi-pane wood sash, fronted with a simple wrought-iron balcony. To either side of this central window grouping is a small octagonal window. There was once a pedimented entry and stoop at the eastern bay, but this has been replaced with a window. A limestone cornice separates the fourth and fifth stories. This building forms the central portion of the school today.

In 1967 the school acquired and demolished the row house to the east (No. 26); in its place architects Adams & Woodbridge added a five-story pavilion surfaced with matching red brick. A sixth story was added to both buildings in 1972. Some fifteen years later the school announced a massive expansion and renovation program, which called for building a new eight-story pavilion to the west (requiring the razing of two 1890 row houses, Nos. 16 and 18, purchased by the school in 1978) and adding four stories to the existing sections. After encountering strong opposition from preservationist groups, led by Carnegie Hill Neighbors, the school agreed to limit the additional stories to two, transferring much of the new space to the rear. The resulting expansion, by Jack L. Gordon Architects, doubled the school's total space to 100,000 square feet, which included a set-back gym and science laboratory on top of the existing floors. In spite of additions and modern elements, the building facade retains its continuity through the use of red brick and limestone string courses, anchored by its majestic Palladian windows. **HD**

28 and 30 East 92nd Street
ARCHITECT:
Henry J. Hardenbergh
DATE: 1892-95
Of a group of six Hardenbergh
row houses that extended from
No. 20 to No. 30, only these
two survive. Designed in the
Renaissance Revival style, the
four-story brownstone facades
exhibit restrained classical
details. Windows are divided
by pilasters with composite
capitals. The buildings are

united by stone cornices over the first stories and modillioned metal cornices and parapets at the roof line. No. 28 has a curved oriel supported by foliate brackets; note the delicate carvings between the windows. At No. 30 a full-height projection at the eastern two bays is ornamented with carved panels. Less visible are the single windows above the (new) stoop; pediments and sills are carved with shells, floral motifs and an escutcheon. The basement levels of both buildings have been substantially altered, and the original stoops have been removed. At No. 28 the surface was refaced with brick and subsequently painted white. Since the mid-1980s No. 30 has been home to a gallery, followed by several restaurants. **HD**

46 and 52-56 East 92nd Street
ARCHITECT: William Graul   DATE: 1887-88

Originally part of a group of six row houses designed for developer Philip Braender (Nos. 48 and 50 were demolished in the 1930s for the John Sloane house), these four survivors retain few similarities other than uniform height. Their stoops have been removed and their entrances relocated to the basement level. Their eclectic style combines Queen Anne and neo-Grec motif. Elements of their design were adapted from a row of seven houses that stood directly to the east and of which only Nos. 58 and 60 remain.

The basement and parlor stories of No. 46 are faced with rough-textured brownstone; pronounced band courses emphasize the chamfered bay, which is dramatized with staggered brickwork at the upper two stories. Carved wood panels accent the arched parlor-story windows. Note especially the third-story openings: Hoods terminate with guttae, and are topped with keystones alternating male and female masks. The unusual scalloped edging of the modillioned bracketed metal cornice is echoed in No. 54, probably inspired by the earlier-built No. 58 East 92nd Street.

 Nos. 52 and 56 have been stripped of ornamentation and stuccoed. No. 54 has fared well: All windows retain their molded surrounds and scored keystones, while those at the second story have eared hoods crowned with cornices. As with No. 46, the best view is reserved for the top story: arched windows with human-mask keystones are flanked with pilasters on triglyph corbels. **HD**

48 East 92nd Street
Originally John Sloane house
ARCHITECT: James C. MacKenzie, Jr.   DATE: 1931-32

Once the site of two neo-Grec/Queen Anne row houses completed in 1888, this elegant five-story townhouse was commissioned by John Sloane, president of the prestigious furniture store W. & J. Sloane, founded by his grandfather in 1843. The house was remodeled for Sloane's daughter and her husband in 1947, and again in 1953 when it was purchased by the Maternity Center Association. It reverted to a private residence in 1997, when it was bought by Carol and George McFadden; they in turn sold it in 1999 to film director Woody Allen, who lived there with his wife, Soon-Yi, and their two daughters until 2004.

The 40-foot wide townhouse is designed in neo-Regency style. The limestone facade rises three stories, then sets back at each of the remaining two, with arched dormers projecting from the metal-sheathed mansard

roof. A historic wrought-iron fence with anthemion-and-thistle motifs fronts the building and the stairs to the basement. Flanking the glass-and-wood door and the western bay are pilasters with anthemion capitals supporting a smooth entablature and dentiled cornice. The tall nine-over-twelve windows of the *piano nobile* have delicate wrought-iron guards echoing the railing design; egg-and-dart moldings embellish projecting lintels. Completing the classical facade is a Greek fret-and-rosette band below the fourth-story parapet. **HD**

47 East 92nd Street
ARCHITECTS: Keeler & Fernald   DATE: 1926-28
Nos. 45 and 47 were originally two of a row of four 1888 brownstones designed by Frank Wennemer. In 1928 they were combined for Robert Louis Hoguet, the president and chairman of Emigrant Industrial Savings Bank. This five-story neo-Georgian townhouse is now a diplomatic residence with its own concealed private driveway to a rear three-car garage. The rusticated stone base of the house has been coated with plaster and painted; pilasters support an entablature running the full width of the building. Multi-pane doors with iron grilles front the main entrance and garage. Brickwork on the upper section is set in Flemish bond and trimmed with limestone. All windows have raised keystones; the fourth-story windows rest on a continuous stone sill. Capping the building is a dentiled cornice and balustrade. **HD**

49 and 51 East 92nd Street
ARCHITECT: Frank Wennemer   DATE: 1887-88
These two Queen Anne brownstones were part of a row of four that included Nos. 45 and 47, built for real-estate developer Philip Braender, who was responsible for more than 1,500 New York City buildings in the late 19th century. Above the parlor floor, both houses retain their varied string courses, elaborately carved lintels at the top story, and bracketed and modillioned metal roof cornices.

No. 49 lost its stoop in 1906. However, much of the basement entrance is historic, including the console-supported cornice, the glazed wood door and grille, the carved band course over the windows, and even the wrought-iron fencing with four newel cages. Although the parlor-floor entrance was converted to a window, the fluted pilasters, transom and decorative wrought-iron railing remain, as do the dentiled window cornices and the panels carved with swags.

No. 51 was altered in 1927; the architect was Frederick R. King. The stoop was removed and a rusticated surface was added to the basement level. Both the ground-level door and window were arched. The wrought-iron railings date from 1927, although the basement window grille is historic. The parlor story was redesigned: In place of the original three openings are two six-over-six windows with neo-Federal-style lintels. **HD**

53 and 55 East 92nd Street
ARCHITECT: Louis Entzer, Jr.   DATE: 1893-94

The same architect who a year earlier designed four mirror-image pairs of brownstones on East 95th Street (Nos. 113-127) created this Romanesque Revival pair for developer D.M.L. Quackenbush. Sturdy and fortress-like, the rough-hewn stone facades display projecting curved bays and rock-faced stone bands. Surprisingly, all windows and doors are square-headed (arches are characteristic of the style). The second-story cornice is corbeled, and under the third-story cornice runs a checkerboard frieze. The upper two stories are faced with buff brick and topped by a metal roof cornice with corbel blocks and an egg-and-dart molding. In 1946 No. 53 was a single-family residence and No. 55 a rooming house. Architect James E. Casale was hired to convert both buildings to two-unit dwellings. Once stoops were removed and parlor-floor entrances converted to windows, a doctor's office was installed in each basement. **HD**

57-61 East 92nd Street
ARCHITECT: Brandt & Co.   DATE: 1886
                       Henry T. Child (No. 57) 1938

Near the middle of the block, John Brandt designed a row of five neo-Grec brownstones, Nos. 57 -65, for developer Jacob Wicks, Jr. Today Nos. 63 and 65 are so different—even in height—that they are described separately.

No. 57 had its stoop and second-story bay window removed, and the entrance shifted to the basement level in 1928. Ten years later, architect Henry T. Child arched the entryway, designed casement windows with an iron balconette for the third story, stripped the windows of their enframements, stuccoed the facade, and removed the cornice. The austere parapet has three bezants (flat discs) that complete the building's Moderne appearance.

Although the stoop has been removed, No. 59 reflects its origins, with corniced and bracketed window frames and subtle string courses. Like its neighbor to the east, it retains its bracketed metal cornice with panels and an anthemion frieze.

No. 61 best illustrates the original neo-Grec character of this brownstone group. A high stoop with cheek walls at the top leads to the parlor floor, where the quoined entrance has double-leaf paneled doors and a multi-pane transom. A fluted corbeled sill supports the parlor-floor window, which is separated from the entrance by an incised pilaster which in turn holds the bracket of the two-sided oriel above it. Classical swags and a low parapet embellish the projecting bay. In the center is a horned and mustached creature, 92nd Street's neo-Grec security guard. **HD**

58 and 60 East 92nd Street
ARCHITECT: Theodore E. Thomson   DATE: 1883

These are the only survivors of seven neo-Grec row houses that extended to Park Avenue. Both retain their original stoops, but there the similarity ends. No. 58 has three stories, with a stone-faced basement and parlor floor; the upper stories are red brick (now painted). Carved wood panels accent arched openings at the parlor floor, and second-story windows are topped with stone voussoirs. At the third story, keystones with classical heads are set in segmentally-arched bricks anchored by stone skew-backs. Like No. 46, the building terminates with a scalloped banding under a modillioned metal cornice.

No. 60 bears little resemblance to the other houses on the block. It is one story taller and several feet narrower. At the foot of the stoop is a historic newel post; steep steps lead to a double glass-and-iron door framed with a heart-motif molding. Pilasters supporting round arches with foliate keystones flank the doorway and parlor-story window; note the stone panel just below with six incised flowers. The most striking feature of the facade is a three-sided oriel at the second floor. It is supported by a fluted corbel resting on a bracket; under each window is a floral carved panel. Additional characteristic neo-Grec features are the rosette-incised pilasters and lintels framing third- and fourth-story windows. Crowning this handsome brownstone is a roof cornice with modillions, grooved brackets and a frieze of small arches. **HD**

62 East 92nd Street
Brick Presbyterian Church Parish House and School
ARCHITECT: Lawrence F. Peck
DATE: 1924

This five-story-and-mezzanine building was designed in the neo-Renaissance style as a residence for Jean Ferry; she and her husband, Mansfield Ferry, a prominent New York attorney, lived there until 1939. During the construction of the Brick Presbyterian Church in that year the church acquired the building and converted for use as a parish house and school.

The entire 92nd Street facade is limestone; above the mezzanine is a dentiled and modillioned cornice, with a string course separating the midsection and top two stories. The entryway is particularly lovely: Over the door is a carved scallop shell embellished with ribbons and tassels, and the door surround has moldings of acanthus leaves and rope coils. Windows on the first level and mezzanine have ornate wrought-iron grilles. The upper-level casement windows have small panes of tinted glass. **HD**

66-70 East 92nd Street
Brick Presbyterian Church Parish House and School
ARCHITECTS: Adams & Woodbridge   DATE: 1948-49

Although part of the Brick Presbyterian Church complex, this Modern four-story-and-penthouse building bears little similarity to the adjoining No. 62, other than the limestone used in the facade. Rising from a brown-granite base, it features a red-marble recessed entryway. Both the wood-and-glass door and ground-story windows have aluminum grilles with cruciform centers.

On the third floor a meeting space is dedicated to the memory of Louise Whitfield Carnegie (Mrs. Andrew), a devoted member of the church for many years. The Chinese wall panels are believed to have come from the sewing room of the Carnegie mansion at 2 East 91st Street, now the Cooper-Hewitt, National Design Museum. **HD**

63 and 65 East 92nd Street
ARCHITECTS: Brandt & Co.   DATE: 1886
                    Edward Webber (No. 63)   1928
                    Charles H. Lench (No. 65)   1934

John Brandt designed these row houses, along with Nos. 57–61, in 1886; however, little remains of their neo-Grec character. In 1928 No. 63 was altered by architect Edward Webber for Luis J. Francke (or his son); at this time the stoop was removed, a window replaced the original entrance, and a basement entrance was added. Today the house presents a neo-Colonial mien, its Bermuda-pink painted brick set off by hunter-green shutters and balconettes at the second and third stories; the second story admits the southern sun through French doors. The house terminates with a parapet and iron fence. No. 65 received a facelift in 1934 at the behest of the Bowery Savings Bank, which commissioned architect Charles H. Lench to convert it into a multi-family building. Now, once again a single-family dwelling, the neo-Georgian house is faced with stucco that has been scored to suggest limestone. The keyed entryway is arched, framing a glazed wood door with an iron grille, and windows are fronted with black window boxes. Above a fourth-story string course, a simple projecting cornice caps the facade. **HD**

115 East 92 Street
ARCHITECT: George F. Pelham DATE: 1927-28
George F. Pelham designed this nine-story neo-Renaissance building with a majestic entry portal and two distinct towers. The entrance is approached through a decorative wrought-iron arch connecting free-standing hexagonal stone columns with stylized capitals. The wood-and-glass doors are deeply recessed, creating a light court, and are flanked by two long windows set in a limestone facade. Carved round arches top windows and doors beneath a traditional dentiled cornice.

The building is clad in multi-tone beige brick. The block towers are divided into three sections separated by projecting corbeled glazed terra-cotta bands above the second and seventh stories. Brick patterns are used throughout the facade, forming window heads or arch motifs. Paired windows on the end bays of the first section are framed by brick quoins and topped by an arched design. The center bays are defined by three stone pilasters with broad-leaf capitals and elongated cartouches linked by a brick arch pattern. This motif is repeated above the ninth-story corner windows.

A brick parapet shows signs of patching and repointing, which suggests that the building originally had contrasting stone quoins framing the outer corners. Two penthouses are set back; the building has a common rooftop terrace for residents. **HD**

116 East 92nd Street
ARCHITECT: Edward Wenz   DATE: 1889

Once a twin of adjoining No. 118, No. 116 was designed as a typical neo-
Grec brownstone row house. The facade (now painted) retains the original
window surrounds; molded lintels and cornices are carried by brackets
incised with floral motifs. Quoined stone blocks frame the first-level
windows. The fifth and terminal story is capped with a bracketed metal
cornice. In 1936 architect Emery Roth redesigned the entrance by creating
a molded stone enframement; sidelights flank the glass-and-wood door.
Another 50 years saw the addition of a fire escape, the removal of the
masonry stoop, and the installation of a low curved metal stoop and brick
basement steps. **HD**

118 East 92nd Street
ARCHITECT: Frank P. Farinella   DATE: 1975-76

Looking at No. 118 today, it's hard to imagine that it started life in 1889
as a twin to the five-story neo-Grec No. 116 next door. In 1976 architect
Frank P. Farinella completely redesigned the building, creating a modern,
same-height apartment house with a brick facade and soldier-brick band
courses, sills and lintels. By reducing the ceiling heights, the architect
produced a seven-story elevator building with four apartments per floor
(a total of twenty-eight units, compared with the original ten!). The residential entrance, slightly below ground level, has a glass-and-wrought-
iron door and sidelight; it is flanked by commercial offices. **HD**

120 and 122 East 92nd Street
ARCHITECTS: No. 120: unknown   DATE: 1871
             No. 122: possibly Albro Howell 1859

This pair of Italianate-style clapboard houses are two of four frame houses
still standing in our neighborhood—a rarity in a city where most structures
of this type were long ago razed in the name of "progress." Each of the two
houses features a wide porch with open-work columns and a cozy front
yard sheltered behind a wrought-iron fence, elements that recall Carnegie
Hill's rural past. The contiguous lots were purchased in 1865 by John C.
Rennert, a wine merchant, from Adam C. Flanagan, who occupied No.
122; the Rennerts moved into No. 120. In 1874 Rennert died and his
widow, Catherine, sold her house to Henrietta Nathan. Today No. 120 is
a multi-family dwelling; as of this writing, No. 122 is being restored as a
single-family house. Both are individual New York City landmarks.

   No. 120 rises three stories above a brick basement painted gray to
match its clapboards. A wooden stoop leads to its porch, which spans the
parlor floor; here, two pairs of French doors are flanked with tall louvered

shutters. The columns supporting the porch are solid; those that carry its modillion-fringed roof echo the design, but in an openwork pattern. The paneled front door has been painted a jaunty lipstick red. Black louvered shutters frame upper-story windows, which are surmounted by modillioned cornices. The cornice at the roof line is supported on evenly spaced brackets with panels between them.

The slightly shorter house at No. 122, which has no basement, was given extra height with the 1927 addition of a boxy, recessed fourth story. Windows on this light sage-green clapboard structure feature segmentally-arched heads topped by cornices; those at ground level are trimmed out, while the windows above are, like those at No. 120, given black louvered shutters, which nicely offset the creamy trim. The renovated front porch—which once listed perilously to the starboard—has a new beadboard ceiling, wood balustrade and openwork columns that support its roof. The paneled front door is recessed within a paneled portico. The facade, which retains its original clapboards, is surmounted by a cornice resting on paired brackets separated, again, by panels. A narrow setback to the east of the house visually links it to the building next door. **HD LM**

121 and 123 East 92nd Street
ARCHITECT: Jacob H. Valentine
DATE: 1869

Designed in the Italianate style, these three-story-plus-basement row houses are among the earliest surviving buildings in Carnegie Hill. In 1898 architect William E. Mowbray replaced the original wood porches with brick entrances and stoops. The seamlessly joined dark-brick facades are mirror images, including even the brightly painted red basement doors. On each building, a flight of stairs with wrought-iron railings leads to an enclosed brick porch; the double wood-and-glass entry doors and transom are framed with rope moldings and topped by a shallow stone cornice. Capping both porches is a metal cornice and wrought-iron railing. All of the windows have stone sills and lintels, now painted white. One continuous wooden cornice with five foliate brackets intersecting rectangular panels surmounts the facade. A short, decorative wrought-iron railing runs across the shared areaway at the sidewalk level. **HD**

124 East 92nd Street
ARCHITECTS: Weber & Drosser   DATE: 1887
William and Geoffrey Platt 1935
In 1887 five adjoining brick row houses were constructed at 124-132 East 92nd Street, designed by the architectural firm of Weber & Drosser. Almost 50 years later, in 1935, the owner of No. 124, Mrs. Helen R. Robinson, hired architects William and Geoffrey Platt to substantially redesign her house. The architects' new design for the three-story, fifteen-foot-wide row house called for removing the cornice and the masonry stoop and relocating the entrance to the basement level. Probably the most noticeable change they made was to the narrow facade, which they converted from brick to classically styled stone, scored at the basement level. They added a frieze of horizontal fluting to span the parapet.

In 2006 new owners replaced the large steel-framed window on the parlor floor with double-hung six-over-six windows that occupy the same enframement space. **HD**

125 East 92nd Street
ARCHITECT: David B. Mann/MR Architects & Decor   DATE: 2006-07
A vacant lot at No. 125 was created when a long-abandoned 19th-century house was demolished in 1991. In 1997 the 92nd Street Y, which had recently purchased the lot, announced plans to construct a five-story building to be used as an adult education facility. The proposal was opposed by Carnegie Hill Neighbors and the Friends of Historic 92nd Street as inappropriate in style and size. Although the New York City Landmarks Preservation Commission ultimately approved revised plans, the Y never acted upon them and finally sold the property.

The new owner commissioned David B. Mann to design this Postmodern five-story limestone townhouse. Casement windows with transoms have simple stone enframements; a top-story setback is largely concealed behind a stone cornice. Fronting the areaway and flanking the three steps to the entry is a limestone wall, softened by plantings at the top. **HD**

126 and 128 East 92nd Street
ARCHITECTS: Weber & Drosser
DATE: 1887-88

Anyone walking along this block in 1890 would have passed five fifteen-foot-wide row houses designed in the Queen Anne style by the architectural firm of Weber & Drosser. Today, two of the five survive almost intact: Nos. 126 and 128. They still sport red-brick facades with brownstone basements and brownstone trim, including quoins, diamond-point sill panels, carved lintels with wing motifs (on the parlor story), panels and bracketed cornices.

Of the two, No. 126 is the more intact, retaining its masonry stoop, iron railings and newels posts, and paneled wood door with a leaded transom. The metal cornice has a prominent central pediment supported by paired brackets. At No. 128 some changes were made in 1947: The stoop was removed and the entrance relocated to the basement areaway. The original entrance was converted to a window that mimics an adjacent window with sill ornamentation. **HD**

127-135 East 92nd Street
ARCHITECT: C. Abbott French & Co.
DATE: 1886-87

Mixing curves, curlicues, carvings, classical and whimsical ornamentation, all but one of these Victorian brownstones remain remarkably intact. Designed as single-family row houses in a neo-Grec style, the quintet features Queen Anne elements and is arranged in an a-b-c-b-a pattern. All five retain their original cornices with scrolled modillions, paneled friezes and guttae. Much of the decorative ironwork is historic. Except at No. 129, all top-story windows are quoined and have incised, eared lintels.

No. 127 (shown at right) is the best preserved. A three-sided oriel at the second story has leaf-carved corners and a cornice with guttae; it is supported by a large carved bracket that sits atop a fluted pilaster terminating in a mischievous face. The stone stoop flares with curved wing walls

West to east on 92nd Street: Nos. 129, 131, 133, and 135

topped by fanciful wrought-iron railings with spiral posts and rosettes. Elliptical arches with keystones and voussoirs cap the entrance and parlor-story window; below the curved sill is a panel carved with vines. Third-story windows have incised lintels and projecting cornices. The building's twin is No. 135; both merit a special visit (with camera) in late May, when the wisteria blooms.

Sadly, No.129 was stripped of ornamentation in 1962: The facade was refaced with a scored material resembling ashlar, the stoop was removed, and a newly created projecting basement entry was enclosed with a wrought-iron fence.

The prominent feature of No.131 is its rounded oriel, embellished with a triglyph frieze, foliate base and supporting bracket. Additional ornamentation includes a pedimented lintel on the second story and incised lintels and projecting cornices on third-story windows. The stoop was removed and the first story was modernized in 1937.

Like Nos. 127 and 135, most of the historic details of No. 133 are intact, including the stoop, iron railings and newel posts. Flanking the entrance and unique to this building are suspended marble columns with composite capitals supporting foliate brackets and a projecting cornice; step back to view the ornamental swag above. At the base of each column a mascaron grins slyly. Note the geometrically incised window surrounds, echoed in the window grilles. Both second- and third-story windows display keyed enframements with eared lintels.

No. 135 is almost identical to No. 127, retaining most historic details (the oriel windows are replacements). The paneled wood-and-glass doors and transom appear to be original. A commercial establishment occupies the basement level. **HD**

130-132 East 92nd Street
ARCHITECTS: Weber & Drosser   DATE: 1887-88
William Lawrence Bottomley 1937-38

Nos. 130 and 132 were originally two of five Queen Anne brick row houses
(Nos. 124-132) designed by Weber & Drosser. In 1937-38 they were
joined, creating a 30-foot-wide neo-Regency townhouse. The owner was
Isabella Greenway, who served as a United States Congresswoman from
Arizona from 1933 to 1937. The Bottomley design included a stucco facade
with the main and service entrances at either end of the basement level. A
large tripartite window grouping in a contoured enframement dominates
the center of the parlor story, spanned by a metal balconette and multi-
pane French doors. Windows have been stripped of ornament, and the
parapet has been removed. A renovation, started in 2006, under the direction of Eric J. Smith Architect, includes replacing the stucco facade with
limestone, recalling, in part, earlier abandoned plans by Bottomley for an
elaborate facade concave to the streetwall and finished in limestone. **HD**

134-138 East 92nd Street
ARCHITECT: Alfred B. Ogden   DATE: 1880-81

These carefully preserved row houses, each three stories plus basement,
were designed and built for carpenter/builder/developer Albro Howell in
a combined neo-Grec/Queen Anne style. (Howell was no stranger to the
area, having built wood-frame houses here since the 1850s.) Just seventeen feet wide, the brick-and-brownstone facades are identical, although
each house wears a coat of paint—gray, strawberry and cream, parading
eastward, like cakes in a pastry-shop window. A single segmentally-arched
opening punctuates the basement level of each. Nine-step brownstone
stoops lead to double paneled-wood doors flanked by carved pilasters;
scrolled brackets support triangular pediments with leafy tympana. On the
upper stories the hooded windows are embellished with incised bouquets
and crisp geometrics. Prominent cornices with rosettes and stylized modillions cap the historic facades. **HD**

140 East 92nd Street
The Mildred
ARCHITECT: Martin V.B. Ferdon   DATE: 1899-1900

Looming above its low-rise neighbors, this seven-story flats building is
designed in the Renaissance Revival style. At the residential entrance on
92nd Street, columns and pilasters with composite capitals support a stone
portico and balustrade. The foliate frieze on the entablature continues
above the rusticated stone base to the corner of Lexington Avenue. Here,
stores occupy the ground level (1392-1396 Lexington Avenue) and one

may observe the rounded corners at both ends of the brick-and-limestone building. Keystones on second-story windows connect to the egg-and-dart molding and string course below the four-story midsection. Windows on the upper stories display such varied decorative elements as eared lintels and splayed voussoirs. Fourth-story windows are arched, and are connected by stone banding. A second string course articulates the crown story, where windows are flanked by pilasters with composite capitals, echoing those at the entryway. Surmounting the facade is a pressed-metal cornice with a foliate frieze and scrolled brackets. **HD**

145 East 92nd Street
ARCHITECT: George F. Pelham   DATE: 1929
A handsome arched entrance and ornate cast-iron grillwork distinguish this neo-Renaissance apartment house. The entryway is set off-center on 92nd Street; pairs of black Doric columns and pilasters on square bases support a full classical entablature and a molded Roman arch with foliate keystone. The five-tiered stoop leads first to a landing of dark-green tile, and then to a pair of French doors with sidelights. The round arch with foliate keystone is repeated above a fanlight.

The building is eleven stories plus a penthouse. Above a one-story limestone base the red-brick facade is defined by band courses above the first, third and ninth stories. There are limestone quoins between the second and third stories; quoins of red brick edge the remaining eight stories. Paired symmetrical cast-iron balconies are set beneath third- and seventh-story windows. The crown is finished with a limestone cornice above a plain band course.

151 East 92nd Street
ARCHITECT: John Wells Green(?)   DATE: 1853(?)
This four-story townhouse is reportedly (but not confirmed to be) the oldest brick dwelling built in Carnegie Hill. The ground-level facade has been faced with stone. The original stoop was removed in the 1940s; French doors attest to the original entrance. Vestigial stone lintels are evident above the upper-story windows. A charming flagstone terrace, shade garden and high iron fence front this historic house.

153 East 92nd Street
ARCHITECT: William Hughes   DATE: 1896

The distinctive feature of this five-story Renaissance Revival building is its round-arched entryway. At the top of six (painted) stone steps, the multi-pane wood-and-glass doors and transom are framed with engaged columns rising from rosette-carved bases; above their composite capitals an arched molding is embellished with fretwork. The entire entry, including the keyed enframement, is painted white with hunter-green accents. Capping the tripartite window is a lintel ornamented with a wave scroll; below, a bracketed sill frames a stone panel depicting a cherub and a pair of vine-trailing dragons. The remainder of the house is of buff brick; rough stone band courses form sills and lintels at each level. A garlanded metal cornice terminates the building.

155, 159, and 163 East 92nd Street
ARCHITECT: Edward A. Mayers   DATE: 1906

Together, these three Renaissance Revival buildings span 130 feet, a substantial part of the block. Each is six stories high, six bays wide, faced in buff brick and identical in design (except for ground-level commercial establishments at Nos. 159 and 163). The entry surround of No. 155 is original: Fluted stone pilasters, painted dark brown, have composite capitals supporting an entablature with blocked panels. Wrought-iron rails also appear to be historic.

Above the first story of each building is a band course in a modified Greek key pattern; a band course tops the second story, and a cornice tops the fifth story. Applied brick quoins define building extremes; the attic section adds horizontal brick banding. A sheet-metal cornice with foliate brackets and swags caps each building. Of particular note is the

window ornamentation: Second-story windows have egg-and-dart moldings, and throughout the facades are splayed stone lintels with carved keystones. Look carefully at the keystones on the fifth story: Eighteen lions silently guard the street below.

160 East 92nd Street

ARCHITECT: Albro Howell   DATE: 1852-53

This modest two-and-a-half-story clapboard residence is said to have been built by Albro Howell, a carpenter-builder who lived down the block at No. 166. The initial owner of No. 160 was Robert N. Hebberd, a book-keeper. Several transactions later, the house was purchased (along with No. 162) by Willard Dickerman Straight and his wife, Dorothy Payne Whitney, who lived at 1130 Fifth Avenue; the two structures were used by the Straights as a garage and living quarters for their servants. During the mid-twentieth century No. 160 was home to luminaries such as jewelry designer Jean Schlumberger and performer Eartha Kitt.

In 1988 the building was designated an individual landmark, outside of the Carnegie Hill Historic District. After a number of years of abandonment and neglect, the house was purchased in 2005 and completely renovated. Architecturally, it incorporates elements of the Greek Revival style—notably the dentiled cornice, the plain frieze, the eyebrow windows at the half story, and the porch supported on four fluted Corinthian columns—with Italianate elements, including scroll brackets on the frieze and half story. The original two-over-four wooden sash were unfortunately replaced with huge single-pane windows at the first floor and "casement windows above. The color palette combines bluish-gray on clapboards, slate-blue on paneled and louvered shutters, and blue accent moldings outlining the panels on the white front door. A flagstone yard and its wrought-iron fence are set off by large cement pots stationed on the sidewalk, each of which is planted with poodle-pompom boxwood. **LM**

162 East 92nd Street

ARCHITECTS: Delano & Aldrich   DATE: 1916-17

Three years after Willard and Dorothy Straight engaged the architects Delano & Aldrich to design their neo-Georgian mansion at 1130 Fifth Avenue, they commissioned the prestigious firm to erect this modest three-story building on East 92nd Street as a private garage and dwelling for their chauffeur.

The red-brick facade is laid in the Flemish-bond style. All apertures have splayed brick lintels. Above the third story runs a limestone band course, a dentil course and a slightly projecting cornice. Wrought iron grilles project from second story windows. Over the paneled-wood door is a simple keystone and plaque bearing the address. In 1940 a fourth story was added with little attempt to match the original structure; a window runs the length of the street facade. The arched, multi-pane vehicle entryway is new. Since the mid-20th century the first story has been used as a sculpture and design studio.

166 East 92nd Street
ARCHITECT: Howard Stokes Patterson   DATE: 1927
Stone band courses separate the one-story base, four-story mid-section and one-story crown of this beige brick neo-Renaissance apartment building. The rusticated stone entry enframement, now painted, is sur-mounted with a dentil course and slightly projecting cornice. Above, a carved limestone window surround has a swag-decorated lintel topped with a broken pediment and pineapple. Two windows in the crown section are capped with arched decorative brickwork and a carved keystones.

170 East 92nd Street
ARCHITECT: Richard Berger   DATE: 1889/90
This five-story-plus-penthouse apartment building exhibits curious patterns of brickwork. Fronting the street is a low brick wall. Most of the street level facade is of narrow dark-brown brick; the remaining surface is of tan brick with stone trim, except for the parapet, which echoes the darker shade. Above second- and fourth-story windows are square panels of decorative brickwork, framed with egg-and-dart moldings and punctuated with curious iron ornaments. Outer-bay windows at the third story have brick voussoirs; stone skew-backs connect to horizontal bands. This effect is repeated at the fifth story; Here, windows are topped with segmentally-arched brickwork and keystones. Flanking the doorway and at the building extremes are four fluted stone pilasters. Three are topped with winged guardians, possibly celestial.

West to east: 1, 3, 5, and 7 East 93rd Street (and a glimpse of No. 11 on opposite page, below)

1-7 and 11 East 93rd Street

ARCHITECTS: A.B. Ogden & Son   DATE: 1891-92

Ten years after the Jacob Ruppert mansion was erected at Fifth Avenue [see page 6], a set of six row houses sprang up diagonally across 93rd Street. The legendary brewer's home is long since gone, but the brownstones—five of them, at least—survive more or less intact. [The facade of No. 9 has been completely altered and is described on the opposite page.] Built for prolific developer Walter Reid, these houses display both Romanesque and Renaissance Revival characteristics and present a harmonious design in spite of individual variations and later changes.

No. 1 incorporates a four-story corner tower to the west, perhaps designed in graceful concert with the more prominent four-story rounded tower of the Ruppert mansion. The curve is echoed in diminishing progression in the two-story oriel of No. 3 and in the one-story oriels of Nos. 5, 7 and 11; Nos. 3, 5 and 11 also display round-arched windows at the fourth stories. Other unifying details include molded band courses, segmental arches at the parlor stories, foliate carving and bracketed metal roof cornices with paneled or foliate friezes. Stoops have been removed and basement-level entrances have been introduced at all but No. 5; however, the stoop at No. 11 was restored in 2007. In addition to its full-height curved bay, No. 1 is distinguished by leaf-and-ribbon window surrounds and a curious bartizan-like form, similar to a turret but more likely a vestigial downspout, rising between the top three stories of Nos. 1

and 3. Delicate leafy panels separate the oriel windows of No. 3.

Designed to mirror each other as the centerpiece of the six houses, Nos. 5 and 7 display foliate moldings around the arched windows of the parlor floors, surrounded by rock-faced rustication and voussoirs. Both oriels are almost identical, with foliate friezes at the top and corbels carved with flowers and ribbons underneath. No. 5, the best preserved of the group, retains its winged stoop and carved newel posts. Squat Romanesque-style colonettes frame the entrance with its exceptionally fine double-leaf iron doors and grilles. Fluted pilasters with Ionic capitals flank third-story windows; fourth-story windows echo the colonettes at the entryway. No. 7 features square-headed windows at both the third and fourth stories, united by continuing cornices. At No. 11, half of a bartizan-like form remains, echoing that at No. 1. Whether through oversight or—more likely—superstition, there is no No. 13. **HD**

9 East 93rd Street
ARCHITECTS: A.B. Ogden & Son
DATE: 1891-92
Chandler Stearns (attributed) 1929-30
Originally one of six 1891-92 brownstones designed by A. B. Ogden & Son, No. 9 underwent a major renovation at the behest of H. Donnelly Keresey, president of Anaconda Wire and Cable. Now a five-story townhouse, the neo-Georgian facade is surfaced in red brick laid in Flemish bond with contrasting limestone trim. The classical entry is framed with marble pilasters with acanthus-leaf capitals, topped with a broken pediment enclosing a carved pineapple, the symbol of hospitality. Carved oil lamps fill the arches of high parlor-story windows, which are capped with keystones. Splayed brickwork tops first- and fourth-story windows, while openings at the third story feature eared limestone lintels. A modillioned cornice runs over the fourth story, above which rises a balustraded parapet. Three pedimented dormers project from a steeply sloped roof. **HD**

4-6 East 93rd Street
Formerly Viola and Elie Nadelman house
ARCHITECTS: A.B. Ogden & Son
DATE: 1888-89
Walker & Gillette 1921-22

This four-story neo-Classical townhouse was originally part of a larger row of brownstones (Nos. 4-12) designed by A.B. Ogden & Son for developer John H. Gray. Nos. 4 and 6 were united in 1922 by Walker & Gillette for Elie and Viola Nadelman, both very involved with the arts in New York. Sculptor Elie Nadelman (1881/82-1946) was born in Warsaw and educated in Paris and Munich; he emigrated to America in 1914 and twelve years later founded New York City's Museum of Folk Art with his wife, Viola Spiess Flannery Nadelman (1877/78-1962), a native New Yorker. Under a Carnegie Foundation grant, the museum opened to the public in 1935; in 1937 the New-York Historical Society acquired its collection. Nadelman's work includes the Art Deco sculpted figures and clock over the 57th Street entrance to the Fuller Building (1929), also designed by Walker & Gillette. Viola Nadelman supervised a retrospective of her husband's work at the Museum of Modern Art in 1948 and served on the advisory committee of the New York School of Applied Design for Women.

The 1922 alterations include removal of the mansard roofs, extending the buildings twelve feet forward, and sheathing the new facade in limestone. A masonry areaway wall fronts the building and joins one of the two curved cheek walls flanking six steps and a stoop at the eastern end. A corniced entry surround frames the double-leaf doors and transom, ornamented with elaborate wrought-iron grilles. (However, one must climb an additional seven steps to reach a second set of doors to the house, which are of glass and iron with a fanlight.) The rest of the facade is austere: Two string courses divide the stories, and window ornamentation consists only of sills or simple cornices. Windows at the fourth story and a restrained dentiled cornice terminate the design. The building underwent a complete interior renovation in 2006-07. **HD**

8-12 East 93rd Street
ARCHITECTS: A. B. Ogden & Son   DATE: 1888-89
                Harvey Stevenson 1940   Roswell F. Barratt 1930-31
                Herbert Lippmann 1936-37

These three brownstones were originally part of a larger row (Nos. 4-12); little remains of their original Romanesque Revival character. All three buildings have had their stoops removed and main entrances shifted to the basement level; the fourth stories are set back behind parapets, capped with pitched roofs between stone-coped side walls.

No. 8 was altered in 1940 by architect Harvey Stevenson for Frederick A. O. Schwarz, grandson of the toy-store founder. Above the rusticated stone basement runs a band with playful aquatic relief carvings. At the parlor story, original round-arched openings display foliate keystones and voussoirs. The higher floors and two-story corbeled bay have been refaced; note the original iron cresting atop the cornice.

Most sophisticated of the trio is No. 10, redesigned in 1931 by architect Roswell F. Barratt for Caramai and John Taylor Johnston Mali. Mr. Mali was in the textile business and served as Belgian consul general in New York; his wife was president of the Oratorio Society of New York. The stuccoed facade is ornamented with Art Deco motifs in subtle modulations of level. Fluted pilasters bracket the bottom three floors, while scalloped bands enframe the middle one, and abstracted trees fill the spandrels above. Note the stuccoed full-width flower box with indented abstract ornaments, which also appear between floors just above.

No. 12 was altered in 1937 by architect Herbert Lippmann for Carl J. Austrian, an attorney who recovered more than $100 million in savings during the Depression for New Yorkers. The Federal-style entry, topped with a dentiled pediment, adds an unexpected element to the rough-faced basement and stuccoed upper facade. Flat keystones project slightly from round-arched windows at the parlor and third stories. The residual oriel is defined by string courses. **HD**

14-24 East 93rd Street

ARCHITECT: Walter Reid, Jr.   DATE: 1892-93

This fine row of Romanesque Revival brownstones, developed by Walter Reid and designed by his son, is almost intact, shaded by mature street trees. The ensemble is unified by material, color and two distinct alternating facade designs, creating a rhythm that individualizes each house as it expresses the harmony of the whole. Stoops survive at Nos. 16, 18 and 22, with bollard-like newel posts carved with leafy designs. No. 16 retains its low areaway walls

East to west: 22, 20, 18, 16, and 14 East 93rd Street

embellished with shields and ribbons. All six buildings have rough-faced basements, and most have historic ironwork over doors and lower-level windows.

Openings at the parlor story are round-arched, framed by voussoirs alternating smooth and rough-faced stone. Delicate foliate panels run the width of the facade above the parlor-floor and third-floor windows of Nos. 14, 18 and 22. As a counterpoint, vertical carved panels adorn the parlor floors of Nos. 16, 20 and 24. Projecting from each second story is a three-bay oriel supported by a carved corbel and enhanced with a foliate upper frieze. The fourth stories of all six buildings have round-arched windows resting on a continuous string course; windows are grouped in twos or threes, capped with cornices and embellished with carved spandrels and engaged columns. All of the houses, with the exception of No. 24, retain their leafy corbeled metal roof cornices, stepped as the street rises gently toward the east. **HD**

15-21 East 93rd Street
ARCHITECT: William Graul   DATE: 1891-92
This quartet of brownstones designed in the Renaissance Revival style differs considerably from the Queen Anne row houses on the south side of 92nd Street (Nos. 46 and 52-56) designed by the same architect for the same developer, Philip Braender, some four years earlier. The 93rd Street group is distinguished by three-sided oriels with supporting corbels above the parlor stories. Close observation will reveal that the placement of the oriels of Nos. 15 and 17 forms a mirror image of those at Nos. 19

West to east: 15, 17, 19 and 21 East 93rd Street

and 21. Charming historic elements remain on all four houses, although the two western buildings have lost their original roof cornices, and No. 17 lost its stoop in 1939. The best preserved are Nos. 19 and 21.

No. 15 was Braender's home in the mid-1890s. Pilasters with fluted capitals flank the parlor-floor entry and separate windows in the oriel. Beneath the parlor-story windows are molded panels. Ornament from the upper two stories has been removed. Little historic detail remains at No. 17 other than the oriel. Stuyvesant Fish, an investment banker, purchased the house in 1914 and in 1939 commissioned architect Harry Silverman to convert it into a multi-family residence. The alterations included creating two basement entrances, installing a large curved window at the parlor floor, and resurfacing the facade with stucco.

Graul designed No. 19 to stand out from the others by using segmentally arched openings for all of the windows and for the entrance, which has a handsome set of iron-and-glass doors with wrought-iron grilles set beneath a grilled transom. The door molding is delicately carved and capped with an ornamental keystone. Note the foliate panels beneath the parlor-story windows, and foliate pilasters separating the oriel windows. The facade of No. 21 is largely intact. Upper-story windows feature cornices and molded surrounds, and are connected by string courses. There is much ornamentation, including foliate carvings beneath windows and under the corbel, fluted pilasters, and a triangular Queen Anne-style pediment set jauntily into the center of the oriel cornice. Both Nos. 19 and 21 retain their original modillioned and bracketed metal roof cornices.

HD

23 East 93rd Street

ARCHITECT: Frederick Jenth   DATE: 1891-92

This four-story brownstone, now painted, was designed in the Renaissance Revival style, although neo-Grec references can be seen in the bracketed window surrounds. Rising from a rock-faced basement, the building is distinguished by its two-story, three-sided bay ornamented with pilasters, cornices, pedimented windows, carved friezes, and iron cresting. Horizontal banding divides each story. The stoop was removed in 1952; above the parlor floor with its segmentally-arched entrance is a square-headed pedimented window. The top two stories feature richly carved window heads, bracketed cornices and sills set on corbeled blocks. Dentils, modillions and paired brackets alternate with an elaborate frieze on the roof cornice. **HD**

West to east: 29, 31 and 33 East 93rd Street

25-33 East 93rd Street and 1316-1320 Madison Avenue

ARCHITECT: Gilbert A. Schellenger DATE: 1889-90

Sloping upwards gently to the east on 93rd Street and then turning north, these seven Renaissance Revival row houses were built by architect Gilbert A. Schellenger. He was responsible also for an earlier, quite different group at 56-62 East 91st Street. With few exceptions, these seven brownstones are remarkably intact. All display similar characteristics: metal roof cornices with paired brackets (the cornice at No. 31 is a replacement), multiple string courses which act as sills, and upper-story windows with projecting cornices carried on fluted brackets and pilasters (the windows at 1318 and 1320 Madison Avenue have keyed enframements).

Fluted pilasters, designed to echo the parlor-story window surrounds, flank the relocated basement entrance of No. 25. No. 27 is the most intact of the group, retaining its rock-faced basement and original cheek walls topped with paneled newel posts. At the top of the nine-step stoop, double-leaf iron-and-glass doors and transom are framed with fluted pilasters; scrolled brackets support a foliate entablature. The stoop and decorative parlor-floor entrance also survive at No. 29; the altered double-width window is gracefully subdivided by curved mullions intersecting a large oval at the upper center. No. 31 has been substantially altered over the years: The stoop was removed in 1920, the facade has been stuccoed and painted, and round-arched windows with fanlights and keystones were installed at the parlor floor. The corner building, No. 33, also known as 1316 Madison Avenue, anchors the seven structures and is by far the largest. The 93rd Street facade retains the brownstone characteristics of its neighbors to the west, adding a full-height angled three-sided bay. The avenue side, however, is faced with random ashlar at the base, and red brick at the top two stories; brownstone quoins define the corners. Pairs of channeled brick pilasters, corbeled at the top, rise from a delicately carved stone base below the parlor-story string course; the disguised flues terminate dramatically at the roof line in corbeled chimney pots. Above the entryway are paired windows with triangular and segmentally-arched pediments; the central bay is capped at the roof with an arched cornice. The lower stories of Nos. 1318 and 1320 were extended and converted to stores during the 1930s; both buildings are painted and have large tripartite windows at the second stories. An iron railing runs along the parapet extension of No. 1318. **HD**

55 East 93rd Street
The Alamo
ARCHITECT: Frederick Jacobson   DATE: 1899-1900
Designed in the Renaissance Revival style, this building originally contained apartments for nineteen families. When the owner/carpenter James Kilpatrick erected the six-story flats structure (which he may have built himself), he used Indiana limestone for the base (now painted), first and second stories, which are boldly rusticated, and stone-trimmed buff brick for the remainder. Most eye-catching is the four-column portico featuring composite capitals and a balustraded entablature inscribed "The Alamo."

Darker-stone string courses articulate the first and fifth stories; a beaded molding runs above the second story. The fenestration pattern consists of single bays at each of the curved corners, and four central bays; all display molded surrounds and lintels that echo the string course design. Additional window embellishments include fluted brackets at the fourth and fifth stories, and splayed keystones at the attic story. The facade terminates in a

festooned metal cornice; its wide projection emphasizes the building's rounded corners.

The public plaza immediately to the west of the Alamo is the site of the real "House on 92nd Street," a five-story row house also designed in 1899 by Jacobson, and made famous by the black-and-white movie of the same name about WWII German spies. That house was demolished in 1971 and replaced in 1983 by the present plaza as a part of the adjacent Carnegie Hill Tower condominium complex at 40 East 94th Street. Its construction settled a controversy between the developer and Carnegie Hill Neighbors: By agreeing to preserve the Alamo and create a public plaza, the developer received a "density" bonus for his 34-story apartment tower. **HD**

56 East 93rd Street
Originally William Goadby and Florence Baker Loew house, now The Spence School

ARCHITECTS : Walker & Gillette
DATE: 1932
Platt Byard Dovell White 2003
This four-story townhouse, often called "the last great mansion," was built for Florence and William Goadby Loew. Mrs. Loew was the sister of the banker George Baker, Jr., whose nearby complex at 67-75 East 93rd Street is now owned by the Russian Orthodox Church Outside of Russia. William Loew was a wealthy stockbroker and socialite who kept a racing stable in Old Westbury on Long Island. The Loews lived in the house until William Loew died in 1955. Subsequent owners have included the theatrical producer Billy Rose and the Algerian Mission to the United Nations. In 1972 it was designated a New York City landmark. In that year the building was purchased by St. Luke's-Roosevelt Hospital, which created the Smithers Alcoholism Treatment and Training Center. Acquired by The Spence School in 1999 (the school's main building is located at 22 East 91st Street), the interior of the mansion was reconfigured by the firm of Platt Byard Dovell White to house the lower school. In order to hide a one-story set-back addition, the sloping tile roof was raised about two feet.

The inspiration for the style of the symmetrical house is modified English Regency; the restrained use of classical ornamentation recalls the work of British architects Robert Adam (1728-1792) and Sir John Soane (1753-1857). The mansion has a central portion whose curving concave walls project to two-story end wings. Both the central part and the wings feature rusticated English basements with windows covered by iron grilles on the first floor and a smooth masonry facade on the floors above. The pedimented portico in the center of the building is supported by columns with composite capitals set off on each side by a low wrought-iron fence with ornamental lanterns. Above the entrance is a slightly projecting central bay with a high recessed arch; a bull's-eye window has radial stone fluting around its upper half. The fluting repeats around the arches of the balustraded Palladian windows on the second stories of the two wings of the house. Each wing has an ornamental stone cornice with a wave molding. The third story is set back; carved curtains grace the central window. **HD LM**

57-61 East 93rd Street
ARCHITECTS: Herter Brothers   1886-88

This trio of three-story-plus-basement row houses was designed in the neo-Grec style. The outer buildings retain much of their jaunty original appearance, while the middle one has undergone significant alterations.

Nos. 57 and 61 are of red brick accented with Dorchester stone trim. Windows have flush stone lintels and are connected with stone impost bands; wider segmentally-arched windows have keystones. Projecting band courses cap the stone basements, and third-story windows rest on corbeled string courses. At one time there were projecting bay windows at the parlor floors, evidenced by the slightly curved ledges on corbels. The ledge at No. 57 now supports a curved iron railing, while that at No. 61 has vertical grilles protecting the entire window expanse. Over the years (1936 for No. 57, 1949 for No. 61), stoops were removed, parlor-floor entries were relocated to the basement level, and cornices were replaced with cement coping. The facade of No. 57 has been painted; the cellar opening retains its original iron grille.

At No. 59 the removal of the stoop in 1926 created a base-

ment-level entrance. However, the major renovation occurred in 1937 at the behest of John Sloane, head of W. & J. Sloane, the prestigious furniture store. Before the work was completed, however, the house was purchased by George T. Pack, an Ohio-born surgeon whose distinguished career led to associations with French and American institutions devoted to the study and prevention of cancer. The American Cancer Society made him an honorary life director.

Sloane, and then Pack, retained the Howes Construction Co. to remodel the facade in a Moderne style, refacing it with a rusticated base and smooth limestone veneer. An enlarged multi-pane bay window with a bowed center dominates the original parlor story. At the upper levels, wood sash windows echo the bay-window design. The areaway ironwork dates from 1937; the gate and first-story grille are of a later date. **HD**

60 East 93rd Street
Originally Virginia Graham Fair Vanderbilt house

ARCHITECT: John Russell Pope DATE: 1930

Shortly after her divorce from William K. Vanderbilt, Jr., Comstock Lode heiress Virginia Graham Fair Vanderbilt commissioned this new residence for herself. One of John Russell Pope's rare works in the neo-French classical style, this skillful evocation of an 18th-century French townhouse, *un hôtel particulier*, blends happily with its slightly younger English Regency-style neighbor to the west [see 56 East 93rd Street].

Mrs. Vanderbilt died in 1935, and from 1937 to 1952 No. 60 housed Byron C. Foy, a vice-president of the Chrysler Corporation, and his wife Thelma (nee Chrysler), as well as their important collection of Impressionist paintings and French 18th-century furniture and decorations. Subsequently the house served as the Romanian Mission to the United Nations. In 1978 it was taken over by the Lycée Français de New York. In 2002 the house was sold to Carlton Hobbs, a London antiques gallery owner, for use as a residence and business showcase. The new owner did extensive internal renovations, restoring many of the rooms to their original Vanderbilt grandeur.

The mansion is three bays wide and is faced in limestone. Deeply coursed limestone piers frame the extremes; the basement facade is coursed as well, forming voussoirs over arched openings. Above the balustraded entablature, a slate-covered mansard roof is accented with three segmentally-arched dormers and flanked with tall chimneys. In the rear the building rises to five stories.

French doors with transoms on the first two stories have delicate wrought-iron window guards. Most striking are the classical keystones, each carved with the likeness of a woman, above the first-story windows and the Palladian doorway at the recessed western section. The double-leaf paneled-wood door is dramatized by garland carvings, a hanging lantern, a carved stone surround and voussoirs. **HD LM**

63 East 93rd Street
ARCHITECT: A.B. Ogden & Son   DATE: 1891
              Frank S. Lindgren   1955-56

Few viewers would guess that this Renaissance Revival brownstone was erected in conjunction with its brick-clad neighbor to the east, No 65. Patrick McMorrow, an early New York residential builder and an innovator in the use of the elevator and fireproof construction, selected the Ogden firm to design both houses with, presumably, compatible facades. No. 63 was built as a three-story-plus-basement single-family residence. Perhaps its most

striking feature is its projecting angled bay, providing views both south and west in spite of the building's fifteen-foot width. Many historic design elements remain: the brownstone facade and the rock-faced stone basement, whimsically carved panels of birds—and a devilish

masque—above the original entrance and under the parlor-story windows, egg-and-dart moldings, and string courses terminating in curlicues.

Some 65 years later, architect Frank S. Lindgren converted the residence, which included a doctor's office, into a two-family dwelling. Probably at that time the stoop was removed and the parlor-story entrance was converted into a window. Capping the building is a bracketed metal cornice, which appears to be a replacement. **HD**

65 East 93rd Street
Formerly William Hamilton Russell house
ARCHITECT: A.B. Ogden & Son   DATE: 1891
              George L. Schelling   1931

This building was designed in 1891 by A.B. Ogden & Son along with No. 63 next door, but little is known about the first 40 years of its life. Erected as a five-story, two-family row house with brownstone facing, by 1930 No. 65 had been subdivided into ten apartments. In the following year architect-builder George L. Schelling converted it to a single-family residence for architect William Hamilton Russell. Over the next 20 years the building would vacillate from being a one- or two-family dwelling to a multi-unit apartment building, which it remains today.

The Modern-style, symmetrical facade dates from Schelling's intervention in 1931, when the brownstone veneer was replaced with rough-textured brown brick. The design of the brickwork is worth noting: Soldier courses above window openings define each story; above the fourth story parades a row of brick dentils and a brick-balustraded parapet. Topping the set-back fifth story is a sloped roof with skylights and end chimneys. On each floor are three steel casement windows with fixed sidelights and transoms. The ground-level openings are unusually high; those at the end bays have wrought-iron gates with a geometric pattern, while the central entrance has glazed wooden doors flanked with historic metal lamps. Wrought-iron transoms cap each opening. **HD**

66 East 93rd Street
ARCHITECT: A.B. Ogden & Son   DATE: 1890-91

The basement and street level of this Queen Anne row house, originally brownstone, are stuccoed; the remaining four stories are of red brick with brownstone trim. The glazed wood-framed doors and multi-light transom appear to be original. Above the first story, the western bay projects slightly and band courses span the facade. Windows display typical Queen Anne decorative elements: carved and corniced lintels, segmented pediments and stone arches. A metal cornice with a foliate frieze, dentils and modillions tops the facade.

In 1939 the building was purchased by Ellin and Irving Berlin, although they never lived here. Irving Berlin was the Russian-born composer of *Alexander's Ragtime Band, White Christmas, Easter Parade, God Bless America,* and other American song classics. **HD**

67-75 East 93rd Street and 1190 Park Avenue
Formerly George F. Baker, Jr. house complex.
Nos. 67 and 69 now privately owned; the other buildings now the Russian Orthodox Church Outside of Russia
ARCHITECTS: Delano & Aldrich
   No. 75 (originally Francis F. Palmer house)   DATE: 1917-18
   Nos. 71-73/1190 Park Avenue (courtyard and ballroom wing) 1928-29
   No. 69 (garage) 1928-29   No. 67 (George F. Baker, Sr. house) 1931

The five-story neo-Federal brick house at No.75, on the corner of Park Avenue, was designed by the renowned architectural team Delano & Aldrich for financier Francis F. Palmer. The site once held one of Carnegie Hill's earliest structures, a frame house built in 1834 with a wrap-around "piazza," or verandah. Named Prospect Hall [see pages 4-5], it was a splendid hotel that served as a way station and day-trip destination for the brand-new

New York and Harlem Railroad. The owner of the building, George
Nowlan, named the property Observatory Place for its unobstructed view
of Long Island and New Jersey. The land was eventually broken up; the
corner lot passed through several owners before its purchase by Palmer.

In 1928 George F. Baker, Jr., bought the Palmer house and brought
back the architects to design a series of additions complementary to the
mansion. (At the time, George F. Baker, Sr. was chairman of the First
National City Bank, now Citibank; upon his death in 1931 his son
assumed the chairmanship, and a $60 million inheritance.) Baker added
a large ballroom wing, 1190 Park Avenue, and a garage with a chauffeur's
apartment above. He converted the courtyard, Nos. 71-73, to a formal
flagstone-paved garden enclosed on the 93rd Street side by a wall.

No. 75 and its wing are distinguished by marble basements lit by
windows protected by their original iron grilles. The rest of the facade is
clad in red brick laid in English bond; square-headed windows display
plain lintels at the first story. Peaked lintels cap second-story windows,
which rest on a marble string course that turns into balconettes on the
facades looking towards the street and avenue. Above the third story runs a
modillioned and dentiled marble cornice and balustraded parapet, behind
which rises a slate mansard roof with fourth-floor pedimented dormers,
fifth-story bull's-eye dormers, and chimneys. The marble entrance portico,
on 93rd Street, is composed of engaged columns carrying an entablature
decorated with bucrania (ox skulls) and swags. The fanlight grille over the
double doors now features a cross. In 1958 the Synod of Bishops of the
Russian Orthodox Church Outside of Russia purchased all but Nos. 67
and 69 East 93rd Street with funds contributed by Serge Semenenko, a

Russian-born Boston banker. A plaque commemorating the gift is embedded in the wall next to the entrance. The complex serves as the headquarters of the Synod of Bishops of the Russian Orthodox Church Outside of Russia.

In adapting the complex for use by the church, the wall at the property line at Nos. 71-73 was opened to create a formal entrance; a highlight of its delicate wrought-iron gate is a gold medallion of the Madonna and Child. The Synod added a staircase and balustraded balcony to access the church's sanctuary (the former ballroom). The balcony is supported by four coupled Ionic columns. An arcaded first story is centered by an arched doorway which is echoed by an arched window higher on the facade.

Set back behind a wrought-iron fence and gate, the northern wing of the house, at 1190 Park Avenue, was built in two sections to accommodate servants' quarters and the ballroom in its courtyard-facing extension. On the Park Avenue facade, first-floor openings, resting on a marble band course, are arched, with scrolled keystones. A marble string course functions as a sill for second-story windows. The street level and second story of the Park Avenue section are now occupied by an independent school.

No. 69, the garage, is distinguished by a colonnade of paired fluted Ionic columns; the two-story structure was designed to harmonize with the rest of the complex. Wide enough to accommodate five cars, the building also served as housing for Baker's chauffeur. The round-arched entrance is lit by an iron lamp supported by curved brackets. Above the second-story windows, which are capped by lintels with Greek key motifs, are inset panels carved with large scallop shells. The courtyard facade is centered with a projecting first-floor window with a pedimented and bracketed enframement, flanked by two smaller windows set in segmental arches.

No. 67 is a four-story house that was intended for George F. Baker, Sr., but he died before he could move in. The red-brick facade, on a marble water table, is highlighted by two doors, both now painted green. The service entrance is capped by a marble lintel with a Greek key motif. The main entrance has a molded enframement bearing a broken pediment supported by dolphins—just one of the motifs, like the scallop shells at the garage and a conch at the ballroom, referring to George F. Baker, Jr.'s interest in nautical pursuits. In fact, title to the house was transferred to his wife, Edith, after he died on his yacht, the Viking, in 1937.

All buildings in the Baker complex are individual landmarks. **HD LM**

68-72 East 93rd Street
ARCHITECT: Max Hensel   DATE: 1890
Constructed of brownstone that has since been painted over, these
Renaissance Revival flats buildings were designed to accommodate six
families each. Later, 1930s building codes mandated the addition of fire
escapes; grilles and railings were also added. Of special interest to the
observant passerby are the delicately carved spandrels separating the deeply
recessed window openings on each building. Those between the second
and third stories, as well as those between the fourth and fifth, run straight
across and feature sinuous scroll-and-vine motifs. The spandrels between
the third and fourth stories, in contrast, are separate, individual panels,
each with its unique design. Those on No. 70, for example, incorporate faux
heraldic shields into the pattern. Like No. 66, its neighbor immediately
to the west, No. 68 was once owned by the famous Broadway composer
Irving Berlin and his wife, Ellin, who converted it to ten units. In point of
fact, the Berlins lived elsewhere—in a far grander abode more suitable to
their lifestyle, on Sutton Place. The building still retains its original
modillioned metal cornice. **HD**

118 East 93rd Street
ARCHITECT: M. Joseph Harrison   DATE: 1925-26
This nine-story buff-brick apartment house is a
rather muted example of the neo-Renaissance style.
Its primary design interest is the two-story cast-stone
entry: Here, wood-and-glass doors are capped with a
molded architrave centered by a cartouche, and are
flanked by wide pilasters with foliate capitals. Inset
bands of darker-toned brick stripe the two-story base
on either side of the entryway, for a rusticated effect.
Incised cast-stone spandrels separate first- and sec-

ond-story windows. A cast-stone cornice underscored by dentils tops the
second story; a more modest cornice separates the seventh story from the
crown section. Zigzag cornices cap lintels over the end bay windows on the
third and ninth floors. **HD**

122 and 124 East 93rd Street
ARCHITECT: Thomas H. McAvoy   DATE: 1877-78
Designed as twins, these three-story neo-Grec brownstones were originally
single-family dwellings. No. 124 is the more intact: A twelve-step stoop
leads to the parlor-floor entrance, which is highlighted with a heavy bracketed
cornice; the double front door is paneled wood with a transom. An
L-shaped iron stair leads to the second-story entrance at No. 122; French

doors are fronted with iron balconettes. Windows on both buildings are one-over-one wood sash, with incised projecting lintels over the second-story openings supported by mini scrolled brackets. Larger scrolled "brackets support the galvanized-iron roof cornice. **HD**

125 East 93rd Street
ARCHITECT: George F. Pelham   DATE: 1924
The rough beige-brick facade of this neo-Medieval, nine-story apartment house features characteristic details favored by the architect: A Tudor arch forms the centered entrance framed by quoins, now painted, and a stone hood molding. The wood French doors have a small, carved dentil band and fanlight.

A white terra-cotta cornice above the second story introduces a pair of terra-cotta balconettes at the third story. Carved escutcheons on each end and small heart-shaped foliate brackets distinguish these purely decorative additions. A single balconette is centered at the eighth story. Brick quoins frame the end-bay double windows creating the impression of vertical towers. The illusion is completed with a square panel with diamond relief beneath a false cant roof line and crenelated parapet. **HD**

126 East 93rd Street
ARCHITECT: John B. McIntyre DATE: 1875-76
From the first story upward, the red-brick facade of this neo-Grec flats building retains much of its historic ornamental detail. Windows are framed with stone; thick sills are supported with brackets; and the peaked, eared lintels are incised with simple geometric elements. An incised band course links third-story windows. The facade is topped with a decorative cornice with brackets and modillions.

Fronting the sidewalk, post-Modern prevails: A boxed stone stoop with peaked newel posts was constructed in 1988. Curved stone stairs lead to the doorway, which now has a coordinating surround comprised of plain engaged columns and a simple pediment inset with an indented arch. However, windows in the historic stone base retain their gentle arches and lintels decorated with scrolls reminiscent of vines. **HD**

128 East 93rd Street
ARCHITECT: Edmund Waring   DATE: 1866

This meticulously-restored Italianate residence, built in 1866 for Henry Shaw, a maker of artificial limbs, was one of the last frame houses to be erected before the "fire line" that prohibited frame buildings south of 86th Street was extended to Harlem. After its completion, the house was sold to Bernard Flach, a manufacturer of moldings for pianos and billiard tables. The simple window lintels and the modillioned, bracketed cornice — one of the last to be executed in wood, before galvanized iron — are features typical of pre-Civil War buildings. The original house had a wooden stoop and front porch, which seem to have existed until 1922.

Consisting of a raised basement faced with brick (added sometime after 1955), two full floors clad in sage-green clapboard, and a slate Second Empire-style mansard roof (added later in the 19th century), the house exhibits an unusually refined harmony of materials and the manner in which they combine to articulate the whole. At ground level, the green paneled front door is framed with a dentiled cornice, fluted pilasters, and side panels with insets that are repeated in a frieze beneath the cornice. The service entrance is narrower; between the two doors is a pair of large multi-pane windows. Nine-over-nine sash windows on the parlor floor and six-over-six windows on the floor above are flanked by green shutters, while the dormer windows are capped with segmental pediments supported both at their sides and in front by slender brackets. All upper-story windows are fronted with slim wrought-iron railings.

The front yard is paved in brick in a herringbone pattern; it is protected by a low brick wall and a tall wrought-iron fence, which serve as a backdrop for boxwood hedges set in planters. **HD**

130 East 93rd Street
ARCHITECT: Herman Sohn   DATE: 1939

This six-story apartment building was originally designed by Thom & Wilson in 1881. In the 1939 alteration, the sole decorative element, other than the black-marble plaque bearing the address number, is brick: rows of brick headers, stretchers, soldier bricks, even angled projecting bricks, all positioned to define various facade areas. Five brick steps lead to the below-street-level wooden door, which is framed with brick. The upper stories are seven bays wide, capped with a brick parapet that steps upward in the center.

131 East 93rd Street
ARCHITECT: Frank Braun   DATE: 1923

A neo-Federal dentiled pediment tops the multi-pane glazed door of this nine-story tan-brick building; a stone cartouche wrapped with fanciful stone ribbons bears the address number. A garlanded band course runs above the second story. These are among the few embellishments on the otherwise austere facade. Crown-story windows have flat stone surrounds; above them runs a rondel-ornamented band course and geometric brickwork. **HD**

134 East 93rd Street
The Royal Carnegie
ARCHITECT: Seymour Churgin/
Architects Design Group of Manhattan
DATE: 1990

With a Postmodern nod to Art Deco design elements, this fifteen-story apartment building rises from a square-block stone base at street level, punctuated with store windows on Lexington Avenue and the first twenty feet of 93rd Street. Above the entrance, the stone is articulated with smooth-faced pilasters flanking a circular window with keystones. A stone band course runs above second-story windows; the remaining facade is of red brick. The entire building sets back at the thirteenth story. It replaces a row of 1862 houses, among the oldest in Carnegie Hill, built by John C. Rennert, a carpenter.

150 East 93rd Street
ARCHITECTS: George & Edward Blum   DATE: 1923

In this eleven-story reddish-brick building we see the inventive Blum brothers in a somewhat traditional mood. The arched terra-cotta entrance surround has multiple moldings of spirals, geometrics, florals and egg-and-dart designs. On the second story, double and triple windows have wide curved lintels carved in terra-cotta with floral motifs. Round-arched window pairs on the third and tenth stories lend the building an overall vertical appearance to relieve its massing. The spiral enframements are embellished with additional floral carvings within the curved lintels. Under the cornice, small brick-and-terra-cotta arches echo the building's classical elements. For a more eccentric Blum approach, walk north one block to 1435 Lexington Avenue.

155 East 93rd Street
ARCHITECT: George A. Bagge & Sons
DATE: 1927

This eleven-story red-brick apartment house displays neo-Renaissance elements combined with brickwork favored during the late 1920s. The two-level limestone entry surround includes a keyed enframement, pilasters and a broken pediment with a cartouche trailing cornucopias. Bricks on the first two levels project at every sixth row, creating monotone striping; further horizontal emphasis is seen in dentiled band courses and string courses above the second, third, ninth and tenth stories. Most windows display simple brick enframements; however, selected window pairs are embellished with arched lintels carved with wreaths and swags. Centered between fourth- and fifth-story windows are large stone panels depicting garlands and urns; the motif is echoed in miniature on second-story lintels. There is no cornice; the height of the parapet alternates to lend verticality to paired window bays.

158-176 and 184-186 East 93rd Street: Brewery Hill
ARCHITECTS: Nos. 158-166: unknown   DATE: 1865
     Nos. 168-174: unknown late 1860s
     No. 176: Gueron & Lepp 1970
     Nos. 184-186: William Jose 1876

These twelve row houses are among the earliest existing structures in Carnegie Hill. Together they form a mostly intact streetscape, combining Italianate and neo-Grec features, with Queen Anne influences in the later houses. The street has long been known as Brewery Hill, as it once led to the Ehret brewery that flourished during the 19th century at the foot of the hill at Second Avenue. (A common conception is that such houses were built for mid-level brewery employees: not true, on this block.) While similar, the houses fall into several groups; the first were built even before Lexington Avenue extended to the area. No. 176 was modernized in 1970. Nos. 178 and 180, formerly housing the Reece school, were demolished in 2007, and No. 182 in 2008; plans are to erect a seven-story condominium. With these exceptions, the row displays an unbroken roof cornice line.

  The first five houses, Nos. 158-166, are of brick (now painted), with stone trim and a two-bay fenestration. Upper windows of all but No. 166 retain their cornices, often associated with the Italianate style. Nos. 158

East to west: 170, 168, 166, 164, 162, 160, and 158 East 93rd Street

and 160 have their original high stoops; that at No. 162 was removed in 2007. Other alterations to the quintet include the creation of a tripartite parlor-level window at No. 164, and an angled stoop at No. 166.

All upper windows of the brownstone-fronted second group, Nos. 168-174, have small brackets under their sills and paneled, bracketed roof cornices, in neo-Grec style. Simple panels with rondels underscore the parlor-story windows of Nos. 168-172. No. 168 is perhaps the best preserved; it retains its stoop, unpainted facade, fanlight, window surrounds and foliate brackets supporting the entrance cornice. At No. 170, the 2004 redesign by Julie Herzig of the ground-level entry displays a graceful round-arched pediment with foliate keystone. The stoop, door enframement and bracketed entry cornice of No. 172 are historic. No. 176 displays a modern red-brick facade, dominated by a full-width round-arched opening, breaking the cornice line (but not the scale) of the row.

The easternmost houses, Nos. 184 and 186, are of red (painted)

brick. The two-bay buildings combine overhanging window cornices with incised eared lintels, and a more complex roof-cornice design, suggesting Queen Anne style. The stoops (original to No. 184, replaced at No. 186 in 2005) lead to double doors with what appear to be historic transoms. Unique in the block—and in Carnegie Hill—and visually terminating the row is the three-sided parlor-level oriel at the carefully restored No. 186.

175-179 East 93rd Street: Brewery Hill
ARCHITECT: Henry Dudley   DATE: 1881

These three four-story apartment houses were built for eight families each, when the Ehret and Ruppert breweries were in full operation down the street, which was known as Brewery Hill. There are no cornices; the roof lines are identical, with bi-level parapets that rise in the center. The facades feature virtually no ornament. No. 175 has been substantially modernized with stone blocks painted beige and windows combining multi-pane and casement styles. A two-step entry leads to an iron-and-glass door. Nos. 177 and 179 retain their brownstone facades, now painted. The top-story windows are segmentally-arched, as are the entry surrounds. Wrought-iron rails front small gardens; the rails are not historic, although there is a vestigial post and one original fence segment. At No. 177 a three-step entryway leads to a wood-and-glass double door topped with a dentil row and transom. Wisteria vines embrace the doorway and partially conceal the fire escape.

No. 179, the furthest down the steep hill, has a five-step entryway with stepped rails on stone cheek walls. Sidelights flank the wood-and-glass door, which is topped with a fanlight. The Marx brothers grew up here. Samuel Marx was a tailor; he and his wife, Minnie, had five sons whose stage names are familiar to many: Chico, Harpo, Groucho, Gummo and Zeppo. According to Harpo (1888-1964), *Harpo Speaks,* "Each morning, the [George Ehret] stallions would charge down the hill at full gallop. When they passed our house, the stallions were wild-eyed and foaming at their bits, and the cobblestones rang like anvils."

180 East 93rd Street
ARCHITECT: Barry Rice   DATE: 2008-09

A seven-story Postmodern apartment house will occupy three lots, formerly Nos. 178-182. The plan calls for a brick facade with limestone trim. The building is under construction at this writing.

181 East 93rd Street
ARCHITECT: George G. Miller   DATE: 1928

Rising from a low granite base, this six-story, brushed-and-scraped light-brown brick building has a rusticated stone entry surround and wooden doors filled with beveled-glass panes. A string course above the first story and a dentil course above the fifth story define the midsection. Protruding brick detailing can be seen around some windows, under several sills, and especially in the crown section, which features high arched window surrounds and a series of small arches at the roof line. The building is a mirror image of 170 East 94th Street.

1 East 94th Street
Formerly Julia and Cass Gilbert house
ARCHITECTS: Louis Entzer, Jr.   DATE: 1895
                Cass Gilbert   1925

Louis Entzer, Jr. designed this five-story townhouse as a pair with No. 3 next door for developers Carrie H. and Francis Joseph Schnugg, who several years earlier had built two groups of row houses on the north side of East 95th Street, now known as Goat Hill. In 1925 the original brownstone front wall was replaced with a neo-Classical limestone facade, and the building was entirely remodeled within, by architect Cass Gilbert for himself and his wife, Julia Finch Gilbert. Some 30 years later, dress manufacturer Jack Borgenicht subdivided the building into two apartments and altered the ground floor to include a garage.

The ground level of the building wears its rusticated limestone with restraint and features, besides the garage, a wrought-iron-and-glass front door. Three tall six-over-nine windows at the parlor-floor level are set off by wrought-iron balconettes resting on modillioned sills; simple delicately molded window enframements are topped with molded cornices. Subtle panels separate the parlor and third stories. Fourth-floor windows are topped with lintels incised with mirrored Greek key motifs at their centers. A string course forms the sill below fifth-floor windows. A modillioned stone cornice and balustrade complete the facade. **HD**

3 East 94th Street
ARCHITECTS: Louis Entzer, Jr.   DATE: 1895
                Mott B. Schmidt   1919
                Ervin Lemberger   1991

Originally designed by Louis Entzer, Jr. as a four-story-with-basement townhouse at the same time as No. 1 next door, No. 3 was renovated by Mott B. Schmidt for Grenville Temple Emmet, a former law partner of Franklin D. Roosevelt, and his wife, Pauline. Emmet served as Roosevelt's United States Minister in the Hague and, later, in Austria, where he died. Schmidt lowered the stoop and simplified the facade in neo-Renaissance style. Architect Cass Gilbert, who lived at No. 1, may have added his own touches to the building in 1925. In 1971 No. 3 was converted

to a day-care center for the Spence-Chapin Adoption Service across the street. In 1991 it was remodeled once again, restoring the round-arched windows at the top story and creating a series of rental units within, including one with an indoor swimming pool. From 2006 to 2008 No. 3 underwent yet more renovations in anticipation of sales of condominiums.

The building gives the appearance of being set back from its neighbor at No. 1 due to a handsome bay that rises from the basement to the roof. The rusticated base features flat-arched windows surmounted by a band punctuated by shallow square cavities. Windows at the parlor level are arched, as are those on the floor above and at the top story. A small nine-pane fixed window is inset over the front door, which is lit by a lantern marked with the numeral 3. All other windows are six-over-nine, which adds to the building's feeling of height. Square cavities repeat under the roof line, which is highlighted by a simple molded cornice and flat parapet. **HD**

4-8 East 94th Street
ARCHITECTS: No. 4: George Hickey   DATE: 1963-65
              Nos. 6-8: George Prentiss Butler, Jr.   1936
              Nos. 4-8: BKSK Architects   2009 (planned)

The history of this 60-foot neo-Classical building is somewhat complex. Nos. 4, 6 and 8 were originally part of a group of four-story row houses designed by A.B. Ogden & Son in 1890. In 1936 George W. Perkins, a powerful figure in Republican politics, hired architect George Butler, Jr. to combine Nos. 6 and 8 to form a neo-Classical red-brick-and-limestone mansion with a four-story street facade, and a fifth story with a set-back mansard roof. The building was acquired by the Spence-Chapin Adoption Service in 1955. In 1963 the agency bought No. 4 and altered the first four stories to conform to the design of Nos. 6-8, adding three stories in the form of a simple red-brick structure, plus mechanicals.

Both buildings rise from a limestone base; the entry at No. 4 has double-leaf paneled doors, while that at Nos. 6-8 is flanked by Doric columns. At the *piano nobile,* a wrought-iron railing with an anthemion design unifies both buildings. Three-story flat pilasters capped with a stylized Greek fret motif divide the complex vertically into six bays. Sunbursts embellish second-story windows. A stone cornice crested with lions' heads and anthemions fronts the recessed attic story on Nos. 6-8.

In 2006 both buildings were sold to a developer for conversion to residential use. Plans for a design by BKSK Architects have been approved by the Landmarks Preservation Commission for removal of the three-story addition to No. 4 and extension of the set-back fifth story of Nos. 6-8, plus the creation of a further recessed sixth story over the entire complex. The proposed building will have a single, unified neo-Classical facade. **HD**

5 East 94th Street
ARCHITECTS: Cleverdon & Putzel   DATE: 1892-93
           Sidney Daub   1951

No. 5 is the westernmost in a string of five Romanesque Revival houses built by Cleverdon & Putzel on the north side of 94th Street. Asymmetry has been introduced to its rough-cut face by means of a three-sided bay reaching from the basement through the second floor to the right of the former parlor-floor entrance. The front door was relocated to ground level in a 1951 renovation, when the building was converted to accommodate multiple apartments. On the parlor floor, an arched window is bracketed by two stilted-arch openings that rest on short engaged columns. Above the second floor, a band course forms the base of a parapet running across the third story, where three arches set off a loggia. A steep gable at the top of the house frames an arched window executed in the Venetian style with smooth voussoirs and lintels resting on paired dwarf columns. A checkerboard pattern enlivens the gable's stonework. **HD**

West to east: 5, 7, 9, and 11 East 94th Street

7–11 East 94th Street
ARCHITECTS: Cleverdon & Putzel   DATE: 1892-93
               No. 7: Polhemus & Coffin   1924
               No. 9 : James E. Casale   1926
               No. 11: Alec Ajzyc Jagoda, Vardlo Associates 1978

These three Romanesque Revival houses are almost identical. Nos. 7 and 9 relocated their former parlor-story entrances to the ground level. The parlor-floor windows at No. 7 simulate French doors. Although No.11 underwent an overhaul in 1978, it appears the best preserved: It is entered from a curved wing wall and L-shaped stoop faced, like the basement, with rough-cut stone. All three houses feature shallow curved oriels, which extend from the second through the third floors; pilasters with ornate capitals separate their bays. The undersides of the oriels are embellished with fanciful foliate carving. Each oriel is crowned by a dentiled cornice and foliate band. The three windows above the oriels are flanked by short pilasters supporting the impost blocks beneath the lintels. Roof-line cornices are accented with colonettes; the one at No. 11 also features tiny Gothic arches and an ornate hollow molding beneath the conventional double-curved molding. **HD**

13 East 94th Street
ARCHITECTS: Cleverdon & Putzel   DATE: 1892-93
            George B. Post & Sons   1940

The easternmost of the Cleverdon & Putzel row of houses [see Nos. 5 and 7-11 East 94th Street], No. 13 was altered several times. The parlor-story entrance has been relocated to ground level, and the facade has been stripped of its Romanesque Revival ornament. The only historic features that remain are its shapely two-story oriel and several string courses. **HD**

10-12 East 94th Street
Joseph H. Choate, Jr. house
ARCHITECT: George B. de Gersdorff DATE: 1919-20

The original 1891 row houses that stood at Nos. 10 and 12 were designed by A.B. Ogden & Son for real-estate developer John H. Gray. However, in 1919-20 architect George B. de Gersdorff combined the two, substantially altering the resulting 40-foot facade in the neo-Georgian style. His client was Joseph Hodges Choate, Jr., later a partner in the firm of Choate, Byrd, Leon & Garretson. The townhouse was converted in 1957 for use by Louise Wise Services, an adoption agency and home for unwed teenage mothers. In 2001 the house reverted back to a private residence.

The stately stone-trimmed red-brick building rises from a coursed stone base. Double iron-and-glass doors with a transom and fanlight grille are topped with a bracketed cornice and decorative frieze. Window openings have splayed lintels with keystones. At the *piano nobile*, round-headed brick arches frame tall, multi-pane French doors opening to iron balconettes. The modillioned and dentiled cornice is surmounted by a balustrade. At the set-back fourth story, a pitched roof holds three copper-clad dormers with alternating triangular and arched pediments. **HD**

14 East 94th Street

ARCHITECTS: McCrea & Sharpe   DATE: 1926

This handsome townhouse was part of an older row—Nos. 10 to 16—designed by A.B. Ogden & Son in 1891. Its facade was redesigned in a neo-Georgian style in 1926 for Walter S. Mack, a vice-president of Bedford Mills, a textile company. At first glance, the five-story house (originally four plus basement) appears elegantly simple and consistent in appearance; a closer look reveals subtle variations from floor to floor. The stucco facade of the upper stories is smooth, contrasting with the rusticated surface at the two-story base. The entry and windows at grade level are segmentally-arched and accented by voussoirs, and a wide inset arch surrounds the central window that dominates the parlor level. Windows on the upper floors are square-headed. Crowning the building is a dentiled cornice and parapet. Over the years since Mack's ownership, No. 14 has been home to luminaries from various areas of the entertainment world: Broadway producer George S. Kaufman was reportedly a resident between 1936 and 1945, and concert pianist Vladimir Horowitz lived and practiced here until his death in 1989. **HD**

16 East 94th Street

ARCHITECTS: A.B. Ogden & Son   DATE: 1891-92
             Unknown   1924-27

The first thing that catches the eye on this completely remodeled four-story-and-basement brick townhouse (there is no trace of the original A.B. Ogden & Son design) is a scroll-edged polychrome ceramic plaque, which is painted with a yellow fleur-de-lis, attached to the facade. Like the ceramic numeral tag that announces the house address, the plaque looks to be a souvenir from a trip to Italy. The otherwise restrained, flat, neo-Federal facade features tall arched windows at the parlor floor fronted by curved wrought-iron balconettes. A bank of squared French windows on the floor above is recessed behind a wrought-iron balcony that spans their width; a heavy, flush stone lintel runs overhead. The windows on the third floor are square-headed, while those on the top floor are arched. The parapet is plain, with simple coping. Entry into the building is through a double front door and a service door, both of which are protected by delicate iron grilles. **HD**

15, 21, 23, and 25 East 94th Street

ARCHITECTS: Cleverdon & Putzel   DATE: 1892-94
                    No. 21: Roy Clinton Morris 1944-46
                    No. 23: Minoque & Palmer 1936-37
                    No. 25: Sterner & Wolfe   1919-20

West to east: 15, 17, 19, 21, and 23 East 94th Street

Along with Nos. 17 and 19 [described on the following page], these Romanesque Revival four-story-plus-basement townhouses were originally designed as an a-b-c-c-b-a group by the same architects who masterminded the neighboring row of five houses (Nos. 5-13) directly to the west.

The gable-roofed "a" house at No. 15 has a loggia spanning the top story, a motif that was later removed from its "a" counterpart down the block at No. 25. No. 15 also features fluted columns between its parlor windows, and a bay resting on a cornice above an incised frieze. Pilasters set off the center window of the bay. The facade is finished off with a dentiled cornice.

The "c" house at No. 21 wears a rough-faced stone facade, pierced by round-arched windows at the parlor and fourth floors. A curved bay sets off the level above the parlor floor. On all floors but the second, Romanesque columns flank the windows. A small bull's-eye window peers from the gabled roof. The easternmost "b" house, No. 23, is faced with stone accented by rough-hewn horizontal bands, and rises to a steep gable containing three arched windows. Triple dwarf columns support the window arches on the third floor.

At No. 25 (originally the Norman P. Ream house), the "a"-style facade has been stripped of most of its ornament, except for pairs of fluted columns flanking a bank of three windows which support a classical entablature. In 1919-20 architects Sterner & Wolfe added tall leaded-glass windows on the parlor floor and leaded-glass casement windows on the floor above. A perforated scored-concrete screen partially obscures the basement to the left of the front door, and the roof is crowned by an unusually high, triglyph-bearing metal cornice. **HD**

17 and 19 East 94th Street
Ramakrishna-Vivekananda Center
ARCHITECTS: Cleverdon & Putzel
DATE: 1892-93
No. 17: Raymond B. Eaton 1939
No. 19: H.P. Alan Montgomery &
John T. Riggs 1919

These two buildings were part of the a-b-c-c-b-a string of Romanesque Revival townhouses [see Nos. 15, 21, 23 and 25] designed by Cleverdon & Putzel. Both buildings continue to display many of the original upper-story "b" and "c" facade features, terminating in twin gables. No. 17 was purchased by the Ramakrishna-Vivekananda Center of New York in 1939, at which time it was converted into a two-family dwelling, plus a chapel. In 2000 the Center purchased No. 19 (and also 22 East 95th Street, to which it backs up) from the soon-to-relocate Churchill School. (No. 22 was resold in 2002).

Bollard-like newels with palmette carvings announce the stately box stoop of No. 17. Double engaged columns with leafy capitals separate parlor-floor windows; single columns flank the new paneled front door. The underside of the curved bay offers additional fanciful carvings; its facade is highlighted by a pattern of indented squares alternating with rosettes, and by two incised friezes. Triple columns set off the three arched windows on the fourth floor. No. 19 reflects the 1919 renovation that had been commissioned by its original owner, Francis Sims McGrath; the work at that time included the removal of the stoop and oriel and the addition of a new, basement-level entrance. In a decorous 2002 renovation, the original leafy newel posts mark stairs leading down into a newly paved areaway behind a new wrought-iron fence and gate. A heavily textured rusticated base and grilles protecting ground-floor windows visually connect the two buildings.

The Ramakrishna-Vivekananda Center is a branch of the Ramakrishna Order of India. Its teachings are based on the ancient system of Vedanta, which combines the religion and philosophy of the Hindus as explained by Sri Ramakrishna (1836-1886), his wife and spiritual companion, Sri Sarada Devi (1853-1920), and his disciple, the Swami Vivekananda (1863-1902). The temple on 94th Street seeks to stimulate individual spiritual growth through lectures, publications and guidance; the Center also maintains a summer cottage at Thousand Island Park in upstate New York, in which the Swami Vivekananda lived and taught in the summer of 1895. **HD**

18-24 East 94th Street

ARCHITECTS: Van Vleck & Goldsmith DATE: 1899

This row of five-story Beaux-Arts townhouses forms an elegant, cohesive ensemble, while enhancing the individuality of each building. Nos. 18 and 22 are similar in design with full limestone facades, two-story oriels, wide curved stoops and centered entrances. These alternate with Nos. 20 and 24, which display red-brick facades, limestone-quoined window enframements, and entrances set at the western sides. All houses are visually united with ornate wrought-iron railings, coursed limestone ground stories, decorative iron balconies at the fourth and fifth stories, and stone roof cornices. Happily, all of the facades survive largely intact.

The ornately carved wooden doors of No. 18 are balanced by narrow windows on each side. There is much intricate detailing above the projecting entryway—a cartouche with the number 18, foliate carvings, and large console brackets which, together with corbels, support the curved two-story bay. A second cartouche enhances the segmentally-arched pediment above the central parlor windows. Elaborate console brackets carry the ends of the cornice atop the fourth floor.

An iron-and-glass canopy protects the entrance of No. 20. The parlor-floor windows are topped by hoods with guttae and bracketed triangular pediments. Third-story windows have bracketed cornices. As with No. 18, the three-sided oriel is supported by brackets and fanned limestone corbels. A triangular pediment tops the parlor-story windows; within

East to west: 24, 22, 20 and 18 East 94th Street

the tympanum is a human masque. Third-story windows have leaded-glass panes. Above the fourth story is a paneled frieze.

No. 24 is the easternmost house in the row. Its four-story bay curves back to meet the facade line of the other buildings, visually completing the Beaux-Arts quartet. Fluted Ionic columns and Doric pilasters flank the entry; above the stone portico is an iron railing fronting a flush window with keystone and arched pediment. Foliate brackets with guttae support a triangular pediment and cartouche above the parlor-story windows. **HD**

40 East 94th Street
Carnegie Hill Tower
ARCHITECT: Edward V. Giannasca DATE: 1983

Soaring 32 stories above Madison Avenue, this beige-brick apartment tower has an angled facade with oversized windows that wrap around the building's corners. The unusual shape gives it even greater visibility in the center of Carnegie Hill's low-scale Queen Anne buildings to the south, and the remains of the Eighth Regiment Armory to the north. An arched chrome-and-glass canopy shields the entrance. A few steps to the east is another unexpected design feature—the mid-block mews between 93rd and 94th streets. This came about as a result of a controversy between the original developer, H.R. Shapiro, and Carnegie Hill Neighbors: In return for preserving the historic Alamo apartment building at 55 East 93rd Street and creating a public plaza, the developer received a "building density" bonus. Philip Birnbaum and Greene & Partners were the architects for the courtyard, which is paved and landscaped.

64 East 94th Street
ARCHITECT: Jules Lewis   DATE: 1958-60
Constructed of red brick, this Modern six-story apartment building features narrow stone courses at the second and sixth stories. Recessed front facade sections minimize the fire escapes. Attractive sidewalk landscaping flanks a two-step-down canopied entrance.

71 East 94th Street
Hunter College Campus Schools
ARCHITECTS: Morris Ketchum, Jr. & Associates   DATE: 1969-71
1339-1351 Madison Avenue
Squadron A (Eighth Regiment) Armory, west facade
ARCHITECT: John Rochester Thomas   DATE: 1888-90; 1895

The original armory faced Park Avenue; early photographs show crenelated round towers at the 94th and 95th Street corners. The armory was designed for the Eighth Regiment, a volunteer squadron of gentlemen riders known as the New York Hussars (First Dragoons). One of the founders was C.P.H. Gilbert, who would become the architect of the Warburg mansion at Fifth Avenue and 92nd Street, now the Jewish Museum. Plans to fill the entire block between Park and Madison avenues had to be scaled back, and the architect, John Rochester Thomas, redesigned the building to fill just 300 feet west of Park Avenue.

In 1889 the exclusive cavalry unit joined the New York State National Guard and adopted the name Squadron A. By 1893 the group was in need of larger drill space and secured funds to extend the armory to Madison Avenue, with Thomas once again creating the architectural design. The brick structure resembled a medieval French fortress. It was styled after the Chateau Gaillard in Normandy, built by Richard the Lion Hearted. A fantasy of brickmason's virtuosity, with arches, corbels, machicolations and crenelations, the western end of the building featured massive square towers and round turrets connected by a crenelated parapet that stretched the full length of the facade and beneath which are four semi-round sentry boxes. The new drill hall was accessed through a large arched opening on 94th Street, with the central pedestrian entrance located on Madison Avenue.

A plaque on a lower Madison Avenue wall bears the dates 1889-1894 and the motto *"Boutez en Avant"* ("Push to the Front"). When Squadron A went on active duty in 1917, it was recognized as the 105th Machine Gun Battalion, serving at Flanders and Ypres. In 1920 the interior of the earlier armory

on the Park Avenue side was combined with that of the 1895 structure, creating a vast riding ring. It soon became one of New York City's most elite social quarters and recreation areas, used for polo matches, dances, and horse shows.

When the armory was mostly bulldozed to make way for the construction of a new junior high school in 1966, community activists protested and the newly formed New York City Landmarks Preservation Commission intervened, halting further demolition and securing historic designation for the Madison Avenue facade. (The Memorial Gates were also saved, and can be seen in the Church of the Heavenly Rest, at Fifth Avenue and 90th Street.) Today that facade has been integrated into the schoolyard of what

has become the Hunter College Campus Schools, a highly selective K-12 public school in the New York City Board of Education system.

The school designed by Morris Ketchum, Jr. at 71 East 94th Street, is an early example of contextual architecture, echoing the fortress-like quality of the original structure with adaptations of crenelations, turrets, towers and corbeled stairwells, and even narrow slit windows. Between the school and the armory is a sunken park and playground; west of the recreational area are stepped brick bleachers from which to view performances or athletic events. A smaller children's playground for community use is located at the north side. Both playgrounds, as well as the school facades, underwent renovations in 2004. The landmarked Madison Avenue facade and tower interiors are undergoing extensive repair at this writing. **LM**

121-137 East 94th Street
ARCHITECT: F.S. Barus   DATE: 1878-79
This charming row of nine neo-Grec brownstones cascades gently down 94th Street. They were constructed for Duffy & Brothers, who were also developers for the square block of row houses running from Third to Lexington avenues between 94th and 95th streets, known as Hellgate Hill. Once all nine were identical, but only Nos. 125 and 133 have survived with their facades largely intact: They have retained their

stoops leading to paneled-wood doors, transoms and entry surrounds, framed by brownstone-paneled piers and bracketed cornices. The windows of the two lower stories are linked visually with panels below the parlor windows; note the carved flowers on the basement lintels. The ground-level windows of all but No. 121 have iron grilles with a Chinese Chippendale pattern. Six houses retain their bracketed and molded sheet-metal roof cornices. **HD**

130 East 94 Street
ARCHITECT: George F. Pelham   DATE: 1923-24
A dramatic two-story limestone entry enframement distinguishes this otherwise restrained nine-story neo-Georgian apartment building. Set against multi-tone beige brick, two pairs of Ionic pilasters support a dentiled cornice over a smooth entablature decorated with four carved wreaths. The base is further defined by a band of header bricks between two stone band courses that extend the entablature. Stone pilasters beneath a broken-arch pediment flank the round-arched wood-and-glass double doors. The lobby retains an elaborate hexagonal-patterned plaster ceiling.

First-story windows have splayed limestone lintels and raised key-stones. A narrow dentiled cornice runs above the eighth story. The facade is topped by a heavier stone cornice over dentil and egg-and-dart courses, and a brick parapet with balustraded stone sections near the corners, visible only from a distance. **HD**

138 East 94th Street
ARCHITECTS: Neville & Bagge   DATE: 1901-02
Viewed from street level, the rusticated limestone base and the entrance of this seven-story building are imposing, suggesting an earlier grandeur. Renaissance Revival details include round-arched openings at two levels, cartouches, carved brackets and a limestone balustrade at the third story. The four-story midsection is red brick with limestone courses between each story. Some window openings have keyed limestone enframements, while others are embellished with balconettes, splayed stone lintels, keystones or pediments. A metal cornice with scrolled brackets tops the crown section. The Lexington Avenue facade has storefronts and an iron fire escape. **HD**

139 East 94th Street

ARCHITECTS: Boak & Paris   DATE: 1927-28

Designed in neo-Renaissance style, this eleven-story building is of red tapestry brick. The ground level has a rusticated limestone base and a limestone entry enframement with an entablature and carved cornice. Flanking the paneled-wood door are engaged columns and curved, brass-topped railings. The second and third stories are quite grand: Limestone pilasters with foliate capitals frame end bays and support a dentiled entablature that spans the length of the building. Second-story window bays display limestone surrounds with foliate keystones and wrought-iron railings; ninth-story windows are embellished with carved limestone pilasters and balconettes supported by foliate brackets. Above the tenth story runs an elaborate arched frieze and cornice. The crown story has limestone window surrounds and quoins at the corners. A decorative iron railing encloses the penthouse level; an unusually high water tank perches precariously at the north end of the roof. The building's storefront windows on Lexington Avenue have been refaced with rusticated limestone surrounds. Architects Russell M. Boak and Hyman F. Paris designed several other buildings in Carnegie Hill. For contrast, walk a few steps east to 152 East 94th Street to see one of their later efforts. **HD**

152 East 94th Street

ARCHITECTS: Boak & Paris   DATE: 1937

Inventive interpretations of classical elements are evident on this eleven-story Art Deco building. Throughout the red-brick facade, look for decorative brickwork: on window lintels, eleventh-floor blind arches, and frames around recessed street-level lights. Terra-cotta ornaments punctuate the base and top of slender brick piers extending from the second to the ninth stories. More classical elements are seen in Greek key designs on the basement window grilles and above the limestone base. Modern cornices decorate the ninth-story wings and eleventh-story central portions.

Of particular interest is the step-down entry. Brass rails top wrought-iron fences of geometric squares, circles and arrowheads, echoed in brass-framed glass doors with wrought-iron arrows and geometrics. Flanking the doors are diamond-patterned iron lanterns. The fluted entry surround has stone piers topped with Greek key capitals, surmounted with a modern interpretation of the classical broken pediment and urn. Geometric motifs are repeated over the facade lights, in iron railings above the entrance, and in railings around the set-back upper terraces.

157-179 East 94th Street
158-180 East 95th Street
Hellgate Hill
ARCHITECTS: Thom & Wilson
DATE: 1878-80

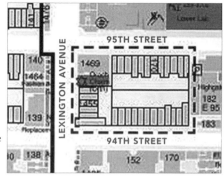

T hese 24 row houses are part of an enclave known today as Hellgate Hill. (The name Hellgate is derived from the Hell Gate brewery between Second and Third avenues, which operated from 1867 until 1935. George Ehret, the founder, tapped the nearby turbulent strait of water in the East River for the name of his flourishing enterprise.) The nearly identical neo-Grec brownstones were part of a square block running from Third to Lexington avenues between 94th and 95th streets and built by the speculative developer Michael Duffy. Thom & Wilson were Duffy's architects for the Lexington Avenue row [see 1449 and 1451-1457 Lexington Avenue] and the cross-street houses as well. Nothing remains of the Third Avenue buildings. The lots on the north end of Lexington Avenue are now occupied by Congregation Orach Chaim and the Renaissance Revival apartment building at the 95th Street corner [see 1459-1461 and 1469 Lexington Avenue]. The facades of most of the 94th and 95th Street houses are surprisingly intact. Many retain their original stoops and their boxy neo-Grec bracketed window trim, and all but one bear their original molded metal roof cornices.

Not visible from the street is a central "companionway" between 94th and 95th streets, leading downhill toward Third Avenue: Staircases connect to many of the houses' rear gardens, providing a unique private greensward, bird sanctuary and play area for the residents' children. Over the years the enclave has been—and continues to be—home to artists, doctors, diplomats and multi-generational families. Not surprisingly, many of the homeowners have forged social bonds as well as those induced by practical concerns. The Hellgate Hill Homeowners Association was formed in 1966 and remains active.

The names of many former residents are well known. On 94th Street, No. 159 was the home of New York City Parks Commissioner August Heckscher, his wife, Claude, and their three sons, from 1949 to 1987. From 1930 to 1954, No. 165 was owned by Carl and Chloe Binger; Dr. Binger's psychiatric testimony at the Chambers-Hiss trial was pivotal. No. 173 was purchased in 1952 by Abstract Expressionist artist Robert Motherwell, who was joined by his second wife, artist Helen Frankenthaler,

West to east: 157, 159, 161, 163, 165, 167, and 169 East 94th Street

in 1957. On 95th Street, Mrs. Cass Gilbert, the wife of the architect, once owned Nos. 160 and 162. Prior to 1951, No. 164 was the residence of Mr. and Mrs. Ellsworth Bunker; Mr. Bunker was a diplomat who served seven presidents and was United States Ambassador to the Organization of American States. No. 174 was the home of the film director Elia Kazan and his wife, Frances. No. 176 was purchased in 1956 by Fritz and Jeanne Bultman, artists and stained glass sculptors; they were already friends of Motherwell as well as of Abstract Expressionist artists Linda and Giorgio Cavallon, who lived next door at No. 178.

157-179 East 94th Street: Hellgate Hill

Nos. 157 and 159 have lost their stoops and much of their upper-window trim. Unique to the group are string courses forming sills under third-story windows; the parlor-story windows of No. 157 are recessed under arches. The stoop remains at No. 161, but not the window trim; in 2007 a set-back fourth story was added as well as a non-functioning garage (without curb cuts).

The overhanging window lintels of Nos. 163-171 have been carefully preserved; stoops remain at all but Nos. 165 and 167. The latter added a fourth story with an eyebrow roof line in 2008. Note the rosettes and triangular pediments over the original parlor-story entrances of Nos. 169 and 171. Only No. 173 has been drastically altered: After a divorce in 1970, Helen Frankenthaler redesigned the house, resulting in the present austere gray-stucco facade, projecting aluminum-framed bay and schematic cornice. Stoops and most ornamentation remain or have been restored at Nos. 175 and 177. All original detailing except the stoop and cornice have been stripped from No. 179, which at this writing offers modest hostel facilities.

East to west: 168, 170, 172, 174, 176, 178, and 180 East 95th Street

158-180 East 95th Street: Hellgate Hill

Stoops, rosettes, lintels and other architectural elements are evident at Nos. 158 and 162. No. 160 has been stripped of all decor. There are no stoops at the next six houses, although most have attractively planted areaways and historic trim at the the upper windows. Note the basement-level archways at Nos. 166 and 168, echoing those on East 94th Street. Stone pilasters flank the parlor-story windows of No. 170 and lower-level openings of No. 174. Best preserved are Nos. 176 and 178; both display their original stoops, carved rosettes, paneled doors and triangular entry pediments. Of particular interest are the incised brownstone blocks carrying the iron newels and fence fronting the areaway of No. 178. The upper stories of No. 180 are intact; next to the ground-level entry a greenhouse-like projection has been added.

170 East 94th Street
ARCHITECT: George G. Miller   DATE: 1928
Facing north instead of south, this six-story apartment building is a mirror image of its backyard neighbor at 181 East 93rd Street.

183 East 94th Street
ARCHITECT: Charles Baxter   DATE: 1877
Residents enter this five-story Italianate-style building via a wrought-iron fence, gate and rear garden; the high red-brick posts are capped with pyramidal stones. Its brightly-painted red-brick facade displays jaunty white stone trim. An auxiliary entrance has elaborate brackets supporting a paneled fascia board with scroll-sawn ornamentation; above is a triangular pediment with a scroll-sawn shield. On the upper floors, all windows have eared lintels, decorative cornices and bracketed sills.

3 East 95th Street
Originally Marion (Mrs. Amory S.) Carhart house

ARCHITECTS: Horace Trumbauer   DATE: 1913-21

Zivkovic Associates Architects and John Simpson & Partners 2005

With its elegant 18th-century-inspired classical details, No. 3 is one of New York's finest examples of a Louis XVI-style house. Mrs. Amory S. Carhart, the widow of a prominent banker and railroad entrepreneur from Tuxedo Park, commissioned the house but never lived in it because of her death in 1919; the property was sold to Charles H. Mackay of Roslyn, NY. It was resold in 1928 to Mabel Drury, who also bought the lot next door, which had belonged to Edith Fabbri, whose mansion at No. 7 is now House of the Redeemer. In 1937, the Lycée Francais de New York purchased No. 3 for use as a school. Twenty years later, the school bought the No. 5 lot and built a modernist extension designed by Henri Durieux. (The No. 5 building was demolished after both lots were sold in 2000.)

No. 3, clad in limestone, is divided horizontally into three sections: a one-story rusticated base; a two-story main section; and a mansard roof. Three bays, each of which contains a tall arch, emphasize the verticality of the structure; one arch frames a central doorway, which exhibits ornate decoration and rich carving. A balcony adorned with a wrought-iron railing in the Louis XVI style sweeps across the second story; it is carried on large foliate brackets, which "dangle like earrings," writes architectural historian Francis Morrone.

Between the second and third floors are carved stone panels exhibiting a symmetrical design of cornucopias, high-stemmed urns, and scrolls; a central panel bears a wreath. Tall, arched French windows punctuate the second floor; above, square-headed windows have eared enframements. Wrought-iron window guards display a second guilloche pattern alternating large and small circles. Three copper-framed dormer windows are set in the mansard roof behind a modillioned cornice, set back by parapet-like extensions of panels below.

When the Lycée sold Nos. 3 and 5 to developers, plans had to be approved by the New York City Landmarks Preservation Commission. The resulting design replaces the old Lycée extension (and eliminates the No. 5 address, as the combined buildings now form a condominium). The limestone-clad structure is the work of British architect John Simpson, a noted classicist and architect of the Queen's Gallery at Buckingham Palace, working in concert with New York-based Zivkovic Connolly Associates. Seamlessly merging with its neighbor, its facade is a faultless example of restrained classicism. Rusticated limestone blocks form voussoirs over

three arched openings on the ground levels, echoing—but not mimicking—the Carhart mansion design. A garland adorns the western entry; a large iron lantern hangs over the wood-paneled eastern door, which is centered with a double-height multi-pane window. At the midsection, three French doors are fronted with iron railings ornamented with acanthus buds and urns. Spandrels above the hooded openings are carved with urns and ribbons, punctuated with rosettes. At the roof line is a slightly projecting limestone cornice with silhouetted rondels above. Also noteworthy is the finely detailed eastern facade overlooking the courtyard of 7 East 95th Street. **HD LM** (Only the original No. 3 building is landmarked).

4 East 95th Street
ARCHITECT: J.E.R. Carpenter   DATE: 1923-24
Of the twelve buildings in Carnegie Hill designed by Carpenter, this nine-story neo-Georgian structure is surely among the most inventive in his use of classical details. The facade is of brick, laid in Flemish bond, with limestone and terra-cotta trim. Framing the entryway are fluted pilasters with acanthus capitals, topped with foliate brackets and a balustrade. At either end of the two-story base are limestone pilasters supporting a full-width (100-foot!) entablature, embellished with rosettes, diamonds and—look closely—Victorian ladies' heads. Below, limestone quoins and brick piers with Doric capitals define window bays; spandrels have elongated interpretations of the

classical Greek key design.

The entire facade is divided into the usual three sections, here joined subtly by four double brick piers. The eighth and ninth stories are quite amazing: Seventeen dwarf columns form balustrades at the end sections; in the center, a paneled band is capped with a string course on which rest nine elaborate terra-cotta pilasters set in shallow niches between the windows. A pitched slate roof has copper-clad dormers and recessed windows, above which can be glimpsed greenery from penthouse terraces. **HD**

7 East 95th Street
Originally Edith and Ernesto Fabbri house, now the House of the Redeemer
ARCHITECTS: Egisto Fabbri, Grosvenor Atterbury   DATE: 1915-17

This elegant five-story brick-and-limestone mansion that is known both as the Fabbri house and the House of the Redeemer was built on an L-shaped plan in the style of an Italian Renaissance palazzo. The house is unusual in Carnegie Hill in that it has an adjoining courtyard, which is guarded by an elaborate wrought-iron railing and gate displaying the Fabbri coat of arms—an arm holding a hammer. Classical urns top the supporting stone pillars.

In 1900 Count Ernesto Fabbri, who came from a well-to-do Italian family, married Edith Vanderbilt Shepard, a great-granddaughter of Commodore Cornelius Vanderbilt. Two years later Mrs. Fabbri bought the property at 7 East 95th Street, which also included the lot next door at No. 5. She sold the western site to the architect Goodhue Livingston in 1914, with the agreement that portions of their adjacent front yards would be left open to furnish air and light; hence the courtyard and garden fence at the west. Livingston's plans to build a mansion never materialized.

Evidence suggests that the basic design of the Fabbri mansion was the work of the brother of Count Fabbri, Egisto Fabbri, a painter and early patron of Cézanne, and that Grosvenor Atterbury was retained to carry out the plan. A two-story section containing the entrance hall continues

along the main section to the rear wing. The entryway, flanked by rusticated pilasters, is set within stone voussoirs framing huge wooden doors that are capped with a wrought-iron fanlight and balustraded balcony. To the right are pedimented windows flanked with pilasters with shell-like capitals. Round-arched leaded-glass windows with fanlights run along the second story, above which are small rectangular openings; the attic story is punctuated by stone-trimmed bull's-eye windows. A modillioned cornice crowns the facade.

The Fabbris were dedicated collectors of Italian Renaissance antiques and many examples remain in the house. They were divorced in 1923, but Mrs Fabbri continued to live and entertain lavishly at No. 7 until 1949, when she donated it and its furnishings to an Episcopal retreat which she created, the House of the Redeemer, setting up a trust fund for its maintenance. It is now nondenominational. The museum-like public rooms have recently been refurbished, making the space especially attractive for social gatherings and group functions; chamber music concerts are open to the public. Especially notable is the second-floor library with splendid woodwork and a frescoed ceiling dating from the fifteenth century, said to be part of the famous Ducal Palace in Urbino. **HD LM**

10-20 East 95th Street
ARCHITECT: Henry Anderson   DATE: 1890

East to west: 20, 18, 16 and 14 East 95th Street

Their long, low stoops, limestone wing walls and stone terraces make this set of six Renaissance Revival houses unique in Carnegie Hill—and, perhaps, the city. Designed for developer P.J. Quirk, these five-story limestone-faced houses have withstood the test of time and are still a delight to the eye. Common to all six buildings are entrances with beaded egg-and-dart enframements, foliate keystones over doors and ground-level windows, and fluted pilasters with foliate capitals supporting triglyph-decorated entablatures at the second story. Third-story windows have molded surrounds and cornices; fifth-story windows are flanked with engaged columns or small pilasters. Swags and wreaths embellish the bracketed metal cornices.

Nos. 10 and 16 are two feet wider than the others; their three-sided oriels are surmounted with parapets that echo the triglyph-and-bezant (flat circle) motif. Be sure to note the pair of angels carved on the underside of the oriel at No. 10, perhaps in defiance of the fire-breathing dragons on the foliate portico of No. 14. Nos. 18 and 20, which are mirror images, feature entrances with fluted columns supporting a bezant-adorned entablature. **HD**

17 and 19 East 95th Street
ARCHITECTS: Neville & Bagge   DATE: 1898-99

These twin six-story buildings, each a substantial 35 feet wide, were
designed in the Renaissance Revival style for builder James Kilpatrick.
Curves abound: The undulating facades swell at their end bays, which
frame curved windows; a wide sheet-metal cornice has curved foliate
brackets, modillions and swags. Arched windows at the second story retain
their original egg-and-dart side rails; and the stoops have curved stone

cheek walls. Identical entryways are flanked
with fluted columns and pilasters, and are
topped with Ionic capitals that support
foliate friezes and iron railings. More details
include an undulating scrolled and dentiled
course above the fifth story, and windows
with pediments, splayed lintels or keystones.
In spite of the abundance of decoration and
movement, the limestone base and mellow
beige brick of the upper stories unify the
design, projecting an overall impression
that is serene and timeless. **HD**

22-28 East 95th Street
ARCHITECT: Thomas Graham   DATE 1899-1901

This handsome quartet of Renaissance Revival row houses was designed by
Thomas Graham, who was also the architect of five row houses at 6-14 East
92nd Street and the apartment-hotel, the Hotel Graham, at 22 East 89th
Street (now part of Saint David's School). While not an exact a-b-b-a
pattern, the buildings share many design characteristics. The cream-
colored brick-and-limestone facades break the severity of the south side of
the street with curved corners, oriels and a continuous sill and cornice
turning inward to the west and outward to the east. The curves are functional
as well as aesthetic: Residents of each house capture a glimpse of Central Park.

On a rise from west to east, the stoops are progressively shorter; a
recently constructed ramp connects the middle two at the top step level.
Unusually tall wrought-iron fences mark the entryways; those at Nos. 24,
26 and 28 are topped with lanterns. Most of the basement and first-floor
openings have historic iron grilles. Nos. 22 and 28 have foliate keystones
over the first-story openings, which are topped with an intermediate
cornice. Nos. 24 and 26 feature double-height oriels at the second and
third stories, resting on carved (but not identical) corbels. Be sure to note
the blustery gentleman gazing from under the oriel at No. 24.

No. 22 was converted in 1952 from a single-family residence to a

two-unit dwelling with a doctor's office; subsequently it was transformed into a school building for the Ecole Française, later the Churchill School, which shared a lot with 19 East 94th Street. In 2000 the Ramakrishna-Vivekananda Center, which for 60 years had owned 17 East 94th Street, purchased the back-to-back lots and buildings. In 2002 No. 22 was resold, to be converted once again to a private residence.

No. 24, converted to a private elementary school in 1943, has housed the Diller-Quaile Music School since 1955. Experiencing a surge in enrollment in the 1980s, Diller-Quaile was seeking a more space when No. 26 became available. They purchased No. 26 in 1992. Although extensive interior alterations were made, including expanded studio space and a new recital hall, the historic character of the facade was preserved— brightened by cheerful red doors. No. 28 was recently restored to a private residence. **HD**

27 and 29 East 95th Street and 1356 Madison Avenue
The Woodbury and The Elmscourt
ARCHITECT: Frederick Jacobson   DATE: 1898-99

This freestanding pair of neo-Renaissance apartment buildings, serenely guarding the northwest corner of 95th Street and Madison Avenue, has paired exterior details that have happily survived more than 100 years. On each, a two-story rusticated limestone base supports four stories of blended tan ironspot Roman brick, with stone quoins at the corners. Most windows have historic one-over-one double-hung wood sash and are topped with carved keystones. Bracketed sheet-metal cornices with modillions and a molded string course top the sixth stories. Linking the two on Madison

Avenue is a wrought-iron fence and gate enclosing a shared courtyard. The entrance to the Madison Avenue building, the Elmscourt, has paired pilasters and a carved surround with a cartouche. The transom is flanked with handsome metal lanterns. Its side-street counterpart, the Woodbury, has a somewhat more elaborate projecting portico: Paired Corinthian columns and pilasters support a carved frieze, balustrade and paired windows with carved lintels. Additional pairs of small pedimented windows supported by corbels flank the entrance. **HD**

53, 57, and 61 East 95th Street
ARCHITECTS: Rouse & Sloan   DATE: 1905
Rising six stories above a limestone base, this trio of
tan-brick Renaissance Revival buildings displays a
sturdy, weathered charm. Porticos are supported with
blocked and curved brackets; the ground-level rustication forms voussoirs over the windows. Cornices
run across the second, fifth and attic stories. Window
pairs on the third to fifth stories have double-brack-
eted sills and splayed lintels with keystones. Rising
at the building extremes are four-story piers capped
with foliate hoods. The terminal metal cornices
project above a dentiled course and block frieze.

112 and 114 East 95th Street
See 1213, 1215, and 1217 Park Avenue.

95th Street between Park and Lexington Avenues: Goat Hill

Goat Hill is thought to have been the name of this area years ago,
presumably because goats grazed on what was then land too hilly
for farming. This block is unique architecturally in Carnegie
Hill, and on the Upper East Side, in that it is intact; its unified groups of
houses display both variety and continuity. All of the houses on the south
side, and some on the north side, reflect the whimsical Queen Anne style
that combined classical elements freely with eclectic architectural styles, such as Dutch and Japanese; those across the
street display sturdy Romanesque Revival characteristics.
The facades mix smooth and decorative brickwork, rough
and smooth stone, and tiny window panes and doors with
multiple panels, resulting in rich textural effects. Many
retain their original stoops and bays. Projections vary,
from three-sided oriels to brick corbels and Dutch gables. Although many
details were the result of mass production, the builders were able to
choose from a variety of materials such as terra-cotta blocks, decorative
masques, intricate ironwork and brick in multiple colors.

The houses were constructed in four groups by three speculative builders.
The south side came first, followed by 1213-1217 Park Avenue that wraps
around the corner to include Nos. 112 and 114. The north side was the last
to be developed, and is divided into two equal groups. Most of the houses
were owner-occupied, mainly by German or Austrian immigrants in the
textile trade. The relatively small size of the buildings—most are 15 1/2 to 18
feet wide—meant that they were less likely to be subdivided into apartments,

and by the late 1940s they began to attract a theatrical and artistic group. Al Hirschfeld, the caricaturist, lived at No. 122 (his salmon-pink house received a cultural medallion from the Historic Landmarks Preservation Center in 2006); Mark Rothko, the Abstract Expressionist painter, lived at No. 118; Karl Schrag, the painter, at No. 127; Betty Comden, the Broadway lyricist, at No. 117; June Havoc, the actress, at No. 115; Vincent Sardi, the restaurateur, at No. 133; Maria Riva, Marlene Dietrich's daughter, at No. 116; and Alfred Drake, the musical theater star, at No. 132.

The Goat Hill Neighborhood Association has been continually active since its formation in 1968. Goat Hill represents what many feel is the essence of Carnegie Hill today: an enclave of surviving history and architectural treasures rarely seen in Manhattan.

East to west: 134, 132, 130, 128, and 126 East 95th Street

116-138 East 95th Street: Goat Hill
ARCHITECT: C. Abbott French & Co.   DATE: 1887-88

The twelve row houses on the south side were built by William J. and John P.C. Walsh. Each house is individualistic, exhibiting Queen Anne elements—patterned brickwork, odd roof lines with curves, corbels, gables, and peaks inset with terra-cotta decoration, and relief carvings. Many share common features such as broad, round-arched openings and sheet-metal-and-wood oriel windows. Four of the row houses retain their sandstone box stoops. The facades are either red-brick and brownstone, or buff-brick and sandstone. Satyr faces range from horned, grinning Satans on the keystones of Nos. 118, 120 and 126, to a Zeus-like head on No. 122, to a leafy terra-cotta monster at No. 124, to more benign faces set in rondels on Nos. 130 and 138. A curious oval window with small panes perches above the entry of No. 134; No. 138 has a great oriel with twelve-pane transoms and curved sides, bordered by checkerboard bricks. **HD**

West to east: 115, 117, 119, 121, 123, and 125East 95th Street

115-127 East 95th Street: Goat Hill
ARCHITECT: Louis Entzer, Jr.   Date: 1891-92

This first group on the north side of the block was built by developer
Francis Joseph Schnugg and his wife, Carrie. Eight houses, now seven, were
designed in Queen Anne style as mirror-image pairs. (No. 113, the twin of
No. 115, was demolished in 1926 for the construction of 1225 Park Avenue.)
Integrated relief stonework runs along the face of No. 119, traverses its
doorway and that of its brownstone neighbor at No. 121, then continues
along that facade; the pattern is echoed at Nos. 123 and 125, although the
brownstone facades vary. The stoops of these pairs share a common center
handrail. To break the rhythm, Nos. 117 and 127, two houses of the same
design but faced with smooth and rock-faced limestone, are placed to separate
the pairs, an interesting architectural device. All of the houses have three-
sided sheet-metal oriels with lively patterns on the undersides; all retain
their original stoops and sheet-metal cornices. A further integrating element
is the original ironwork that separates the areaways from the sidewalk. **HD**

129–143 East 95th Street: Goat Hill
ARCHITECTS: Frank Wennemer   DATE: 1889-90
            No. 133: Clinton, Russell & Clinton   1932

The second group of eight, also built for the Schnuggs, is more varied in
style, decoration and degree of preservation. The houses were originally
designed as pairs, with neo-Grec and Romanesque elements. The basement
and parlor levels were of stone, with the upper stories alternating tan and
red brick with brownstone accents. All but three of the stoops have been

removed; however, the remaining railings and iron newels are original. No.
129 was stripped of its facade in the 1930s but it has since been restored; the
restoration included decorative panels below the parlor- and third-story
windows. Nos. 131 and 135 are similar, with stone cornices decorated with
garlands; note the fire-breathing creatures guarding No. 135. No. 133 was
remodeled in 1932 by Charles Kenneth Clinton, of Clinton, Russell and
Clinton, for James Ripley, the owner of a dock-building company. Clinton
added a mansard roof and a brick facade that projects to the lot line, with
a street-level entrance. Carved friezes embellish the parapet of No. 137.
An oculus window at the attic story of No. 139 is capped with a gabled stone
cornice. No. 141 has added a story and removed its cornice altogether. The
red-brick-and-brownstone facade of No. 143 is beautifully intact; its eastern
bay projects to the stoop line, visually terminating the historic row. **HD**

140 East 95th Street (1466-1472 Lexington Avenue)

ARCHITECTS: Springsteen & Goldhammer   DATE: 1929

Unique in Carnegie Hill, this six-story, tan textured-brick building exhibits
Mediterranean and medieval elements that surprise at every level. The
entrance on 95th Street is framed by pairs of twisted stone columns with
elongated acanthus-leaf capitals supporting Gothic-carved, dentiled impost
blocks. Over the glazed-wood door is a trefoil arch with keystone; a dentil-
supported molding finishes the upper edges of the stepped stone enframement. At the second story, corner windows have stone surrounds with triangle
motifs, topped with shields and peaked finials. Brick-and-stone spandrels,
peaked at the center, separate third- and fourth-story windows. The building
is guarded by stuccoed towers at the corner bays.

For the best view of the upper facade, step
across Lexington Avenue. Between the towers, a
crenellated cornice tops fifth-story windows;
pitched roofs with red tiles project over the sixth
story. The corner tower has stone balconies with
wrought-iron railings; spiral columns, similar to
those at the entrance, divide the arched openings
of the loggia. Capping the tower is a red pyramidal
roof and gold finial. There are two secondary
towers: That on Lexington terminates in an
asymmetrical gable, also tiled, while the one at
the west end of 95th Street includes a chimney.
Completing the odd mixture are stone waterspouts
projecting from the building corners. **HD**

158-180 East 95th Street, Hellgate Hill See 157-179 East 94th Street

7 East 96th Street
Originally Ogden Codman, Jr. house; now the Manhattan Country School
ARCHITECT: Ogden Codman, Jr.
DATE 1912-13

The 1989 New York City Landmarks Preservation Commission plaque on the limestone facade of this four- (now five-) story building reads: "This 1912-13 house, based on 18th century French architecture, was designed by Ogden Codman, Jr., for his own use. Codman was a talented architect and decorator, who created elegant structures noted for their harmonious scale and lack of excessive opulence. The building is distinguished by wrought-iron balconies, dormer windows, and a porte cochère leading to a courtyard and garage." The building was modeled after a Parisian townhouse or *hôtel particulier* in the style of the early Louis XV period. Codman had originally planned a group of similar neo-French Renaissance houses on the north side of the street at Nos. 7, 9, 11, 13 and 15; only Nos. 7 and 15 were built. (Note: The garage of No. 7 originally had a turntable that would turn a vehicle and point it toward the street, eliminating the difficulty of backing out.) The townhouse was subsequently owned by Mrs. William Moore who enlarged the penthouse in 1927; a corporation, the president of which was Princess Alexis Guy Oblensky, during the 1940s and '50s; and the Nippon Club in the late 1950s. Gus and Marty Trowbridge bought and restored the house in 1966, adapting it to accommodate the Manhattan Country School.

A quintet of granite bollards lines the low granite base. Windows at the rusticated ground story are embellished with wrought-iron grilles. Garlands, now weathered, link stone brackets with bezants and guttae supporting a delicate wrought-iron balcony. Tall round-arched openings at the *piano nobile* have French doors with fanlight transoms, scrolled keystones and bottle-green curved shutters. Beneath the shuttered third-story windows are simplified limestone swags. Round-headed dormers with unusually graceful enframements rise above the modillioned limestone cornice. An iron fence fronts the slate mansard roof; another fence tops the set-back penthouse. **HD LM**

8 East 96th Street

ARCHITECT: Rosario Candela   DATE: 1927-28

This reddish-purple-brick neo-Renaissance apartment house rises fifteen stories. The building rewards careful scrutiny: Much, but not all, visual interest is concentrated at the two-story base. Its three entrances (Nos. 6, 8 and 10) and central bays are set within double-story arched surrounds, dramatized by wide rope moldings. At ground level, paneled-wood doors are framed with terra-cotta panels ornamented with vines, urns and rams' horns. Octagonal wrought-iron lanterns flank the central entrance, which

is guarded from above by terra-cotta lions' heads. At the second story are tripartite windows; those within the arches are capped with brick-encircled Tudor roses. End-bay windows are framed with rope surrounds and foliate lintels. Double rows of quoin-like bricks extend the full height of the facade. The cornice has been replaced with a rebuilt parapet, which has retained original carved panels at both ends. **HD**

9 East 96th Street

ARCHITECTS: Gronenberg & Leuchtag   DATE: 1926

This fifteen-story tan-brick apartment house is one of four in Carnegie Hill designed by this architectural team (the others are at 108 East 91st Street, 1230 and 1235 Park Avenue), and displays a combination of neo-Medieval and neo-Renaissance ornament. The main entrance of No. 9 is surrounded with foliate forms and rope coils, set below a dentil band topped with an acanthus-leaf molding. Historic octagonal lanterns flank the multi-pane wood doors. Above a simple band course are pairs of double-height arched windows, richly ornamented with terra-cotta surrounds and cast-stone engaged columns. Single windows are set within eared lintels and quoins; between the openings are small terra-cotta panels. A grand cornice of acanthus leaves and dentils separates the third story from the building's midsection.

 Third-story windows have narrow iron balconies; decorative cast-stone balconies project from the seventh, ninth, and thirteenth stories. All sills have small dentils. Above the thirteenth story are more pairs of double-height arched windows, echoing (but not duplicating) those below; note the carved hood moldings, rope-coiled engaged columns and large rosette spandrels between arches. The facade terminates with an arched frieze and a stone cornice. **HD**

12 East 96th Street
Originally Robert L. Livingston house, now La Scuola d'Italia Gugliemo Marconi
ARCHITECT: Ogden Codman, Jr.   DATE: 1916

This narrow Beaux-Arts townhouse bears characteristics similar to those at Nos. 7 and 15 across the street, designed by the same architect. It was built for the banker, broker and active clubman Robert L. Livingston. After his death in 1925, his wife, who was related to Mrs. I. Townsend Burden, another affluent Carnegie Hill resident, continued to live at No. 12 until it was purchased in 1939 by the Emerson School. Since 1991 it has housed La Scuola d'Italia Gugliemo Marconi, the only Italian/American school in North America.

The five-story building (plus two additional stories at the rear, barely visible from the street) is of limestone which is rusticated at ground level and along both sides. Notable are the graceful fruit garlands beneath each window sill and draped beside keystones under the second-story balcony, which is supported by large consoles. A wrought-iron railing fronts the round-arched windows at the *piano nobile;* wood casements with transoms are used throughout. Above the modillioned stone cornice rises a slate mansard roof, from which project segmentally-arched dormers with verdigris trim. **HD**

14 East 96th Street
ARCHITECTS: Levin Deliso White Songer   DATE: 1981

Located in the center of the block, this 21-story "sliver" building, just 22 feet wide, replaced a brick townhouse and caused considerable concern among neighborhood groups, ultimately leading to the enactment of New York City's "sliver law." Designed in a Modernistic style, the white-brick ground story is recessed; sidelights flank the metal-and-glass entry. Ribbon-like windows pierce the painted-concrete facade. The east side, visible from a distance, has a bold pattern of concrete-outlined brick rectangles. **HD**

15 East 96th Street
Originally Lucy Drexel Dahlgren house
ARCHITECT: Ogden Codman, Jr.   DATE: 1915-16

Designed to be one of a group of complementary buildings at 17 and 12 East 96th Street, this four-story limestone townhouse was created for socially prominent Lucy Drexel Dahlgren. According to architectural historian Henry Hope Reed, the inspiration for the elegantly restrained

neo-French Renaissance exterior was a house on Rue Sainte-Catherine in
Bordeaux. The Dahlgren house was later owned by Pierre Cartier, the jeweler;
in 1945 it was sold to the nearby Church of St. Francis de Sales for use as a
convent. In 1981 it returned to private ownership.

Three segmentally-arched openings are
surrounded with rusticated limestone. The
carved, paneled doorway is reached through a
porte cochère that opens onto an interior courtyard. (The well-preserved interior has been
described as "stately" and includes an octagonal
dining room.) Stone brackets support a shallow
balcony with a wrought-iron railing at the
central pedimented window. The windows in
the side bays are separated by carved panels. All
windows on the *piano nobile* have French doors
and multi-pane transoms. A modillioned
limestone cornice sets off the attic story, which
has three segmentally-arched dormers framed
by limestone coping. **HD LM**

16-24 East 96th Street
The Queenston
ARCHITECTS: Clinton & Russell   DATE: 1905-06
This six-story Renaissance Revival apartment building was originally
planned for 25 flats; the first-story apartment on the Madison Avenue
side was converted to two stores in 1928.

The dark-red-brick facade is enlivened by a two-story rusticated
limestone base, limestone pilasters marking the end bays, and a limestone-
faced central section on 96th Street. Stone banding and window surrounds
and stone lintels and sills also enrich the facades. Clustered stone brackets

at the sheet-metal cornice form
capitals for the limestone-and-
brick pilasters that separate the pairs
of windows. Two bays retain historic
fluted mullions. Some upper-floor
windows have balconettes with
wrought-iron railings. The main
entrance has a grand limestone
enframement of engaged Doric columns on granite plinths flanking an
arched opening with carved spandrels. A glazed double-leaf wood door is
surrounded by sidelights and a multi-pane transom; above is a segmentally-
arched pediment and a wood-framed tripartite window. **HD**

17 East 96th Street
ARCHITECTS: Sugarman, Hess & Berger   DATE: 1923-24

Neo-Renaissance ornament, concentrated at the base and crown sections, characterizes this fifteen-story apartment building. Above the two-story stone base, pairs of pilasters define the central bays and entryway and support an entablature containing blocks of guttae. A modified Greek key motif tops second-story windows. Circular spandrels between windows and pilasters are carved with winged classical heads; above the glazed-wood doors is a low-relief panel depicting a shield, garlands and ribbons. Classical profiles can be spotted on vertical panels above.

The austere midsection of the textured brown-brick facade is divided into two-story sections by molded band courses underscored with vertical bricks; restrained embellishments can be seen in third-story window surrounds. Interest revives above the thirteenth story: Pilasters support a band course that projects at the central window to form a shallow balcony. Similar pilasters appear at the attic story, where they flank a rusticated central arch. All windows on 96th Street have replacement double-hung sash. The east and west elevations are faced with the same brick, and banding at every two stories also echoes the facade. **HD**

21 East 96th Street
ARCHITECTS: H. Thomas O'Hara Architects & Barry Rice   DATE: 2005

With a nod to its historic surroundings, this eleven-story red-brick-and-limestone building displays neo-Classical elements in a Postmodern format. Broad arches at the entry side are echoed in the duplex water-tower housing; all arches have vestigial keystones. The series of two-story grooved limestone window surrounds, enframing complex sets of six panes in four sizes, lend a sense of verticality and dignity to the narrow building. The condominium has just one apartment per floor, as in traditional pre-war buildings.

49 East 96th Street
ARCHITECT: Thomas W. Lamb   DATE: 1929-30

Designed by an architect best known for his theater designs, this nineteen-story apartment house represents the Art Deco period both in its exterior details and its circular lobby. The double-story entrance surround of lapped stone is accented, above the doorway, with diagonally carved geometrics and a rondel. The diagonal motif repeats itself as bracing on street-level wrought-iron grilles at the windows, and is echoed once again on the iron-and-glass door. Horizontal stone banding frames the windows on the first four stories.

The fifth story marks the start of a classic Art Deco ziggurat effect, where seven central windows feature half-round balconettes forming visual column bases. From this floor to the seventeenth, the central window bays are slightly recessed and floors are separated by decorative brick spandrels. The impression created is of vertical lines soaring upward, to terminate with projecting piers at the top two stories. Setbacks occur progressively at the fifteen, seventeenth and eighteenth stories. A tiered vertical block forms a stone spire rising above the parapet.

Original tenants of the building included Alfred Barr, the founding director of the Museum of Modern Art, and one of the penthouses was briefly the home of television newscaster Geraldo Rivera.

50 East 96th Street
Woodward Hall
ARCHITECT: George F. Pelham DATE 1905-06

The tan-brick facade of this six-story Renaissance Revival apartment house rises above a one-story rusticated limestone base; it was altered in 1929 by the firm of Schwartz & Gross to convert the ground-floor apartments to stores. The off-center main entrance features an arched opening with a

double row of rusticated voussoirs; the carved entry surround is embellished with ribbon-wrapped acanthus leaves. Massive scrolled brackets support a balustraded stone balcony above. Rusticated brick pilasters define the building extremes and divide the facade into single and double bays, creating a pronounced vertical impression in spite of its boxy shape. Eared stone lintels over all windows accent the darker monotone facade, which is further ornamented with mid-story panels carved with leaves and cartouches. Above the fifth story, windows are arched with keystones; a secondary cornice announces the crown story. A sheet-metal frieze and its rusted cornice complete the facade. **HD**

53-55 and 57-59 East 96th Street
ARCHITECT: George F. Pelham   DATE: 1906
At only six stories high, this matched pair of neo-Federal and Renaissance Revival-style apartment houses lends light and informality to this busy cross street. The building complex is balanced by another Pelham apartment house, the Van Cortlandt at 1240 Park Avenue, providing symmetry (intentional?) along the north side of 96th Street. The first stories are clad in smooth limestone with the brick remainder alternating gray headers and red stretchers laid in Flemish bond. A low stoop flanked by short square pillars announces the identical main entrances, surmounted by large foliate brackets supporting a heavy lintel. Beyond the utilitarian glass doors, the original plaster frieze and moldings remain, as well as classical columns in the small lobby areas. Limestone belt courses and paneled window enframements delineate the second and sixth floors. Other windows have eared lintels with ornamented keystones. The roof line is finished with a large black sheet-metal cornice and dentil molding.

60 East 96th Street
ARCHITECT: Emery Roth
DATE: 1927-28
Anchoring the south side of the block between Madison and Park avenues are two similar neo-Renaissance buildings, Nos. 60 and 70—so similar, in fact, that one might (incorrectly) attribute them to the same architect. Of beige brick set in common bond style, the end bay sections of both buildings have horizontal brick banding above the second story. Both use sets of double-height, triple windows at the upper stories, and broken pediments at the roof lines. Both have sixteen stories plus a penthouse. And both draw abundantly upon escutcheons as design motifs.

This building was among Emery Roth's last in Carnegie Hill. The grand two-story entry section is of limestone. Wide rope moldings frame wood-and-glass double doors, around which are floral carvings, escutcheons and guttae. The numeral 60 is flanked by carvings of marine creatures. Rising above is an urn set in a niche and a triangular pediment. The second-story window pairs are topped with round arches and rosettes. Centered on the third story is a flamboyant terra-cotta escutcheon. More escutcheons are visible on panels between arched triple windows at the fourteenth and fifteenth stories, which are divided by spiral-engaged pillars echoing the door moldings. Crown-story windows at the building extremes have balconettes supported by scrolled brackets, topped with broken triangular pediments and posts carrying large spherical blossoms.

65 East 96th Street
The Gatsby
ARCHITECT: George F. Pelham DATE: 1924

The north side of 96th Street between Madison and Park avenues boasts five distinctive apartment houses—49, 53-55, 57-59, and 65 East 96th Street, and 1240 Park Avenue— from three architectural eras, best viewed in the glow of late-afternoon sun. Rising fifteen stories between Renaissance Revival buildings designed some twenty years earlier by George F. Pelham, No. 65 exhibits the restrained neo-Renaissance details prevalent in the 1920s.

Two pairs of double-story fluted limestone pilasters flank the entryway; above the projecting dentil-lined cornice are classical urns. Over the recessed wood-and-glass door is another dentil row and cornice, topped with a limestone cartouche. More Renaissance details can be seen in the carved spandrels and elaborate curved grilles on the first story, and foliate brackets supporting a broad limestone balustrade above the eighth story. Rising from a stone base, the reddish-brown-brick facade has double rows of quoins, which are of limestone on the two-story base section and projecting bricks on the remaining stories. Band courses top the second, fifth and thirteenth stories. At the crown section, windows have balustrades, carved limestone surrounds, dentils and molded lintels. A final row of dentils runs beneath the roof cornice.

Yes, it's named for *The Great Gatsby*. No, neither he nor his creator ever lived here but, according to the doorman, F. Scott Fitzgerald's son did (actually, his daughter, Scottie) and that accounts for the building's name, which is a recent addition.

70 East 96th Street
ARCHITECT: Rosario Candela   DATE: 1928-29
Bearing striking similarities to its next-door neighbor [see 60 East 96th Street], but with 25% fewer units, this sixteen-story-plus-penthouse building was designed by the Sicilian architect famous for his spacious apartment layouts. The building decor can be characterized as neo-Renaissance with

medieval accents. The entry is very elaborate: Wood-and-glass double doors are framed with limestone panels and triple rows of moldings, topped with terra-cotta acanthus leaves and an escutcheon. Above are more carvings, side posts and an egg-and-dart molding surrounding another escutcheon. Street-level windows have terra-cotta foliate hoods with centered escutcheons; the shield motif is repeated in wrought-iron window grilles. Nestled just below the second-story dentil course are—look carefully—terra-cotta goddesses. In the central portion of the building, third-story windows have round-arched hoods with triple moldings; inside each is a large shield and a geometric pattern of smaller escutcheons. Triple windows at the thirteenth and fourteenth stories have bracketed balconies supporting engaged spiral pillars, and are separated by terra-cotta panels carved with—what else?—escutcheons; window hoods and circular motifs echo those at the first story. Crown-story double windows at the building extremes have bracketed balconies and broken segmental pediments. A frieze of rounded red tiles marks the roof line, which is protected with iron railings and limestone-topped brick posts.

108 East 96th Street
ARCHITECTS: Schuman Lichtenstein Claman Efron   DATE: 1986/1994
In the spring of 1986, the 31-story mid-block tower on 96th Street between Park and Lexington avenues "topped out" with the traditional American flag and branch (signaling that no fatalities had occurred during construction). Then CIVITAS, an East Side advocacy group, made a belated discovery: The top twelve stories were not permitted under existing zoning laws. The city's Department of Buildings quickly revoked the permit and the uninhabited building languished amid a storm of controversy, suits, countersuits and appeals. 108 East 96th Street, originally named Park View, became known as "the Too-Tall Building." Five years later, in 1991, the developer agreed to remove the top twelve stories in exchange for being allowed to build outward. In what may be unique in the history of New York City construction, starting in March 1993 the offending twelve stories were dismantled. It was not until May 1994 that a new permit was granted for the "construction" of the existing nineteen-story condominium.

The resulting structure is of red brick with a double-height limestone first story. Limestone string courses connect window lintels and balcony bases at each level. The overall look is a Postmodern nod to the simplified Queen Anne-style flats buildings that still dot the city [see, for example, 1361 Lexington Avenue].

112 East 96th Street
96th Street Library
ARCHITECTS: Babb, Cook & Willard
DATE: 1905

The 96th Street Library is one of 86 branches of the New York City Public Library system. It is one of the so-called Carnegie libraries, built with a $5.2 million donation by Andrew Carnegie in 1901. Carnegie stipulated that a board of architects approve all library designs, and this one typifies the style they preferred: neo-Classical, three-stories high, with a limestone facade. The first two stories project slightly from the corners, separated from the attic story by a simple cornice. At the first level, pairs of scrolled brackets support two round-arched windows that are capped with scrolled keystones embellished with acanthus leaves. The entryway is enclosed in the third arch: Double doors and sidelights are framed with an enriched-talon molding; above, a classical pediment is broken with a cartouche bearing, appropriately, an open book. Further classical details can be seen in the eared architraves and cornices atop second-story windows, the wide dentil band under the final cornice, and the limestone balustraded parapet.

115-117 and 119 East 96th Street
ARCHITECTS: Bernstein & Bernstein DATE: 1904

Look closely: These two six-story brick buildings are identical, except for the facade colors and the street-level stores of No. 119. The Renaissance Revival window embellishments vary from floor to floor—note the leafy brackets supporting triangular pediments with richly carved infill, curved hood lintels with cartouches, splayed lintels with scrolled keystones, and spandrels centered in each building's midsection. Both buildings terminate with a bracketed and modillioned metal cornice.

At No. 115-117 the street level remains residential (although there are stores in the basement). Segmentally-arched windows are topped with radiating brickwork, ornamental strips, and keystones with shell-like bonnets. The entire brick facade appears to be a replacement: Light-colored band courses and quoins framing the third-story windows are not stone, but brick: *trompe l'oeil* on busy 96th Street!

128-136 East 96th Street

ARCHITECT: Louis Entzer, Jr.   DATE: 1892

Robust and fortress-like, this quintet of five-story Romanesque Revival buildings mixes smooth and rough-cut stone with several shades of brown brick. The central bays project slightly; windows are deeply recessed. The ground stories of all but No. 136 retain their low stoops and curved cheek walls, pairs of engaged columns with foliate capitals, and round arches capped with voussoirs. Note the peaked pediments over entries, now truncated for fire escapes. At the upper levels, Nos. 128, 130 and 136 are almost identical: Each is four bays wide, with multiple rough-stone bands connecting second- and third-story windows, and wide foliate bands uniting round-arched attic-story windows. Each building is capped with a molded metal cornice embellished with floral motifs and dentils.

No. 132 and 134 break the pattern subtly. Rough stone masonry prevails throughout. Flanking the double entry are square columns, over which are suspended engaged spiral shafts terminating in corbel stones. The upper stories are six bays wide, with round-arched windows at the fourth level.

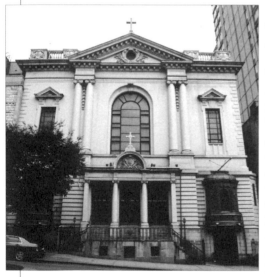

135 East 96th Street
Church of St. Francis de Sales

ARCHITECTS: O'Connor and Metcalfe   DATE: 1895-1903

The cornerstone of this Roman Catholic church was laid on December 8, 1895. The first mass was held on August 30, 1896 in the original or "Basement Church," and services continued in this location until the "Upper Church" was dedicated some seven years later. Designed in Baroque Italian Renaissance style, the symmetrical limestone facade has both freestanding and engaged columns with composite capitals. The lower-level colonnade supports an entablature, a cornice with modillions and a curved pediment with a richly carved cartouche in the tympanum. Molded metal oriels flank the elaborate entrance and interrupt the deep facade rustications.

On the upper level, a soaring arched window is flanked by pairs of engaged columns and narrow windows with triangular pediments. Limestone quoins mark the building's corners. The roof cornice and modillions complete the imposing design, crowned with a large triangular pediment, a marble balustrade and tiled roof.

A broad, steep flight of stairs originally led from the sidewalk to the raised entrance. In 1953, in response to difficulties encountered by parishioners, the design was modified to a double stairway rising from both sides for a less demanding climb. The reconfiguration was done by the architectural firm of John O'Malley. The architect was Edward V. Giannasca, who 40 years later would design the Carnegie Hill Tower at 40 East 94th Street.

More than 25 stained-glass windows may be viewed from the main sanctuary and adjacent galleries; most were installed from 1904 to 1907. The window depicting the church's namesake, St. Francis de Sales, who was canonized under Pope Clement VIII in 1509, is located toward the front of the church on the right side.

138 East 96th Street
(1486 Lexington Avenue)
ARCHITECT: Frank Wennemer
DATE: 1890

This five-story Romanesque Revival building corners Lexington Avenue, rising slightly as a bastion to its neighbors to the west. Light-brown brick is accented with darker-brick bands at each level. Smooth stone lintels top second- and third-story windows; a dentiled cornice runs above the fourth story. Round-arched windows at the top story echo those of the contiguous western buildings. Above the street-level commercial space, interest is concentrated on the 96th Street facade, which contrasts Nos. 128-136 with recessed central bays. The wide projecting sections are ornamented with foliate panels at the second and fourth stories and vertical channels at the fifth story. Viewed from the street, the projecting molded metal roof cornice cuts a striking skyline as it traces the building's contours.

166 East 96th Street
ARCHITECT: Howard Stokes Patterson   DATE: 1927-28

The relative isolation of this Art Deco building—flanked by the Seabury Playground on the south and west, and P.S. 198, the low elementary school (painted orange!) on the east—makes it seem taller than its sixteen stories would suggest. Its verticality is reinforced by double rows of stacked

bricks rising from a brushed limestone base to the
roof line. The entryway displays flamboyant Art
Deco styling: Square fluted pedestals support
enormous wrought-iron lanterns, which flank a
molded gray-marble entry surround. Double-
glass doors have wrought-iron grillwork in a bold
geometric pattern. Above the second-story
windows a wavy limestone horizontal band is
interrupted with vertical geometric ornaments,
echoed at the roof. The 96th Street facade and
part of the west facades are reddish-brown brick;
the remaining walls are of yellow brick.

201 East 96th Street
Islamic Cultural Center of New York
ARCHITECTS: Mosque: Mustafa K. Abada, Skidmore, Owings & Merrill
Minaret: Altan Gursel, Swanke Hayden Connell   DATE: 1989-96
The Islamic Cultural Center was the first building erected as a mosque in
New York City. Funded by the governments of Kuwait, Saudi Arabia and
Libya, it is a striking Postmodern structure just outside of Carnegie Hill.
   The geometric form follows Islamic law, as does the position of the

alter niche, or mihrab, within
the mosque, which dictates the
29° angle from the Manhattan
street grid. (Draw a straight
line to the east around the
globe and you'll reach the holy
city of Mecca, Saudi Arabia.)
An adjoining slender 130-foot
minaret serves only as a design
element, since the congregation
is too dispersed for an effective
call to prayer. Gilded crescent
moons atop both the copper-
clad dome of the mosque and
the minaret also face Mecca.
   Both structures are clad
in rosy granite in a series of
squares of various sizes. Four
steel trusses on the mosques's
exterior frame six large granite
panels. Each is surrounded by

translucent glass, providing natural light to the interior. A cubic frame surrounding the square above the entrance portal bears Islamic inscriptions in carved relief. Three large glazed windows feature geometric Islamic designs on a fired ceramic surface, giving them an opaque pale-green color. A series of sixteen articulated metal bars steps up to the base of the dome. Clear glass between each level provides a halo of light above the prayer hall.

The mosque's alignment creates a traditional and spacious forecourt for worshippers to gather before prayer. Two steps rise to a pair of fifteen-foot-high bronze doors of carved relief squares. Beyond the doors, layers of suspended glass panels form a translucent arch, reminiscent of traditional stalactite portals. The building's interior is a perfect square with no columns in the prayer hall. Here, up to 1,000 worshippers have unobstructed views of the walls and interior dome. Following the guidelines set by the Muslim committee, architect Mustafa K. Abada created a women's balcony to honor the separation of the sexes. Small lights suspended on brass rods float in a circle eighteen feet above the floor and recall the low-slung oil lamps of landmark mosques in the Middle East.

6 East 97th Street
ARCHITECTS: Ellis, Aaronson & Heidrich   DATE: 1928
Flanking the limestone entryway of this six-story, neo-Georgian red-brick building are simple pilasters that support a dentil course and cornice. Above the paneled-wood door is a fanlight topped with a keystone and rosettes. Second-story windows have iron balconettes; all windows have eared limestone lintels. The central portion of the building is recessed for fire escapes. For a surprise treat, step across the street and look up: Above the fifth story is a slate-covered mansard roof, with arched dormers framed by copper pilasters capped with classical pediments.

9 East 97th Street
Hortense Court
ARCHITECT: Edward Wenz
DATE: 1899
The entryway of this six-story Renaissance Revival building is very grand indeed: Pairs of marble columns with Ionic capitals support a projecting entablature with floral panels framing the

building's name. Ionic pilasters flank the wrought-iron glass-and-brass door, which is surrounded by a carved limestone egg-and-dart molding. The base and second story are of horizontally banded limestone; the upper stories are of tan brick with limestone quoins at the extremes. Marble balustrades at ground level are echoed on the balcony fronting second-story windows. The center window bays are paired, with pilasters and segmentally-arched carved pediments at the second story, and splayed lintels on the upper stories. Rounded outer bays project from a carved, corbeled base; carved friezes separating each story have centered cartouches. Alas, what must have been a grand cornice has been removed.

12 East 97th Street
ARCHITECT: Lafayette Anthony Goldstone
DATE: 1928
The broad central section of this eleven-story red-brick building is substantially recessed, with steps and a bi-level awning leading down to a further recessed entryway. On either side of the door is a lushly planted shade garden over which project corner window bays. Above the door is a simple escutcheon bearing the number 12, a narrow dentil course, and brackets supporting a balconette. At the left and center (but not to the right), the two-level limestone base features classically carved, arched windows accented with keystones. Simple limestone string courses run above the second, third and eighth stories. Brick and limestone posts punctuate the roof line. Below the eleventh-story parapet a frieze with rosettes and vertical incisings completes the restrained design.

15 East 97th Street
St. Nicholas Russian Orthodox Cathedral in New York
ARCHITECT: John Bergesen   DATE: 1902
Originally conceived to function as the most important center of the Orthodox Church in North America, St. Nicholas Cathedral (also known as the Cathedral Church of His Holiness Patriarch of Moscow and All Russia in North America and the Representation of the Moscow Patriarchate) was erected as a permanent home for a congregation, formed in 1894, that formerly met in a rented house on the Lower East Side. The church, which attained the status of cathedral in 1903, was designed as a space where Russian émigrés seeking liturgical and spiritual traditions

could find a sense of peace and solace. The revolution of 1917 and the long years of canonical disorder that ensued concentrated the ministry of the cathedral more strictly to the diaspora of the Russian Orthodox Church, which today is undergoing a great renewal.

The building, funded by money collected by Imperial permission throughout the Russian Empire, derives from a traditional form of Baroque architecture as it evolved in Moscow. The most familiar feature translated to this cathedral structure is the verdigris-hued standing-seam rooftop with its five copper onion-dome cupolas topped by gilt crosses.

Architectural adornments abound. Noteworthy are the della Robbia-like majolica arch insets depicting winged cherubs; the tripartite stained-glass window at the center of the facade, the center portion of which is arched; and the various engaged columns and pediments that set off other windows. The entrance to the brick-clad building, which is set upon a granite founda-tion, is contained within a central two-story gabled bay. Flanking the facade are wide brick pilasters, each topped by a small, onion-  domed turret. A blue-and-gold diamond-patterned band stretches across the facade at the base of the roof. The cathedral complex includes an attached three-story rectory, which is visually linked to the cathedral by garlands of colored brick, terra cotta, and majolica. The entire complex is an individual landmark, outside of the Carnegie Hill Historic District. **LM**

17 East 97th Street
The Mannados
ARCHITECT: David Stone
DATE: 1904-06

This six-story apartment building is somewhat austere, compared with others designed in the elaborate Renaissance Revival style of the period. There are subtle details: Applied brick quoins line the corners and end bays of the red-brick midsection; contrasting limestone window surrounds echo the paneled crown and banded base sections. Central windows have splayed lintels, while those at the second-story end bays are topped with triangular and arched pediments. Limestone string courses run above the first and second stories, and a leafy band course tops the fifth story. Shops line the Madison Avenue side. At the off-center main entrance on 97th Street, recessed green-marble engaged columns flank a glass double door and transom; each has decorative grillwork. The limestone entablature supports a series of mutates (low blocks) and a balustraded balcony.

51 East 97th Street
ARCHITECT: George F. Pelham   DATE: 1904

Many features of this six-story Renaissance Revival building are similar to those favored by George F. Pelham during the first decade of the 20th century. Above the rusticated limestone base, red brick dramatizes carved stone detailing such as elaborate second-story window enframements, oval windows with horn and-fruit surrounds and mascarons (virtually identical to those on Pelham's apartment house at 1240 Park Avenue), and splayed lintels with keystones. Double windows are treated as single elements with elaborate stone reveals, capped with fleur-de-lis, fruited horns, broken segmental pediments and cartouches. Beneath the modillioned stone cornice runs a triglyph-and-rondel frieze. On 97th Street, a segmental arch with

voussoirs tops the off-center residential entrance; lions' heads under scrolled brackets support an entablature embellished with leaves and a cartouche. The original doors have been replaced with institutional glass and metal. Rising above foliate panels, street-level windows (now bricked up) are divided by engaged columns with composite capitals.

Unusual for Pelham buildings is the rounded corner at 97th Street; the base of the triple bay is richly carved with vines and birds, and ornate panels separate windows at each story.

4 East 98th Street
St. Bernard's School
ARCHITECTS: Delano & Aldrich
DATE: 1915

Founded as an elementary school for boys in 1904, St. Bernard's original quarters were at 570 Fifth Avenue. The school moved in 1910 to 111 East 60th Street and in 1915 took possession of the present neo-Federal-style building. The wings were added in 1919; further expansions included a fifth floor in 1988, and two-and-one-half additional floors in 1997. Today St. Bernard's educates boys from kindergarten through ninth grade.

The building is of red brick rising from a granite water table. Two continuous limestone belt courses separate the first and second stories; additional band courses below the fifth, sixth and seventh stories unify the three sections.

On the main building, four square-headed windows trimmed with geometrically decorated lintels and sills flank the classical entrance, which consists of engaged Doric columns, double doors with a round-arched fanlight, scrolled keystone, swags and guttae, topped with a dentiled triangular pediment. (Each schoolboy shakes the hand of the headmaster every morning at this handsome door.) Centered over the pediment is a stone cartouche containing an insignia, flanked with tripartite windows; this symmetrical design is repeated at the third story, with a single window replacing the cartouche. At the fourth story, five small windows with curved wrought-iron balconies rest on a continuing stone sill. A single multi-pane window runs the entire length of the fifth-story central facade. Simple square-headed windows pierce the top two stories, which terminate with a peaked central roof.

The first level of the three-bay-wide east wing consists of a round-arched doorway with sidelights and a double segmentally-arched window with decorative grillwork. At the fourth story, two arched windows flank a stone escutcheon. The west wing is wider and relatively unadorned; all windows are square-headed except for those at the fifth story, which are segmentally-arched, echoing the east wing openings. A round-arched entry marks the westernmost access to the school.

5-17 East 98th Street
Mount Sinai School of Medicine
ARCHITECT: Robert D. Kohn   DATE: 1925-26

Originally built as a residence for nurses at Mount Sinai Hospital, in 1954 this fourteen-story building added classrooms, an infirmary and a gymnasium. Today it houses the administrative facilities and doctors' offices of the Faculty Practice Associates of the Mount Sinai School of Medicine.

The brown-brick building, which combines neo-Renaissance and Art Deco elements, consists of three sections, with the recessed center mass twice the width of the projecting east and west bays. Visually, the first two floors are divided into four equal parts. Rising from a low granite base, each double-story limestone section is flanked with quoins and includes three high-arched windows and slightly tapered geometric keystones. These are topped with pairs of double-hung windows and, at the end sections, geometric brackets supporting a cornice, above which is a decorative iron railing. At the western bay the triple windows become triple doors, altogether creating a grand series of twelve framed arches running the full expanse of the 150-foot-wide structure.

The third-story windows on the east and west bays have limestone surrounds and geometrically shaped lintels. Above the tenth story runs a wide, multi-colored brick band course with limestone geometrics. In the center, two large projecting limestone ovals frame medallions. A row of limestone diamonds set within diagonal brickwork stretches over the thirteenth story. Crowning the center section are three Palladian windows. The limestone roof line rises to geometric peaks, which are repeated in the east and west tower enclosures.

16 East 98th Street
ARCHITECT: George Keister   DATE: 1924

The first two levels of this understated nine-story building are rusticated limestone, which forms voussoirs over street-level windows. Pilasters with foliate capitals flank the entry, above which is a marquee. Rising above a cornice, the five-story midsection is red brick; vertical rows of applied brick define outer window bays. More classical details are revealed as one looks upwards: Escutcheons with carved shells punctuate a limestone string course over the sixth story; the seventh-story cornice, embellished with modillions and dentils, supports a wrought-iron railing extending the full width of the facade. Eighth-story outer bay windows have broken segmental pediments. At the center of the two-story crown section, three Corinthian pilasters flank central windows and support a terminal limestone entablature; balustrades complete the outer edges.

CARNEGIE HILL WALKS

A t a brisk pace it would take twelve minutes to walk from 86th Street to 98th Street. A stroll might take two hours…or two weeks. Carnegie Hill is rich in architectural attractions, many among the oldest in the city. Some have been widely publicized, and some rarely mentioned outside of this guide book. Several of these walks are plotted by specific streets or areas, but most are themed, so some sites will be mentioned more than once. The walks are self-guided: They take from one to two-and-one-half hours, but of course you can set your own time frame. This guide focuses on exterior architectural styles and features, but why not stop at a museum café or a restaurant, visit a gallery, a boutique, a bookstore. Step inside one of the many churches or religious institutions (but check ahead for hours open to visitors). Take in the view from the reservoir, reached through the Engineers' Gate at Fifth Avenue and 90th Street. If you have a child in tow, Madison Avenue abounds with shops to pique young interests and historic buildings to pique your own—as well as a playground on 95th Street just behind the remains of the castle-like Squadron A Armory. For descriptions of each of the buildings mentioned on a walk, please turn to the appropriate pages in this guide.

The Landmarked Rhinelander Queen Anne houses at 146-156 East 89th Street.

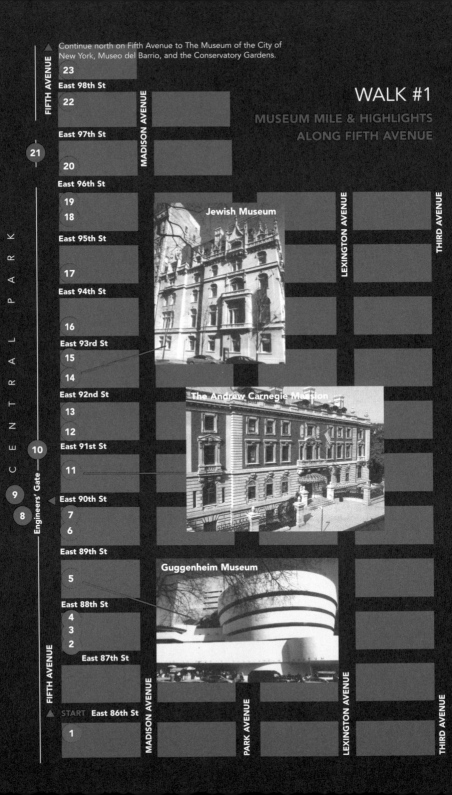

Continue north on Fifth Avenue to The Museum of the City of New York, Museo del Barrio, and the Conservatory Gardens.

WALK #1

MUSEUM MILE & HIGHLIGHTS
ALONG FIFTH AVENUE

FIFTH AVENUE

MADISON AVENUE

LEXINGTON AVENUE

THIRD AVENUE

PARK AVENUE

CENTRAL PARK

East 98th St

East 97th St

East 96th St

East 95th St

East 94th St

East 93rd St

East 92nd St

East 91st St

East 90th St

East 89th St

East 88th St

East 87th St

Engineers' Gate

Jewish Museum

The Andrew Carnegie Mansion

Guggenheim Museum

START East 86th St

23

22

21

20

19

18

17

16

15

14

13

12

11

10

9

8

7

6

5

4

3

2

1

MUSEUM MILE & HIGHLIGHTS ALONG FIFTH AVENUE
Time: 2 hours, plus museum visits

Carnegie Hill residents revere their neighborhood for its proximity to Central Park as well as for its architectural treasures. Residents and visitors alike enjoy the diversity of Carnegie Hill's fine homes, apartment houses and cultural attractions, many of which lie along the stretch of Fifth Avenue known as Museum Mile. Let's start at 86th Street. All buildings with Fifth Avenue addresses are discussed on pages 23 to 37 of this guide. Most museums have cafés and all have gift shops; best call or check their websites for days open and viewing hours.

On the southeast corner of 86th Street you'll see the **Neue Galerie ❶**, an elegant Beaux-Arts mansion by Carrère & Hastings commissioned in 1914 by industrialist William Starr Miller; for nine years it was the residence of Grace Wilson Vanderbilt, widow of Cornelius Vanderbilt III. It now houses a definitive collection of early 20th-century Austrian and German Expressionist art. That it does so with such aplomb is due to the expertise of the restoration's architect, Annabelle Seldorf, and the generosity of cosmetics heir Ronald Lauder. You can enjoy a delicious bite, or a gourmet meal, at

Neue Galerie

the Viennese Café Sabarsky or the Café Fledermaus.

As you walk north you will pass the 1928 neo-Renaissance **1060 Fifth Avenue ❷**, one of twelve luxury apartment houses in the neighborhood designed by J.E.R Carpenter. Next door is the oldest apartment house on our stretch, **1067 Fifth ❸**, an exquisite 1917 French Gothic building designed by C.P.H. Gilbert; it was the second luxury apartment building to be built on the entire avenue (after McKim, Mead & White's No. 998 at 81st Street in 1910). At **2 East 88th Street ❹** (page 103) the sleekly Moderne apartment house, designed by Pennington & Lewis in 1930, is topped with piers bearing enormous stone heads resembling Greek goddesses; for best viewing step across Fifth Avenue.

Instantly recognizable is Frank Lloyd Wright's iconic **Solomon R. Guggenheim Museum ❺**, the showcase for modern art that stretches between 88th and 89th streets. Its vigorous 1959 coil is offset by a self-effacing blond slab by Gwathmey Siegel, which caused an uproar when unveiled to the public in 1992. Today the museum complex elicits no adverse commentary, and welcome restoration work underscored its rightful spot on the National Register of Historic Places. Popular, too, are the museum's airy café and lively shop; its underground theater (yes, it is circular) hosts a variety of programs.

A few steps north, at 1083 Fifth, the suave Beaux-Arts Archer M. Huntington house, now the **National Academy Museum** ⑥, was modified in 1915 by Ogden Codman, Jr (a neo-Renaissance wing was added at 3 East 89th Street). Dedicated to American art, the academy maintains an active art school next door at 5 East 89th Street. Painters of an *en plein air* persuasion can be seen with their art supplies as they head toward the Engineers' Gate, across from Hardie Phillip's 1930 "Gothic Deco" **Church of the Heavenly Rest** ⑦ (page 122) at 90th Street.

The **Engineers' Gate** provides access to Carnegie Hill's bucolic "back yard," Central Park, and the Jacqueline Kennedy Onassis Reservoir. Lingering nearby, shaded by trees, stands a statue of **Fred Lebow** ⑧, founder of the New York Road Runners Club, which is quartered at 9 East 89th Street. His spirit presides over the annual New York Marathon, as well as many other road races for worthy causes. At the stairs to the reservoir is a bust of **John Purroy Mitchell** ⑨,

National Academy

at 34 New York City's youngest mayor, from 1914 to 1918. Shortly after his term ended, while training for World War I, Mitchell fell from an Army Air Force plane, apparently from having neglected to fasten his seat belt. In the wall at 91st Street is a bas-relief monument to **W. T. Stead** ⑩, a renowned British journalist who died on the Titanic, while, it is said, reading and smoking a cigar in the first-class smoking room.

The prominence and influence of the owners of the exuberantly detailed **Andrew and Louise Carnegie mansion** ⑪ (page 137), designed by Babb, Cook & Willard in 1903, gave our neighborhood its name. Straddling the block from 90th to 91st streets, the complex— now the **Cooper-Hewitt, National Design Museum,** a branch of the Smithsonian Institution dedicated to the industrial, graphic and decorative arts—includes two landmarked mansions on East 90th Street, the Beaux-Arts McAlpin-Miller house at No. 9 and the McAlpin-Minot house at No. 11. It also embraces one of the few grand enclosed gardens in the city. At 91st Street is a second magnificent dwelling by C.P.H. Gilbert, the Italian Renaissance **Otto and Addie Kahn mansion** ⑫ (page 136), now the Convent of the Sacred Heart. It is followed by **1107 Fifth** ⑬, an

Otto Khan mansion

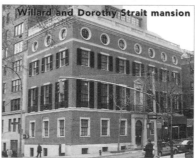

Willard and Dorothy Strait mansion

apartment house designed in 1925 by Rouse & Goldstone for Marjorie Merriweather Post Hutton to house her 54-room triplex "mansion in the sky;" a separate entrance on 92nd Street led to her private elevator. Next up the avenue are the spires and finials of a third C.P.H. Gilbert masterpiece, the 1908 Felix and Frieda Warburg mansion, now the **Jewish Museum 14**. Since 1963 the museum was linked to an eyesore of an addition. In a skillful 1993 "restoration" the architect Kevin Roche seamlessly appended gallery space, creating a facade to echo the French Gothic Chateau style of the original exterior.

Two neo-Renaissance J.E.R Carpenter buildings, **1115 15 and 1120 Fifth 16**, stand across from each other on 93rd Street and are commonly referred to as "twins," although close scrutiny will reveal their distinct personalities.

At 94th Street stands **1130 Fifth 17**, the 1915 neo-Georgian mansion designed by Delano & Aldrich for Willard and Dorothy Payne Whitney Straight. Now a private residence, it formerly housed the International Center for Photography. Continuing

north you will spot a diminutive J.E.R. Carpenter building at **1143 Fifth 18**, now owned by the French Embassy, and two more imposing Carpenters, **1148 and 1150 Fifth,** at the north and south corners of 96th Street **19 20**. Cross Fifth Avenue and check out the pocket park at 97th Street: Presiding over the tiny space is a full-size copy of a self-portrait of **Albert Bertel Thorvaldsen 21**, with hammer in hand. The Danish/Icelandic sculptor's claim to fame in the United States is his "Resurrected Christ" which was replicated on Temple Square in Salt Lake City. Two final Carpenter apartment houses, **1165 22 and 1170 Fifth 23**, tip their elegant hats—and canopies—to each other across 98th Street.

If you are in the mood to continue, walk up to the **Museum of the City of New York** at 103rd Street and the **Museo del Barrio** at 104th Street; both are well worth your time. For a final treat and a delightful respite, discover the magnificent three-part **Conservatory Garden,** entered through the Vanderbilt Gates at Fifth Avenue and 105th Street.

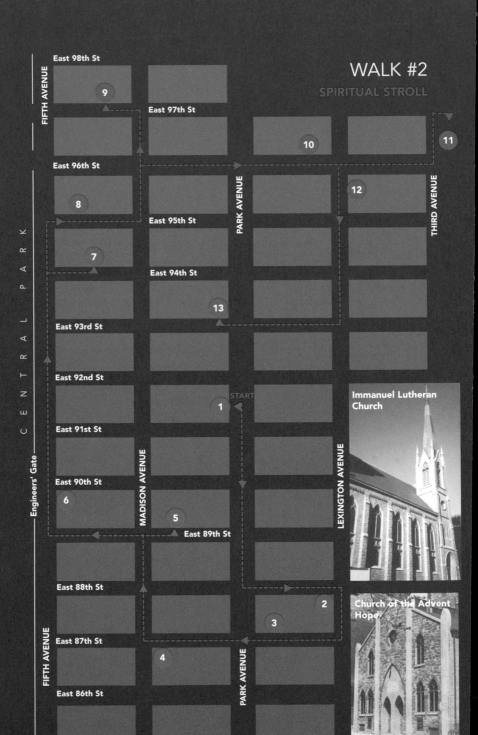

WALK #2
SPIRITUAL STROLL

Immanuel Lutheran Church

Church of the Advent Hope

SPIRITUAL STROLL
Time: 1 hour 45 minutes, plus visits

Park Avenue Synagogue

Within the modest confines of Carnegie Hill are no fewer than thirteen religious institutions! This walk relishes the variety of their architectural styles. The interiors are equally interesting; some buildings are open during the day, while others are closed to the public except during worship services so best call ahead.

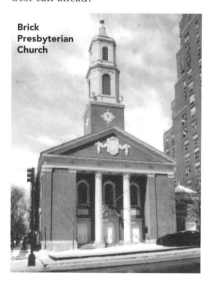
Brick Presbyterian Church

Our stroll begins at the neo-Georgian **Brick Presbyterian Church 1** (page 59) on Park Avenue between 91st and 92nd streets, designed by York & Sawyer in 1938. From there, walk down to 88th Street and turn east; the 1886 neo-Gothic **Immanuel Lutheran Church 2** (page 109) at the corner of Lexington Avenue is one of the earliest buildings in Carnegie Hill. Head down Lexington one block and turn west on 87th Street; on the north side, just before Park, you will pass the diminutive Seventh-Day Adventist **Church of the Advent Hope 3** (page 97). On the south side stretching to Madison Avenue is the Moorish-style **Park Avenue Synagogue 4** (page 95), designed in 1926 by Walter S. Schneider, with its 1980 modern addition opening on Madison Avenue. Head up Madison to 89th Street; turn east here and you will spot Hubert, Pirsson's 1870 Gothic-style **Church of St. Thomas More 5** (page 117), since 1950 a Roman Catholic church. It was originally the Episcopal Church of the

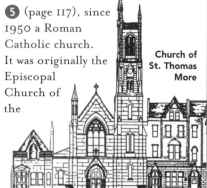
Church of St. Thomas More

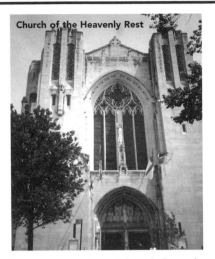

Church of the Heavenly Rest

Beloved Disciples and later belonged to the nearby **Church of the Heavenly Rest** 6 (page 122) two blocks to the west, on the corner of 90th Street and Fifth Avenue. From the "Gothic Deco"-style Heavenly Rest, designed by Hardie Phillip in 1930, stroll up Fifth past the Andrew Carnegie garden and mansion and the Jewish Museum; turn east on 94th Street. In mid-block, at Nos. 17-19, is the **Ramakrishna-Vivekananda Center** 7 (page 208), occupying two 1893 Romanesque Revival townhouses. One block north, at 7 East 95th Street, is the Italian Renaissance-style **House of the Redeemer** 8 (page 220), a non-denominational retreat; it was designed in 1917 for Edith and Ernesto Fabbri by Grosvenor Atterbury and Fabbri's brother, Egisto. Continue to Madison and turn west on 97th Street, near Carnegie Hill's northernmost boundary, to the amazing onion-domed **St. Nicholas Russian Orthodox Cathedral** 9 (page 242), on 97th Street off Fifth, designed by John Bergesen in 1902. Go back to 96th Street. Between Park and Lexington stands the Baroque-style **St. Francis de Sales** Roman Catholic church 10 (page 238), built between 1895 and 1903. Continue east: Just across Third Avenue, set at a 29° angle (to face the holy city of Mecca), are the Modern **Islamic Cultural Center** mosque and minaret 11 (page 240), completed in 1996. From the mosque, wend your way down Lexington: Between 94th and 95th streets stands **Congregation Orach Chaim** 12 (page 84), designed by Schwartz & Gross in 1907. Turn west at 93rd Street to Park Avenue: There you can view the **Russian Orthodox Church Outside of Russia** 13 (page 192), the neo-Federal George F. Baker, Jr., house complex designed from 1917 to 1931 by Delano & Aldrich.

Ramakrishna-Vivekananda Center

House of the Redeemer

St. Nicholas
Russian Orthodox
Cathedral in
New York

Islamic Cultural Center
of New York

Church of St. Francis de Sales

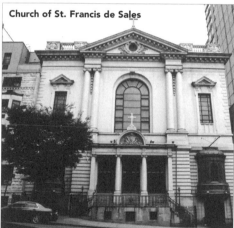

Congregation
Orach Chaim

Russian
Orthodox Church
Outside of Russia

257

WALK #3
MARCH UP PARK

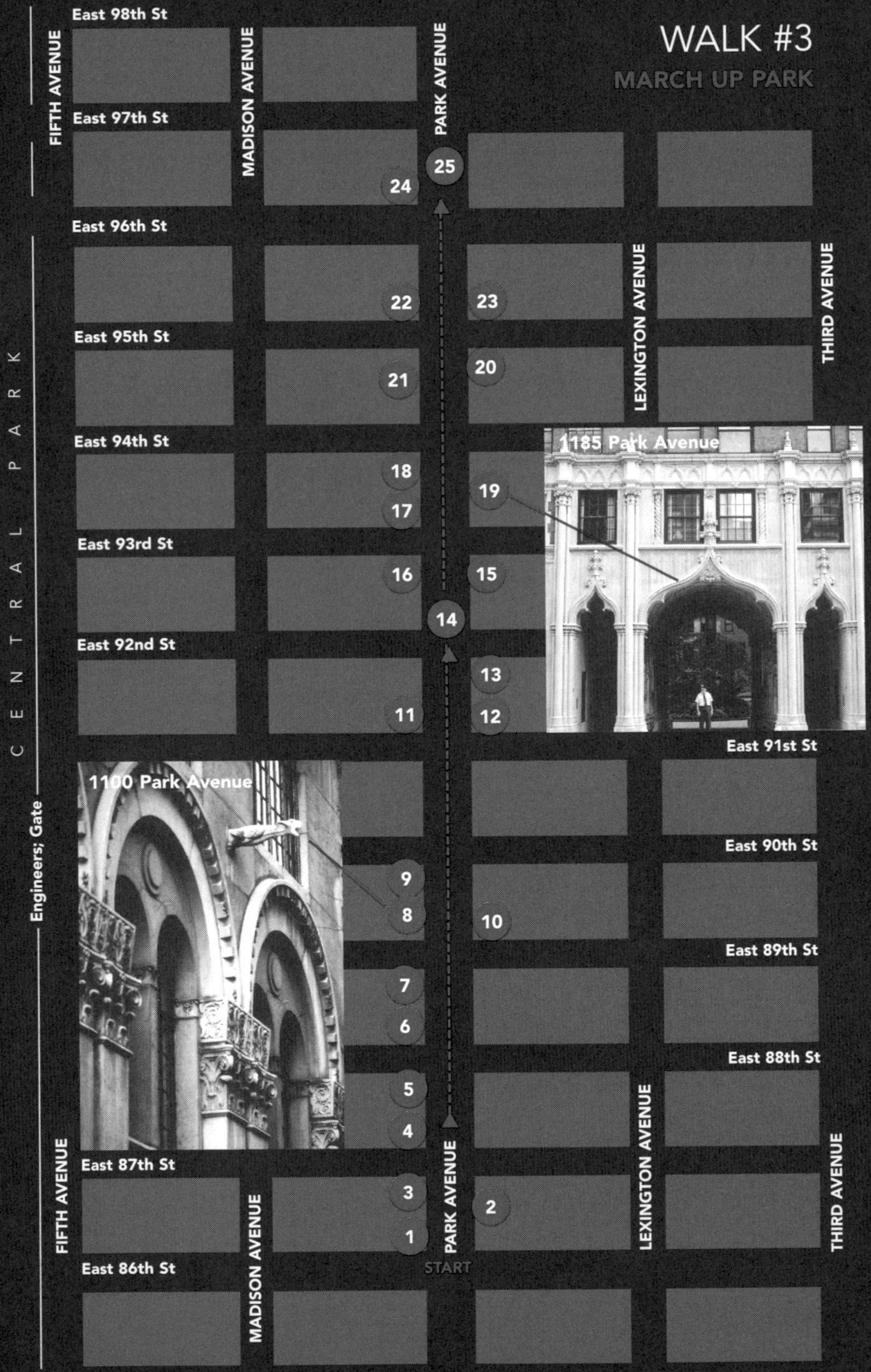

East 98th St

FIFTH AVENUE

MADISON AVENUE

PARK AVENUE

East 97th St

24   25

East 96th St

LEXINGTON AVENUE

THIRD AVENUE

22   23

East 95th St

21   20

East 94th St

1185 Park Avenue

18
17   19

East 93rd St

16   15

East 92nd St

14

13
11   12

East 91st St

1100 Park Avenue

East 90th St

9
8   10

East 89th St

7
6

East 88th St

5
4

FIFTH AVENUE

Engineers; Gate

CENTRAL PARK

East 87th St

MADISON AVENUE

3
1   2

PARK AVENUE

LEXINGTON AVENUE

THIRD AVENUE

START

East 86th St

MARCH UP PARK
Time: 1 hour 15 minutes

B y the end of the 1880s the cuts from the Grand Central railroad tracks were roofed over with new planted center sections and Fourth Avenue was optimistically renamed Park Avenue. However, it was not until after 1906, when the railroad switched from coal to electricity, that apartment houses began to rise, and luxury buildings followed a decade later. This ten-block walk from 86th Street to 96th Street revels in a handsome sweep of buildings by some of New York's most influential architects, and offers a few unexpected treats as well. Details count more than the overall impression of prosperity on this tour: As you walk, note how the character of each apartment house is revealed in the application of ornament, especially around the entry and at the crown stories. (All Park Avenue buildings are described in detail on pages 48 to 72.)

1040 Park Avenue

For pure spectacle, plan your walk for late April into mid-May, when tulips paint the malls and Kwansan cherry trees are laden with deep-pink blossoms.

Delano & Aldrich's tortoises and hares race along the third-story frieze of **1040 Park Avenue** at 86th Street ❶. The building is topped with what was in 1924 an innovation: a glass-walled penthouse commissioned by its first occupant,

Looking north up Park Avenue from 86th Street

1088 Park Avenue

1105 Park Avenue

the magazine publisher Conde Nast. Four classical heads eye passersby from above the third-story windows of **1049 Park ❷**, designed by Mills & Bottomley in 1919. **1050 and 1060 Park ❸❹**, designed by J.E.R. Carpenter, act as neo-Renaissance bookends on the western corners of 87th Street. **1070 Park ❺** is one of nine Park Avenue buildings designed by Schwartz & Gross and one of two with exuberant neo-Venetian Gothic detailing; note the double ogee arches, mythical creatures and triple-story window bays.

Diminutive **1082 Park ❻** is an 1887 row house that not only held out against the luxury apartment-house tide of the 1920s, but also covered its facade with "neo-Florentine" glazed-polychrome terra-cotta tiles in graphic defiance.

Mott B. Schmidt's **1088 Park ❼**, among the avenue's most distinguished buildings,

1070 Park Avenue

was built in 1925; a double-height entry portal and vaulted lobby lead to a garden courtyard. DePace & Juster's mellow-toned **1100 Park ❽** has a pronounced medieval character; note the graceful round-arched windows and gargoyles above the entrance. Next door are nestled two of the oldest buildings in Carnegie Hill, **1108 and 1110 Park ❾**. Built in 1856, their storefronts are a rarity on the avenue, grand-fathered before the 1920s building boom. On the southeast corner of 89th Street is **1105 Park ❿**. Built in 1923, it is the first of four Park Avenue buildings by the legendary architect Rosario Candela. Of note are the "expectant" caryatids—perhaps an unplanned effect—above the entrance.

At 91st Street the **Brick Presbyterian Church ⓫** tops its steeple with a golden weather vane; the neo-Georgian building was designed by York & Sawyer in

1938. Opposite are **1141-1149 Park** ⓬, the remaining cluster of a row of neo-Grec brownstones designed by John Sullivan in 1886; only No. 1147 retains traces of its original character. **1155 Park** ⓭, built in 1914, is among the earliest luxury apartment houses on the avenue, designed in neo-Renaissance style by Robert T. Lyons. Centered in the mall at 92nd Street is **"Night Presence IV"** ⓮, the 22 1/2-foot-high bolted-steel sculpture by Louise Nevelson.

Note the rich classical detailing of **1175 Park** ⓯, designed in 1925 by Emery Roth. Directly across the avenue at **1172 Park** ⓰ is a second Candela building: You may need binoculars to spot the lions' and rams' heads at the cornice. At the northwest corner at **67-75 East 93rd Street** ⓱ (page 192) is the 1917 neo-Federal house complex designed by Delano & Aldrich for Francis F. Palmer (later owned by George F. Baker, Jr.), now the Russian Orthodox Church Outside of Russia. Abutting it is a third Candela, **1192 Park** ⓲; the hand-carved limestone ornamentation replicates the original 1926 design—which was of pre-cast concrete.

1240 Park Avenue

Spanning the entire east side from 93rd to 94th streets is **1185 Park** ⓳, a 1929 neo-Venetian Gothic building designed by Schwartz & Gross. Through its triple-ogee-arched drive-in portal is a courtyard from which radiate

1220 Park Avenue

entrances to six separate sections of the complex. At 95th Street, note the newly restored 1890 brownstone at **1217 Park** ⓴; whimsical creatures embellish the facade. Directly across is the Hunter College Campus School, which stands on the former Squadron A Armory site ㉑ (page 211). A final Candela awaits at **1220 Park** ㉒; step across the street to view its much-photographed water-tank enclosure. **1225 Park** ㉓, designed by George F. Pelham in 1926, displays fortress-style battlements, perhaps to echo those at the armory. At the northwest corner of 96th Street is **1240 Park** ㉔, a 1905 Pelham flats building designed in flamboyant Renaissance Revival style. Our walk terminates at 96th Street in a newly restored **pocket park** ㉕ overlooking the railroad tracks of MetroNorth, which yawn northward at 97th Street from the tunnel drilled in 1837 into the bedrock under the avenue.

East 98th St
East 97th St
East 96th St
East 95th St
East 94th St
East 93rd St
East 92nd St
East 91st St
East 90th St
East 89th St
East 88th St
East 87th St
East 86th St

FIFTH AVENUE
MADISON AVENUE
PARK AVENUE
LEXINGTON AVENUE
THIRD AVENUE

CENTRAL PARK

Engineers' Gate

WALK #4

THOSE QUIRKY QUEEN ANNES

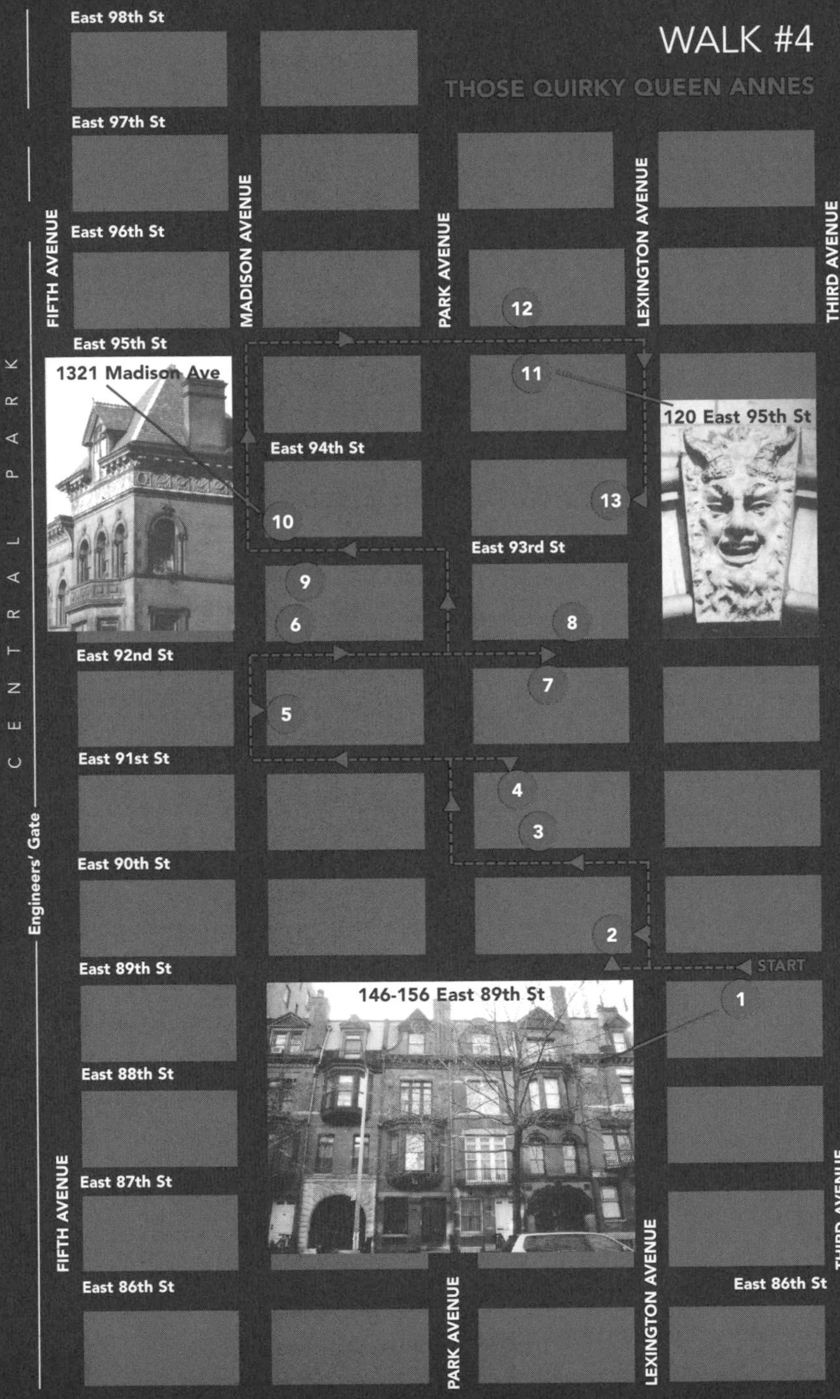

1321 Madison Ave

120 East 95th St

146-156 East 89th St

START

1
2
3
4
5
6
7
8
9
10
11
12
13

THOSE QUIRKY QUEEN ANNES
Time: 1 hour 15 minutes

Eccentric and playful, Queen Anne row houses date from 1880 to 1890 and are characterized by asymmetry and an eclectic hybrid of forms.

Start on 89th Street near Third Avenue. Six narrow red-brick houses, **Nos. 146-156** ❶ (page 120), were commissioned by William Rhinelander; the design by Hubert, Pirsson & Co. exhibits amazing variety in arches, oriels, chimneys and peaked pediments. Continue west: **1340-1350 Lexington Avenue and 121 East 89th Street** ❷ (pages 74, 110), by Henry J. Hardenberg, constitute the smallest Historic District in the city; note the peaks and pots peppering the roof lines. Walk up Lexington and turn west to view **113 East 90th Street** ❸ (page 129), once a private firehouse, now the Allan Stone Gallery. One block north are **48-54 East 91st Street** ❹ (page 144), designed by A.B. Ogden & Son. No. 54 is the best preserved; curved newels and iron railings carved with Tudor roses guard the stoop.

Head west to view two Queen Anne gems at **1281 and 1283 Madison Avenue** ❺ (page 39). The only survivors of a row designed by Frederick T. Camp, the top stories sport spiky pointed gables, shields, rosettes and finials. Around the corner are **49 and 51 East 92nd Street** ❻ (page 165),

designed by Frank Wennemer; their wrought-iron newel cages, carved lintels, swags and metal roof cornices are historic. Continue east: **134-138 East 92nd Street** ❼ (page 175), also by Ogden, and **127-135 East 92nd Street** ❽ (page 173), by C. Abbott French, offer curves, curlicues and whimsical ornamentation—like the sly mascarons grinning from No. 133.

Ogden's **66 East 93rd Street** ❾ (page 192) displays carved lintels and stone arches; this townhouse was once owned by Ellin and Irving Berlin. At the northeast corner, **1321 and 1323-25 Madison** ❿ (page 44), designed by James E. Ware, are a delight to the eye, from the balustraded stoop to the three-sided bays to the corner tower.

Walk north past the Squadron A Armory remains; turn east on 95th Street. A final treat awaits—Goat Hill, unique in the city, with nineteen Queen Anne row houses, most in pristine condition. **116-138 East 95th Street** ⓫, also by C. Abbott French, and **115-127 East 95th Street** ⓬, (pages 225-226), by Louis Entzer, Jr., are lively and individual, with masks, patterned brickwork, oriels, gables and stepped parapets. To finish your walk, turn south on Lexington to **1428 and 1432** ⓭ (page 81) to view two workaday Queen Annes: Above the shopfronts are incised pediments, devilish faces and a sunburst.

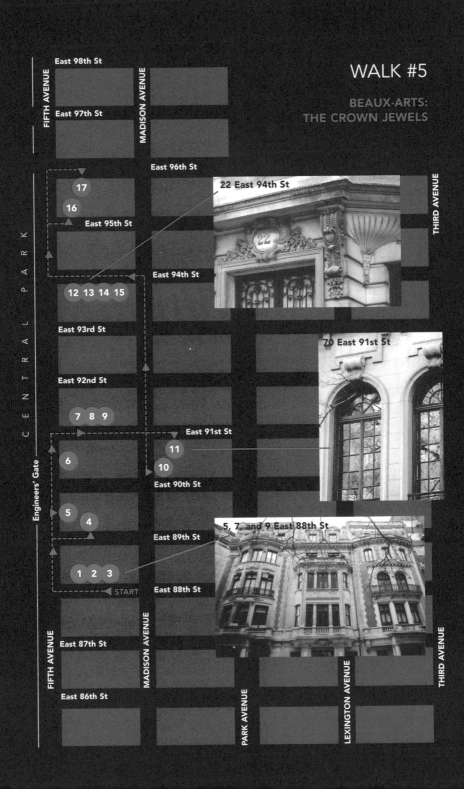

WALK #5

BEAUX-ARTS:
THE CROWN JEWELS

22 East 94th St

70 East 91st St

5, 7, and 9 East 88th St

BEAUX-ARTS: THE CROWN JEWELS
Time: 1 hour 30 minutes

National Academy Museum

I ntroduced at the turn of the twentieth century, Beaux-Arts is considered to be the pinnacle of classical architectural style. It derives from the same 1500s European model as the earlier Renaissance Revival style, but is more ornate and used mostly for homes of the wealthy and grand public buildings. Facades are often of limestone and may include bow fronts, large brackets to support balustraded balconies, and elaborately carved swags, scrolls and cartouches. Carnegie Hill is proud to host fifteen Beaux-Arts buildings, many of which are individual landmarks.

We start our walk with **5, 7, and 9 East 88th Street ❶❷❸** (page 104). These brick-and-limestone beauties by Turner & Kilian were built in 1903 "on spec" rather than for a wealthy patron; note the porticoed entrances, fine grillwork and lavish marble trim. One block north is **9 East 89th Street ❹** (page 113). This is the only surviving building designed by the German Expressionist painter Oscar Bluemner; its eccentricities include long wedge-shaped keystones and massive scrolled brackets ending in guttae. Since 1981 it has been the headquarters of the New York Road

Runners Club. Around the corner at **1083 Fifth Avenue ❺** (page 27) is the elegant National Academy Museum, also designed by Turner & Kilian and modified in 1915 by Ogden Codman, Jr., for Archer M. Huntington, stepson of the railroad tycoon, Collis P. Huntington. Codman also designed the adjoining 3 East 89th Street wing, creating a grand circular hallway and sweeping spiral staircase, with a life-size statue of Diana, sculpted by Huntington's second wife, Anna Hyatt.

At the corner of Fifth Avenue and 91st Street stands the magnificent **Andrew and Louise Carnegie Mansion ❻** (page 137), now the Cooper-Hewitt, National Design Museum. Completed in 1903 as a retirement residence for Andrew and Louise Carnegie by the architects Babb, Cook & Willard, the style is considered a hybrid, combining a "homey" brick neo-Georgian facade with robust limestone Beaux-Arts details. A visit to the sumptuous interiors, conservatory and lush garden is a must.

7 East 91st St

9 East 91st St

Directly across are **7, 9, and 11 East 91st Street** ⑦⑧⑨ (pages 139-141). No 7, now part of Convent of the Sacred Heart, was designed in 1903 by Warren & Wetmore, architects of Grand Central Station. It was commissioned by William D. Sloane and his wife, Emily Vanderbilt Sloane (granddaughter of Commodore Cornelius Vanderbilt), as a wedding present for their daughter Florence to James A. Burden. The high arched doorway was wide enough for a carriage, which could exit to the side court of No. 9, designed for the Sloanes' other daughter, Emily Vanderbilt Sloane, upon her marriage to John Henry Hammond. The 137-foot tract of land for both buildings was purchased from Andrew Carnegie. The mansion at No. 9 was designed by Carrère & Hastings in 1903,

fashioned after a 16th-century Italian Renaissance palazzo. In the music room on the *piano nobile* Benny Goodman, who would become the Hammonds' son-in-law, performed the Mozart Clarinet Quintet. The building is now the Consulate of the Russian Federation in New York. No. 11, also owned by the Consulate, was designed by Trowbridge & Livingston for John B. and Caroline Wilmerding Trevor. Note the deeply-set arched windows and iron balustrades at the *piano nobile.*

Continue east on 91st Street and turn right; on the opposite corner is **1261 Madison Avenue** ⑩ (page 38), one of the the city's first luxury apartment buildings, designed by Buchman & Fox in 1901. The magnificent portico is composed of garlanded brackets supporting a swan's neck pediment and

1261 Madison Avenue

cartouche. Return to 91st Street; just east is **No. 70** ⑪ (page 149), designed by Robert T. Lyons in 1905. Its arched French windows with narrow wrought-iron balconies are typical of Louis XV-style Parisian apartments. Return to Madison and head north. The elegant quartet of five-story Beaux-Arts townhouses, **18-24 East 94th Street** ⑫⑬⑭⑮ (page 209), was designed by Van Vleck & Goldsmith in 1899. Nos. 18 and 22 are similar, with full limestone facades, two-story oriels and curved stoops; Nos. 20 and 24 display red-brick facades and limestone-quoined window enframements.

3 East 95th Street ⑯ (page 218) was originally a single building designed by Horace Trumbauer for Mrs. Amory S. Carhart in the style of a Louis XVI house. The mansion

was purchased in 1937 by the Lycée Francais, which added a modernist extension. When the Lycée sold both buildings in 2000, John Simpson, architect of the Queen's Gallery at Buckingham Palace, in collaboration with Zivkovic Architects, designed a replacement for the annex; the resulting merger is a faultless example of restrained classicism echoing—not mimicking— the original Carhart facade.

Our final stop is **12 East 96th Street** ⑰ (page 230), a narrow Beaux-Arts townhouse designed by Ogden Codman, Jr. for Robert L. Livingston in 1916; the building now houses La Scuola d'Italia Gugliemo Marconi. Graceful fruit garlands draped between keystones and large brackets with guttae embellish the limestone facade.

24 East 94th St

8 East 94th St

18 East 94th St

12 East 96th St

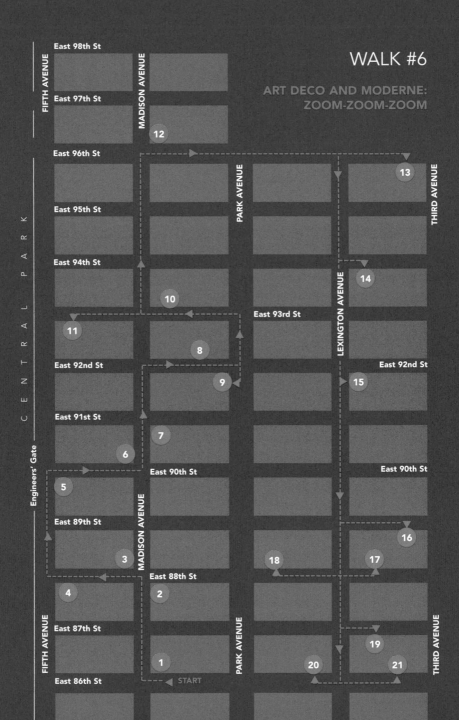

WALK #6

ART DECO AND MODERNE:
ZOOM-ZOOM-ZOOM

ART DECO AND MODERNE: ZOOM-ZOOM-ZOOM
Time: 2 hours 30 minutes, if one continuous walk

2 East 88th St

S leek and stylish, Art Deco buildings add a whipped-cream flourish to Carnegie Hill's mostly conservative pudding. The area boasts quite a few first-rate examples—including two which are sometimes referred to as Moderne, one church, and three commercial structures. All were built within a narrow time frame, between 1927 and 1938. The locations are scattered; you may wish to divide your walk into north-south or east-west segments.

49 East 86th Street ❶ (page 88) is an understated Moderne building by Pennington & Lewis at the corner of Madison Avenue.

19 East 88th St

Two blocks north is Sugarman & Berger's **40 East 88th Street** ❷ (page 106); note the decorative stone-work lining the upper-story terraces. For sheer flamboy-ance, **19 East 88th Street** ❸ (page 106) is hard to beat. Built in the depths of the Great Depression, it combines bold sculptural forms, stylized flowers, steel-banded

balconies with ocean-liner rails, and even flying but-tresses. **2 East 88th Street** ❹ (page 103), another Pennington & Lewis Moderne standout, is best viewed from across Fifth Avenue; four serene goddesses enclose the water tank. At Fifth and 90th Street, Hardie Phillip's **Church of the Heavenly Rest** ❺ (page 122) is an austere Gothic masterpiece with Art Deco massing and details: note the elongated angels above the entrance.

Returning to Madison, George F. Pelham's Deco-Medieval **21 East 90th Street** ❻ (page 127) displays surprising splashes of color throughout the facade. One block north. at **46 East 91st Street** ❼ (page 143), is another Pelham with lively red-and-buff-brick vertical bands.

Continue north up Madison and turn right on 92nd Street. **No 57** **8** (page 166) has a Moderne replacement facade; note the bezants at the parapet. On the corner of 92nd Street is **1150 Park Avenue** **9** (page 62), a late Moderne-style Pelham, Jr. Walk north up Park onto East 93rd Street and swing by **No. 65** **10**

10 East 93rd St

(page 192) and **No. 10** **11** (page 183), which display Art Deco and Moderne replacement facades.

123 East 86th St

The northern highlight is **49 East 96th Street** **12** (page 232): Thomas Lamb's 1930 design mixes bold geometrics with an exciting ziggurat effect. Two blocks away, **166 East 96th Street** **13** (page 239) emphasizes its verticality with fluted columns and geometric flare-ups piercing the parapet. Return to Lexington Avenue and head south: **152 East 94th Street** **14** (page 214), designed by the inventive Boak & Paris team, has a step-down entry with squares,

1395 Lexington, 92nd St Y

circles and arrowheads in the grillwork. Two blocks south on Lexington, the **92nd Street Y** **15** (page 79) displays pronounced Art Deco touches in its brick piers rising from shallow stone balconies.

A final Art Deco cluster starts at **160 East 89th Street** **16** (page 122), a late Boak & Paris design. On East 88th Street, **No. 161** **17** (page 110) uses decorative brickwork and **No. 111** **18** (page 108) frames its door with stepped purplish-gray marble. The Alan Garage at **154 East 87th Street** **19** (page 100) is required viewing, with colorful terra-cotta geometrics, lion heads, and automobile tires as part of the design. Return to 86th Street: Just west is Citibank at **No.123** **20** (page 91); note the Walker & Gillette stylized eagles above the central window. Finally, walk east: Above the street-level stores at **No. 157** **21** (page 91), five piers culminate in female busts crowned with stylized sunbursts.

40 East 88th St

157 East 86th St

21 East 90th St

111 East 88th St

160 East 89th St

160

49 East 96th St

49

166 East 96th St

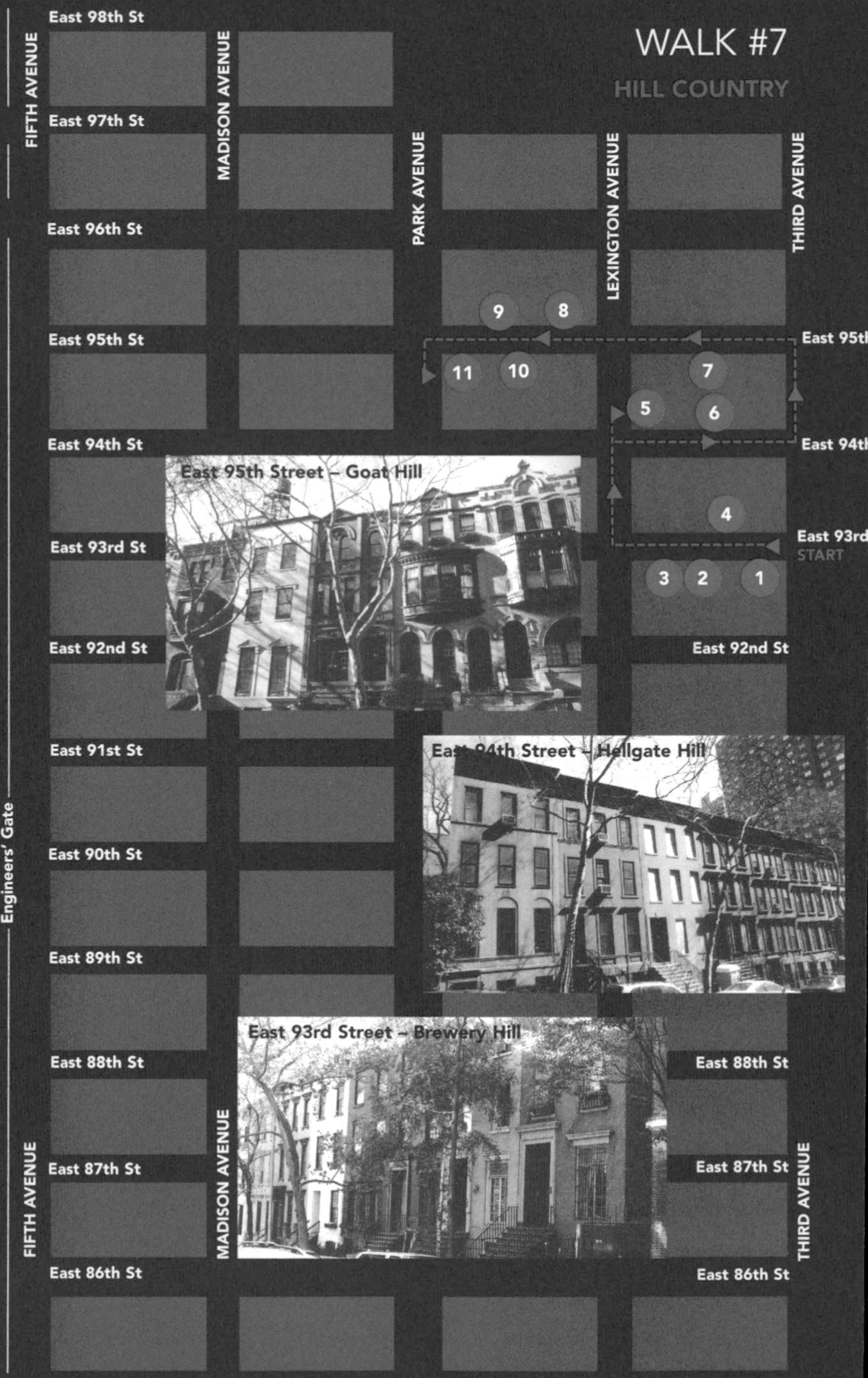

WALK #7
HILL COUNTRY

East 98th St
East 97th St
East 96th St
East 95th St
East 94th St
East 93rd St
East 92nd St
East 91st St
East 90th St
East 89th St
East 88th St
East 87th St
East 86th St

FIFTH AVENUE
MADISON AVENUE
PARK AVENUE
LEXINGTON AVENUE
THIRD AVENUE

CENTRAL PARK
Engineers' Gate

East 95th Street – Goat Hill

East 94th Street – Hellgate Hill

East 93rd Street – Brewery Hill

East 95th
East 94th
East 93rd
START

East 92nd St
East 88th St
East 87th St
East 86th St

9 8
11 10
7
5 6
4
3 2 1

HILL COUNTRY
Time: 1 hour 15 minutes

Three streets in the upper reaches of Carnegie Hill are home to some of the earliest row houses in the city. Each block is on a steep incline; each has its own character and informal "hill" name. The houses display Italianate, neo-Grec, Queen Anne and Romanesque Revival features. Most have been lovingly preserved.

Brewery Hill (page 199) leads down from Lexington Avenue to what were once the Ehret and Ruppert breweries on Second Avenue, that flourished in the 19th century. Start your walk just in from Third Avenue at **184 and 186 East 93rd Street** ❶, a pair of 1876 neo-Grec brownstones. **Nos. 168 - 176** ❷ were built in the late 1860s. (No. 176 added a modern facade in 1970.) The red-brick Italianate houses, at **Nos. 158-166** ❸, date from 1865. Across the street are **Nos. 175-179** ❹ (page 201). No. 179 was home to Samuel Marx, a tailor, his wife Minnie, and their five sons, whose stage names are familiar—Chico, Harpo, Groucho, Gummo and Zeppo.

1451-1457 Lexington ❺ (page 82) are what remain of the western section of **Hellgate Hill**, a U-shaped enclave encompassing the north side of 94th Street ❻ and the south side of 95th Street ❼ (page 215). The area was once a square block of neo-Grec row houses designed by Thom & Wilson in 1878-1880; the Third

Avenue side has been demolished. Not visible is a "companionway" between the two streets, with staircases connecting the rear gardens. Walk down 94th Street; most of the original houses survive. Only No. 173, once the residence of artists Robert Motherwell and Helen Frankenthaler, has been drastically altered. Twelve similar houses line the uphill march on 95th Street.

Cross Lexington and continue up 95th Street, known as **Goat Hill** (page 224), presumably because goats once grazed there. On the north side **Nos. 129-143** ❽ were designed in pairs by Frank Wennemer, with neo-Grec and Romanesque Revival elements; No. 143 is beautifully intact. **Nos. 115-127** ❾ were designed in Queen Anne style as mirror-image pairs by Louis Entzer, Jr. The 1887-88 Queen Anne houses on the south side, **Nos. 116-138** ❿, designed by C. Abbott French, exhibit odd roof lines, oriels and satyr-like faces. The caricaturist Al Hirschfeld lived in the salmon house, No. 122. Two Queen Annes at the west end of the row, Nos. 114-116, together with newly restored **1217 Park Avenue** ⓫ (page 68), are part of an 1890 group wrapping around the corner onto Park. Goat Hill represents what many feel is the essence of Carnegie Hill today: an enclave of surviving history and architectural treasures rarely seen in Manhattan.

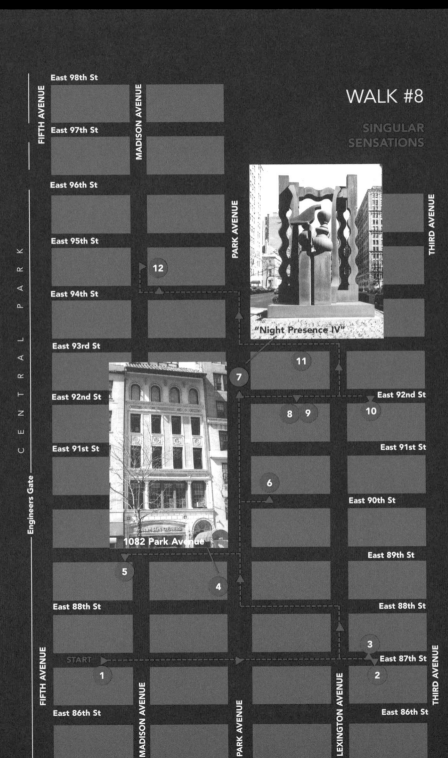

WALK #8

SINGULAR
SENSATIONS

"Night Presence IV"

1082 Park Avenue

East 98th St
East 97th St
East 96th St
East 95th St
East 94th St
East 93rd St
East 92nd St
East 91st St
East 90th St
East 89th St
East 88th St
East 87th St
East 86th St

East 92nd St
East 91st St
East 90th St
East 89th St
East 88th St
East 87th St
East 86th St

FIFTH AVENUE
MADISON AVENUE
PARK AVENUE
THIRD AVENUE
LEXINGTON AVENUE
CENTRAL PARK
Engineers Gate

START

1
2
3
4
5
6
7
8
9
10
11
12

SINGULAR SENSATIONS
Time: 1 hour, 30 minutes

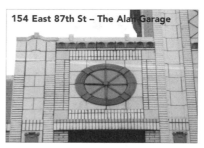

154 East 87th St – The Alan Garage

Carnegie Hill possesses a number of unusual structures, twelve of which we have singled out in this walk. Some are truly one-of-a-kind, while others recall a vanishing breed, be it a horse-drawn-era firehouse or, rarer still, a wooden house.

Let's begin on 87th Street on the block between Fifth and Madison avenues. **12 East 87th Street** ❶ (page 93) is one of the city's most original buildings. Called The Capitol, it was designed as an eight-story luxury apartment house with one fourteen-room, four-bath apartment per floor. Architects George & Edward Blum—early 20th-century champions of textile-like pattern and ornament in design—clad the facade in white brick (in 1911!) and glazed terra-cotta incised with an abundance of decorative motifs, including friezes of shells and rosettes. Continue east past Lexington to encounter two more unusual structures. **154 East 87th Street,** the Alan Garage ❷ (page 100), was designed by Frank J. Schefcik in 1930. The Art Deco facade offers an exuberant display

of terra-cotta motifs, including automobile tires, as well as signage spelling out the name of the garage and the directionals UP and DOWN. Across the street at **159 East 87th Street** ❸ (page 101) is the Italianate/Romanesque Revival "13 Hook & Ladder 13" firehouse built around 1860, now used as a storage

159 East 87th St, Andy Warhol's studio

facility. Its fame derives from the go-go 1960s when it served as Andy Warhol's studio and gallery, when he lived around the corner at 1342 Lexington Avenue.

Next, walk west across 88th Street and turn north up Park Avenue to view another tile-faced building at **1082 Park** ❹ (page 52). The "neo-Florentine" polychrome-tile design was conceived in 1925 by designer Augustus N. Allen for shop-owner Simon Ginsberg as a jazzy antidote to the staid apartment buildings rising along the avenue. Continue up Park and

22 East 89th St – The Hotel Graham

128 East 93rd St

detour to Madison Avenue: At **22 East 89th Street** you will see the Romanesque Revival **Hotel Graham** ❺ (page 115), built in

**113 East 90th St –
Allan Stone Gallery**

1891 and heralded as the Upper East Side's first apartment hotel. Now owned by Saint David's School, it retains its grand arched entry, curvaceous wings and lavishly embellished windows. Return to Park and head east to **113 East 90th Street,** another former firehouse, now the widely respected **Allan Stone Gallery** ❻ (page 129). Displaying a playful combination of Queen Anne and Romanesque Revival elements, the gallery retains its fire-engine-size arched entryway (now a window) and a peaked parapet. Two blocks up at Park Avenue at 92nd Street you will see the massive bolted-steel

"Night Presence IV" ❼ (page 63) by Louise Nevelson, who once lived in the neighborhood. Turn east to view the first two of Carnegie Hill's four wooden frame houses, rarities that somehow escaped early fire-code razing. **120** and **122 East 92nd Street** ❽ ❾ (page 170), built in 1871 and 1859, are Italianate in style and retain wide porches with openwork columns. Further east, **160 East 92nd Street** ❿ (page 178) is a smaller clapboard house in Greek Revival style with fluted Corinthian columns. It was designed in 1852 by carpenter-builder Albro Howell, who lived

120 and 122 East 92nd St

down the block, and may also have designed No. 122. Over the decades the house was occupied by the jeweler Jean Schlumberger and by the singer Eartha Kitt. The fourth wooden house, at **128 East 93rd Street** ⑪ (page 197), was designed by Edmund Waring. Italianate in style, the 1866 house stands back from the street behind a bricked front yard. Details to note are the slate mansard roof and dormer windows.

160 East 93rd St

Retrace your steps to Park Avenue and continue along 94th Street. Stretching along Madison Avenue from 94th to 95th streets are the remains of the **Squadron A (Eighth Regiment) Armory** ⑫ (page 211), constructed from 1888 to 1895 to accommodate the drills of the First New York Hussars, a volunteer squadron of "gentleman riders." The brick armory once encompassed much of the square block between Madison and Park avenues. Mimicking a medieval French fortress, it was designed by John Rochester Thomas with turrets, towers, corbels and crenelations—some of which are echoed in the 1970 contextual design building for the Hunter College Campus Schools.

Squadron A (Eighth Regiment) Armory
Madison Avenue at 94th-95th streets

THE ARCHITECTS

A few of Carnegie Hill's better known architects, shown left to right:
William Adams Delano, Chester Holmes Aldrich, J.E.R. Carpenter,
John Russell Pope, Henry J. Hardenbergh, Horace Trumbauer,
Whitney Warren, Charles Delavan Wetmore, Frank Lloyd Wright.

Carnegie Hill is graced with a wide variety of buildings, from modest row houses and flats to grand apartment houses and mansions. These are the work of upwards of 200 architects and architectural firms within the 48 blocks that comprise our neighborhood. In the late 19th century and the first three decades of the 20th century, when residential building boomed, developers produced well over 400 individual buildings and rows of houses here. Many of the earlier architects were basically self-taught; patterns dictated the design of the structures, floor plans and exterior trim, although within such constraints these diligent draftsmen often demonstrated charming variety and originality.

By contrast, the architects retained by the wealthy capitalists and entrepreneurs who commissioned some of the city's loveliest apartment buildings and mansions in Carnegie Hill are amongst the city's—and the nation's—finest practitioners of their art. Much has been written about the most renowned; their biographies here, by necessity, have been whittled to a mere paragraph or two.

In writing the biographies, we have indicated the architects' dates when known. If no biography is included, we were unable to unearth information other than the address of the particular Carnegie Hill building(s) attributed to the architect. In our research we tapped many sources. If a building is located within the Expanded Carnegie Hill Historic District designation report of 1994, we turned first to the biography provided by the New York City Landmarks Preservation Commission (LPC). We also consulted LPC reports on architects active in other designated historic districts in New York City, supplementing them with information gleaned from books, newspapers, magazines and websites. Sources include, among others, our original *Carnegie Hill: An Architectural Guide* of 1989, articles from *The New York Times* archives and obituaries, the Society of Architectural Historians American Architects' Biographies, the *American Institute of Architects Guide to New York City* by Elliot Willensky and Norval White, Christopher Gray's Office for Metropolitan History, Carter B. Horsley's *Upper East Side Book,* Robert A.M. Stern's *Architecture* (or *Metropolitan Architecture*) and *Urbanism* series, the Macmillan *Encyclopedia of Architects, Architects in Practice in New York City* by Dennis Steadman Francis and James Ward, Wickipedia, websites of the New-York Historical Society, Columbia University and other educational facilities, *Time* magazine, realty companies, and of the architectural firms if they are extant; and even several personal interviews.

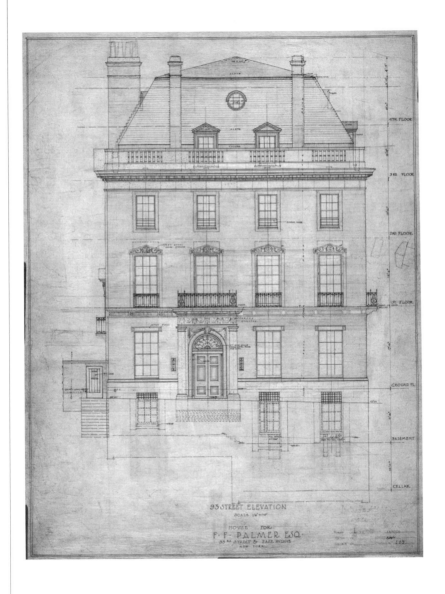

The 1917 south elevation by architects Delano & Aldrich of 75 East 93rd Street, Francis F. Palmer house (later George F. Baker house, now part of the Russian Orthodox Church Outside of Russia).

ADAMS & WOODBRIDGE

Lewis Greenleaf Adams (1897-1977)

Frederick James Woodbridge (1900-?)

Fellow members of the American Institute of Architects, Adams and Woodbridge joined forces in 1945. **Lewis Greenleaf Adams,** born in Lenox, Massachusetts, graduated from Yale and the Ecole des Beaux-Arts in Paris and began his career in 1926 as a draftsman at the firm of Delano & Aldrich. He was there for three years before entering a partnership, Adams & Prentice, that lasted until 1941. In 1954-55 he served as president of the Architectural League of New York. Minneapolis-born **Frederick James Woodbridge,** after graduating from Columbia, worked in the offices of McKim, Mead & White. He interrupted his association with that firm for four years to study at the American Academy in Rome and served as architect for two excavations, at Antioch and Carthage. In 1929 he left McKim, Mead & White to become a partner in the firm of Evans, Moore & Woodbridge, where he stayed until 1942. The post-war partnership of Adams & Woodbridge concentrated primarily on institutional buildings, including the Adirondack Museum in Blue Mountain Lake, New York, and an infirmary and dormitory for Hamilton College in Clinton, New York. In Manhattan, Adams & Woodbridge designed the Episcopal Church Center on Second Avenue and 44th Street, a dome for the Cathedral of St. John the Divine, and a new wing for Trinity Church on Wall Street. In Carnegie Hill the firm designed the addition to the Nightingale-Bamford School at 26 East 92nd Street, and the Brick Presbyterian Church parish house and school at 66-70 East 92nd Street.

GAETANO AJELLO (1883-1983)

Sicilian-born Gaetano Ajello emigrated to the United States in 1902. By 1906 he was working on the Schwab mansion on Riverside Drive and 73rd Street and three years later had received commissions in Manhattan for four buildings, all designed in the Italian Renaissance style, near Columbia University. In 1912 he became affiliated with the Paterno and Campagna families, fellow Sicilians and influential developers who built over 100 apartment houses. For them and other clients Ajello followed a more subdued, neo-Classical style. Of his 38 projects the most recent to attain landmark status, designated in June 2006, is the Claremont Theater on Broadway and 135th Street. Salient features of an Ajello building include a central escutcheon incised with the initials of the building's owner and a cornerstone bearing his own name: G. Ajello, Architect. He retired in the mid-1920s and until his death at age 100 invented and patented designs in various fields: for airplanes, railroads—and shoes. The apartment house at 17 East 89th Street was Ajello's only Carnegie Hill building, and his last commission.

AUGUSTUS N. ALLEN (?-1957)

Active from the first decade of the 20th century through the 1920s, Augustus N. Allen is known for designing grand estates for wealthy families on Long Island and in New Jersey, as well as office buildings in midtown Manhattan. Among his notable buildings are the Latham Hotel at 4 East 28th Street, designed in 1906; the neo-Classical John Jermain Memorial Library in Sag Harbor on Long Island, built in 1910; and a 26-story Renaissance Revival office building at 292 Madison Avenue, completed in 1923. In the same year he designed a sumptuous 3,500-square-foot office for financier John W. Campbell in a corner of Grand Central Terminal; styled after a 13th-century Florentine palazzo with a 25-foot-high hand-painted ceiling, an enormous fireplace and leaded windows, the office was restored in 1999 as the Campbell Apartment, a public bar and lounge. In Carnegie Hill he designed the polychrome-tile facade of 1082 Park Avenue.

HENRY ANDERSON

Henry Anderson was a New York City architect specializing in residential buildings in the Renaissance Revival and neo-Renaissance styles at the turn of the 20th century. Starting his practice in 1882, he soon became head draftsman for Simon I. Schwartz (later of the firm of Schwartz & Gross). Anderson produced designs for a number of apartment buildings on the Upper West Side, including the Semiramis, the Don Carlos, and the Aylesmere, all in 1901. His commercial work is best represented by a warehouse at 143-147 Franklin Street in Tribeca (1899). In Carnegie Hill he designed the six houses at 10-20 East 95th Street.

WILFRED E. ANTHONY (1878-1948)

Wilfred Edwards Anthony practiced architecture in New York City from 1914 to 1940. In 1930-31 he designed several religious buildings, including one for the Holy Name Society at 141 East 65th Street and another for the St. Catherine of Sienna Church at 411 East 68th Street. Three years earlier, in Carnegie Hill, he enlarged and redesigned the facades of 105 and 107 East 91st Street.

GROSVENOR ATTERBURY (1869-1956)

Grosvenor Atterbury was famous as an innovator of prefabricated public-housing projects and as an urban planner. He was born in Detroit and educated at Yale and Columbia and at the Ecole des Beaux-Arts in Paris. Upon returning to New York City, he worked for the firm of McKim, Mead & White. Much of his early work concentrated on fashionable residences for wealthy industrialists, including H.O. Havemeyer, a benefactor of the Metropolitan Museum of Art, for which Atterbury restored the American

Wing in 1936. Philanthropic ideals inspired Atterbury to develop a system of prefabrication based on standardized precast concrete panels; it was first applied to the model housing community of Forest Hills Gardens in Queens, begun in 1909 under the sponsorship of the Russell Sage Foundation. He also designed a railroad station for the community. In Manhattan he designed the Russell Sage Foundation building on Park Avenue at 64th Street (1916), St. James Episcopal Church on Madison Avenue and 71st Street (1937), and the Amsterdam Houses, a huge housing project on the West Side behind what is now Lincoln Center (1938). Atterbury was also involved with the restoration of City Hall. He served as an architectural consultant on hospitals and was an associate professor of architecture at Yale. In Carnegie Hill he designed 6 East 87th Street, now the Liederkranz Club, and collaborated with Egisto Fabbri, architect brother of his client Ernesto Fabbri, on the design of 7 East 95th Street, the Edith and Ernesto Fabbri house, now the House of the Redeemer.

FELIX AUGENFELD (1893-1984)

Born in Austria, Felix Augenfeld trained in Vienna and was briefly a member of the Loos Bauschule, whose members included fellow modernist Richard Neutra. From 1922 until 1938 Augenfeld maintained a studio with Karl Hofmann; their clients included Sigmund Freud, for whom Augenfeld designed an ingenious lounging chair. In 1938 both designers left Austria for London; the following year Augenfeld moved to New York City and within two years opened his own office. He worked primarily on interiors and furnishings; between 1945 and 1950 he created a number of designs for the Wisconsin-based American Chair Company. His architectural credits include only two houses in the United States: a beach house that he built for himself on Fire Island in 1957, and the Carnegie Hill townhouse at 10 East 87th Street that he designed with architect Jan Hird Pokorny.

BABB, COOK & WILLARD

George Fletcher Babb (1843-1916)
Walter Cook (1846-1916)
Daniel Wheelock Willard

The partnership of Babb, Cook & Willard combined the talents of three fellows of the American Institute of Architects who worked together to design the magnificent mansion belonging to steel magnate and philanthropist Andrew Carnegie, for whom Carnegie Hill is named. **George Fletcher Babb** was born in New York. At the age of fifteen he joined the office of T.R. Jackson; a year later he became associated with Nathaniel G. Foster, with whom he worked until 1865, when he moved to the office of Russell Sturgis as senior draftsman. One of his projects was the redesign of the studio in

Cornish, New Hampshire, of Augustus Saint-Gaudens, sculptor of the Lincoln Memorial in Washington, D.C. **Walter Cook,** also born in New York, graduated from Harvard and studied architecture in Munich and Paris. Babb and Cook joined forces in 1877; in 1884 **Daniel Wheelock Willard,** a graduate of M.I.T., joined them to form Babb, Cook & Willard. Among their commissions were the DeVinne Press Building at 393 Lafayette Street and buildings for the New York Life Insurance Company in New York City and in St. Paul and Minneapolis, Minnesota. In addition to the Andrew and Louise Carnegie mansion at 2 East 91st Street, now the Cooper-Hewitt, National Design Museum, the firm designed two branches of the New York Public Library, so-called Carnegie libraries, in Morrisania in the Bronx and at 112 East 96th Street in Carnegie Hill.

C. DALE BADGELEY (1899?-1990)

A winner of the Prix de Rome, C. Dale Badgeley was educated at Ohio State University and Columbia. During his career he designed skyscrapers in Caracas, Venezuela, and several buildings on the campus of the American University in Beirut, Lebanon, as well as private residences. In New York City he designed the rehabilitation of Bryant Park and other city parks. Badgeley is best known for his design of the overall plan of the 1939-40 New York World's Fair. In Carnegie Hill he remodeled the facade of 103 East 91st Street, adding a stark neo-Georgian limestone extension.

BARNEY & CHAPMAN
John Stewart Barney (1869-1924)
Henry Otis Chapman (1862-1929)

Partners for twenty years, from 1894 until 1914, John Stewart Barney and Henry Otis Chapman were responsible for a number of Manhattan's most architecturally noteworthy religious institutions, including the Church of the Holy Trinity at 316 East 88th Street, just outside of Carnegie Hill, and Grace Chapel at 412 East 14th Street; both are designated landmarks. Together the pair also designed several hotels, including the Navarre on Seventh Avenue and 39th Street. A native New Yorker, **Barney** graduated from Columbia and the Ecole des Beaux-Arts in Paris. He designed the Revillon Building on West 28th Street in association with Stockton B. Colt. Upon his retirement from the firm, he devoted the remainder of his life to painting. **Chapman,** who was born upstate in Otisville, studied architecture at Cornell; he, too, completed his training in Europe. He designed the Union Sulfide Building on Rector Street and two buildings for the United States Mortgage and Trust Company. In Carnegie Hill the firm designed 157 East 89th Street and 11 East 90th Street, the latter for William and M. Louise McAlpin in 1902-03.

F.S. BARUS
Little is known of Frederick S. Barus other than that he practiced architecture in Manhattan during the 1870s. During that time he was responsible for a row of Italianate-style brownstones on East 65th Street (and an adjoining row of tenements on Lexington Avenue), as well as the row of nine neo-Grec houses at 121-137 East 94th Street in Carnegie Hill.

CHARLES BAXTER
A native New Yorker, Charles Baxter designed a number of neo-Grec row houses on the Upper East Side and in Mount Morris Park in Central Harlem, in what are now designated Historic Districts. In addition to doing residential work, he was the architect of St. Nicholas Church and St. Anselm's Monastery in the Bronx. In Carnegie Hill he designed 105-109 East 88th Street and 183 East 94th Street.

RICHARD BERGER
Richard Berger is on record for designing several buildings in SoHo in Manhattan, including a cast-iron warehouse at 112 Prince Street, in the neo-Grec/Renaissance Revival style in 1889. In Carnegie Hill he designed 169 East 87th Street and 170 East 92nd Street.

JOHN BERGESEN
A New York architect of Russian origin, John Bergesen was a partner around the turn of the 20th century with the firms of Young, Bergeson & Cornell and of Brewster & Bergesen. In Carnegie Hill he designed the extraordinary St. Nicholas Russian Orthodox Cathedral in New York at 15 East 97th Street.

BERNSTEIN & BERNSTEIN
Michael Bernstein
Mitchell Bernstein

In the early 1890s **Michael Bernstein** had his own architectural practice at 111 Broadway; his work at the time included an office building at 18th Street and Broadway and the Schley Music Hall at 112 West 34th Street (renamed the Savoy and demolished in 1952). After forming a partnership with another architect, he returned to working independently before becoming head draftsman for **Mitchell Bernstein.** The two formed a partnership with offices first on Trinity Place and then on East 23rd Street. Together they were responsible for a number of Renaissance Revival mixed-use buildings, including seven in Carnegie Hill: 1324 and 1469 Lexington Avenue, 162 East 90th Street, 160 East 91st Street, and 115-117 and 119 East 96th Street.

SYLVAN AND ROBERT L. BIEN

Sylvan Bien (1893-1959)

Robert L. Bien (1923-2002)

In the early 1900s Austrian-born **Sylvan Bien** emigrated to San Francisco, where he assisted on the design of the Panama-Pacific Exposition. In 1916 he moved to New York City. In 1919 he joined the firm of Warren & Wetmore; subsequently he was affiliated with Shreve, Lamb & Harmon and, later, with Emery Roth. From the early 1930s until his death he maintained his own practice, specializing in apartment buildings and hotels, including the Carlyle on East 76th Street at Madison Avenue. **Robert L. Bien** was educated at the Cornell College of Architecture and at Stamford University and joined his father's practice in 1949. At that time the firm had become entrenched in the ubiquitous Modern style, which in the 1960s evolved into the so-called "white bricks." A few later examples of the Biens' version of the genre added bay windows or notes of color. In Carnegie Hill the Biens designed 11 East 86th Street, 40 East 89th Street, and 1199 Park Avenue.

BKSK ARCHITECTS

Stephen F. Burns

Harry C. Kendall

George B.M. Schieferdecker

Joan Krevlin

Formed in 1985, the firm of BKSK Architects focuses on high-end residential, commercial and institutional design, with emphasis on historic preservation and environmental sustainability. **Stephen F. Burns,** a graduate of Princeton University, **Harry C. Kendall,** a graduate of Washington University, and **George B.M. Schieferdecker,** a graduate of Middlebury College, all received their architectural master's degrees from Columbia University. Burns, a specialist in the integration of architectural and landscape design, is currently a New York City Landmarks Preservation Commissioner. **Joan Krevlin** earned her art history degree and master's degree in architecture from Washington University. Among the firm's recent projects are the Queens Botanical Garden Visitor & Administration Center in Flushing, New York, and the design of condominium buildings at 124 Hudson Street and 120 East 72nd Street. Under construction at this writing is the firm's facade re-design and conversion to residential use of Nos. 4-8 East 94th Street in Carnegie Hill.

OSCAR BLUEMNER (1867-1938)

Oscar Bluemner was best known as an Expressionist painter, although he trained as a portrait painter and an architect. Born in Hanover, Germany, he won prizes at the Royal Technical Academy in Berlin, where photographer and art dealer Alfred Stieglitz had also studied. Immediately upon graduating in 1892, Bluemner emigrated to Chicago; in 1900 he moved to New York City, where he set up an architectural office. Two years later he designed a pair of Carnegie Hill townhouses, 7 and 9 East 89th Street, in the Beaux-Arts style. (No. 7 no longer exists.) In 1904 he designed the Bronx Borough Courthouse, now a designated landmark, in association with Michael J. Garvin. His plans were stolen by his partner; he sued, and after ten years won the case. That experience so disillusioned him that he discontinued practicing architecture, other than designing a handful of country houses that he termed "bungalows" for private clients. Bluemner devoted the rest of his life to painting: He was an exhibitor in the Armory Show of 1913 and was involved in the prestigious 291 Gallery of Alfred Stieglitz, who became one of his sponsors. Following the death of his wife in 1926, Bluemner moved to Braintree, Massachusetts, where he lived until his suicide in 1938. Some of his work is in the permanent collection of the Whitney Museum of American Art; a retrospective, "A Passion for Color," was mounted at the Whitney in the fall of 2005. His surviving Carnegie Hill building at 9 East 89th Street is now the headquarters of the New York Road Runners Club.

GEORGE & EDWARD BLUM

George Blum (1870?-1928)
Edward Blum (1876-1944)

George Blum was born in New York; his brother **Edward** was born in Paris. Of French parentage, the Blum brothers had a dual-city upbringing, with the family finally settling in New York in 1888. George received his architectural degree from Columbia in 1895; both brothers studied briefly (but not together) at the Ecole des Beaux-Arts in Paris and in 1909 set up an architectural practice in New York. Their first apartment building, the Phaeton at 539 West 112th Street, was completed in the same year; its unexpected subtle tone variations, criss-cross brickwork and bursts of colored tiles foreshadowed the idiosyncratic designs to follow. Over the next two decades they would produce a string of 120 apartment buildings with curious towers, neo-Medieval accents and highly textural facades employing custom-crafted terra-cotta panels, intricate metalwork, clinker bricks, mosaics and art tiles. Among their more intriguing projects is the white-brick-and-terra-cotta Hotel Theresa on Seventh Avenue and 125th Street in Harlem (1913), now the Theresa Towers where Fidel Castro met Soviet leader Nikita Khrushchev in 1960. They also designed loft buildings for the garment industry and several synagogues. In Carnegie Hill they designed the Capitol at 12 East 87th Street, 150 East 93rd Street, 1075 Park Avenue and 1435 Lexington Avenue.

BOAK & PARIS

Russell M. Boak (1896-?)

Hyman F. Paris

Bronx-born **Russell M. Boak** entered the office of architect Emery Roth right after eighth grade and went to work as a draftsman. **Hyman F. Paris** practiced architecture as early as 1913; he was registered in New York City by 1922 and he, too, was a draftsman for Roth. Boak and Paris are thought to have formed their partnership in 1927. The firm was active in the 1930s and worked throughout Manhattan and in the Bronx, often for developer Samuel Minskoff. Their work from that decade exhibited a number of stylistic elements—Gothic, Romanesque, neo-Renaissance— but, most tellingly, they developed a special flair for the then-popular Art Deco/Art Moderne style, which is perhaps best represented by their Metro Theater (formerly the Midtown) on Broadway and 99th Street, now a designated landmark. A standout of their elegantly restrained buildings is the fenestration: steel casement windows, with pairs often set at the corners, allowing two contiguous exposures to a room. The firm dissolved in 1942, when Paris presumably retired; Boak went on to work with architect Thomas O. Raad in the 1940s and 1950s. Boak & Paris are well represented in Carnegie Hill with apartment houses at 110 East 87th Street, 160 East 89th Street, and 139 and 152 East 94th Street.

WILLIAM A. BORING (1859-1937)

After studying at the University of Illinois and Columbia, William Alciphron Boring spent three years at the Ecole des Beaux-Arts in Paris. Upon his return to New York City in 1890 he joined the firm of McKim, Mead & White. In 1891 he formed a partnership with Edward Lippincott Tilton; their best-known work is the new Immigration Station at Ellis Island in New York harbor, now on the National Register of Historic Places. Among their other commissions were the Hotel Colorado in Glenwood Springs, Colorado, and the Marine Barracks in the Brooklyn Navy Yard. Working independently, Boring designed apartment buildings at 520 (since demolished), 521, and 540 Park Avenue in Manhattan. In Carnegie Hill he added a mansard roof to 66 East 91st Street.

WILLIAM LAWRENCE BOTTOMLEY (1883-1951)

A native New Yorker, William Lawrence Bottomley received a degree in architecture from Columbia in 1906 and continued his studies at the American Academy in Rome and the Ecole des Beaux-Arts in Paris. In 1920 in New York City he and architect Edward C. Dean were commissioned by Charlotte Hunnewell Sorchan to renovate two back-to-back rows of ten houses on East 48th and 49th streets, to create what became the Turtle Bay Gardens Historic District. Bottomley also altered the facades of four contiguous townhouses on East 70th Street, including those of a merged pair owned by James P. Warburg, son of financier Paul Warburg. As a partner in the firm of Bottomley, Wagner & White, he co-designed the 1931 neo-Georgian River House and River Club at 435 and 447 East 52nd Street (and the club's dock for yachts). Bottomley worked extensively in Virginia, notably in Richmond, where he designed many houses, twenty of which survive. He is credited with two books, *Spanish Details*, which he wrote, and *Great Georgian Houses of America*, which he edited. In Carnegie Hill he is responsible for the neo-Georgian facade of 1211 Park Avenue and for combining 130 and 132 East 92nd Street into a townhouse with a neo-Regency facade. In 1919, together with J.L. Mills (about whom nothing is known), he designed 1049 Park Avenue, which in 1922 was awarded the Gold Medal by the New York Chapter of the American Institute of Architects for "Best designed Apartment Hotel erected during the past three years."

JOHN BRANDT

John Brandt began his architectural practice in 1879. He was joined by Louis Brandt in 1892; they formed the firm of L. & J. Brandt and maintained their partnership until 1908. John continued practicing until 1925. Under the firm name of Brandt & Co., he is credited with designing 1361 Lexington Avenue and 120 and 122 East 91st Street in Carnegie Hill between 1885 and 1889. He also designed a row of five neo-Grec houses at East 92nd Street; Nos. 59 and 61 survive relatively intact.

FRANK BRAUN

First listed as a practicing architect in 1907, Frank Braun is on record as maintaining an office in Manhattan until 1913. However, his Carnegie Hill apartment house at 131 East 93rd Street was completed in 1923.

BUCHMAN & FOX

Albert C. Buchman   (1859-1936)
Mortimer J. Fox   (1875?-1948)

Albert C. Buchman received his education at Cornell and Columbia. In 1887 he formed a partnership with Gustav Deisler, followed two years later by a partnership with Hermann J. Schwarzmann (See Schwarzmann & Buchman). **Mortimer J. Fox** graduated from the City College of New York and Columbia. The partnership of Buchman & Fox was formed in 1899 and lasted until 1917. The firm designed a number of New York department stores, including the old Bonwit Teller and the West 18th Street addition to B. Altman. Buchman & Fox was responsible also for the annex to the New York Times

Building on West 43rd Street. In 1917 Fox left the firm to become a director of the Columbia Bank, later Manufacturers Trust; in later life he left banking to pursue his avocation, landscape painting. Buchman formed a partnership with Ely Jacques Kahn and went on to design many office buildings and one hotel, the Sherry-Netherland on Fifth Avenue at 59th Street. In Carnegie Hill Buchman & Fox designed 1261 Madison Avenue, now a designated landmark.

JOHN C. BURNE

Established in New York City by 1877, John C. Burne specialized in speculative houses and apartment buildings throughout Manhattan and in Park Slope in Brooklyn. His early buildings were designed primarily in the neo-Grec style; his subsequent work favored the Renaissance Revival style, as in the flats building at 1350 Madison Avenue in Carnegie Hill.

J. CLEVELAND CADY (1837-1919)

Providence-born Josiah Cleveland Cady graduated from Trinity College in Hartford, for which he later designed a number of buildings. By 1864 he had set up practice in New York City and eight years later he established his own firm, J.C. Cady & Co., which would later assume the name Cady, Berg & See in recognition of his partners, Louis D. Berg and Milton See. A former student of Henry Hobson Richardson, Cady applied the so-called Richardson Romanesque principles to many of the firm's designs, including the Carnegie Hill row houses at 57-65 East 90th Street. The firm's reputation rested on several outstanding works in the city, including the old Metropolitan Opera House at Broadway and 39th Street and parts of the American Museum of Natural History. Cady was the architect for a number of Presbyterian churches in New Jersey as well as for the Park Avenue Methodist Church, just south of Carnegie Hill at 85th Street. He designed buildings for several universities—fifteen for Yale alone, including the Crittendon Library. In 1918, a year before his death, he bequeathed his 400-volume library of architectural books to Trinity College.

FREDERICK T. CAMP (1849-1905)

In practice with Gilbert Bostwick Croff by the late 1870s, Frederick Theodore Camp seems to have specialized in flats buildings in Manhattan and the Bronx. He worked in a variety of architectural styles; in Carnegie Hill he is represented by two Queen Anne row houses at 1281 and 1283 Madison Avenue and the buildings at 1273 Madison Avenue (now demolished), 1080 and 1082 Park Avenue, and 1434-1440 Lexington Avenue.

ROSARIO CANDELA (1890-1953)

A first-generation Italian immigrant, Sicilian-born Rosario Candela arrived in New York at the age of nineteen and received his architectural degree from Columbia seven years later, in 1915. Through his first employer, Gaetano Ajello, Candela connected with developers Anthony Campagna and Joseph Paterno; all three were fellow Sicilians who made their names with apartment buildings throughout Manhattan, especially on the Upper East and West sides. Candela was exclusively a residential architect. His first design on the Upper East Side was the circumspect 1105 Park Avenue at 89th Street. As his fame grew, his designs became more sophisticated and urbane. A particularly fertile time for him was the eight-month period from March through October, 1929, when he designed six of his grandest apartment houses, including 770, 778, and, most famously, 740 Park Avenue; the latter is documented in the book *"740 Park: The Story of the World's Richest Apartment Building"* by Michael Gross. Other sterling examples of his work include 1 Sutton Place South and 834, 960, and 1040 Fifth Avenue (1040 was the home of Jacqueline Onassis), as well as the Stanhope Hotel at 995 Fifth Avenue, which has been converted into residences. Candela favored the terraced setback and "temple-like" water-tower enclosure, innovations that allowed not only for penthouse apartments where once clustered garret-like servants' quarters, but also for more graceful roofscapes. He was the architect of seven Carnegie Hill apartment houses: 1105, 1172, 1192, and 1220 Park Avenue, 12 East 88th Street, and 8 and 70 East 96th Street.

J.E.R. CARPENTER (1867-1932)

A designer of luxury apartment houses (sixteen in the Upper East Side Historic District alone), James Edwin Ruthvin Carpenter was born in Columbia, Tennessee, and graduated from M.I.T. After studying at the Ecole des Beaux-Arts in Paris, he set up practice in Norfolk, Virginia, concentrating on commercial buildings. In New York City he trained in the office of McKim, Mead & White. In 1909 he received a commission from the Fullerton-Weaver Company, a real-estate development firm, for a nine-story apartment building at 116 East 58th Street (since demolished). Three years later he set up practice on his own; his first project was 907 Fifth Avenue, for which he received a Gold Medal from the New York Chapter of the American Institute of Architects. From 1912 until his death in 1932 he worked both as an architect and as a real-estate investor and advisor, often with his wife and his brother, John. While admired for the restraint of his facades, Carpenter received his greatest acclaim for his "off-the-foyer" floor plan, which transformed the entrance hall or gallery of an apartment into an important focus of the interior design, as well as for his insistence on separating public reception rooms from those reserved for private use.

In 1923 he was instrumental in helping to overturn a height restriction—of 75 feet—on Fifth Avenue, an effort that spurred further development along the avenue. Other buildings that he designed in New York City include the original offices for CBS at 435 Madison Avenue and the Lincoln Building at 60 East 42nd Street. Carpenter was prone to designing similar buildings facing each other across a side street; such pairs in Carnegie Hill are 1115 and 1120, 1148 and 1150, and 1165 and 1170 Fifth Avenue, and 1050 and 1060 Park Avenue. His other Carnegie Hill apartment houses are 1060 and 1143 Fifth Avenue, 14 East 90th Street, and 4 East 95th Street.

CARRÈRE & HASTINGS
John Merven Carrère (1858-1911)
Thomas Hastings (1860-1929)

The quarter-century partnership of Carrère and Hastings had its seeds in Paris, where they met as students and earned their diplomas at the Ecole des Beaux-Arts. **John Merven Carrère,** born in Rio de Janeiro to a Baltimore coffee merchant, received his early education in Switzerland, while **Thomas Hastings,** a native New Yorker, studied briefly at Columbia. The two decided to form their own practice in 1886 while working in New York City as draftsmen for the firm of McKim, Mead & White. An early client was oil magnate Henry Flagler, who commissioned them to design hotels and churches in Florida as well as his own house in Palm Beach. Their reputation was secured in 1897, when they won a design competition for the New York Public Library on Fifth Avenue at 42nd Street (they subsequently designed fourteen branches, so-called Carnegie libraries). The Beaux-Arts New York Public Library is now a designated New York City landmark, as are a number of their other Manhattan commissions, including the approaches and arch of the Manhattan Bridge; the First Church of Christ, Scientist, on 96th Street and Central Park West; the Henry Clay Frick mansion, now the Frick Collection, at Fifth Avenue and 70th Street; and 1048 Fifth Avenue, now the Neue Galerie New York, just below the 86th Street boundary of Carnegie Hill. Their design for Grand Army Plaza on Fifth Avenue and 59th Street is a designated Scenic Landmark. Their most noteworthy designs outside of New York City are Woolsey and Memorial halls at Yale University, the Vanderbilt estate in Centerport on Long Island, and the House and Senate Office Buildings in Washington, D.C. After Carrère's death in an automobile accident in 1911, Hastings continued to practice under the firm's name, designing buildings for Standard Oil, the Macmillan Company, and the Cunard Line, all in Manhattan. In Carnegie Hill the firm designed 9 East 91st Street, originally the John Henry and Emily Vanderbilt Sloane Hammond house and now the Consulate of the Russian Federation in New York.

WALTER B. CHAMBERS (1866?-1945)

Brooklyn-born Walter Boughton Chambers received his education at Yale and the Ecole des Beaux-Arts in Paris, followed by training in Munich. Back in New York City, he joined the firm of Ernest Flagg in 1895. During his eleven years there the firm designed, among other buildings, the Oliver Gould Jennings residence at 7 East 72nd Street and the firehouse at 44 Great Jones Street, both designated landmarks. After 1906 Chambers worked independently, specializing in apartment buildings as well as private houses. In Carnegie Hill he collaborated with J.E.R. Carpenter on the design of 1148 Fifth Avenue.

SEYMOUR CHURGIN

The earliest record of Seymour Churgin's architectural practice in New York City is his 1979 redesign of the interior of the Engineers' Club at 32 West 40th Street, a building originally financed by Andrew Carnegie and designed by Carnegie's architects, Whitfield & King: Churgin's task was to divide the large clubrooms into apartment-size units. He undertook a similar assignment for St. George's parish house at 207 East 16th Street. During the 1980s and 1990s his firm, subsequently known as the Architects Design Group of Manhattan, was responsible for numerous apartment buildings, including the 366 West 11th Street Condominiums, 382 Third Avenue, 309 East 49th Street, 245 East 84th Street, and an eighteen-story building at 86th Street and Second Avenue. His only design in Carnegie Hill is the Royal Carnegie at 134 East 93rd Street.

CLEVERDON & PUTZEL

   Robert J. Cleverdon
   Joseph Putzel

Although their partnership, founded in 1882, lasted over a quarter of a century, little is known of either **Robert J. Cleverdon** or **Joseph Putzel** other than the quality and quantity of their work, especially in the mercantile sector. Their work included townhouses, row houses, and apartment and commercial buildings in Mount Morris Park, on the Upper West Side, and especially downtown. One of their projects was the Astor Building at 583 Broadway. In Carnegie Hill the firm designed two rows of Romanesque Revival houses at 5-13 and 15-25 East 94th Street.

CLINTON & RUSSELL

   Charles William Clinton (1838-1910)
   William Hamilton Russell (1856-1907)

CLINTON, RUSSELL & CLINTON

   William Hamilton Russell (1885-1958)
   Charles Kenneth Clinton

The two partnerships, one following the other, practiced architecture for almost half a century, from 1894 until 1940. **Charles William Clinton,** born in New York City, apprenticed to Richard Upjohn, then practiced alone for three decades before joining Russell. **William Hamilton Russell,** who was also born and raised in the city, received his architectural training at the Columbia University School of Mines, now its architecture school, following which he joined the firm of James Renwick, his great-uncle. From 1883 until 1894 the firm was known as Aspinwall, Renwick & Russell. The partnership of Clinton & Russell, formed in 1894, maintained an active practice, designing many hotels, including the Astor Hotel on Times Square (since demolished), and apartment houses, notably the Apthorp at 78th-79th Street and Broadway and the Graham Court at Seventh Avenue and 116th Street, both for the Astor family. The Apthorp and the Graham Court are designated landmarks. Clinton & Russell designed the 71st Regiment Armory at 33rd Street and Park Avenue, built in 1905, a grand structure and tower modeled after the town hall in Siena; it was demolished in the late 1960s. After Russell's death in 1907 Clinton continued and the firm of Clinton, Russell & Clinton was later established by the architects' sons. In Carnegie Hill Clinton & Russell designed 16-24 East 96th Street, the Queenston. Clinton, Russell & Clinton designed a new facade and addition to 133 East 95th Street.

OGDEN CODMAN, JR. (1863-1951)

Architect and interior designer to the Gilded Age's social elite, Ogden Codman, Jr. was born to a wealthy and socially prominent Boston family. He spent his teenage years in France and was educated, albeit briefly, at M.I.T. Following apprenticeships with two uncles, architect John Hubbard Sturgis and decorator Richard Ogden, Codman struck out on his own in 1893, designing houses in the French neo-Classical style for family friends in Boston, New York City and Newport, one of the era's premiere watering holes. A major project there was the interior design of the second and third floors of Cornelius Vanderbilt II's mansion, The Breakers. In Newport he met Edith Wharton, with whom he wrote *The Decoration of Houses* after working with her on her country houses in Newport and in Lenox, Massachusetts; the book espoused their philosophy that architecture and interior design should be integrated into a harmonious whole. Codman collaborated with Wharton on her Manhattan townhouse as well. His other New York City projects included the East Wing of the Metropolitan Club on Fifth Avenue and 60th Street; outside of the city, he designed the interior of the Rockefeller estate, Kykuit, in Pocantico Hills. In 1920 he returned to France, where he remained until his death. In all, Codman designed 22 houses, including five in Carnegie Hill, three of which are designated landmarks: 7 East 96th Street, his own house, now the Manhattan Country School, 15 East 96th Street, and the facade of 1083 Fifth Avenue, now the National Academy Museum. He also designed 3 East 89th Street, the wing to 1083 Fifth Avenue; and 12 East 96th Street, now La Scuola d'Italia Gugliemo Marconi.

C. HOWARD CRANE & KENNETH FRANZHEIM
C. Howard Crane (1885-1952)
Kenneth Franzheim (1890-1959)

Born in Hartford, **C. Howard Crane** set up an architectural practice there before moving to Detroit in 1904. He made his name designing theaters—close to 250—throughout the United States. In Manhattan, he is represented by the Music Box at 239 West 45th Street and the Guild, later the ANTA and the Virginia and now the August Wilson, at 245 West 52nd Street; both are designated landmarks. **Kenneth Franzheim** was born in Wheeling, West Virginia. After graduating from M.I.T., he worked for Boston architect Welles Bosworth and then worked in Chicago, where he became associated with Crane, ultimately managing Crane's New York City office. The two became partners in 1924; in that year they designed 1158 Fifth Avenue in Carnegie Hill.

When the firm dissolved a year later, Crane returned to Detroit; he designed more than 50 theaters in the Detroit area alone. In 1932 he moved to Milan, where he designed Italy's first skyscraper, and finally to London, where he took up industrial design and helped modernize a number of English factories. Meanwhile, in New York City, Franzheim produced designs for large public projects, including airports in fifteen cities. In 1937 he moved to Houston. After a four-year stint in Washington, D.C. during World War II, he divided his time between Houston and Mexico City, where he was an honorary member of the Mexican Society of Architects.

RICHARD HENRY DANA IV (1879-1933)
The grandson of the poet Henry Wadsworth Longfellow, Richard Henry Dana IV was, like his forebear, born and raised in Cambridge, Massachusetts, where he received his degree from Harvard, the sixth generation of his family to do so. He completed his architectural studies at Columbia and the Ecole des Beaux-Arts in Paris. From 1908 to 1916 he was a visiting lecturer at the Yale School of Architecture; he received an honorary B.F.A. degree from Yale in 1910. He opened his own practice in 1921 and designed, among other projects, the Yale campus in China and, in Manhattan, the clubhouse for the National Society of Colonial Dames in the State of New York at 215 East 71st Street. An avid proponent of the Colonial Revival style, he served on the editorial committee for *Great Georgian Houses of America,* published in 1933. In Carnegie Hill he designed 108 East 89th Street, the Dalton School.

LUCIEN DAVID (1900-?)

Born and raised in France, Lucien David was educated at the Sorbonne and the Ecole des Beaux-Arts in Paris, following which he moved to the Far East, where he designed, among other buildings, the Santa Theresa Church in Hong Kong and an apartment house in Shanghai. In 1945 he emigrated to the United States and opened his own firm. Four years later he formed a partnership with Helen Graham Park that lasted two years. In 1960 he was initiating architect in the conversion of the Carnegie Hill row house at 1209 Park Avenue into the Town House International School.

GEORGE B. DE GERSDORFF (1866-?)

A native of Salem, Massachusetts, George B. de Gersdorff was educated at Harvard and M.I.T. before going to Paris in 1890 to study at the Ecole de Beaux-Arts. In 1894 he joined the firm of McKim, Mead and White. Nine years later he opened his own firm. In Carnegie Hill he converted the two row houses at 10 and 12 East 94th Street into a neo-Georgian townhouse.

DELANO & ALDRICH
William Adams Delano (1874-1960)
Chester Holmes Aldrich (1871-1940)

William Adams Delano was born in New York City and graduated from Yale and the Columbia University School of Architecture, completing his training at the Ecole de Beaux-Arts in Paris. Providence-born **Chester Holmes Aldrich** studied architecture at M.I.T. and the Ecole des Beaux-Arts. The two met at the offices of Carrère & Hastings and formed their own firm in 1903. The following year they received their first important commission, the Walters Art Gallery in Baltimore. Their major work in Manhattan catered to a wealthy clientele and included the Chapin School on East End Avenue at 84th Street and several Upper East Side private clubs: the Colony Club at Park Avenue and 62nd Street, the Knickerbocker Club at Fifth Avenue and 62nd Street, and the Union Club at Park Avenue and 69th Street. Their roster of country estates includes Kykuit, the house of John D. Rockefeller in Pocantico Hills; Oheka, the summer house of Otto Kahn in Cold Spring Harbor on Long Island, (cited at the time as the second largest residence in the United States); and the Vincent Astor residence in Port Washington, also on Long Island. The firm was responsible for the Art Deco Marine Air Terminal at LaGuardia Airport, now a designated landmark; the Post Office Department Building in Washington, D.C.; and the American Embassy in Paris. In 1933 Aldrich became the resident director of the American Academy in Rome; he died there seven years later. Delano continued to practice architecture until 1950, and in 1953 was awarded the Gold Medal of the American Institute of Architects.

In 1949 he served as architectural consultant to the Commission on the Renovation of the White House. Also an artist, he exhibited his work at the Fogg Art Museum at Harvard University.

The partnership of Delano & Aldrich produced many fine Georgian-style buildings in Carnegie Hill: 9 East 86th Street; 1040 Park Avenue; 15 East 88th Street; 12-16 East 89th Street, originally the Cutting houses, now Saint David's School; the facade of 67 East 91st Street; 20-24 East 92nd Street, the Nightingale-Bamford School; 162 East 92nd Street; 67- 75 East 93rd Street, formerly the George F. Baker house complex and now the Russian Orthodox Church Outside Russia; 1130 Fifth Avenue; and 4 East 98th Street, St. Bernard's School.

DEPACE & JUSTER

Little is known about this firm except that they practiced in New York City around 1930. Among their works are an apartment house at 444 East 52nd Street (1929), and St. Roch's Church and Rectory in the Bronx (1931). In Carnegie Hill they designed 1100 Park Avenue.

DEUTSCH & SCHNEIDER
Maurice Deutsch (1884-1957)
Walter S. Schneider (?-1948)

A noted architect and engineer who received his degree from Columbia, **Maurice Deutsch** designed the track layout of New York City's Grand Central Terminal. He was interested in low-cost housing and chaired a sub-committee for Mayor Fiorello LaGuardia researching property improvement. He is credited with the design of a number of apartment buildings on the Upper West Side. **Walter S. Schneider** was responsible for the renovation of the Sutton Mews apartments and gardens, lifting the buildings from tenement status to residences compatible with those on upscale Sutton Place nearby, along the East River. He designed three synagogues: B'nai Jeshurun at 270 West 89th Street, Unity Synagogue, later Mt. Neboh, at 130 West 79th Street (no longer in existence), and the Moorish-style Park Avenue Synagogue at 50 East 87th Street in Carnegie Hill.

WILLIAM M. DOWLING (1899-1954)

A graduate of the Beaux-Arts Institute of Design in Chicago, William M. Dowling was in charge of the plans and construction for the Lord Baltimore Hotel in Baltimore and the Abraham Lincoln Hotel in Reading, Pennsylvania, in the 1920s. He designed Regent House and Goodhue House in New York City and the Hilltop Acres development in Yonkers. From 1941 to 1943 and again shortly after World War II, he was senior housing control architect for the New York State Division of Housing and, later, associate chief architect at Norman K. Winston-Holzer Associates, where he directed the planning and construction for the 3,700-unit Bay Terrace cooperative apartments in Bayside in Queens. He designed 19 East 88th Street in Carnegie Hill.

HENRY DUDLEY (1813-1894)

Henry Dudley was born and educated in England and emigrated to the United States in 1851. He was one of the charter members of the American Institute of Architects and designed its original seal. As principal architect of the New York Ecclesiological Society and the Protestant Episcopal Church, he designed 162 churches, the majority of which are in New York State. He specialized in Gothic Revival, primarily the early English style. St. Paul's Episcopal Church in Syracuse, New York, and Christ Episcopal Church in New Brunswick, New Jersey, are outstanding examples of his work. The brownstone apartment houses at 175-179 East 93rd Street are his only buildings in Carnegie Hill.

MICHAEL DUFFY

Nothing is known of Michael Duffy's background; he was both an architect and a builder active in the last quarter of the 19th century. As a developer working with architects Thom & Wilson, he was responsible for nearly 40 identical neo-Grec brownstones lining the square block known as Hellgate Hill, bounded by Lexington and Third avenues and 94th and 95th streets in Carnegie Hill. Although the Third Avenue houses have been demolished, 24 of the others survive. The three houses at Nos. 1460-1464 on the west side of Lexington Avenue between 94th and 95th streets are all that remain of a row of eleven neo-Grec brownstones that he designed and built in 1878.

EGGERS & HIGGINS

Otto Reinhold Eggers (1882-1964)
Daniel Paul Higgins (1886-1953)

Cooper Union-educated **Otto Reinhold Eggers** was born in Manhattan and served his apprenticeship at the Beaux-Arts Institute of New York, in the atelier of Henry Hornsbostel. **Daniel Paul Higgins** had to leave school after eighth grade in order to help support his family, and eventually completed his architectural (and accounting) studies in his spare time at New York University. Eggers and Higgins met in the offices of John Russell Pope, where both worked. When Pope died in 1937, they incorporated as Eggers & Higgins, as they were prevented from continuing to use Pope's name. The firm was responsible for important institutional buildings, including the completion of Pope's designs for the Thomas Jefferson Memorial and the West Building of the National Gallery of Art, and the Dirkson Senate Office Building, all three in Washington, D.C. Commissions for universities include the Morehead Planetarium at the University of North Carolina at Chapel Hill, the first planetarium constructed in the South; the Myron Taylor Hall for Cornell Law School; and buildings on the campus of Indiana University. In New York City their projects included the Damrosch Park Bandshell in Lincoln Center and the General Assembly Hall at the 1964-65 New York World's Fair in Flushing Meadows in Queens. They were initiating architects of the apartment building at 4 East 89th Street in Carnegie Hill.

LOUIS ENTZER, JR.

Louis Entzer, Jr. worked in New York City from 1892 into the early 1900s, specializing in apartment buildings and houses. He had offices in Carnegie Hill at 19 and 78 East 96th Street, among other locations. The Queen Anne row houses at 115-127 East 95th Street are among his earliest known work; he also designed 1 and 3 East 94th Street (which were subsequently given new facades), 53 and 55 East 92nd Street, and 128-136 East 96th Street.

FRANK P. FARINELLA

A graduate of Seton Hall University in South Orange, New Jersey, Frank P. Farinella received his architecture and engineering degrees from Van Rensselaer Polytechnic Institute in Troy, New York. A builder and engineer as well as an architect, in 1955 he founded Farinella Construction and became known as "the king of two-family houses." The company built more than 2,000, the first of which was in Irvington, New Jersey; he lived there with his bride while renting out the second unit. He later formed a partnership with architect Edward J. Hurley; the firm is best known for conversion and restoration work, including the conversion of the New York City Police Department's Ninth Precinct building at 135 Charles Street into Le Gendarme apartments, the Ansonia Clock Company in Brooklyn into the Ansonia Court apartments, and the restoration of the main entrance and *porte cochère* of the landmarked Ansonia apartment hotel on West 73rd Street. Farinella's work in Carnegie Hill is a new facade for 118 East 92nd Street.

H.I. FELDMAN (1896-1981)

Hyman Isaac Feldman was born in Russia and came to the United States in 1900. He studied at Cornell, Yale and Columbia before establishing his own practice in New York City in 1921. An active proponent of the Art Deco style, he is represented by many residential and commercial buildings, including hotels, throughout the metropolitan area — more than 4,000, by one estimate. One of his projects, the Cranlyn Apartments in Brooklyn

Heights, received the first award for best apartment-house design from the Brooklyn Chamber of Commerce in 1932. A writer as well as an architect, Feldman published articles on subjects ranging from economics to real estate. In Carnegie Hill he replaced Eggers & Higgins as architect of 4 East 89th Street and designed Trafalgar House at 120 East 90th Street.

MARTIN V.B. FERDON (1860-1950)

Born in Manhattan into a venerable New York-New Jersey family, Martin van Buren Ferdon had set up an architectural practice in New York City by 1885. Alone, and later with James A. Ellicott, he was responsible for a number of commercial buildings in Greenwich Village and Tribeca as well as several apartment houses and strings of row houses on the Upper West Side. Many of his designs were in the Romanesque Revival style; among them is the former Everard Storage Warehouse on West 10th Street, which was converted into apartments in the 1970s. He also designed a private stable on West 17th Street. In Carnegie Hill he designed the Mildred, a Renaissance Revival flats building at 140 East 92nd Street.

FLEMER & KOEHLER

J.A. Henry Flemer (?-1900)
Victor Hugo Koehler

J.A. Henry Flemer joined **Victor Hugo Koehler** in 1889, three years after Koehler had established an architectural practice in New York City. Together they immediately designed a group of seven row houses at 1209-1217 Park Avenue and, around the corner, 112 and 114 East 95th Street in Carnegie Hill; of these, Nos. 1213, 1215 and 1217 and Nos. 112 and 114 retain much of their original facades. The partnership lasted until Flemer's death in 1900. In 1901 Koehler became associated with James M. Farnsworth. Continuing to use the name Flemer & Koehler, together and separately they had a varied practice. Their institutional work a five-story nursing school for Beth Israel Hospital at Jefferson and Cherry streets in downtown Manhattan, the Richmond Hill High School in Queens, and the Chaari Zedek Synagogue in Brooklyn. Koehler gained a reputation for theater design and is credited with designing a theater on Broadway and 45th Street in 1901, the Lyric Theater at 213 West 42nd Street in 1903, and the Lafayette Theater on Seventh Avenue between 131st and 132nd streets in 1912-13.

HENRI FOUCHAUX (1856-1910)

Of French extraction, Henri Fouchaux was born in Coytesville, New York. He joined the firm of Schickel & Ditmars as a superintendent established his own firm in 1886. Proficient in a variety of architectural styles, he designed commercial and residential buildings throughout New York City, including the Pierce, now the Powell, Building in Tribeca and a store-and-loft on West 19th Street on Ladies Mile. Fouchaux-designed apartment houses can be found throughout the Upper West Side, Jumel Terrace, and Hamilton Heights, where his 41 Convent Avenue is a designated landmark. In Carnegie Hill he added one story and redesigned the facade of 1311 Madison Avenue.

FOX & FOWLE ARCHITECTS (now FXFOWLE ARCHITECTS)
Robert F. Fox, Jr. (1943-)
Bruce S. Fowle (1937-)

The firm of Fox & Fowle Architects, established in 1978, changed its name to FXFOWLE to reflect the expansion of its business and its merger in 2000 with Jamhekar Strauss. **Robert F. Fox, Jr.** graduated from Cornell and received his master's degree from the Harvard Graduate School of Design, after which he worked in the offices of Emery Roth & Sons. **Bruce S. Fowle** received his architectural degree from Syracuse University and worked for Edward Larrabee Barnes. The two met at Brown, Daltas & Associates, an architectural firm based in Rome, but soon left to open their own firm. As Fox & Fowle they were responsible for a wide range of projects, including corporate headquarters, hotels, commercial and residential buildings, and cultural, not-for-profit and educational facilities, such as the neo-Georgian addition at 16-18 East 91st Street in Carnegie Hill that they designed for the Spence School in 1987.

C. ABBOTT FRENCH & CO.
Charles Abbott French

The firm of C. Abbott French & Co. was in practice from 1887 to 1890, after which its name was changed to French, Dixon & DeSaldern to reflect Charles Abbott French's partnership with two other architects, Robert C. Dixon, Jr. and Arthur DeSaldern. Although nothing is known of French's training, records reveal that in 1892 he designed an "ideal country seat" for himself in the Old English style—it cost over $100,000—in Summit Ridge, New Jersey, while his office was on West 57th Street. When his partners left in 1894, French resumed his solo practice until 1907. He designed a number of commercial and residential projects throughout Manhattan, many in the Renaissance Revival and Queen Anne styles. The former is perhaps best represented by the New-York Cab Company Stable, later a garage and now a designated landmark, on Amsterdam Avenue and 75th Street. In the late 19th century stables rented out horse-drawn carriages to denizens of their neighborhoods, and even then the New-York Cab Company carriages were painted bright yellow. In Carnegie Hill the firm designed the row houses at 127-135 East 92nd Street and 116-138 East 95th Street, as well as 1402 Lexington Avenue.

FRED F. FRENCH CO.
Fred Fillmore French (1883-1936)
H. Douglas Ives (1888-1945)

Real-estate tycoon **Fred Fillmore French** was born in New York City. His father died when he was a child, and as a boy he held a number of jobs, including peddling papers and washing windows, to help support his family. A Pulitzer scholarship enabled him to graduate from high school; he then spent a year at Princeton. After taking an engineering course at Columbia, he "temped" in the building profession, working his way up the ladder until he formed his own company in 1910. His partner, **H. Douglas Ives**, was born and received his architectural training in Canada; he moved to New York City after World War I and worked briefly for Cass Gilbert before joining French's firm as chief architect. The Fred F. French Co. made its name with Tudor City, the largest housing development to date (1925) in Manhattan. Adhering to his own catch phrase "You can't overbuild in New York," French went on to mastermind the development of the massive 1,600-apartment Knickerbocker Village complex between the Manhattan and Brooklyn bridges. His eponymous building at Fifth Avenue and 43rd Street is a designated landmark. His Carnegie Hill apartment houses are 1140 and 1160 Fifth Avenue.

GIANNASCA GALLO ARCHITECTS
Edward V. Giannasca (1931-)
Paul J. Gallo

Bronx-born Edward V. Giannasca grew up in Queens, lived in Brooklyn, and received his architectural training at the Pratt Institute and the Institute of Design and Construction in Brooklyn. He interned with Joseph Mathieu, an architect specializing in ecclesiastical work; one of his earliest projects was the reconfiguring of the steep steps of the Church of St. Francis de Sales at 135 East 96th Street in Carnegie Hill. In 1961 he formed a partnership with Paul J. Gallo. The firm's practice includes architectural and interior designs for religious institutions, schools and colleges, medical centers, commercial and industrial buildings, and residential developments. Giannasca's commercial work in Manhattan is represented by a seventeen-story hotel conversion to an office building at 551 Madison Avenue; in Brooklyn his work includes a new complex for the Church of St. Bernard; and he designed the Oak Park townhouse community in Douglaston in Queens. He has received design excellence awards from the New York City Department of Public Works, the Brooklyn Real Estate Board, and the Queens Chamber of Commerce. He maintains an office near Carnegie Hill, and designed Carnegie Hill Tower at 40 East 94th Street.

CASS GILBERT (1859-1934)

A pioneer in skyscraper design and a celebrity architect in his own time, Cass Gilbert was born in Zanesville, Ohio. He grew up in St. Paul, Minnesota, where as a teenager he apprenticed briefly as a draftsman before completing his studies at M.I.T. After a trip to Europe, where he immersed himself in Roman, Gothic and Renaissance architecture, he joined the firm of McKim, Mead & White. Two years later he returned to St. Paul to open his own practice with a fellow M.I.T graduate, James Knox Taylor. During their eight-year partnership Gilbert designed residences, churches, railway stations and municipal buildings, including the Minnesota State Capitol. Having won an 1899 design competition for the U.S. Custom House on Bowling Green in New York City, he moved to Manhattan and embarked on a series of major commissions, among them the Broadway-Chambers Building, the New York Life Insurance Building, the support towers of the George Washington Bridge, the Brooklyn Army Terminal, and the Woolworth Building, which, when it was completed in 1913, was the tallest building in the world. Gilbert's work outside the city is equally impressive. It includes the St. Louis Art Museum, created for the 1904 World's Fair; the Detroit Public Library; and the U.S. Supreme Court Building in Washington, D.C. He also designed master plans for several college campuses. In Carnegie Hill he remodeled 1 East 94th Street with a new neo-Classical facade as a residence for himself and his wife, Julia Finch Gilbert.

C.P.H. GILBERT (1861-1952)

Charles Pierrepont Henry Gilbert was born in New York City and educated at Columbia and the Ecole des Beaux-Arts in Paris. After plying his trade for a few years in Arizona and Colorado mining towns, he returned to New York and established a practice with George Kramer Thompson, with whom he designed a number of buildings in the Romanesque Revival style in Park Slope in Brooklyn. By the late 1890s he was specializing in mansions for the socially prominent in Manhattan, Brooklyn, Westchester and on Long Island; throughout his career he designed more than 100. Although best remembered for his "signature"French Gothic or Francois I, Gilbert was accomplished in the Gilded Age's most-favored styles. His notable buildings include the Cushman Building, a twelve-story mansard-roof tower at 1 Maiden Lane; the Beaux-Arts DeLamar mansion at 233 Madison Avenue, now the Polish Consulate; and the neo-French Gothic Fletcher mansion at Fifth Avenue and 79th Street, now the Ukrainian Institute in America. Both of the latter are designated landmarks. In Carnegie Hill are three more of his magnificent buildings, the first two of which are also landmarked: the Francois I chateau at 1109 Fifth Avenue, now the Jewish Museum; the neo-Italian Renaissance palazzo at 1 East 91st Street, designed in conjunction with Scottish architect J. Armstrong Stenhouse, now the Convent of the Sacred Heart; and the neo-French Gothic apartment house at 1067 Fifth Avenue.

HORACE GINSBERN (1900-1969)

A graduate of Columbia, Horace Ginsbern was a founder and trustee of the Building Industry League of New York. Over the course of three decades he designed numerous apartment houses in the metropolitan area, including 1045 Fifth Avenue and 252 East 61st Street. Ginsbern was one of the architects for New York City's first public-housing project, the Harlem River Houses on Seventh Avenue between 151st and 153rd streets, as well as the architect for the Jewish Child Care Association's mental-health facility on East 87th Street. His only building in Carnegie Hill is 151 East 90th Street.

LAFAYETTE ANTHONY GOLDSTONE: See Rouse and Goldstone

JACK L. GORDON ARCHITECTS (JLGA)

Jack L. Gordon received his architectural training at the Pratt Institute, earning his degree in 1962. His firm, Jack L. Gordon Architects (JLGA), founded in 1969, has a client list with emphasis on the fields of education, entertainment, health care and historic preservation; the latter includes the restoration of 254-260 Canal Street, one of the earliest cast-iron buildings in New York City and now a designated landmark. Work for educational facilities in the city includes the Jewish Theological Seminary, restoration of the High School for the Performing Arts, and the 1989-91 addition to the Nightingale-Bamford School at 16-18 East 92nd Street in Carnegie Hill.

THOMAS GRAHAM (1866-1938)

Before launching his own architectural firm in 1890, Thomas Graham spent five years with a family real-estate development firm, Charles Graham & Sons. Both an architect and a builder, Graham was an enthusiastic proponent of a new concept in multi-family living: the apartment hotel, which typically included a reception area and public and private dining rooms for the use of the tenants. Apartments in these buildings did not have kitchens. Graham maintained his office in the basement of the Hotel Graham, an apartment hotel that he designed and built—and gave his name to—at 22 East 89th Street in Carnegie Hill; it was the first apartment hotel on the Upper East Side. Today the Romanesque Revival building, which remains residential except for a street-level store, is owned by its next-door neighbor, Saint David's School. Graham also designed the row houses at 6–14 East 92nd Street and 22–28 East 95th Street.

WILLIAM GRAUL

Little is known of William Graul except that he may have been born in Reading, Pennsylvania, and received a Medal of Honor for service in the Civil War. He was practicing architecture in New York City by 1868. His earliest efforts appear to have been tenements on Orchard Street on the Lower East Side. He later designed apartment buildings, stores and lofts in Greenwich Village and Tribeca. His surviving Carnegie Hill buildings include four Queen Anne brownstones at 46 and 52–56 East 92nd Street and four Renaissance Revival row houses at 15–21 East 93rd Street.

GRONENBERG & LEUCHTAG

> Herman Gronenberg
> Albert Leuchtag

Herman Gronenberg and **Albert Leuchtag,** of whose backgrounds nothing is known, were successful architects by the 1920s. The three-dozen apartment buildings, hotels and theaters that they designed in New York City include apartment houses on Riverside Drive, the Park Central Hotel on Seventh Avenue and 56th Street, the Times Square Hotel at 255 West 43rd Street, which is on the National Register of Historic Places, and the Commodore Theater in Williamsburg in Brooklyn. The firm was responsible for four apartment houses in Carnegie Hill: 108 East 91st Street, 9 East 96th Street, and 1230 and 1235 Park Avenue.

GWATHMEY SIEGEL & ASSOCIATES ARCHITECTS

> Charles Gwathmey (1938-)
> Robert Siegel (1939-)

The youngest architect to receive the A.I.A.'s prestigious Brunner Prize, **Charles Gwathmey,** son of artist Robert Gwathmey, was born in Charlotte, North Carolina and trained at the Yale School of Architecture. From 1965 to 1991 he pursued a teaching career; in 1968 he formed a partnership with **Robert Siegel,** who was born in New York City and received degrees in architecture from the Pratt Institute and Harvard. One of Gwathmey's first projects—which brought him fame—was a weekend complex for his parents in Amagansett on Long Island. The firm's commissions range from master plans for universities to libraries and art museums to furniture and tableware. Their work in New York City includes the headquarters for Morgan Stanley Dean Witter & Company; the undulating glass-walled Astor Place Tower in the East Village; the International Design Center in Long Island City in Queens; and the conversion of a building at the Kaufman Studios, also in Long Island City, into the Museum of the Moving Image. They designed the interiors of the offices and the showroom for Giorgio Armani and the administrative offices for Lincoln Center. Among their notable works are the Museum of Contemporary Art in Miami and the seven-story annex to the Guggenheim Museum at 2 East 89th Street, as well as restoration of the original Frank Lloyd Wright building, in Carnegie Hill.

WALTER HAEFELI (1875-1938)
Swiss-born Walter Haefeli was educated in Zurich and emigrated to the United States, where he first designed loft buildings. His later projects included the Old Lyceum Building on West 110th Street, 16-24 West 71st Street, and a Renaissance-style apartment house at 562 West End Avenue. In Carnegie Hill he designed renovations for 72 East 91st, the John Foster Dulles House.

HENRY J. HARDENBERGH (1847-1918)
Henry Janeway Hardenbergh was born in New Brunswick, New Jersey, and received his initial training, starting at age eighteen, in the office of Detlef Lienau in New York City, where he was a student draftsman. In 1871 he established his own firm. His first projects were for Rutgers College; these included a chapel (with Tiffany windows) and a library. It was the Dakota apartment house on Central Park West and 72nd Street, so named because it rose on land that was then empty of development, that brought him recognition. Hardenberg's greatest achievements in the city are his luxury hotels, notably the Plaza on Fifth Avenue at 59th Street, the Albert (now apartments) on University Place, and the Manhattan (since demolished) on 42nd Street. He was commissioned by the Astor family to design the Astor Office Building on Wall Street, the original Waldorf Hotel on Fifth Avenue and 33rd Street, and the nearby Hotel Astoria; the latter two were razed to create the site for the Empire State Building.

Hardenbergh also designed the building for the American Fine Arts Society, of which he was the founder, at 215 West 57th Street; it now houses the Art Students League and is a designated landmark, as is the Plaza. His projects outside of New York City include the Copley Plaza Hotel in Boston, the Willard Hotel in Washington, D.C., and the Palmer Stadium at Princeton University. In Carnegie Hill he designed the Queen Anne row houses at 1340-1350 Lexington Avenue and 121 East 89th Street, designated the Hardenbergh/Rhinelander Historic District in 1998, as well as 28 and 30 East 92nd Street.

GEORGE E. HARNEY (1840-1924)
George E. Harney was born in Lynn, Massachusetts. After apprenticing with Alonzo Lewis, he opened his own architectural practice in Newburgh, New York, in 1863. In Newburgh he designed St. Margaret's Church, the Lincoln Home and Hospital, and the extension and transepts for the Dutch Reformed Church. Upon moving to New York City in the late 1870s, he went

into practice with William Paulding. In Manhattan he designed the Commercial Union Building on William Street and the Mercantile Library on the site of the Old Clinton Hall on Astor Place. His residential projects included several houses on Fifth Avenue and, in Newark, New Jersey, Ballantine House, a 27-room mansion commissioned by the beer-brewing family. Harney authored several pattern books of the day; complete with floor plans, these extolled picturesque styles for country houses. Reprints of these volume—*Cottage Residences; Stables, Outbuildings and Fences;* and *Victorian Cottage Interiors*—are still available. In Carnegie Hill he designed the red-brick firehouse and stable at 113 East 90th Street, now the Allan Stone Gallery.

M. JOSEPH HARRISON
By 1908 M. Joseph Harrison was an established architect in New York City, where he practiced until 1941. In 1923 he designed a small commercial building at 187 Franklin Street in what is now the Tribeca West Historic District. Little else is known of his work other than his nine-story apartment house at 118 East 93rd Street in Carnegie Hill.

ALFRED B. HEISER
Nothing is known of Alfred B. Heiser except that he practiced architecture in Newburgh, New York. He was chairman of the board of the first Adventist Home for the Aged, which he designed for the Seventh-Day Adventist Church in 1953 in Newburgh. In 1956 he designed the Church of the Advent Hope at 111 East 87th Street in Carnegie Hill.

JAMES HENDERSON
James Henderson maintained an architectural practice in Manhattan from 1887 to 1890. In Carnegie Hill he designed Renaissance Revival row houses at Nos. 64- 68 East 91st Street, of which No. 68 survives without significant alterations.

MAX HENSEL
Max Hensel's architectural practice in Manhattan dates from 1887. His residential work can be seen in the West End-Collegiate and Upper West Side/Central Park West Historic Districts as well as in Carnegie Hill, where he designed the Renaissance Revival flats buildings at 68-72 East 93rd Street.

HERTER BROTHERS
Peter Herter (1847-?)
Francis William Herter (1853-1933)
Peter and Francis **William Herter** were born and trained in Germany and arrived in New York City in the early 1880s. Until 1893 much of their work

was concentrated on the Lower East Side. More important as developers than designers, they built a large number of tenements—more than 100—that were noteworthy for having stoves and baths in each apartment, at the time considered luxuries and therefore unnecessary amenities for the poor. They also designed and built the Eldridge Street Synagogue, now a designated landmark. Following a period of financial distress, from 1893 to 1899, they set up separate practices, Francis on his own and Peter with his son, Peter John, as P. Herter & Son and, three years later, as the Herter Realty Company. In Carnegie Hill the original Herter brothers designed the neo-Grec row houses at 57-61 East 93rd Street.

F. BURRALL HOFFMAN, JR. (1882-1980)

F. Burrall Hoffman, Jr. was born in New Orleans; his family were descendants of the socially prominent New York family, the Knickerbockers. After graduating from Georgetown University, Harvard (where he was a member of the Hasty Pudding Club) and the Ecole des Beaux-Arts in Paris, he joined the firm of Carrère & Hastings. Three years later, in 1910, he established an architectural practice with H.C. (Henry Creighton) Ingalls. Among Ingalls & Hoffman's projects in New York City were three Manhattan theaters: the Henry Miller at 124 West 43rd Street, the Little Theatre, now the Helen Hayes, at 240 West 44th Street—both are designated landmarks—and the old Neighborhood Playhouse, now the Harry du Jur Playhouse at the Henry Street Settlement House at 466 Grand Street on the Lower East Side. The firm's most impressive commission, created with Diego Suarez, was Villa Vizcaya, an Italian Renaissance palazzo—complete with Venetian-style barber-pole moorings—on the oceanfront property of farm-machinery magnate James Deering in Miami. A project in Hoffman's later years was the Susan B. Wagner Wing for Gracie Mansion, which he designed in collaboration with Mott B. Schmidt and Edward Coe Embury in 1966. He also designed private houses and country estates in the metropolitan area; notable are the Van Cortland mansion in the Bronx and 17 East 90th Street in Carnegie Hill, the Wanamaker Munn House and now part of the Spence School. Both are designated landmarks.

WILLIAM I. HOHAUSER (1896-?)

A native New Yorker, William I. Hohauser was educated at Stuyvesant High School (for whom he designed a new building in 1954), Cooper Union and Columbia, where he received a degree in civil engineering. After a brief stint as an architect at the Brooklyn Navy Yard, he was primarily involved in large-scale housing projects throughout New York City, such as the Fort Greene Houses in Brooklyn, the Bronx River Houses, and the Stephen Foster Houses in Manhattan. His largest housing project is the

Reverend Dr. Martin Luther King, Jr. Towers, comprising ten separate buildings on Lenox Avenue at 116th Street in Central Harlem. Hohauser designed a number of theaters, including the Normandie at 51 East 53rd Street in Manhattan (since demolished) and the Avon in Stamford, Connecticut, and was the architect for the Liggett Drugstore chain. One of his apartment buildings is the Modern-style 870 Fifth Avenue. In Carnegie Hill he designed the Art Deco commercial building at 157 East 86th Street.

ALBRO HOWELL
Albro Howell was a carpenter/builder and developer, rather than an architect, who maintained an office downtown from 1835 to 1881, first on Beekman Street and later on Cliff Street. In 1851 he moved uptown to Yorkville, where he concentrated on developing the south side of 92nd Street between Park and Third avenues. He built a house for himself at No. 166 (since demolished), where he lived until 1854. Around 1853 he built the clapboard house at No. 160 in a combined vernacular Greek Revival and Italianate style. The building is one of the oldest intact 19th-century wooden houses north of Greenwich Village and is a designated landmark. In Carnegie Hill Howell is associated with six intact houses. In addition to 160 East 92nd Street, two are attributed to him as the possible designer: 1390 Lexington Avenue, built in 1855, originally located on East 92nd Street and then moved around the corner when Lexington Avenue was cut through in 1869; and 122 East 92nd Street, an Italianate wood frame house built in 1859. The three row houses at 134-138 East 92nd Street were designed by architect A.B. Ogden, with Howell as developer.

HUBERT, PIRSSON & CO.
Philip Gengembre Hubert (1830-1911)
James W. Pirsson (1833-1888)

Philip Gengembre Hubert was born in Paris and at the age of nineteen came to the United States and settled in Cincinnati, Ohio. After the Civil War he moved to New York City, where he was hired by **James W. Pirsson** to design six single-family houses at Lexington Avenue and 43rd Street. Pirsson, the son of a well-known New York City piano manufacturer and musician who helped found the New York Philharmonic Society, received his training from an English architect named Wheeler. Hubert and Pirsson formed a partnership around 1870. They initially designed low-cost tenements but soon branched out to more upscale row houses. They made their name with the early luxury cooperative apartment buildings they called home clubs, leading Hubert to claim to have originated the concept of cooperative ownership. Among the most notable were the Central Park Apartments (since demolished), nicknamed the Navarro Flats or Spanish Flats (after the developer, Jose Francesco de Navarro), on West 58th and 59th streets and Central Park South between Sixth and Seventh avenues; in the mid-1880s these eight contiguous buildings formed the city's largest apartment complex. Another home club was the Chelsea Hotel, built in 1883, at 222 West 23rd Street, which featured, among other amenities, duplex artists' studios, a private ballroom on the top floor and a private restaurant with its own French chef. In contrast, their landmarked Queen Anne row houses at 146-156 East 89th Street in Carnegie Hill are intimate and picturesque. On a more celestial note, Hubert, Pirsson & Co. designed the Church of the Puritans on West 130th Street and the Gothic-style Episcopal Church of the Beloved Disciple, now the Roman Catholic Church of St. Thomas More, at 59-65 East 89th Street in Carnegie Hill.

ALFRED HUTTIRA
Nothing is known of Alfred Huttira other than that in 1890 he designed the modest brick apartment building at 150 East 87th Street in Carnegie Hill.

ARTHUR C. JACKSON (1865-1941)
Arthur C. Jackson was born in Utica, New York, and trained at Harvard and Columbia and at the Ecole des Beaux-Arts in Paris. In 1898 he joined the firm of Carrère & Hastings in New York City, where he worked on the plans for the New York Public Library. After seven years at Carrère & Hastings and two with Heins & LaFarge, he opened his own practice in 1911. At first he designed public and commercial buildings, including the Utica Public Library, the Fifth Avenue branch of the New York Equitable Trust Company, the National Surety Company Building at the junction of Albany and Washington streets, and an annex to the Chubb Bros. Building. Later he concentrated on residential design. Besides a neo-Classical townhouse at 17 East 70th Street, now a designated landmark, Jackson designed the neo-Renaissance house at 11 East 89th Street, originally the Lawrence L. Gillespie house and now the Trevor Day School, in Carnegie Hill.

STEPHEN B. JACOBS (1939-)
With bachelor's and master's degrees in architecture from the Pratt Institute in 1963 and 1965, Stephen B. Jacobs joined the firm of Whittlesey, Conklin & Rossant, where he was involved with the planned community of Reston, Virginia. He established his own firm, the Stephen B. Jacobs Group, in 1967. The firm's projects range from public works and preservation conversions to the design of hotels and condominiums in New York City, Miami, Providence, and Montreal. Jacobs is a lecturer on architecture and preservation at

Columbia University and other educational institutions. In 2002 he designed the Little Camp Memorial at Buchenwald in Weimar, Germany. His Manhattan hotel projects include the renovation of the Gotham, at Fifth Avenue and 55th Street, into the Peninsula in 1982; the Library Hotel at 299 Madison Avenue and the Giraffe at 365 Park Avenue, both in 2000; and the Gansevoort at 18 Ninth Avenue, in the Meatpacking District, in 2004. The firm has designed numerous residential buildings in downtown Manhattan and Brooklyn. An early project was the 1973-74 design of 155 East 88th Street in Carnegie Hill.

FREDERICK JACOBSON
Virtually nothing is known of Frederick Jacobson except that he practiced architecture in Manhattan and Brooklyn from 1891 through 1921. Among his commercial buildings are 414-416 West Broadway, in the SoHo-Cast Iron Historic District, and alterations to loft buildings along Ladies Mile on Sixth Avenue. In Carnegie Hill he designed the Alamo, a Renaissance Revival flats building at 55 East 93rd Street, and the Woodbury and the Elmscourt at 27-29 East 95th Street and 1356 Madison Avenue.

ARTHUR B. JENNINGS (1849-1927)
Born in North Brookfield, Massachusetts, Arthur Bates Jennings graduated from City College of New York and trained under George B. Post and Russell Sturgis before setting up his own practice in 1876, which he maintained until 1921. His early work was residential. Subsequently he designed churches, which became a specialty, and institutional buildings as well as buildings for colleges and universities; his work can be found across the country from Portland, Maine, to Seattle. He was responsible for the design of the Webb Institute of Naval Architecture in Glen Cove on Long Island, and the Hanover Fire Insurance Company building at 34 Pine Street in downtown Manhattan. Jennings lived with his family on 136th Street and Broadway and in Summit, New Jersey, in houses of his own design. A number of his houses can be found in Summit and nearby Short Hills. In Carnegie Hill he designed the row of neo-Grec brownstones at 115–121 East 91st Street.

FREDERICK JENTH (1840?–1897)
Frederick Jenth worked as a mason until 1875, when he began to practice as an architect. He maintained an office at 191 Forsyth Street in New York City until 1895. A commercial building that he designed at 177 Franklin Street in 1887 displays neo-Grec characteristics, which are reflected in his 1891-92 Renaissance Revival row house at 23 East 93rd Street in Carnegie Hill.

PHILIP JOHNSON (1906-2005)

Cleveland-born Philip Cortelyou Johnson graduated from Harvard in 1927 and joined the then-new Museum of Modern Art. As founding chairman of its Department of Architecture and Design, he curated a number of highly influential exhibitions, most notably "Modern Architecture: International Exhibition," and co-authored a book, *The International Style*, with Henry-Russell Hitchcock. In 1940 he entered Harvard's Graduate School of Design to train as an architect; he received his degree three years later. His first project, his own Glass House in New Canaan, Connecticut, is a classic example of the Modernist aesthetic espoused by Mies van der Rohe, with whom he collaborated on the Seagram Building on Park Avenue at 52nd Street. Johnson's Asia House at 112 East 64th Street strongly reflects Mies's influence. His other projects in New York City include the sculpture garden at MoMA and the New York State Theater at Lincoln Center. In collaboration with John Burgee, and later Raj Ahuja, he designed the Investment Diversified Services (IDS) center in Minneapolis; PPG Place, for the Pittsburgh Plate Glass Company; Pennzoil Place in Houston; and the Crystal Cathedral in Garden Grove, California, for the televangelist Robert H. Schuller. His most famous building is the ATT, now Sony, headquarters on Madison Avenue at 56th Street in New York City, whose "Chippendale" broken-pediment top has become a hallmark of the Postmodern style. His subsequent association with Alan Ritchie produced an office-and-retail building at the site of Checkpoint Charlie in Berlin. Residential work included the apartment house tower, the Metropolitan, at 181 East 90th Street in Carnegie Hill. Toward the end of his life Johnson designed ancillary buildings on his New Canaan property, among them a gatehouse and a guesthouse. The property can be visited by appointment.

HUGO KAFKA (1843-1913)

A native of Austria-Hungary, Hugo Kafka received a degree in architecture from the Polytechnikum in Zurich and the Medal of Art at the Vienna International Exposition in 1873. The following year he came to Philadelphia and joined the firm of Herman Schwarzmann, chief architect of the Centennial Exposition of 1876. Two years later he was practicing architecture in New York City under the name of Hugo Kafka & Co. In 1884 he was one of several architects participating in a design competition for the Squadron A (Eighth Regiment) Armory between 94th and 95th streets in Carnegie Hill; in the same year he designed 11 East 92nd Street. Another of his projects was the Joseph Loth Silk Ribbon Factory at 1818 Amsterdam Avenue, now a designated landmark. Kafka was associated with a number of firms until the turn of the century, when he established the firm of Hugo Kafka & Sons with Hugo Kafka, Jr., an architect, and Fred P. Kafka, a structural engineer.

KAVY & KAVOVITT

Kavy & Kavovitt maintained an office on Court Street in Brooklyn. Their apartment-house designs include 24 East 67th Street (1960), a 32-story tower at 345 East 93rd Street (1977), and 160 East 88th Street in Carnegie Hill.

KEELER & FERNALD
Frederick S. Keeler

Frederick Keeler started his architectural practice in 1908. In 1920 he formed a partnership with a man whose last name was Fernald; the firm designed an Art Deco building at 835 Washington Street. In 1928 they combined 45 and 47 East 92nd Street in Carnegie Hill into a single-family house. The partnership lasted until 1935, after which Keeler practiced independently again through 1940.

GEORGE KEISTER

Active in New York City from 1889 to 1925, George Keister was especially sought after for his theater designs. Like many architects of his time, he began by designing neo-Grec and neo-Renaissance-style tenements but soon branched out. Among his non-theatrical projects are the 400 block on East 136th Street in the Bronx; several apartment buildings on Morningside Heights, including Claremont Court and the Montebello; and the First Baptist Church at 265th Street and Broadway. On West 113th Street, near the Columbia University campus, he designed the so-called Keister House, home of the Sigma Chi fraternity and once the home of Lou Gehrig. The building was to be demolished by Columbia to make way for a dormitory, but the facade was saved and incorporated into the new design. Keister also designed the Gerard Apartments residence hotel at 123 West 44th Street, now a designated landmark, and a townhouse at 305 West 71st Street. Many of his theaters were demolished; surviving examples include the Belasco at 111 West 44th Street and the Apollo at 253 West 125th Street in Harlem. He was responsible for two buildings in Carnegie Hill: the neo-Georgian townhouse at 9 East 90th Street, originally the McAlpin-Miller house, and the apartment house at 16 East 98th Street.

MORRIS KETCHUM, JR. (1904-1984)

Morris Ketchum, Jr. was born in New York. He received his undergraduate and architectural degrees from Columbia and studied at the School of Fine Arts in Fontainebleau, near Paris. Ketchum worked for Edward Durrell Stone and others before starting his own firm, Morris Ketchum, Jr. & Associates. He is best known for large-scale commercial commissions such as shopping centers, notably Shoppers World in Framingham, Massachusetts, and the Jacksonville Downtown Center in Florida. In New

York City he designed the World of Birds and the World of Darkness buildings at the Bronx Zoo, P.S. 45 in Brooklyn, a dining hall for Queens College, and a monument to President John F. Kennedy on Grand Army Plaza in Brooklyn. Ketchum also designed the United States Embassy and ambassador's residence in Rabat, Morocco, and the Nordiska department store in Stockholm. He wrote numerous articles as well as a book, *Blazing a Trail,* about his own work. He served as vice-chairman of the New York City Landmarks Preservation Commission from 1972 to 1979. His design of the Hunter College Campus Schools at 71 East 94th Street in Carnegie Hill echoes the fortress-like quality of the original Squadron A (Eighth Regiment) Armory.

ROBERT D. KOHN (1870-1953)

Captivated by Art Nouveau, which he studied at the Ecole des Beaux-Arts in Paris after graduating from Columbia, Robert D. Kohn applied detailing in that style to a number of his New York City buildings. His first project demonstrating this penchant was the New York Post Building (1906-07), facing St. Paul's Chapel on Vesey Street; of particular note are the sculpted caricatures of newspaper editors by Gutzon Borglum on one of the higher floors. His better-known buildings are the Meeting House for the Society for Ethical Culture (1911) on Central Park West and 64th Street (Kohn had collaborated with Carrère and Hastings on the adjacent school building), and the Fieldston School in Riverdale in the Bronx (1926), which he designed in association with Clarence S. Stein. Kohn, Stein, and Charles Butler were responsible for Temple Emanu-El on Fifth Avenue at 65th Street, a project that also involved the firm of Mayers, Murray & Phillip, and for a massive addition to Macy's department store. Independently, Kohn designed a Beaux-Arts townhouse at 46 East 74th Street. He also designed the Tower Press Building in Cleveland, Ohio, and, with Butler, a store in Brooklyn for A. I. Namm & Son. At the northern boundary of Carnegie Hill he designed the Mount Sinai Hospital residence for nurses, now the Mount Sinai School of Medicine, at 5–17 East 98th Street.

LOUIS KORN (1873?- ?)

Louis Korn was born in New York City and received his degree in architecture from Columbia in 1891. After a year's apprenticeship with John B. Snook Sons, he opened his own practice. An early project was a loft building at 91 Fifth Avenue, followed by lofts at 141-145 Wooster Street and at 20 and 40 West 22nd Street. In 1901-02 he designed an apartment hotel at 12 Fifth Avenue and two apartment houses, the Regina and the Alabama, on East 11th Street. Korn's best-known design, entered in a competition, won him the commission, in 1904, for an Italian-Renaissance palazzo for the Progress Club, a Jewish social club on Central Park West at 88th Street. The building was purchased by the Walden School in 1932; it was demolished in the late 1980s to make way for a luxury apartment house. In 1899 he designed the Hotel Chastaignary, now the Hotel Wales, at 1295 Madison Avenue in Carnegie Hill.

NATHAN KORN (1893?-1941)

Nathan Korn received degrees from Cooper Union and Columbia. His buildings on record include 6 West 77th Street, the Bolivar at Central Park West and 83rd Street, and the Buckingham Hotel apartments on the Avenue of the Americas at 57th Street. Two of his 1920s luxury apartment buildings on Fifth Avenue, Nos. 944 and 956, reveal his affinity for the neo-Italian Renaissance style, as does his 1133 Park Avenue in Carnegie Hill.

CHARLES KREYMBOURG (?-1941)

Charles Kreymbourg had an architectural office at 2534 Marion Avenue in the Bronx, and much of his residential work was concentrated in that area and the Inwood section of Upper Manhattan. In 1921 he designed three tenements on the Grand Concourse at Fordham Road, and he is credited with the design of several Art Deco apartment buildings, including 165 Seaman Avenue, 57 and 83 Park Terrace West, and 48 Park Terrace East. In Manhattan he designed the neo-Georgian apartment building at 105 East 38th Street in Murray Hill and 161 East 91st Street in Carnegie Hill.

THOMAS W. LAMB (1871-1942)

The architect of more than 300 theaters across the country and around the world, Thomas White Lamb was born in Scotland and emigrated to Canada before moving to New York City, where he studied at Cooper Union. Among his most famous theaters was the second New York Academy of Music at 140 East 14th Street. (Built in 1927, renamed the Palladium, it was the site of the Beatles' first appearance on the Ed Sullivan show in 1964 and has been since demolished). He also designed the Cort at 138 West 48th Street; the Mark Hellinger, now the interdenominational Times Square Church on Broadway and 52nd Street; the first Madison Square Garden between 26th and 27th streets; and the Audubon Ballroom on Broadway between 155th and 156th streets in Washington Heights, where Malcolm X was assassinated. (Columbia University redeveloped the building as the Audubon Business and Technology Center, rising six stories behind the Ballroom's restored facade.) Internationally, Lamb was responsible for theaters in Canada, Cairo, Mumbai, Calcutta, Johannesburg, and London, where he designed the first American-style movie theater in Europe. In 1920, Lamb built a summer getaway for himself, the shingle-and-cobblestone Cobble Mountain Lodge, in the Adirondacks; the house remains privately owned. In 1927 he designed the Pythian Temple, a lodge for the fraternal order of the Knights of Pythias, at 135 West 70th Street, with an Art Deco facade of movie-set Egyptian images; the building has since been converted into a condominium. Three years later he designed the Art Deco apartment house at 49 East 96th Street in Carnegie Hill.

JOHN LAMBEER, JR.
All that is known of John Lambeer, Jr. is that in 1906 he designed a neo-Federal-style stable at 112 East 91st Street in Carnegie Hill.

THOMAS LEHRECKE
Thomas Lehrecke's first design on record is for a house that he built for his family in Tappan, New York, in 1963 as a prototype for a development. By 1969 he was a partner in the firm of Oppenheimer, Brady & Lehrecke; in that year, in association with architect Philip Birnbaum, he designed the 40-story apartment tower at 45 East 89th Street in Carnegie Hill. Five years later the firm designed an addition to the Amsterdam Houses behind Lincoln Center on the West Side. Lehrecke was subsequently affiliated with the firm of Gruzen & Partners, where he was involved in the design of the United States Embassy in Moscow in 1981, working with Skidmore Owings & Merrill.

CHARLES H. LENCH
Between 1921 and 1940 Charles H. Lench was a practicing architect in New York City; he was also the owner of the Alliance Realty Company. He designed a building at 34 West 54th Street and an Art Deco apartment building in the Upper West Side/Central Park West Historic District. The only example of his work in Carnegie Hill is the 1934 conversion of 65 East 92nd Street, a single-family house, into a multi-unit building with a neo-Georgian facade. The house has since reverted to a private residence.

JOHN P. LEO (1858-1923)
John P. Leo practiced in New York City as an architect and a builder, and in 1895 he was president of the Employers & Builders League. His 40-year practice included private residences and apartment buildings. He was active in civil defense, serving as a captain in the National Guard and a colonel in the Police Reserves. In Carnegie Hill he designed the flats building, the Trent, at 124 East 91st Street.

LEVIN DELISO WHITE SONGER

The firm of Levin Deliso White Songer designed 59-61 Christopher Street in the Greenwich Village Historic District. In Carnegie Hill they were responsible for the mid-block sliver building at 14 East 96th Street.

HERBERT LIPPMANN

Herbert Lippmann had an office in Manhattan from 1920 to 1925, and worked with architect Henry Churchill in the design of the Lowell Hotel at 28 East 63rd Street. In Carnegie Hill he designed a new facade for 12 East 93rd Street.

ELECTUS LITCHFIELD & ROGERS

Electus Darwin Litchfield (1872-1952)

Pliny Rogers (1882-1930)

Born in New York, **Electus Darwin Litchfield** graduated from the Brooklyn Polytechnic Institute. After a year at the Stevens Institute of Technology in Hoboken, New Jersey, he worked at the firms of Carrère & Hastings and Lord & Hewlett, and in 1908 joined Tracy & Swarthout as a partner. **Pliny Rogers** was born in Saginaw, Michigan, and received his architecture degree from Cornell. He became a draftsman with Tracy & Swarthout, where he met Litchfield; over the next ten years Litchfield and Rogers collaborated on many projects including the St. Paul Public Library and the James J. Hill Reference Library in St. Paul, Minnesota. During World War I they designed Yorkship Village, a "model town" near Camden, New Jersey, for 1,700 workers in the shipbuilding industry. The town, now known as Fairview, is listed on the National Register of Historic Places. In 1919 they set up the firm of Electus Litchfield & Rogers. After the partnership dissolved in 1926, Litchfield divided his time between designing public buildings across the country and serving on city-planning commissions in New York. Among his projects are the U.S. Post Office, Courthouse and Custom House in Albany and the Astoria Column in Astoria, Oregon—all on the National Register of Historic Places—and the Red Hook Housing Project in Brooklyn. Rogers designed a number of apartment houses and the Country Club of Troy, New York. In 1922 Litchfield and Rogers designed the neo-Federal apartment house at 4 East 88th Street in Carnegie Hill.

ROBERT T. LYONS

A designer primarily of apartment houses and hotels, Robert T. Lyons was an established architect in New York City by 1897. He was responsible for a number of buildings for developers Bing & Bing, including the apartment house at 565 Park Avenue and the Gramercy Park Hotel on Lexington Avenue and 21st Street. He designed the Beaux-Arts St. Urban apartments at 285 Central Park West, the Lorington on Central Park West at 70th Street, and the Coronet on West 58th Street. His commercial work includes the Jones Building at Duane and Elm streets and the Mela Building on the corner of Crosby and Spring streets. Two clubs, the City Athletic Club on West 54th Street and the Tammany Central Association Clubhouse on East 32nd Street, were also of his design. His other apartment houses include 25 East 67th Street, 112 East 74th Street, and in 1913, together with Warren & Wetmore, the seventeen-story 903 Park Avenue at 79th Street, then the world's tallest apartment building. In Carnegie Hill he designed a new facade for 70 East 91st Street, and the neo-Renaissance apartment house at 1155 Park Avenue.

STEPHEN C. LYRAS (1913-1983)

A graduate of New York University and the University of Pennsylvania School of Fine Arts, Stephen C. Lyras became a member of the American Institute of Architects in 1948. Working in partnership with the Greek-born architect John M. Kokkins, he designed hospitals and other facilities to be built in Greece under the United States war relief effort following World War II. In New York City he was a developer as well as a designer of apartment buildings, including 1065 Park Avenue in Carnegie Hill.

JAMES C. MACKENZIE, JR. (1887-1963)

James Cameron Mackenzie, Jr. was born in Lawrenceville, New Jersey. After graduating from Columbia and the Ecole des Beaux-Arts in Paris, he apprenticed at the firm of McKim, Mead & White. A parallel career of military activism informed much of his work; he served in various capacities — both on active duty and as a consultant—from 1916 on, and in 1949 achieved the rank of brigadier general while producing a number of projects for the military, including the Naval Air Base at Port Lyautey in Morocco and the Naval Training Center in Memphis, Tennessee. Mackenzie designed the headquarters for the Reader's Digest in Chappaqua, New York. In New York City he was responsible for the Harlem YMCA, now both a New York City designated landmark and a National Historic Landmark, as well as for two housing projects for the New York Housing Authority: Sheepshead Bay in Brooklyn and the Jacob Riis Houses on the Lower East Side of Manhattan. In Carnegie Hill he designed the neo-Regency townhouse at 48 East 92nd Street.

IRVING MARGON (1888?-1958)

Irving Margon's architectural practice in New York spanned more than 50 years. He designed residential buildings on the Upper East Side, including 965 Fifth Avenue, now a designated landmark, and 5 East 64th Street, a neo-Classical townhouse. He is listed as one of the architects of the twin-towered apartment building the El Dorado, also a designated landmark, on Central Park West and 90th Street. In Carnegie Hill he designed 120 East 89th Street.

JOHN W. MARSHALL

John W. Marshall was an architect and builder who worked with developers, both independently and in partnership, on the Upper East Side during the 1870s, 1880s and 1890s. His firm affiliations include Marshall & Hoffman; Marshall, Knowlden & Smith; Marshall & Nisbit; and Marshall & Walter. When the U.S. Federal Building, now a designated landmark, was built in 1892-99, Marshall served as superintendent of construction. In 1871 he built a row of eight houses on East 73rd Street; in the same year he was responsible for 162 and 164 East 88th Street in Carnegie Hill.

MAYNICKE & FRANKE

Robert D. Maynicke (1849-1913)

Julius Franke (?-1936)

The firm of Maynicke & Franke was responsible for over 100 buildings throughout New York City. **Robert D. Maynicke** was born in Germany and upon his arrival in New York, completed his architectural education at Cooper Union. Practicing independently, he designed the Brown Building at New York University and the Germania Bank Building on the Bowery, now a designated landmark, as well as several buildings along Ladies Mile on Broadway. **Julius Franke** graduated from the City College of New York and studied at the Ecole des Beaux-Arts in Paris. When he returned to New York City, he and Maynicke formed a partnership. Among the firm's major commissions were the International Toy Center at 200 Fifth Avenue, the New York Times Building at 229 West 43rd Street, and the Merchants' Exchange Building on Fifth Avenue and 17th Street. After Maynicke's death in 1913, Franke continued to practice under the firm name; his projects included additional work on the Warren & Wetmore-designed Hecksher Foundation for Children, now the Hecksher Building, at 1230 Fifth Avenue, which houses the Museo del Barrio, the Central Park Conservancy, and the Urban Park Rangers. In his retirement Franke moved to the Bavarian Alps and devoted himself to painting. Before he left the city, he helped draft the present New York City building code. In 1921 he designed the neo-Renaissance apartment house at 1349 Lexington Avenue in Carnegie Hill.

THOMAS H. MCAVOY (?-1887)

There are few records for Thomas A. McAvoy other than that he practiced architecture in New York City from 1874 until 1887. In Greenwich Village he designed the houses at 189 and 241 Waverly Place. His Carnegie Hill brownstones, at 122 and 124 East 93rd Street, were designed in 1877-78 in the neo-Grec style.

ALMERON WALLACE MCCREA (1873-1954)

Nothing is known of the education and background of Almeron Wallace McCrea. The earliest records of his work indicate that he redesigned the approaches to the Brooklyn Bridge after its completion. A specialist in residential architecture, he designed new facades for Upper East Side row houses during the 1920s. In 1926, under the firm name of McCrea & Sharpe, he designed a new facade for 14 East 94th Street in Carnegie Hill. Three years later, practicing independently, he redesigned the facade of 11 East 90th Street, originally the Minot-McAlpin house. He continued to practice until 1936.

JOHN B. MCINTYRE

John B. McIntyre maintained an office in Manhattan from 1875 until 1895. His commercial work included designs and alterations for stores and loft buildings in Tribeca; he also designed a small neo-Grec flats building at 126 East 93rd Street in Carnegie Hill. After his office was relocated to Long Island City in 1899, he was the architect of the Boys' Building (since demolished) of the New York Catholic Protectory in the Parkchester section of the Bronx.

GEORGE G. MILLER

During the late 1920s and the 1930s George G. Miller was active in northern Manhattan and the Bronx. The facades of his apartment buildings are often characterized by ornamental brickwork, typical of the end of the Arts and Crafts movement and the rising prevalence of Art Deco. Working independently, he designed 674, 686, and 687 West 204th Street, 119-131 Payson Avenue, and 56 Cooper Street in the Inwood section of Manhattan. In the late 1930s he designed a number of apartment houses in northern Manhattan with Albert Goldhammer. In Carnegie Hill he was the architect for 111 East 88th Street as well as the back-to-back twin buildings at 181 East 93rd Street and 170 East 94th Street.

MR ARCHITECTURE + DECOR
David B. Mann (1955-)

A native New Yorker, David B. Mann earned his bachelor's degree from Pratt Institute in 1981. After working with several design firms in New York City he joined the architectural firm of Fox & Fowle, where he was responsible primarily for designs for commercial lobbies and convention centers. In 1995 he founded his own practice, MR Architecture + Decor. The firm concentrates on modern interior design for retail stores, lofts, and residential apartments, as well as homes in upstate New York and on Long Island. In Carnegie Hill Mann designed the modern townhouse at 125 East 92nd Street.

HARRY B. MULLIKEN (1877?-1952)

Henry Burritt Mulliken was born in Sterling, Illinois, and received his degree from the Columbia University School of Architecture. He first practiced with Chicago architect Daniel H. Burnham and soon thereafter returned to New York City to join the firm of Ernest Flagg. He formed a partnership with Edgar J. Moeller in 1902. Mulliken & Moeller designed a number of hotels, many on the West Side, including include the former Aberdeen apartment hotel at 17 West 32nd Street, now the Best Western Manhattan Hotel and a designated landmark; the Woodstock on West 43rd Street; the Iroquois on West 44th Street; the Ameritania on Broadway and 54th Street; and the Bretton Hall on Broadway between 85th and 86th streets. Among their apartment houses are the Severn Arms on Amsterdam Avenue and 72nd Street; the Van Dyke, a block north at 73rd Street; and Orwell House and Rossleigh Court, twin buildings on Central Park West between 85th and 86th Streets. Two years before forming his partnership with Moeller, Mulliken designed Madison Court at 1361 Madison Avenue in Carnegie Hill.

NECARSULMER & LEHLBACH and GEHRON & ROSS

Edward Necarsulmer (1874-1959)
Edward Lehlback (1884-1944)
William Gehron
Sidney F. Ross

Of the two firms involved with the design of the north building of the 92nd Street Y at 1395 Lexington Avenue in Carnegie Hill, little is known of Necarsulmer & Lehlbach other than a shortlist of their buildings: 88 Lexington Avenue, 70 West 40th Street, and 115 West 45th Street, and the altered facade of the Franklin Simon store on Fifth Avenue at 37th Street. **Edward Necarsulmer** graduated from Columbia and the Ecole des Beaux-Arts in Paris and extended his stay in Europe on a McKim Traveling Fellowship before opening a practice in 1903.

William Gehron's associations varied throughout his career. As Gehron, Ross & Alley (with David Levy as associate architect), he and **Sidney F. Ross** were responsible for the complex that comprises the Jewish Theological Seminary on Broadway and 123rd Street, including the Jacob H. Schiff Memorial Library, the Teachers' Institute, and the Louis S. Brush Memorial Dormitory. Gehron & Ross designed the Memorial Bridge in Rochester, New York; the Forum, a building dedicated to the performing arts in the Capitol Complex in Harrisburg, Pennsylvania; and Washington Hall, the cadet mess hall at the United States Military Academy at West Point. With Andrew J. Thomas, Gehron designed the Queens Borough Hall and, with Alfred Easton Poor, the Criminal Courthouse, in the same Civic Center complex.

NEVILLE & BAGGE

Thomas P. Neville

George A. Bagge

Thomas P. Neville and **George A. Bagge** established their partnership in 1892. An enormously prolific firm that specialized in both store and loft buildings and in apartment houses, Neville & Bagge was responsible for a long list of Renaissance Revival buildings on the West Side, including 325, 490, 498, 590, and 789 West End Avenue. The firm also designed 300 West 113th Street for Columbia University and a number of apartment houses best known by their names: Riverside Mansions, the Roxborough Apartments, the Netherlands, the Columbus, and the Dorchester. From 1898 to 1902 they designed four flats buildings in Carnegie Hill: 61 East 86th Street, 138 East 94th Street, 17 and 19 East 95th Street, and 1326 and 1391 Madison Avenue, and twenty years later they redesigned the commercial building at 173 East 86th Street. In 1924 Bagge formed a partnership with his son, George A. Bagge & Sons; the firm was active for twelve years, during which time they designed the neo-Renaissance apartment house at 155 East 93rd Street.

LAWRENCE J. O'CONNOR (?- 1900)

Interested primarily in ecclesiastical architecture, Lawrence J. O'Connor was responsible for a number of Roman Catholic churches throughout New York City and State, and in New Jersey. Among his projects are the church that became the Cathedral of the Immaculate Conception, in Syracuse; the Church of the Immaculate Conception, in Yonkers; St. Michael's Catholic Church at 434 West 34th Street in Manhattan; and the Church of St. Francis de Sales at 135 East 96th Street in Carnegie Hill.

H. THOMAS O'HARA, JR. (1959-)

Prior to forming his own firm in 1997, H. Thomas O'Hara, Jr. was affiliated with Schuman, Lichtenstein, Claman and Efron and with Costas & Kondylis Associates. Over a twenty-year period with these firms he was chief architect for both residential and commercial buildings, including the Astor Terrace apartment complex at 94th Street and Second Avenue, and for the conversion of the Trump International Hotel and Tower on Central Park West into hotel and apartment condominiums. Since 1997 O'Hara's firm has collaborated with well-known architects, including Michael Graves, Philip Johnson and Robert Stern. O'Hara is responsible for major apartment buildings in Manhattan and Brooklyn Heights; his 18-story condominium tower at 1510 Second Avenue, opened in 2008, features a glass curtain wall, as does his planned apartment house at 1055 Park Avenue in Carnegie Hill. In 2005 he collaborated with Barry Rice on the design of 21 East 96th Street.

A.B. OGDEN & SON
Alfred B. Ogden (c.1834-1895)
Samuel B. Ogden (c.1865-1925)

Alfred B. Ogden and his son, **Samuel B. Ogden,** both native New Yorkers, maintained an architectural practice together from 1885 to 1895. Alfred Ogden had been involved primarily in the woodworking business until 1878, when he received his first major commission, a hospital (since demolished). By the time his son joined him, he had proved to be a designer of multi-family dwellings throughout the city in virtually every genre: tenements, row houses, flats buildings and apartment houses. A.B. Ogden & Son also designed stables, lofts, and industrial buildings such as the Estey Piano Company Factory on Lincoln Avenue in the Bronx, now a designated landmark. Upon his father's death on Christmas Day in 1895, Samuel changed the name of the firm to A.B. Ogden & Company and moved into a building of his own design at 954 Lexington Avenue. In 1900 he moved with his family to Brooklyn and appears to have closed down the firm, except for an occasional commission in that borough. The Carnegie Hill output by A.B. Ogden & Son was prolific and includes 1296-1304, 1305-1309, 1313, and 1340 Madison Avenue; 121-123 East 88th Street; 171-175 East 90th Street; 26, 48-54, and 49-55 East 91st Street; 1, 3, 9, and 15-25 East 92nd Street; 1-11, 4-12, 63, and 66 East 93rd Street; and 4-16 East 94th Street. Many of the buildings have undergone substantial facade changes. Alfred B. Ogden designed 134-138 East 92nd Street, and A.B. Ogden and Co. designed the Wellington at 1290 Madison Avenue.

LAWRENCE F. PECK (1882-1951)
Lawrence F. Peck practiced architecture in New York City from 1912 until 1930. In 1923 he designed the townhouse at 62 East 92nd Street in Carnegie Hill; since 1939 the building has served as part of the parish house and church school complex for the Brick Presbyterian Church.

GEORGE F. PELHAM (1866-1937)
GEORGE F. PELHAM, JR. (?-1957)
George Frederick Pelham credited with being responsible for more apartment buildings in Manhattan than any other architect of his time, and Carnegie Hill is the beneficiary of as many as 24 of his commodious designs. Born and educated in Ottawa, Pelham was the son of an architect who moved his family to New York City when George was in his teens. After training under private tutors, he apprenticed as a draftsman for a few years before establishing his own architectural practice in 1890. Like many of his contemporaries, he designed tenements and row houses before

hitting his stride as a pre-eminent designer of nineteen- and twenty-story apartment buildings. Among his more ambitious projects is the Tudor-inspired fifteen-building "garden community" of Hudson View Gardens on Pinehurst Avenue between 183rd and 185th streets; this development is one of Manhattan's earliest co-ops and was built specifically to attract middle-class families to what was then considered a suburb. Pelham designed the hotel Plaza Athenée at 37 East 64th Street and, just before retiring, the Central Hanover Bank and Trust Company at Sixth Avenue and 35th Street. His apartment houses encompass styles from Renaissance Revival to neo-Tudor Gothic, neo-Medieval, neo-Georgian, neo-Renaissance, and Art Deco.

The Carnegie Hill buildings attributed to George F. Pelham are 1136 Fifth Avenue; 1392-1398 Madison Avenue, 1120, 1130, 1160, 1225, and the Van Cortlandt at 1240 Park Avenue; 56 East 87th Street, 47 East 88th Street; 115 East 89th Street; 21, 51, and 115 East 90th Street; 46, 150-152, and 162 East 91st Street; 115 and 145 East 92nd Street; 125 East 93rd Street; 130 East 94th Street; Woodward Hall at 50 East 96th Street; 53-55, 57-59, and 65 East 96th Street; and 51 East 97th Street.

George F. Pelham, Jr. was born in New Rochelle, New York, and received his education and training at the New York School of Fine and Applied Art and at the Art Students League. He joined his father's firm in 1918 and was made a partner four years later; in 1928 he set up his own firm. He was responsible for a multi-tower group of apartment houses, Castle Village, in Washington Heights. Over the years he designed hundreds of apartment houses as well as commercial buildings and churches. In 1951 he dissolved his firm to practice with Paul Tishman & Company and, two years later, with Kelly & Gruzen. In Carnegie Hill he designed three apartment houses: 1056 Fifth Avenue, 1150 Park Avenue, and 115 East 86th Street.

PENNINGTON & LEWIS

Hall Pleasants Pennington (1889-1942)
Albert William Lewis

Hall Pleasants Pennington was born in Baltimore and educated at Princeton and the Ecole des Beaux-Arts in Paris. In France during World War I he designed hospitals for the American Red Cross. After the war he joined his architect father, Josias, in his Baltimore-based firm. During the 1920s he moved to New York City; a house of his design from this period is 9 East 79th Street. He practiced with **Albert William Lewis,** forming the firm of Pennington & Lewis in 1929. Within a year they designed two Carnegie Hill apartment houses in the Moderne style at 49 East 86th Street and 2 East 88th Street. Pennington was involved with the design of the Hall of Pharmacy at the 1939-40 New York World's Fair,

and he consulted on the design of the Norman-castle-style Frederick
Osborn House at the Russel Wright historic site at Cat Rock in upstate New
York. He also designed his own neo-Classical house on Long Island's
North Shore. Nothing is known of Albert William Lewis apart from his
association with Pennington and, after 1935, with Willis N. Mills, who
joined their firm. Pennington, Lewis & Mills specialized in the design of
apartment houses and were the architects of the Federal Building at 90
Church Street.

PETER PENNOYER ARCHITECTS
Peter Pennoyer (1957-)
A native New Yorker, Peter Pennoyer graduated from Columbia and earned
his Master's degree from Columbia Graduate School of Architecture,
Planning and Preservation in 1984. While at graduate school he worked as
a designer at the Manhattan office of his Columbia professor, the architect
Robert A.M. Stern. He started his own practice in 1984 as principal of
Pennoyer, Turino Architects in New York City; in 1990 he formed Peter
Pennoyer Architects. Pennoyer's work is firmly rooted in a respect for
classical design, with projects including renovations of the Mark Hotel and
the Knickerbocker and Colony Clubs in New York City, and many town-
houses on the Upper East Side. He serves on the boards of the Institute of
Classical Architecture and Classical America, the Morgan Library &
Museum, and the Mrs. Giles Whiting Foundation. Together with Anne
Walker, he is the author of *The Art and Architecture of Delano & Aldrich, The
Architecture of Warren & Wetmore, The Architecture of Grosvenor Atterbury,* and an intro-
duction to a reprint of Frank M. Snyder's *Building Details.* In 2007 the firm
restored the neo-Grec facade of 50 East 91st Street in Carnegie Hill.

HARDIE PHILLIP (1887-1973)
Scottish-born F. Hardie Phillip received his education and architectural
apprenticeship in Edinburgh. He spent two years in Malaysia before
emigrating to the United States in 1910. His first job was with the firm of
Cross and Cross; from there he joined the firm of Bertram Grosvenor
Goodhue, where he advanced to the position of chief designer. When
Goodhue died, Phillip joined two other associates, Francis L.S. Mayers
and Oscar H. Murray, to form the firm of Mayers, Murray & Phillip. At
the time Phillip was involved with the design of the Episcopal Church of
the Heavenly Rest and its adjoining parish house and chapel at 90th Street
and Fifth Avenue in Carnegie Hill, which he saw through to completion.
The firm designed a number of important buildings throughout the
nation, including the Nebraska State Capitol, the National Academy of

Science in Washington, D.C., and the Los Angeles Public Library. In Manhattan, Mayers, Murray & Phillip designed the Community House of St. Bartholomew's Church at Park Avenue and 50th Street, now a designated landmark, and collaborated with Kohn, Stein & Butler on the design of Temple Emanu-El on Fifth Avenue at 65th Street. Phillip was architect-in-charge of the redesign of the Honolulu Academy of Arts, now a designated landmark, as well as the design of the C. Brewer Oriental Institute at the University of Chicago.

In 1933 Mayers, Murray & Phillip were appointed architects to the Bureau of Indian Affairs and were responsible for public buildings on reservations throughout the United States. Their most significant building was the octagonal pueblo-style Navajo Nation Council Chamber in Window Rock, Arizona, built in 1934 and since then the center of government for the Navajo Indian nation; it was designated a National Historic Landmark in 2004. The firm disbanded in 1940 and Phillip practiced independently in New York before moving permanently to California in the early 1950s.

PLATT BYARD DOVELL WHITE

Charles Adams Platt (1932-)
Paul Spencer Byard (1939-2008)
Ray H. Dovell
Samuel G. White

Charles Adams Platt, born in 1932, is the third generation of a family of distinguished architects. His father, William Platt, designed the National Academy School of Fine Arts at 5 East 89th Street in Carnegie Hill and his grandfather and namesake, Charles Adams Platt, designed the Freer Gallery in Washington, D.C. Platt, an architect and artist, began practicing in 1963; in 1965 he formed the firm of Smotrich & Platt, the precursor of Platt Byard Dovell White. He served as chairman of the Preservation Committee of the Municipal Arts Society, of which he was a director for 25 years; a member of the New York City Landmarks Preservation Commission for five years; the director of New 42 Inc.; and a member of the Gracie Mansion Conservancy. Platt is a visiting critic at Cornell University and an adjunct associate professor at the Columbia University Graduate School of Architecture, Planning and Preservation.

Paul Spencer Byard was a graduate of Yale and received degrees from Harvard Law School, Clare College, Cambridge, and the Columbia University Graduate School of Architecture, Planning and Preservation, where he taught as an adjunct associate professor. His legal career included associate counsel of the New York State Urban Development Association as well as private practitioner. He began practicing architecture in 1977, and joined Charles A. Platt Partners in 1989. Bayard was a director of the Municipal Art Society and the New York Landmarks Preservation Conservancy as well as president of the Architectural League. He authored several books on architecture including *The Architecture of Additions: Design and Regulation.*

Ray H. Dovell worked as an architectural designer for New York firms in the Middle East before joining Smotrich & Platt in 1984. He is also a recognized furniture designer. His educational affiliations include Columbia University, where he is a design juror; the City College of New York; and the Pratt Institute.

Samuel G. White is the great-grandson of Stanford White. He is the author of the books *The Houses of McKim, Mead & White* and *McKim, Mead & White, The Masterworks.* He began practicing architecture in 1974; a founding partner of the firm of Buttrick, White & Burtis, he has designed educational, institutional and residential buildings. He is an adjunct assistant professor of fine arts at New York University and lectures regularly to preservationist groups, including Carnegie Hill Neighbors.

Among Platt Byard Dovell White's notable achievements are two new wings of the Saginaw, Michigan Art Museum, the Green-Wood Columbarium in Brooklyn, and the color-lighted New 42nd Street Studios at 229 East 42nd Street; their five-story Reece School at 25 East 104th Street, built in 2006, introduces color via tinted glass. Their restoration and adaptive reuse projects include the Louis Armstrong House Museum in Queens, the Foundation Building of Cooper Union at Astor Place, the Chanel Building on West 57th Street, and the Loew Mansion at 56 East 93rd Street in Carnegie Hill as the new home of the Spence School's lower school. Also in Carnegie Hill the firm designed the ten-story (originally planned as seventeen-story) apartment building at 47 East 91st Street.

WILLIAM AND GEOFFREY PLATT

William E. Platt (1897-1984)

Geoffrey Platt (1905-1985)

Sons of New York artist and architect Charles Adams Platt, **William** and **Geoffrey Platt** entered their father's firm after completing their education at Harvard and Columbia, William in 1924 and Geoffrey in 1930. Upon their father's death in 1933, they renamed the firm William and Geoffrey Platt. The following year the firm was awarded first prize in an international competition for re-planning the business center of Stockholm. Other major commissions included additions to the chapel at the Suresnes American Cemetery and Memorial outside of Paris; buildings for Deerfield Academy in Deerfield, Massachusetts, and for Smith College in nearby Northampton; and together with landscape architect Ellen Biddle Shipman, Longue View, a plantation house near New Orleans, which is now a national landmark. In Manhattan the Platts worked on alterations to Fort Clinton in Battery Park as well as on the old Aquarium and the Subtreasury Building. They designed the Steuben Building on Fifth Avenue and 56th Street for Corning Glass, incorporating 3,800 blocks made of that company's signature Pyrex. In 1965 Geoffrey Platt was elected the first chairman of the New York City Landmarks Preservation Commission. In Carnegie Hill William Platt designed 5 East 89th Street, the National Academy School of Fine Arts; the firm designed 163 East 86th Street and a modern classical facade for 124 East 92nd Street.

JAN HIRD POKORNY (1925-2008)

Revered in his homeland, the Czech Republic, and among his émigré compatriots in the United States, Jan Hird Pokorny made his home in New York City in 1940 and became a United States citizen in 1945. He earned a master's degree at Columbia University's architecture school and later served on the faculty. Both a modern architect and an ardent preservationist, he was an often-outspoken member of the New York City Landmarks Preservation Commission. He and his firm, Jan Hird Pokorny Associates, restored many buildings in the city, notably 181-193 Front Street and the South Street Seaport Museum at 207 Front Street in Schermerhorn Row. Their other projects include the restoration of the Battery Maritime Building and the Brooklyn Historical Society, both of which won awards from the New York Landmarks Conservancy, and the New Library, Speech and Theater and Auditorium buildings for Lehman College in the Bronx with David Todd & Associates. In 2001 the New York State Association of Architects honored Pokorny with the Quintessential Architect award, a prize given only twice in its history. In Carnegie Hill he designed 10 East 87th Street in collaboration with architect/designer Felix Augenfeld.

GEORGE MORT POLLARD (1865-?)

Born in Brooklyn, George Mort Pollard received his education at the College of the City of New York (now City College). After establishing his architectural practice in New York City he formed a partnership with Joseph L. Steinman in 1897. The firm soon established a reputation for designing buildings that combined living and studio spaces for artists, often as duplex units. Among their best know works are the Art Nouveau artists enclaves at 130 and 140 West 57th Street and the neo-Renaissance studio building at 39-41 West 67th Street. Working independently, Pollard designed the Gothic-style Hotel des Artistes at 1 West 67th Street in 1917. Pollard's only work in Carnegie Hill is the modest facade of 1413 Lexington Avenue.

POLSHEK PARTNERSHIP ARCHITECTS

James Stewart Polshek (1930-)

Born in Akron, Ohio, James Stewart Polshek enrolled at Case Western Reserve University with intentions of becoming a psychiatrist. After taking a course in modern architecture he transferred to Yale University, graduating in 1955 with a Master of Architecture degree. He worked for architect I.M. Pei prior to forming the firm of Polshek Partnership in 1963. From 1972 to 1987 Polshek served as dean of the Columbia University Graduate School of Architecture, Planning and Preservation. Although the portfolio of the New York-based firm is prodigious—with hundreds of commissions focusing on cultural, educational, governmental and scientific institutions, as well as residential towers—it was the 1999 opening of the Rose Center for Earth and Space at the American Museum of Natural History that put Polshek in the public eye. Other much-publicized projects include the site design for the William Jefferson Clinton Presidential Center in Little Rock, Arkansas, the redesign of the Brooklyn Museum's main entrance, the sleek Scandinavia House on Park Avenue at 38th Street, and the new Zankel Hall theater beneath Carnegie Hall. The firm's only Carnegie Hill project is the 1998 two-story building linking the Andrew Carnegie mansion to its McAlpin-Miller house at 9 East 90th Street.

POMERANCE & BREINES

Ralph Pomerance (1908-1995)

Simon Breines (1906-2003)

Born in Manhattan, **Ralph Pomerance** was graduated from the Carnegie Institute of Technology and opened his own office in 1933. Two years later he formed a partnership with Simon Breines in an architectural practice that would span nearly 60 years. An early project of Pomerance was the Swedish Pavilion at the 1939-40 New York World's Fair, designed in collaboration with Swedish architect Sven Markelius. **Simon Breines,** a native New Yorker, received his degree in architecture from Pratt Institute. He was the founding director of the New York Landmarks Conservancy and, as an advocate for pedestrian-friendly urban design, was a co-author with William J. Dean of *"The Pedestrian Revolution: Streets Without Cars."* Pomerance & Breines have more than 400 buildings to their credit, both public and private. Included are the Grand Concourse Public Library in the Bronx and apartment buildings at 209 East 56th Street and 800 Second Avenue. Best known for housing complexes and medical buildings—for Bellevue, Mount Sinai, and Jacobi Medical Center—in 1967 the firm designed the seventeen-story Baum-Rothschild Staff Pavilion at 1249 Park Avenue, part of the Mount Sinai complex, as well as the contiguous apartment house at 1245 Park Avenue in Carnegie Hill.

JOHN RUSSELL POPE (1874-1937)

The son of a portrait painter, John Russell Pope was born in New York and studied at the City College of New York. Upon receiving his degree in architecture from Columbia, he was awarded a scholarship to the newly-founded American Academy in Rome. After two years of travel in Italy and Greece, he studied at the Ecole des Beaux-Arts in Paris. He returned to New York City in 1900 and apprenticed with Bruce Price; three years later he went out on his own. Renowned for his work in the classical style, he was responsible for Union Station in Richmond, Virginia, now the Science Museum of Virginia; the Baltimore Museum of Fine Art; and the National Archives Building, the Jefferson Memorial, and the West Building of the National Gallery of Art in Washington, D.C. (The latter two were completed by the firm of Eggers & Higgins after his death.) Pope also designed, in Washington, D.C., the Masonic Temple of the Scottish Rite, the Pharmaceutical Building, and Constitution Hall for the Daughters of the American Revolution. He conceived the master plan for Yale University and the master plan for Dartmouth College. His work abroad includes the Duveen Sculpture Gallery at the British Museum and the Sculpture Hall of the Tate Gallery in London as well as the War Memorial in Montfaucon, France. In New York City he designed the Theodore Roosevelt Memorial at the grand entrance to the American Museum of Natural History and, at the Frick Collection, the lovely courtyard garden with its paired Ionic columns, the oval chamber, the East Gallery and the ornate auditorium. Among his private houses were the Marshall Field III residence in Huntington, New York; alterations to the Newport, Rhode Island, mansion Belcourt for Oliver and Alma Belmont; and several houses for the Vanderbilt family, including 60 East 93rd Street in Carnegie Hill for Virginia Graham Fair Vanderbilt. He also designed 22 East 91st Street, the Spence School.

WALTER REID, JR.

The son of a real-estate developer, Walter Reid, Jr. was active as an architect between 1892 and 1913, working both with his father and with the firm of A.B. Ogden & Son. In Carnegie Hill he collaborated with Ogden on 1, 3, and 9 East 92nd Street and designed the row houses at 14-24 East 93rd Street.

BARRY RICE (1966-)

A native of Brisbane, Australia, Barry Rice graduated from the University of Queensland and received his diploma in architecture from the Polytechnic of Central London. He established his architectural practice in 1999 and is an associate partner at Robert A.M. Stern Architects in New York City. His projects include new buildings, renovations and interiors in New York City, San Francisco, and Chicago, and private residences on Long Island and in Pawling, New York. In Manhattan he is responsible for an eight-story sliver building on West 86th Street; condominiums in Chelsea, in East Harlem, and at 19 St. Mark's Place; and several major renovations on Park Avenue. In Carnegie Hill he collaborated with H. Thomas O'Hara, Jr. on the design of 21 East 96th Street and is the architect of the planned 180 East 93rd Street.

KEVIN ROCHE JOHN DINKELOO AND ASSOCIATES

Kevin Roche (1922-)
John Dinkeloo (1918-1981)

Kevin Roche was born in Dublin. A graduate of the National University of Ireland, he emigrated to the United States in 1948. After taking graduate courses at the Illinois Institute of Technology under Mies van der Rohe, he moved to New York City to work for the United Nations Planning Office. **John Dinkeloo,** born in Holland, Michigan, was an engineer. He graduated from the University of Michigan School of Architecture and started out at the firm of Skidmore Owings & Merrill in New York City. In 1950 first Roche and then Dinkeloo joined the firm of Eero Saarinen. When Saarinen died ten years later, Roche and Dinkeloo continued at the practice and completed ten major commissions that were under way, including the iconic St. Louis Gateway Arch and, in New York City the TWA Terminal at Idlewild Airport, now JFK International Airport; the IBM Pavilion at the 1964-65 New York World's Fair; and "Black Rock," the dark-glass CBS Headquarters building at 51 West 52nd Street. In 1966 the partnership of Kevin Roche John Dinkeloo and Associates, based in Hamden, Connecticut, was formed. The firm was responsible, in New York City, for the Ford Foundation Building at 321 East 42nd Street; a master plan for the Metropolitan Museum of Art and new wings and additions to the Museum; United Nations Plaza on First Avenue at 44th Street; and the renovation of the Central Park Zoo. After Dinkeloo's death in 1981, Roche stayed at the firm with its name unchanged. The firm has a great number of major commissions, national and international, to its credit. In 1989 Roche designed the addition to the Jewish Museum at 1109 Fifth Avenue in Carnegie Hill. In 2003 the firm designed the Museum of Jewish Heritage at 36 Battery Park Place in downtown Manhattan.

ROSENBERG KOLB

Eric Rosenberg
Michele Kolb

Eric Rosenberg graduated from Colgate University and received his architectural degree from North Carolina State University. After working with architectural firms in St. Louis and New York he formed his own New

York City-based firm in 1983. **Michele Kolb,** a graduate of Parsons School of Design and Columbia, was associated with Pentagram Design, Gwathmey Siegel and Associates, and Vignelli Associates before forming a partnership with Rosenberg in 1987. In addition to architectural design the firm's commissions include interior, product and graphic design for retail and hospitality spaces, corporate offices, residences, and international projects. In Carnegie Hill they designed a new facade for 164 East 91st Street.

ERWIN ROSSBACH

Erwin Rossbach, together with Thomas W. Lamb, designed the 63rd Street Music Hall between Central Park West and Columbus Avenue; started in 1909 and completed in 1914, it was an almost exact reproduction of the Drury Lane Theatre in London. Later named Daly's 63rd Street Theater, it was demolished in 1957. Rossbach also designed a new limestone facade in the Art Nouveau style for 16 West 45th Street in 1909. A year earlier he was the architect of 120 East 88th Street in Carnegie Hill.

EMERY ROTH (1871-1948)

Emery Roth emigrated to the United States from his native Hungary at the age of thirteen when his innkeeper father died, leaving the family destitute. Moving to Chicago and then to Bloomington, Illinois, he apprenticed for three years at an architectural firm and also worked as a carpenter/builder. He unsuccessfully sought work in Kansas City and returned to Chicago, working his way up from office boy to draftsman in the firm of Burnham & Root, which designed the 1893 World's Columbian Exposition in Chicago. At the close of the Exposition he moved to New York City and took a position with Richard Morris Hunt, where he drafted interior drawings for The Breakers, Cornelius Vanderbilt II's mansion in Newport, Rhode Island. Roth then joined with Ogden Codman, Jr. In 1895 he opened his own practice; his first major work in New York City was the Hotel Belleclaire at 2171 Broadway, now landmarked. He soon specialized in the design of luxury apartment houses, including the San Remo, the Beresford, and the El Dorado on Central Park West, the latter designed in association with Margon & Holder; all three are designated landmarks. In the 1930s his sons, Richard and Julian, joined their father and the firm was renamed Emery Roth & Sons. One of Roth's last projects was the Normandy Apartments at 140 Riverside Drive, also a designated landmark. In Carnegie Hill he designed 21 East 87th Street, 114 East 90th Street, 60 East 96th Street, 1125 and 1133 Fifth Avenue, 1112 and 1175 Park Avenue, and new facades for 1143, 1145, and 1149 Park Avenue. Emery Roth & Sons designed 50 East 89th Street.

ROUSE & GOLDSTONE
ROUSE & SLOAN

William Lawrence Rouse (1874-1963)
Lafayette Anthony Goldstone (1876-1956)
John T. Sloan

William Lawrence Rouse, a native New Yorker, trained at the Stevens Institute of Technology in Hoboken, New Jersey. Early in the 20th century he formed a partnership with **John T. Sloan,** about whom information is uncertain. The firm of Rouse & Sloan designed the Hendrik Hudson Apartments at Riverside Drive and 110th Street and the Peter Stuyvesant Hotel at 86th Street and Central Park West. In 1905 the firm designed the three identical buildings at 53, 57 and 61 East 95th Street in Carnegie Hill.

(An architect, John Sloan, is on record as having studied at New York University; after supervising construction for the United States Army from 1908-1920 and designing the Pershing Square Building at 100 East 42nd Street, he formed a partnership with T. Markoe Robertson in 1924. Sloan & Robertson designed the Chanin Building at 122 East 42nd Street, the Graybar Building at 420 Lexington Avenue, and many institutions, and apartment houses in New York City. However, it seems questionable that this John Sloan played a part in the design of 53-61 East 95th Street, as he would have been just seventeen at the time of the buildings' completion.)

Lafayette Anthony Goldstone arrived in New York City from Poughkeepsie at the age of fifteen to join his brothers, Julius and Frederick, and to study with architect William Henry Cusack. Apprenticeships with Carrère & Hastings, Bates & Barlow, and Cleverdon & Putzel followed; he remained with the latter for six years. After serving in the Spanish-American War, he supervised the construction of tenements designed by George F. Pelham on the Lower East Side and later joined the firm of Norcross Brothers. When Rouse and Goldstone formed their partnership in 1910, they were sought after as architects of luxury apartment houses on the Upper East and West sides. They were responsible also for commercial buildings, hotels and banks. In Carnegie Hill Rouse & Goldstone designed 1107 Fifth Avenue. After the firm split up in 1926, Goldstone was associated for a time with Frederick L. Ackerman. Notable apartment houses by Goldstone alone include 4, 44, and 50 East 72nd Street, 125 East 74th Street, 730 Park Avenue and, in Carnegie Hill, 12 East 97th Street.

FRANK J. SCHEFCIK

Other than his designs for the Alan Garage and the Franklin Hotel at 154-164 East 87th Street in Carnegie Hill, there are few records of the work of Frank J. Schefcik. In 1920 he submitted applications to build garages on East 32nd Street and West 56th Street.

GILBERT A. SCHELLENGER (?-1921)

Gilbert A. Schellenger's place of birth and training are unrecorded, but he is known to have been practicing architecture by the early 1880s. During that decade and the one following, he produced an enormous number of residential buildings throughout Manhattan—tenements, row houses, flats buildings and small apartment houses—designed mainly in groups and in many of the then-popular revival styles. More than 200 of his residential buildings are on the Upper West Side. A number of his buildings are now designated landmarks, including the William Diller house at 309 West 72nd Street, the 354-355 Central Park West Houses, and 80 Wooster Street, a former warehouse that is said to be the first building in SoHo that was converted into artists' lofts. In Carnegie Hill he designed Renaissance Revival brownstones at 56–62 East 91st Street, 67 and 69 East 91st Street, 25–33 East 93rd Street and 1316-1320 Madison Avenue, and the modest five-story building at 1067 Park Avenue.

MOTT B. SCHMIDT (1889-1977)

Mott B. Schmidt was born in Middletown, New York, and raised in Brooklyn. He graduated from the Pratt Institute and opened his own architectural office in 1912. After World War I he concentrated on designing city and country houses for an affluent clientele; his first such commission was for an English Regency-style townhouse for Grenville T. Emmet at 39 East 63rd Street. Houses that he designed for Vincent and Helen Astor at 130 East 80th Street, now the Junior League of New York, and for Emily Trevor at 15 East 90th Street in Carnegie Hill, are designated landmarks.

His other significant projects include the apartment building at 19 East 72nd Street; a Sutton Place townhouse for Anne Morgan and, also on Sutton Place at No. 1, a mansion for Mrs. William K. Vanderbilt, now the residence of the Secretary-General of the United Nations; a country house for himself in Bedford, New York; and a residence on the estate of John H. Cowperthwaite in Bedminster, New Jersey, now the Trump National Golf Club. Late in his career Schmidt, in association with John Barrington Bayley, the co-founder of Classical America and an architect for the New York City Landmarks Preservation Commission, designed the neo-Georgian Susan B. Wagner Wing for Gracie Mansion in collaboration with F. Burrall Hoffman and Edward Coe Embury. In Carnegie Hill, Schmidt also designed the neo-Georgian townhouse at 57–61 East 91st Street, originally the Guy and Cynthia Cary house, now part of the Dalton School; the neo-Classical courtyard building at 1088 Park Avenue; and the 1919 renovation of 3 East 94th Street.

WALTER S. SCHNEIDER

In 1919 Walter S. Schneider designed the B'nai Jeshurun Synagogue at 257 West 88th Street in collaboration with Henry Beaumont Herts, a prominent theater architect. Both were members of the congregation at the time; they developed a square facade of roughened granite modeled on an Egyptian temple. Eight years later Schneider designed the Moorish-style Park Avenue Synagogue at 50 East 87th Street in Carnegie Hill.

LEONARD SCHULTZE (1877-1951)

Born in Chicago, Leonard Schultze came to New York to study at the City College of New York. After further study at the Metropolitan Museum of Art, he joined the firm of Warren & Wetmore, eventually assuming the position of chief designer of Grand Central Terminal. In 1921 he formed a partnership with S. Fullerton Weaver. Schultze & Weaver earned their reputation as designers of luxury Jazz Age hotels, including the Breakers in Palm Beach, the Atlanta Biltmore, the Sevilla Biltmore in Havana, and the Los Angeles Biltmore, now the Millennium Biltmore. In New York City they were responsible for the Sherry-Netherland and the Pierre hotels, on Fifth Avenue at 59th and 61st streets, and the Waldorf-Astoria on Park Avenue at 49th Street, which upon completion in 1929 was the largest hotel in the world and is now a designated landmark. After Weaver's death in 1939, Leonard Schultze & Associates designed more hotels and became actively involved in town planning. Major commissions were the Parkmerced 2,500-apartment "city within a city" in San Francisco, designed for the Metropolitan Insurance Company of New York, and the Park Fairfax development outside Washington, D.C., built to house federal workers during World War II. In Carnegie Hill the firm designed 47 East 87th Street and 15 East 91st Street.

SCHUMAN LICHTENSTEIN CLAMAN EFRON (now SLCE ARCHITECTS)

Sidney Schuman (1908-?)
Samuel Lichtenstein (1908-?)
Peter Claman (1928-)
Albert Efron

Sidney Schuman and **Samuel Lichtenstein** met as draftsmen at the Bell Telephone Company and formed their architectural partnership in 1941. Their design work concentrated on apartment buildings, institutions and hotels, notably Temple Israel of the City of New York at 112 East 75th Street and the Coronado Hotel at 151 West 70th Street. As the firm added partners it changed its name to reflect its growth: first to Schuman, Lichtenstein & Claman, then to Schuman Lichtenstein Claman Efron, now SLCE Architects. Schuman retired in the early 1990s; Lichtenstein practiced well into his eighties. The firm's recent projects include a post-Modern apartment tower at 1012 East End Avenue and, with Cesar Pelli & Associates, the Bloomberg Tower at Lexington Avenue and 59th Street, Element 555 at West 59th Street, 1 Beacon Court at 151 East 58th Street, and the German Mission to the United Nations on First Avenue and 49th Street. In Carnegie Hill Schuman & Lichtenstein designed 7 East 86th Street, 55 East 87th Street, and 1372-1378 Lexington Avenue. Schuman Lichtenstein Claman Efron designed 108 East 96th Street, completed in 1994.

SCHWARTZ & GROSS

Simon I. Schwartz (1877?-1956)

Arthur Gross (1877-1950)

Classmates and fellow graduates of the Hebrew Technical Institute, a vocational school on Stuyvesant Place that operated from 1884 to 1939, **Simon I. Schwartz** and **Arthur Gross** formed their architectural practice in 1902. (Their early building records show a B.N. Marcus as a co-partner.) Their hugely prolific firm specialized in luxury apartment houses and hotels; representative examples, in a variety of styles ranging from Renaissance Revival to neo-Venetian Gothic to Art Deco, can be found throughout the city. Notable among their designs are the Colosseum Apartments at 435 Riverside Drive (1910), the Dorset at 150 East 79th Street (also 1910), and the Pennsylvania Building at 225 West 34th Street (1925). They designed the first conspicuously Art Deco apartment building on Central Park West, at No. 55, in 1930. As the firm's reputation grew, the partners, especially Schwartz, became actively involved in the financing and development of their buildings, such as the Surrey Hotel at 20 East 76th Street, of which Schwartz was the president and director. Other of the firm's hotels include the Mark at 992 Madison Avenue)now undergoing conversion) and the Fitzpatrick Manhattan on Lexington Avenue at 56th Street. Eleven buildings in Carnegie Hill are the work of Schwartz & Gross: 55 and 103 East 86th Street; 1045, 1070, 1085, 1095, 1111, 1125, 1165, and 1185 Park Avenue; and 1459 Lexington Avenue, Congregation Orach Chaim.

SCHWARZMANN & BUCHMAN

Hermann J. Schwarzmann (1843-1891)

Albert C. Buchman (1859-1936)

Born in Munich, **Hermann J. Schwarzmann** was the son of a fresco painter; he emigrated to Philadelphia and began work as an engineer of waterworks in Fairmont Park. His reputation was assured when he was named architect-in-chief of the Centennial Exposition of 1876, which was held in Philadelphia and for which he designed Memorial Hall, the Horticultural Building, and the Women's Building. In 1880 he moved to New York City. In 1885, working with Raphael Guastavino, he designed the Temple B'nai

Jeshurun, a Byzantine-Moorish-style synagogue on Madison Avenue between 64th and 65th streets, since demolished. **Albert C. Buchman,** a graduate of Cornell and the Columbia University School of Mines, now a now its architecture school, began to collaborate with Schwarzmann in 1881; they formed a partnership in 1885 and designed 70 and 72 East 91st Street (later altered) and the row houses at 123–133 East 91st Street in Carnegie Hill. The partnership lasted until 1888, after which Buchman formed several new partnerships, including Buchman & Fox (which see).

EDWARD I. SHIRE (1874-1973?)
A native New Yorker, Edward Isaac Shire received his education at the City College of New York and at Columbia, graduating in 1896. After two years with the firm of Shire & Kaufman, he continued his architectural studies at the Ecole des Beaux Arts in Paris. Upon his return to New York City in 1900, he formed his own firm. Shire's widely varied projects included health facilities, mortuary structures and buildings for religious and educational institutions, as well as residential and interior design work. His portfolio included the townhouse at 126 East 70th Street and several other houses on the Upper East Side in addition to the Carnegie Hill townhouse at 53-55 East 91st Street, now the First Program of the Dalton School, for which he designed a neo-Georgian facade.

JOHN SIMPSON (1954-)
John Simpson, an eminent British architect specializing in the classical style, received his diploma in architecture from University College in London and set up practice in 1980. A member of the Royal Institute of British Architects, he endorsed the New Classicism in the 1980s and cemented his reputation with Ashfold House in West Sussex. He is especially noted for his work for the Royal Family, including the Market Building for Poundbury, the Prince of Wales's mixed-urban development in the town of Dorchester in Dorset, and renovations to the Queen's Galleries and Royal Kitchens at Buckingham Palace, which were completed for the Golden Jubilee in 2002. In Carnegie Hill he collaborated with Zivkovic Connolly Architects on the design of the 2005 addition to the Mrs. Amory S. Carhart house at 3 East 95th Street.

SKIDMORE OWINGS & MERRILL (SOM)
Founded in Chicago in 1936 by Louis Skidmore and Nathaniel Owings, the firm became Skidmore Owings & Merrill with the arrival of John Merrill three years later. In 1952 Gordon Bunshaft joined the firm and was responsible for the design of the iconic Lever House on Park Avenue at 53rd Street. Today the firm maintains offices in eight cities around the

world, including New York. Their output has been staggering, with more than 10,000 architectural, engineering, and planning projects, in more than 50 countries—which have garnered more than 800 design awards. Among their signal accomplishments is the Sears Tower in Chicago, now the tallest building in the United States. The firm also designed Chicago's John Hancock Tower as well as the million-square-foot Bank of America World Headquarters in San Francisco and the International Terminal at San Francisco Airport. The firm's major commissions in New York City, besides Lever House, include the Metropolitan Opera House at Lincoln Center; One Chase Manhattan Plaza and the Goldman Sachs & Co. building downtown; the Bertelsmann Building in Times Square; Worldwide Plaza on Eighth Avenue and 52nd Street; 9 West 57th Street, with its snappy red 9 out front; the Time Warner Center on Columbus Circle; and the Islamic Cultural Center of New York, just outside of Carnegie Hill at 96th Street and Third Avenue. In Carnegie Hill SOM converted the department store Gimbels East at 120 East 87th Street into a seventeen-story luxury apartment building, Park Avenue Court.

SNELLING & POTTER
  Grenville T. Snelling (?-1920)
  Howard Nott Potter (?-1937)
The partnership of Snelling & Potter, formed in about 1895, was active for fifteen years. The firm is on record as having designed a Gothic-style church building for St. John's Episcopal Church in Jacksonville, Florida, completed in 1906, as well as a remodel of Trinity Episcopal Church in St. Augustine four years earlier. **Grenville T. Snelling** was an instructor at Columbia University as well as a practicing architect. In 1909 the firm provided a new facade for 66 East 91st Street in Carnegie Hill. Snelling practiced independently until 1913 and **Potter** until 1922.

JOHN B. SNOOK (1815-1901)
John Butler Snook was born in England and trained under his father, a carpenter/builder, before emigrating to New York City, where he practiced that trade until he joined with William Beer to form an architectural partnership in 1837. In 1842 he joined forces with Joseph Trench; they later formed the partnership of Trench & Snook. Their firm was responsible for the A.T. Stewart Dry Goods Store at 280 Broadway, the nation's first department store, later the Sun Building, now a designated landmark. When Trench left the firm to move to California, Snook expanded his practice to become one of the largest in New York City. Among his most notable projects was the design of the original Grand Central Station, completed in 1871. At that time he also designed a Second Empire-style townhouse at 1388

Lexington Avenue in Carnegie Hill. In 1877 he celebrated the firm's fiftieth anniversary by taking in his three sons, James (1847-1917), Samuel (1857-1915), and Thomas (1863-1953), and a son-in-law, John W. Boylston, and changing the firm name to John B. Snook & Sons. Upon the death of John Snook, Samuel assumed leadership of the firm until 1907. After Samuel's death, Thomas took over and was later joined by Thomas E. Snook, Jr., and the name of the four-generation firm was changed once again, to John B. Snook Sons. In all, the Snooks were responsible for over 500 buildings in the city, including schools, churches, tenements, private houses and commercial buildings.

GEORGE W. SPITZER

George W. Spitzer is on record as having maintained an architectural practice in New York City from 1887 through 1917. Several of his Romanesque Revival houses are in Hamilton Heights, and a store and loft building that he designed in 1901 is in the Ladies Mile Historic District, at 11 West 20th Street. His only Carnegie Hill building is the 1897 Renaissance Revival Hotel Ashton, now an apartment house, at 1306-1312 Madison Avenue.

SPRINGSTEEN & GOLDHAMMER

George W. Springsteen (1879-1954)
Albert Goldhammer

The firm of Springsteen & Goldhammer was formed in 1919 and remained active until around 1934. **George W. Springsteen** was born in Brooklyn and received his education at Cooper Union and the Pratt Institute. He apprenticed at the office of Rouse & Goldstone and later worked in at least two partnerships before joining forces with **Albert Goldhammer**. Much of Springsteen & Goldhammer's work consisted of low-cost housing, especially in the Bronx. In the late 1930s Goldhammer designed a number of apartment houses in northern Manhattan with George G. Miller. In 1938 he alone designed several buildings, including a synagogue for the Society for the Advancement of Judaism at 15 West 26th Street. In Carnegie Hill Springsteen & Goldhammer designed 140 East 95th Street.

CHARLES STEGMAYER

Charles Stegmayer was in practice by 1890. His designs include a flats building at 137 East 73rd Street; the Holland Hotel on West 10th Street, one of a number of seamen's hotels near the Hudson River waterfront in the far West Village; and 1495 Third Avenue at 84th Street, constructed in 1906, notable for its cast-iron facade and grand arched central window. In Carnegie Hill he designed 173 East 86th Street; 175 East 87th Street, now the Doyle Galleries; 125 East 88th Street; and 168 East 91st Street.

J. ARMSTONG STENHOUSE (1863-1931)

Born in Scotland, Joseph Armstrong Stenhouse apprenticed in Dundee and practiced in Aberdeen before relocating to London and then New York City. In London he designed several blocks of mansions in the West End, a specialty he transferred to Manhattan where he was responsible for a number of grand Fifth Avenue houses—especially their interiors, including furnishings, for which he demonstrated a remarkable flair. He worked on mansions for financiers George Blumenthal, on Park Avenue and 70th Street, and Jacob Schiff. With C.P.H Gilbert he designed 1 East 91st Street, originally the Otto and Addie Kahn mansion and now the Convent of the Sacred Heart, in Carnegie Hill. Upon his retirement Stenhouse returned to the British Isles, settling in the English country-side, in Sutton Courtney, Berkshire.

FREDERICK J. STERNER (1862-1931)

London-born Frederick Junius Sterner came to the United States at the age of sixteen with his father; they moved first to California and then to Chicago, where his father became a liquor merchant. During the 1880s Sterner worked as a draftsman in Chicago; by 1890 he had moved to Denver, where he practiced architecture, first in partnership with Ernest Phillip Varien and then with George W. Williamson, for the next 30 years. His firms were responsible for important public buildings and private houses, notably the Antlers Club and Glen Eyrie in Colorado Springs, the latter a house that is now on the National Register of Historic Places.

In 1906 he moved to New York City, where his brother, Albert, a well-known painter, lived. He won recognition remodeling brownstones into houses of artistic merit with special plantings and gardens, including his own, at 139 East 19th Street, near Irving Place, which he shared with his sister, Maude. Both were involved with the design of the Greenbrier Hotel in West Virginia, Frederick as architect and Maude as interior designer. Later houses that Sterner renovated—and lived in—included 154 East 63rd Street, 150 East 62nd Street and, finally, a house on the corner of 65th Street and Lexington Avenue. In 1924 he moved back to London with his sister. He died in Rome. In Carnegie Hill Sterner designed the neo-Georgian townhouse at 109 East 91st Street for Mrs. I. Townsend Burden, Jr., and, with John Wolfe, of whom nothing is known, a new facade for 25 East 94th Street.

HARVEY STEVENSON (1894-?)

Harvey Stevenson was born in Croton-on-Hudson, New York. He was educated at Yale and apprenticed with various New York City firms, including McKim, Mead & White, before establishing his own practice.

Among his commissions were a house for Gary Cooper and, in 1923, the restoration of Boscobel in Garrison, New York. He was also responsible for the Administration Building at the 1939-40 New York World's Fair. His work in Carnegie Hill involved a few alterations to 8 East 93rd Street.

LEO STILLMAN (1904-1989)

A Russian émigré noted for his Art Deco designs in the 1930s, Leo Stillman studied at the City College of New York and at the Beaux-Arts Institute of Design. He was a prolific architect, specializing in low-rise apartment-house complexes throughout the metropolitan area; his later work demonstrated an affinity for poured-concrete construction techniques. Among his New York City projects are the Park Terrace Gardens in Upper Manhattan, Walden Terrace in Rego Park in Queens, Oxford Knolls in the Bronx, 144 and 200 East 84th Street, and 11 East 88th Street and in Carnegie Hill.

SUGARMAN, HESS & BERGER

M. Henry Sugarman (1888-1946)
Arthur P. Hess
Albert G. Berger (1879-1940)

The three architects who comprised the firm of Sugarman, Hess & Berger worked independently and together throughout the 1920s and 1930s in New York City, New Jersey, and Philadelphia. **M. Henry Sugarman,** a native New Yorker, was educated at the Columbia University School of Architecture and the National Academy of Design; he also studied in England and France. He acquired practical experience in New York City with architect J.E.R. Carpenter and practiced for a time in Alabama and South Carolina. In 1923 he joined with **Arthur P. Hess,** about whom little is known, and **Albert G. Berger.** Hungarian-born Berger received his architectural and engineering training at the University of Budapest; in 1904 he emigrated to the United States and worked as a draftsman at the firm of Schwartz & Gross. In 1924 Sugarman, Hess & Berger designed the neo-Renaissance apartment house at 17 East 96th Street in Carnegie Hill.

After Hess left in 1926, the firm of Sugarman & Berger specialized in hotels and apartment houses; their many commissions included the Fifth Avenue Hotel at 1 Fifth Avenue, the New Yorker Hotel at Eighth Avenue at 34th Street, and 935 Park Avenue. In Philadelphia they designed the 1900 Rittenhouse Square Apartments, now on the National Register of Historic Places. Their Carnegie Hill buildings include 1311-1329 Lexington Avenue, 25 East 86th Street (1178-1188 Madison Avenue, 20 East 87th Street), 125 East 87th Street, and 40 East 88th Street.

JOHN SULLIVAN

Nothing is known of architect/builder John Sullivan except that he was responsible, in Carnegie Hill, for three neo-Grec row houses at 1141, 1143, and 1147 Park Avenue and for two groups of row houses on East 91st Street, of which only Nos. 103, 113, 166, and 168 survive.

THOM & WILSON

Arthur M. Thom
James W. Wilson

Hugely prolific as late-19th-century architects of residential buildings in Manhattan, **Arthur M. Thom** and **James W. Wilson** are also among the most elusive in terms of identification. Working in collaboration with real-estate developers, they designed numerous French flats, groups of row houses, and small apartment buildings in Greenwich Village and the Upper East Side. They were the architects of the Harlem Courthouse at 170 East 121st Street, now a designated landmark. In Carnegie Hill they designed the neo-Grec Hellgate Hill brownstone row houses for speculative developer Michael Duffy in 1878-80. Originally a full square block between Lexington and Third avenues and 94th and 95th streets, the surviving 24-house enclave includes 157-179 East 94th Street, 158-180 East 95th Street, and 1451-1457 Lexington Avenue.

JOHN ROCHESTER THOMAS (1848-1901)

Born in Rochester, New York, John Rochester Thomas studied in Europe. Upon returning home, he opened his own practice in 1868. In 1882 he moved to New York City. Primarily an architect of religious institutions—he designed over 150 churches—he is represented in the city by the Calvary Baptist Church at 123 West 57th Street and the Ephesus Seventh-Day Adventist Church on Malcolm X Boulevard and 123rd Street, now a designated landmark. Besides the Squadron A (Eighth Regiment) Armory between Madison and Park avenues and 94th and 95th streets in Carnegie Hill, he was responsible for the Old Stock Exchange and the Hays Building at 21 Maiden Lane in downtown Manhattan. A proponent of humane architecture for prisoners, he designed a number of state reformatories, including those in Elmira, New York, and Rahway, New Jersey, and presented a paper about prison architecture before the Congress of the National Prison Association in 1893. Among his other work outside the city is Brooks Hall at the University of Virginia. In 1896 Thomas created the winning design, out of 133 entries, in a competition for a new New York City Hall; the legislature subsequently voted against demolishing the older structure but commissioned him to adapt his design to plans for a new Surrogate's Courthouse/Hall of Records at 31

Chambers Street, a project he was working on at his death. It was completed by the firm of Hogan & Slattery in 1911.

THEODORE E. THOMSON

Theodore E. Thomson was active in New York City from 1874 to 1913 and at one time maintained an office in Brooklyn. He designed an apartment building at 100 West 14th Street and was responsible for several Renaissance Revival buildings on the West Side, including 527 Sixth Avenue and 134 and 138 West 74th Street. In Carnegie Hill he designed a group of seven neo-Grec row houses on East 92nd Street, of which Nos. 58 and 60 survive.

TREANOR & FATIO
William A. Treanor (1888-1946)
Maurice Fatio (1897-1943)

Maurice Fatio was born and educated in Switzerland and at the Ecole des Beaux-Arts in Paris; he arrived in New York City in 1920. **William A. Treanor** studied engineering at the Pratt Institute and practiced in two firms before joining forces with Fatio in 1921. In Manhattan Treanor & Fatio designed a mansion on Beekman Terrace and an apartment house on Beekman Place as well as an apartment building at 222 East 71st Street; they were also responsible for the 55th Street Playhouse. In 1925 Fatio relocated to Palm Beach, Florida, and assumed the lavish lifestyle of a society architect, while Treanor remained behind to run the New York office. Treanor & Fatio designed suburban and summer residences for the Vanderbilt family as well as for Otto Kahn and Mrs. Mortimer Schiff. A Moderne house of Fatio's design in Palm Beach received the Paris Medal of Honor in 1937, and the firm's Olympia School in Hobe Sound is on the National Register of Historic Places. In 1923 the firm designed a neo-Georgian facade for 63 East 90th Street in Carnegie Hill.

TROWBRIDGE & LIVINGSTON
Samuel Beck Parkman Trowbridge (1862-1925)
Goodhue Livingston (1867-1951)

Samuel Beck Parkman Trowbridge was born in New York and educated at Trinity College in Hartford and at the Columbia University School of Mines, now its architecture school. After graduating, he furthered his training at the American School of Classical Studies in Athens and at the Ecole des Beaux-Arts in Paris. Upon his return to New York City, he apprenticed with George B. Post. **Goodhue Livingston,** also born in New York, graduated from the Columbia University School of Mines, where he and Trowbridge met. He, too, apprenticed with Post. Livingston,

Trowbridge, and a fellow Columbia graduate, Stockton B. Colt, founded the firm of Trowbridge, Colt & Livingston in 1896. Colt left after three years, and Trowbridge and Livingston practiced together until Trowbridge's death. Their major commissions in New York City include public and commercial buildings in downtown Manhattan: the Bankers Trust Building; the Drexel, Morgan & Co., later J. P. Morgan & Co., building; the Chemical National Bank building; a 20-story addition to the New York Stock Exchange; and the Equitable Trust Company Building. They also designed the B. Altman department store on Fifth Avenue at 34th Street and the St. Regis Hotel on 55th Street and Fifth Avenue, both designated landmarks, and the old Hayden Planetarium at the American Museum of Natural History. On a smaller scale, they designed a house for John S. and Catherine Rogers, now the New York Society Library. at 53 East 79th Street. Their commissions outside the city include the Mellon National Bank in Pittsburgh, the Palace Hotel in San Francisco, the national headquarters of the American Red Cross in Washington, D.C., the Oregon State Capitol, and the Mitsui Bank in Tokyo. Trowbridge was a founder and trustee of the American Academy in Rome. After his death, Livingston remained active in the firm until 1946. In Carnegie Hill Trowbridge & Livingston designed the Beaux-Arts town-house at 11 East 91st Street for John B. and Caroline Wilmerding Trevor, Jr.; it is now the Consulate of the Russian Federation in New York.

HORACE TRUMBAUER (1869-1938)

A native and life-long resident of Philadelphia, Horace Trumbauer bypassed architecture school and, at the age of sixteen, started out in the firm of G.W. and W.D. Hewitt, where he remained until 1890. After opening his own firm, he designed modest residences in the suburbs outside of Philadelphia and in nearby New Jersey. Within a few years he was designing on a far grander scale in and around Philadelphia and in Newport, Rhode Island, and other of the Gilded Age's most fashionable resorts. Although primarily a residential architect, Trumbauer designed clubs, hotels and cultural-institution buildings. In 1906 he was joined by Julian F. Abele. Abele was the first African American to graduate from the University of Pennsylvania's Department of Architecture, in 1902; he was Trumbauer's partner and chief designer at the firm for more than 30 years. Their commissions in Philadelphia include the Philadelphia Museum of Art, the Free Library of Philadelphia, the North Broad Street Railway Terminal, Irvine Auditorium at the University of Pennsylvania, and the Widener Office Building, one of several commissions for the Widener family, who also engaged the firm to design the Widener Memorial Library at Harvard University.

In New York City Trumbauer was responsible for the Ritz-Carlton

Hotel (in association with Warren & Wetmore), the Wildenstein Art
Gallery at 19 East 64th Street, and sumptuous townhouses, including the
James B. Duke mansion at Fifth Avenue and 78th Street, now the New
York University Institute of Fine Art and a designated landmark. Late
in his career Trumbauer designed a master plan for Duke University,
including seventeen buildings of his own design; this commission came
from Peter A.B. Widener, the founder of the American Tobacco Company
and a benefactor of Duke. Sadly, most of Trumbauer's mansions in
Manhattan, including those built for James Speyer at 87th Street and Fifth
Avenue and for I. Townsend Burden at 2 East 92nd Street, both in
Carnegie Hill, were demolished to make way for large apartment buildings. Surviving is 3 East 95th Street, the Louis XVI-style house (also a designated landmark) that Trumbauer designed for Mrs. Amory S. Carhart.
In 2005 it was joined to a new four-story building designed by British
architect John Simpson in association with Zivkovic Connolly Architects.

TURNER & KILIAN
James R. Turner
William G. Kilian

The partnership of **James R. Turner** and **William G. Kilian** was active
from 1900 through 1907. During that period the firm designed 1083
Fifth Avenue, now the National Academy Museum, and a group of
Beaux-Arts townhouses at 5-9 East 88th Street in Carnegie Hill. Kilian
continued practicing through 1940.

JACOB H. VALENTINE (1823-1903)
Jacob H. Valentine was born on Allen Street on Manhattan's Lower East
Side; during the 1880s he maintained an office at 151 East 128th Street.
Little else is known of this architect, who was responsible for many
Italianate, neo-Grec, Queen Anne, and Renaissance Revival buildings on
both the Upper West and Upper East sides; few of his building facades
survive today. In 1869 he designed the mirror-image brick row houses at
121 and 123 East 92nd Street, among the earliest surviving buildings in
Carnegie Hill. He is attributed with the 1879 design of the brownstone
row houses at 164 and 166 East 90th Street and 164 East 91st Street.

VAN VLECK & GOLDSMITH
Joseph Van Vleck, Jr. (1876-1942)
Goldwin Goldsmith (1871-1962)

The firm of Van Vleck & Goldsmith was active in Manhattan and New Jersey
from 1897 to 1913. All that is known of **Joseph Van Vleck, Jr.** is that he was
a born in Montclair, New Jersey, and graduated from Columbia. **Goldwin**

Goldsmith, born in nearby Paterson, received a Ph.D. from the Columbia University School of Architecture after a brief apprenticeship at the firm of McKim, Mead & White. Following graduation and a year of study at the Ecole des Beaux Arts in Paris, he and Van Vleck formed their partnership. Among their early works were several buildings in Montclair, including the First Methodist Episcopal Church, now a landmark. In New York City the firm designed two of three houses, also designated landmarks, on Fifth Avenue between 83rd and 84th streets that were known as the Pratt mansions and are now occupied by the Marymount School. Van Vleck & Goldsmith also designed residences at 1026, 1027, and 1028 Madison Avenue as well as the row of Beaux-Arts townhouses at 18-24 East 94th Street in Carnegie Hill.

In 1913 Goldsmith moved to Kansas and established the University of Kansas School of Architecture. He taught there until 1928, when he became chairman of the Architecture Department at the University of Texas at Austin. In 1935 he wrote the book *Architects' Specifications: How to Write Them,* which became a standard text.

WALKER & GILLETTE
Alexander Stewart Walker (1876-1952)
Leon Narcisse Gillette (1878-1945)

The partnership of Walker & Gillette was formed in 1906 and lasted for almost 40 years. **Alexander Stewart Walker** was born in Jersey City, New Jersey, and received his architectural degree from Harvard in 1898. **Leon Narcisse Gillette** was born in Malden, Massachusetts, and graduated from the universities of Minnesota and Pennsylvania. He worked in New York City at several firms including Babb, Cook & Willard, and then studied further at the Ecole des Beaux-Arts in Paris. He worked briefly for the firm of Warren & Wetmore before joining Walker. Walker and Gillette cemented their reputation with residential designs, specifically for wealthy and socially prominent clients on Long Island, among them H.H. Rogers in Southampton, William R. Coe in Oyster Bay, and George F. Baker in Glen Cove.

Their major commissions in Manhattan included the First National Bank at 2 Wall Street, the Battery Maritime Building at the southern tip of Manhattan, the Art Deco Fuller Building on Madison Avenue and 57th Street, wings for the New-York Historical Society; and 980 Park Avenue, now the Italian Consulate—all are designated landmarks—as well as the Chemical Bank & Trust Co. on East 50th Street. The firm also designed Playland in Rye, New York, the first planned amusement park in the United States; the planned community of Venice, Florida; and the Industrial Trust Building in Providence, Rhode Island, still the tallest building in that city, as well as buildings (and murals) for the 1939-40 New York World's Fair and a bank in Havana, Cuba.

In Carnegie Hill they designed the Art Deco Citibank building at 123 East 86th Street. Their residential work in Carnegie Hill includes a new facade uniting 4 and 6 East 93rd Street, formerly the Viola and Elie Nadelmn house. and the English Regency-style 56 East 93rd Street, now the Lower School of the Spence School.

JAMES EDWARD WARE (1846-1918)
James Edward Ware practiced architecture in New York City for nearly a half century, initially on his own and later with his sons, Franklin B. and Arthur, as James E. Ware & Sons. Born in New York, Ware studied at the City College of New York and opened his practice in 1869. As a pioneer in designing the modern fireproof warehouse, he was responsible for the Manhattan Storage and Warehouse buildings at Lexington Avenue and 42nd Street and at Seventh Avenue and 52nd Street. He championed humane living conditions for the poor and won a competition to design a model tenement with a window in every bedroom; his so-called "dumbbell tenement" was a prototype for tenements mandated by the Tenement House Law of 1879, until new legislation outlawed them in 1901. Ware participated in the design of buildings for the Mohonk Mountain House in New Paltz, New York.

In Manhattan he designed the Madison Avenue Presbyterian Church at 73rd Street, the 12th Regiment Armory on Columbus Avenue and 61st Street, the Fifth National Bank at Third Avenue and 23rd Street, a row of gabled houses at 11-14 Mount Morris Park and West 121st Street, and the Osborne, an apartment house at Seventh Avenue and 57th Street. Ware's work in Carnegie Hill was done between 1889 and 1891. His Romanesque Revival row houses at 1285-1293 Madison Avenue are remarkably well preserved; he and his family lived in No. 1285. He also designed five Queen Anne houses on Madison Avenue between 93rd and 94th streets, of which Nos. 1321 and 1323-1325 survive.

EDMUND WARING
Edmund Waring had his own architectural practice from 1855 to 1858, with an office at 20 Chrystie Street. His son, William E. Waring, joined him in 1859 and the firm became E. Waring & Son, existing until 1867, after which Edmund Waring practiced on his own until 1882. In Carnegie Hill he designed the Italianate-style frame house at 128 East 93rd Street, one of the last wooden houses to be built before fire laws prohibited such structures.

WARREN & WETMORE

Whitney Warren (1864-1943)

Charles Delavan Wetmore (1867-1941)

A Gilded Age partnership that produced over 300 buildings, Warren & Wetmore enjoyed spectacular success, in part because of social and familial ties to prominent families such as the Vanderbilts. **Whitney Warren,** a native New Yorker and Vanderbilt cousin, graduated from Columbia and traveled to Paris at the age of eighteen to study at the Ecole des Beaux-Arts. Enamored of Europe, he remained there for a decade before returning to New York City to work briefly for the firm of McKim Mead & White. **Charles Delavan Wetmore** was born and educated in Elmira, New York, and attended Harvard College and Harvard Law School; he then studied architecture and designed three dormitories for the campus before joining a law firm. In 1898 Warren persuaded him to give up law and form a partnership; Warren acted as principal designer while Wetmore managed the financial and legal end of the business. Warren & Wetmore established their reputation with their first commissions: the New York Yacht Club at 37 West 44th Street, now a designated landmark, and Grand Central Terminal (with the firm of Reed & Stern), which became the focal point for a number of ancillary buildings that Warren & Wetmore designed, including the Commodore, the Vanderbilt (with its Guastavino-ceilinged Della Robbia Bar), and the Biltmore hotels, and the New York Central Building at 230 Park Avenue, now the Helmsley Building and also a landmark. Their other hotels include an addition to the Plaza; the Belmont in Providence, Rhode Island; the Ambassador in Atlantic City; the Broadmoor in Colorado Springs; the Royal Hawaiian in Honolulu; and the Bermudiana in Hamilton, Bermuda. The firm designed the Steinway Building at 109 West 57th Street, Aeolian Hall at 689 Fifth Avenue, a building for Con Edison, and the old Chelsea Piers, as well as luxury apartment houses including 854 Fifth Avenue and together with Robert T. Lyons, 903 Park Avenue, and townhouses, country estates and country clubs.

Warren & Wetmore was responsible for a number of railroad stations in this country and in Canada. Warren took the most pride in his design for the reconstructed university library in Louvain, Belgium, which had been destroyed in World War I. For many years he presided over the annual ball of the Beaux-Arts Institute of Design, of which he was a founder. After retiring from the firm in 1931, he continued to act as a consultant; Wetmore remained the senior partner until his death. The firm designed two buildings in Carnegie Hill: 161 East 90th Street and 7 East 91st Street, the Beaux-Arts mansion for James A. and Florence Adele Burden, Jr., now part of the Convent of the Sacred Heart and a designated landmark.

WEBER & DROSSER

Adam Weber
Hubert Drosser

Little is known of either partner, other than that both were probably born in Germany. In 1885 **Adam Weber** designed four neo-Grec row houses at 1380-1386 Lexington Avenue in Carnegie Hill, then part of Yorkville. The following year he formed a partnership with **Hubert Drosser** that lasted until until 1896. Together Weber and Drosser designed 1364 and 1377-1379 Lexington Avenue, and a group of five row houses, Nos. 124-132 East 92nd Street, of which Nos. 126 and 128 survive. They were responsible also for the German Renaissance-style Scheffel Hall, a beer garden and social center at 190 Third Avenue near 14th Street, another then-thriving German enclave in New York City. The firm is on record as having designed the Ice Railway power house and track at the 1893 World's Columbian Exposition in Chicago.

WECHSLER & SCHIMENTI

Max Wechsler (1906-1993)
Michael Schimenti (1915- ?)

The firm of Wechsler & Schimenti provided the architectural and engineering expertise for a number of mid-20th-century high-rise apartment buildings, theaters, and office and commercial buildings in Manhattan, as well as remodels of former structures, including a brownstone at 7 East 63rd Street. **Max Wechsler,** a native New Yorker, studied at Columbia University and New York University; **Michael Schimenti,** also born in New York, was educated at Cooper Union, the Mechanics Institute, the New York Structural Institute and the Ecole des Beaux-Arts in Paris. Before joining forces with Wechsler in 1947, he worked as a draftsman for William I. Hohauser. Among the firm's well-known apartment towers are the 55-story Corinthian at 330 East 38th Street, designed in conjunction with Der Scutt Architects; 200 Central Park South, which presents a curved facade on the corner of Seventh Avenue; and 985 Fifth Avenue on the northeast corner of 79th Street. In Carnegie Hill the firm designed the Modern apartment buildings at 1050 and 1080 Fifth Avenue and, with the firm Wechsler, Grasso & Menziuso, 169 East 91st Street.

FRANK WENNEMER

Frank Wennemer practiced architecture in New York City from about 1890 to 1911. An early designer of elevator apartment buildings on the Upper East Side, he also designed two carriage houses, now landmarked, at 170 and 172-174 East 73rd Street. His row houses in Carnegie Hill incorporated the popular styles of the day—Romanesque Revival, neo Grec, and Queen Anne—and include 127, 129, and 168-172 East 90th Street, 49 and 51 East 92nd Street, 129-143 East 95th Street, and 138 East 96th Street.

EDWARD WENZ

Edward Wenz's architectural practice, which was primarily residential, was established in 1887. He designed row houses and flats buildings on the Upper West Side, in addition to Queen Anne and neo-Grec buildings in Carnegie Hill, which include the Summit at 1428 Lexington Avenue, 1432 Lexington Avenue, 62 East 87th Street, 116 East 92nd Street, and Hortense Court at 9 East 97th Street.

WHITFIELD & KING

Henry D. Whitfield (?-1949)

Beverly S. King

Henry D. Whitfield graduated from Harvard in 1898. He was the brother of Andrew Carnegie's wife, Louise, and benefited by being given the position of in-house architect of the Carnegies. Nothing, however, is known of his training, nor of that of his partner, **Beverly S. King,** with whom he practiced from 1903 until 1910. Whitfield, with and without King, designed libraries on behalf of Carnegie in Barnesville, Georgia; St. Petersburg, Florida; and Honolulu; some have been designated land-marks or are on the National Register of Historic Places. Whitfield also designed, on behalf of Carnegie, the Rensselaer Polytechnic Institute in Troy, New York. In New York City Whitfield & King designed the Engineers' Club at 32 West 40th Street, now an apartment house, as well as the Grand and Quarropas Building at 160 Fifth Avenue, where Whitfield kept his office. Working independently, Whitfield designed the Heads and Horns Building, completed in 1922, at the Bronx Zoo. For his brother-in-law, he designed a garage at 55 East 90th Street in Carnegie Hill—one of the first garages in New York City. It has since been expanded and now houses the Horace Mann School for Nursery Years.

FRANK WILLIAMS & PARTNERS ARCHITECTS

Frank Williams (1936-)

Frank Williams is a graduate of the University of California at Berkeley. He received a master's degree from Harvard in 1965 and taught at Columbia University for four years. After working for Skidmore Owings & Merrill in San Francisco, he opened his own architectural firm in New York City in 1969. Frank Williams & Partners Architects has been responsible for some 20 hotels and mixed-use residential towers in New York City, including the Rihga Royal Hotel at 151 West 54th Street, the Belaire at 524 East 72nd Street, 515 Park Avenue, the Park Belvedere at 101 West 79th Street, and Trump Palace at 200 East 69th Street, at 57 stories the tallest all-residential tower in the city. Williams collaborated with I.M. Pei on the design of the Four Seasons Hotel at 57 East 57th Street. Worldwide the firm has designed towers in Dubai, Bangkok, Seoul, Shanghai, and Beijing. Their ongoing project is the Mercury City Tower, a 70-story complex in the center of Moscow with strong references to the Russian Constructivism Movement of the 1920s. In Carnegie Hill the firm designed the Gotham, a mixed-use residential tower at 170 East 87th Street. Williams is the author of several books on architecture and has received many awards.

OSWALD WIRZ
Swiss-born Oswald Wirz arrived in New York City in 1880 and established a firm with Robert Nickel five years later. The partnership lasted only a year; Wirz then worked briefly on his own before being hired by builder James G. Wallace, with whom he remained until 1895. While at Wallace Brothers he designed a headquarters for the firm—the Wallace Building at 56-58 Pine Street, now landmarked—which was, at twelve stories, then considered a skyscraper (four stories were added in 1919). The building was recently converted into corporate apartments and is now the Cambridge Club. Wirz also designed 120 Liberty Street and the Beard Building at 125 Cedar Street. His last recorded affiliation was with George W. Spitzer, whose firm he joined in 1899 as head draftsman. In Carnegie Hill he designed the Renaissance Revival flats buildings at 114-118 East 91st Street.

WRAY & BUSSELL
Joseph Wray
Samuel D. Bussell
Nothing is known of **Joseph Wray** and **Samuel D. Bussell,** who were both architects and developers, other than that they are credited with three high-stoop brownstone row houses at 30-34 East 62nd Street, in addition to the pair of 1889 Renaissance Revival buildings at 63 and 65 East 91st Street in Carnegie Hill.

FRANK LLOYD WRIGHT (1869-1959)
More has been written about Frank Lloyd Wright than any other American architect, and with just cause: During a career-spanning seven decades, he designed more than 1,000 buildings — homes, offices, churches, schools, libraries, bridges, museums—in virtually every format; of the 542 that were completed, 409 still exist. Born in Richland Center, Wisconsin, he studied briefly at the University of Wisconsin in Madison; the few courses in basic mathematics and mechanical drawing that he took comprised the extent of his formal architectural education. Soon he moved to Chicago, where he served a short apprenticeship with J.L. Silsbee; this led to six years at the firm of Adler and Sullivan, where he was responsible for much of their residential work. Here he developed his iconic house form with a low,

horizontal silhouette; well-known examples of his "prairie style" include the Coonley House in Riverdale, Illinois, and the Robie House in Chicago. He also designed the Unity Temple in Oak Park, Illinois, where he then lived, and the Larkin Building in Buffalo, New York (since demolished).

As Wright's fame grew, so did the magnitude and number of his commissions — which increasingly reflected his personal design dictates. Among his most famous designs are Falling Water, the dramatic cantilevered house he designed for Edgar Kaufmann in Bear Run, Pennsylvania; the Price Tower in Bartlesville, Oklahoma; the Imperial Hotel in Tokyo (since demolished); and the headquarters for Johnson Wax in Racine, Wisconsin. One of his unrealized projects was a mile-high skyscraper in Chicago. Wright was a prolific lecturer and writer; his books include an autobiography and his seminal text, *On Architecture*. His architectural legacy lives on at his studio and school in Taliesin West in Scottsdale, Arizona, where he spent his last years, and at what is undoubtedly his most famous work, the Solomon R. Guggenheim Museum at 1071 Fifth Avenue in Carnegie Hill.

YORK & SAWYER

Edward Palmer York (1865-1928)
Philip Sawyer (1868-1949)
William Louis Ayres (1874-1947)

A firm that established its reputation with its designs for banks (50 in all), large office buildings and other institutions, York & Sawyer was active from the turn of the century into the 1950s. **Edward Palmer York** was born in Wellsville, New York, and graduated with a degree in architecture from Cornell, after which he came to New York City to join McKim, Mead & White. It was there that he met **Philip Sawyer** and **William Louis Ayres,** who 40 years later would be architect-in-charge of Carnegie Hill's Brick Presbyterian Church at 1140-1144 Park Avenue. Sawyer, born in New London, Connecticut, originally studied civil engineering; he served with the U.S. Geological Survey in New Mexico and directed an irrigation survey of the Yellowstone River in Wyoming. Later he trained in architecture at Columbia and the Ecole des Beaux-Arts in Paris. Ayres was born in Bergen Point, New Jersey, and received his degree in electrical engineering from Rutgers University. In 1901 he joined York and Sawyer, who had formed their partnership in 1898.

In New York City the firm was responsible for a number of buildings that are now designated landmarks, including the Federal Reserve Bank of New York, at 33 Liberty Street downtown; the Greenwich Savings Bank at Broadway and 36th Street; the Bowery Savings Bank at 110 East 42nd Street, now an upscale event hall run by the Cipriani family; the Central Savings Bank at Broadway and 73rd Street; the New-York Historical Society; and the

New York Athletic Club on Central Park South. Institutional commissions include buildings for the Manhattan Eye, Ear and Throat Hospital, Roosevelt Hospital, the Beaux-Arts Babies' Hospital at Lexington Avenue and 55th Street (now an office building), and the medieval-style Academy of Medicine at 103rd Street and Fifth Avenue. They also designed the law school buildings at the University of Michigan; the engineering school buildings at Cornell University; and buildings for Vassar, Smith, and Middlebury colleges, the University of Washington, and Rutgers University, as well as for the Riggs National Bank. They designed the U.S. Department of Commerce Building in Washington, D.C., and the U.S. Post Office, Custom House, and Courthouse in Honolulu, which are on the National Register of Historic Places.

ZIVKOVIC CONNOLLY ARCHITECTS
Don Zivkovic
Brian Connolly

Founded in 1988 as Zivkovic Associates Architects, the New York City firm of Zivkovic Connolly Architects has completed projects for a diverse clientele. **Don Zivkovic** earned a degree in architecture from the University of Western Australia and a Master's degree in Architectural history from Columbia University. He is past director of the Architects' Council of New York City and president of the Society of American Registered Architects. **Brian Connolly,** a graduate of Trinity College in Dublin, Ireland, joined the firm in 1989; he is a fellow at the Institute of Classical Architecture and Classical America. The range of their projects includes, on the one hand, a modern embassy in Manhattan for the Government of Botswana and, on the other, the rehabilitation of a 19th-century landmark banking-hall at Cornhill, in London, England, as well as work at the UN, West Point and Lincoln Center. The firm is noted for its finely designed townhouses and country residences, including Bacchus House in Greenwich Village, the new Mt. Taurus house and estate in Cold Spring, New York, and a 30-acre stone-manor estate in Greenwich, Connecticut. Their work has received numerous awards and is published internationally. In 2007 the firm received the prestigious Palladio Award for the design, in collaboration with John Simpson of London, of the addition to the Mrs. Amory S. Carhart house at 3 East 95th Street in Carnegie Hill, for which they were also the renovation architects.

GLOSSARY OF
ARCHITECTURAL TERMS

acanthus An ornamentation suggesting the leaves of the acanthus, a family of prickly herbs in the Mediterranean region.

anthemion An architectural ornament of floral forms derived from the honeysuckle or palm leaves in a cluster radiating upward.

arcade A series of arches supported on piers or columns.

architrave The lowest part of a classical entablature. See entablature.

archivolt An ornamental molding around an arch.

areaway A sunken space affording access, air and light to a basement.

ashlar Square-cut finished stone, laid evenly.

balconette A small balcony, usually accessed by French doors. Also called a Juliet balcony.

balustrade A series of short upright posts or pillars (balusters) that support a railing running along the edge of a porch, balcony or roof.

band course See belt course.

barrel vault A continuous, unbroken semicircular arched ceiling or roof of stone or brick, sometimes imitated in plaster or wood.

bartizan A small turret-like structure projecting from a building.

battlement A parapet with open spaces that surmounts a wall, used for defense or decoration.

bay A vertical division of a facade, marked off by fenestration or other structural component.

bay window A projecting unit of the exterior of a building containing windows, rising from the ground or with some form of support. See oriel.

bellflower A showy plant with alternating leaves and bell-shaped flowers, used in architectural decoration.

belt course A narrow horizontal band of masonry that is usually of a different color or material from the rest of the exterior, used to divide a facade into horizontal sections. It may be flat-surfaced, molded or richly carved. Also called a band course or string course.

bezant A flat disk used as an architectural ornament.

blind arch An arch that frames a wall section, as opposed to framing an opening.

bollard A short heavy post of metal, wood or concrete, often set in a series to delimit an area or restrict access by vehicles.

bracket A support, usually decorative, that projects from a wall under a cornice, balcony, lintel, sill or pediment.

bull's-eye window A small circular window, often at the top story. Also known as an oculus window.

cantilever A structure or beam supported only at one end.

capital The top member, usually decorated, of a column or pilaster.

cartouche An ornamental frame, oval or scroll-like, flat or convex, often bearing a crest or inscription.

casement A window that is hinged on the side.

chamfer A surface formed by beveling the edge of two adjoining planes, often at 45°. Also, a channel or groove in wood or stone.

chamfered corner The beveled edge of a building or corner window, often seen in Art Deco-style buildings.

colonette A small, short column, often ornamental.

colonnade A regular row of columns supporting a beam, entablature or series of arches.

column A vertical cylindrical support. In classical design it is composed of a base (except in the Greek Doric order), a long, gradually tapered shaft and a capital.

console A compound-curved bracket that supports a carved figure, shelf or other horizontal element.

contextual New architectural design that relates to antecedent buildings in the immediate neighborhood.

coping A cap or cover on a wall parapet that protects the masonry from water.

corbel A block or brick projecting from a wall to support a cornice, beam or other horizontal member.

corbeling, corbeled An overlapping arrangement of bricks in which each course steps outward and upward from the face of a wall.

cornice A projecting horizontal molding at a rooftop, the top of an entablature or other segment of a facade.

course A continuous horizontal row of bricks or range of masonry throughout a wall.

crenelation (crenellation) A notched or indented opening in a battlement or parapet.

cresting A decorative element, often of iron, usually running along the ridge of a roof.

crown section The uppermost or attic section of a building's facade, usually delineated by a band course. The typical neo-Renaissance building consists of a base section, midsection and crown section.

cupola A small domed roof on top of a larger roof.

dentil A small rectangular block used in a series beneath a cornice or other architectural element.

diaper A pattern of small repeating figures connecting with or growing out of one another.

dogtooth A design composed of closely-spaced pyramidic ornaments formed by sculptured leaves radiating from a raised center; the pattern is diamonds within squares.

Doric The oldest and simplest of the classical orders, recognizable by its capital consisting of a square block resting on a circular one. The column may be smooth or fluted. The Greek Doric has no base, differentiating it from the Roman order.

dormer A vertical roofed structure, usually housing a window, projecting from a sloping roof that makes the attic space inside usable as a room.

drip molding A projecting molding around the top of a door or window frame, often channeled vertically and then at right angles at the sides to deflect rain. Also called a drip lintel.

ear A small extending piece on each side of a top of a door or window enframement. Also called a crossette, eared enframement or eared lintel.

egg-and-dart molding A convex molding pattern of alternating ovals (eggs) and downward-pointing arrowheads (darts).

engaged column A column attached to or built into a wall.

English bond A pattern of bricklaying with alternating rows of headers (ends) and stretchers (long sides).

entablature In classical architecture, the major horizontal part supported by columns or pilasters, consisting of the architrave, frieze, and cornice.

eyebrow dormer A curved dormer with no sides.

escutcheon A shield-shaped decoration, sometimes displaying a coat of arms or other motif.

facade The main exterior face of a building.

fanlight A semicircular or semi-elliptical window above a door, usually inset with glazing bars radiating like a fan.

fascia A plain band in the architrave of an entablature.

fenestration The arrangement of windows in a building.

festoon A decorative representation of a garland of flowers, fruit, leaves or piece of cloth suspended between two points. Also called a garland or swag.

finial The crowning ornament on a pointed element, such as a spire.

fleur-de-lis A stylized three-petal iris flower.

Flemish bond A pattern of bricklaying in which each course consists of alternating headers and stretchers. The courses alternate so that each header is centered above the stretcher below it, and vice versa.

foliate (foliated) Ornamented with leaves. Brackets often display foliate carving.

French flat(s) An early term for a post-Civil War apartment with generously-sized rooms all on one floor, or a building with such living units. Often such an apartment house had a common kitchen and dining room like a hotel.

French window A casement window that opens down to the floor like a door; usually in pairs. First used at Versailles in the 1680s.

fret, fretwork A pattern of horizontal and vertical lines repeated to form a band. Also called a meander or Greek key pattern.

frieze The decorated band on an entablature between the architrave and the cornice; a similar band in a belt course or below a roof cornice.

gable The triangular wall area beneath a pitched roof.

gambrel roof A pitched roof with two slopes on each of its two sides, the lower slope being steeper than the upper slope.

gargoyle A water spout in the form of a grotesque human or animal figure, projecting from a building; a grotesquely carved figure.

Greek key A geometrical ornament consisting of horizontal and vertical lines, repeated to form a pattern. Also called a fret or fretwork.

grille A decorative grating, usually of iron, used to protect an opening.

guilloche An ornamental border design formed of two or more interlaced bands around a series of circular voids.

guttae A group of small peg-like ornaments in the Doric entablature, projecting below a horizontal cross-member, especially below triglyphs.

header A brick positioned so that its short end is exposed.

hipped roof A roof with four uniformly pitched sides; the roof has no gables.

historic In architecture, dating from or preserved from the original construction.

hood A projection that shelters an element such as a door or window; hood molding.

imbrication A pattern resembling the regular overlapping of tiles or shingles, usually cut in a scalloped shape.

impost block A block, capital or molding from which an arch springs.

incised Having a surface that has been cut into with decorative designs. Popular in neo-Grec and Queen Anne architecture.

Ionic order An order of classical Greek architecture with capitals resembling rams' horns or scrolls (volutes). See volute.

jigsaw carving A curved wooden ornament cut with a thin narrow saw blade, often seen in Queen Anne-style houses. Also called scroll-sawn.

keyed enframement A block, often used in a series, that projects beyond the edge of the frame of a door or window and is joined to the surrounding masonry. See quoin.

keystone A central wedge-shaped stone at the crown of an arch or vault that locks the other pieces in place; also used as a decorative element. See voussoir.

lintel A horizontal beam or stone bridging an opening, and usually carrying the load above the opening.

loggia An arcaded or colonnaded gallery open on one or more sides, sometimes attached to a larger structure.

lunette A crescent-shaped or semicircular window on a wall surface.

mansard roof A roof having two slopes on all four sides, the lower slopes being steeper than the upper slopes.

marquee A permanent canopy, often of metal and glass, projecting over an entrance.

mask An often grotesque representation of a head or face. Also called a mascaron.

modillion A projecting horizontal scroll-shaped bracket or console, arranged in pairs or in a series to support a cornice.

molding A decorative band used to trim openings, wall planes or structural elements.

mullion A slender vertical strip separating the panes of glass in a window or other opening.

muntin A thin strip separating the panes of glass in a window.

mutules Oversized, widely spaced dentil-like flat projections or blocks.

newel The main post that supports the handrail at the foot of a flight of stairs or a stoop.

oculus window See bull's-eye window.

ogee An S-shaped double curve used in arches or moldings, found in Moorish and French architecture.

order An accepted style of classical architecture, consisting of an entablature and its supporting columns. The five orders are Doric, Ionic, Corinthian (all of Greek origin), Tuscan (of Etruscan origin), and Composite (of Roman origin).

oriel A bay window carried on corbels or brackets.

Palladian window A tripartite window with a large arched central opening flanked by smaller rectangular windows, separated by posts or pilasters.

palmette A stylized palm-leaf shape used as a decorative element in classical architecture.

pantile A roofing tile whose cross section is an ogee curve or an arc of a circle. Tiles are laid with the down curve of one overlapping the upturn of the next one. Often seen in Mediterranean architecture.

parapet A low, solid protective wall at the edge of a roof or other raised area.

patera A circular or oval disk-like ornament, often decorated with acanthus leaves.

pediment An ornamental gable, usually triangular, above a door or window, framed by a cornice below and two raking cornices above. A broken pediment has raking cornices that do not meet at the peak, usually to make room for a sculpture or ornamental element.

piano nobile The parlor floor (in Italian, the "noble floor"), usually the level above the ground floor, with higher ceilings than other stories in the house.

pier A vertical structural element, usually placed at intervals to support or strengthen a wall.

pilaster A flattened engaged column, usually with capital and base.

plinth A base supporting a column, pilaster or statue.

pointed arch An arch having a pointed crown. Also called a Gothic arch or lancet arch.

porte-cochère A covered entrance large enough for wheeled vehicles.

portico A small porch with a roof supported by columns, often in front of the entrance to a building.

putti Figures of Cupid-like baby boys used in architectural adornment. (The singular is putto.)

quatrefoil A four-lobed foliation.

quoin A structural block, usually of masonry and of alternating lengths or sizes, used in a series to reinforce the corners of a building. Often imitated for decorative purposes, as at the sides of windows or doors. See keyed enframement.

relief A carved or molded ornament projecting from a flat surface.

reveal The side of an opening for a door or window between the frame and the outer surface of a wall.

ribbon windows Grouped horizontal windows, often casement-style. In Art Deco buildings, windows running the full width of a facade for a "streaming" effect.

rock-faced Masonry that retains or simulates the irregular texture of natural stone.

rondel (roundel) A circular figure or object, often used decoratively.

rope molding A twisted molding resembling a rope or cable.

rosette A round floral ornament.

round arch A semicircular arch.

row house One of a group of an unbroken line of attached houses that share common side walls (party walls).

rubble stone Irregularly shaped rough-textured stone laid in a random manner.

rustication Stonework with heavily beveled or deeply recessed joints, usually at the lower floors of a building.

sash The framework in which panes of glass are set in a window. Sash may be divided with muntins (e.g., six-over-six double-hung sash).

scroll Ornamentation resembling the curves of a loosely-rolled parchment scroll.

segmental arch An arch in the form of a segment of a semicircle.

shaft The main body of a column between the base and the capital.

sidelight A vertically framed window, often subdivided into panes, flanking a door.

skew-back A slanting surface or stone supporting a segmental arch.

soffit The exposed underside of an architectural element such as an arch, balcony, vault or roof.

soldier course A course of bricks laid vertically.

spandrel The triangular wall segment between arches. Also, a panel between the top of one window and the sill of another window directly above it.

splay A slant-sided surface or masonry panel cut into a building wall above a door or window. Lintels are often splayed.

stoop Steps with railings, of iron or masonry, that lead up to a front door (from the Dutch "stoep").

stretcher A brick laid horizontally with its length parallel to the wall.

string course See belt course.

stucco A rough coating for exterior walls made from Portland cement, lime, sand and water. (Portland cement is named after Portland, England, for its resemblance to limestone quarried there.)

swag See festoon.

swan's neck pediment A broken pediment formed by a pair of S-curves above the horizontal cornice and rising to a pair of scrolls on either side of the center, from which a finial often rises.

terra cotta Hard-fired clay, glazed or unglazed, molded into ornamental elements.

transom The crossbar separating a door from a window or fanlight above it; the window above the crossbar of a door.

tracery Ornamental work with branching lines or foils, often used in the top of a Gothic window.

trefoil A three-lobed decorative form used in Gothic-style architecture. Often repeated within a Gothic arch or tracery. Quatrefoil, cinquefoil.

triglyph A block on a Doric frieze having two vertical grooves down

the center and a half groove at either end, creating three narrow panels. Always used in a series.

Tuscan order The simplest form of the five classical orders, consisting of non-fluted columns with Doric-like capitals supporting a plain entablature.

tympanum The space within the moldings of a pediment, often ornamented with sculpture. (The plural is tympana.)

vault An arched stone or brick ceiling or roof.

verdigris A green or bluish-green coating that forms on weathered copper, brass and bronze.

Vitruvian scroll A series of scrolls forming a stylized wave pattern. Also called a wave scroll.

volute A carved spiral form in classical architecture, often used in large pairs on Ionic capitals or in smaller pairs on Corinthian columns.

voussoir A wedge-shaped stone of an arch, other than the keystone.

wing wall A wall of a stoop that widens at the bottom and usually curves outward.

wrought iron Iron that is forged or hammered, as opposed to cast or molded.

ziggurat A rhythmic ascension, usually symmetrical, achieved by the building up of successively smaller stepped-back blocks. The ziggurat is characteristic of Art Deco design.

INDEX TO BUILDINGS

HOW TO USE THIS INDEX

The index reflects the order of building write-ups in this Guide. First, we list the avenues, starting at Fifth Avenue at 86th Street, with address numbers progressing north. The south-to-north sequence is repeated for Madison, Park and Lexington avenues. Cross streets start at 86th Street and Fifth Avenue, with numbers increasing as they progress east, up to Third Avenue. We return to Fifth Avenue and repeat the west-to-east sequence for 87th Street, 88th Street, and so on. In some cases Carnegie Hill buildings have both an avenue and a street address; our Guide and index reflect the residential address, unless otherwise noted.

The column **Address / Building Owner or Institution** lists the original or former owner (if historically noteworthy), followed by the name of the museum, house of worship, school or other public building at that address. Because of space constraints the names may be truncated; we ask your forbearance. Full names are included in the building write-up.

** The column **Architect(s)** rarely allows space for more than one name, so when you see a double asterisk ** it means that the cited architect is the original designer, and that there are other architects who collaborated initially or who made substantial facade changes in subsequent years. The building write-up covers all known architects associated with the building.

* The column **Year Completed** lists the final year of the original construction, even though the building may have undergone several reincarnations in subsequent decades. A single asterisk * indicates that the date is an estimate.

• A dot • in the column **CH Historic District** indicates that the building falls within the Expanded Carnegie Hill Historic District, as designated by the New York City Landmarks Preservation Commission in 1994.

• A dot • in the column **Landmarked** indicates that the building is an individual landmark, designated by the Landmarks Preservation Commission.

x If the column **Page** shows an **x** rather than a page number, it means that there is no write-up. Of the more than 430 buildings and building groups in Carnegie Hill, there a few about which we could find little or no information. Again, we ask your forbearance, and invite readers to provide us with historical building facts that we can include in future editions of the Architectural Guide.

Address / Original Owner or Institution	Architect(s)	YEAR COMPLETED	CH HISTORIC DISTRICT	LANDMARKED	PAGE
1326 Madison Ave	Neville & Bagge	1900	•		45
1339-1351 Madison Ave: see 71 East 94th St					
1340 Madison Ave	A.B. Ogden & Son	1894	•		45
1350 Madison Ave	John C. Burne	1894	•		46
1356 Madison Ave: see 27-29 East 95th St					
1361 Madison Ave / Madison Court	Harry B. Mulliken	1901	•		46
1391 Madison Ave	Neville & Bagge	1904			47
1392-94 & 1396-98 Madison Ave	George F. Pelham	1906			47

PARK AVENUE

1040 Park Ave	Delano & Aldrich	1924			48
1045 Park Ave	Schwartz & Gross	1923			48
1049 Park Ave	Mills & Bottomley	1919			49
1050 Park Ave	J.E.R. Carpenter	1923			49
1055 Park Ave	H. Thomas O'Hara	2009			50
1060 Park Ave	J.E.R. Carpenter	1929			50
1065 Park Ave	Stephen C. Lyras	1974			50
1067 Park Ave	Gilbert A. Schellenger	1885			51
1070 Park Ave	Schwartz & Gross	1928			51
1075 Park Ave	George & Edward Blum	1923			52
1080 Park Ave	Frederick T. Camp**	1887			52
1082 Park Ave	Frederick T. Camp**	1887			52
1085 Park Ave	Schwartz & Gross	1926			53
1088 Park Ave	Mott B. Schmidt	1925			54
1095 Park Ave	Schwartz & Gross	1930			54
1100 Park Ave	DePace & Juster	1930			55
1105 Park Ave	Rosario Candela	1923			55
1108 & 1110 Park Ave	unknown	1856			56
1111 Park Ave	Schwartz & Gross	1926			56
1112 Park Ave	Emery Roth	1927			57
1120 Park Ave	George F. Pelham	1930			57
1125 Park Ave	Schwartz & Gross	1926			58
1130 Park Ave	George F. Pelham	1927			58
1133 Park Ave	Nathan Korn	1924			58
1140-1144 Park Ave / Brick Presbyterian Church	York & Sawyer	1938	•		59
1141-1149 Park Ave	John Sullivan**	1886	•		60
1150 Park Ave	George F. Pelham, Jr.	1940	•		62
1155 Park Ave	Robert T. Lyons**	1914	•		63
Park Ave Mall (92nd St) "Night Presence IV"	Louise Nevelson (artist)	1972	•		63
1160 Park Ave	George F. Pelham	1926	•		64
1165 Park Ave	Schwartz & Gross	1926	•		64
1172 Park Ave	Rosario Candela	1926	•		64

Address / Original Owner or Institution	Architect(s)	YEAR COMPLETED	CH HISTORIC DISTRICT	LANDMARKED	PAGE
CROSS STREETS: 86TH STREET					
7 East 86th St	Schuman & Lichtenstein	1960	•		87
9 East 86th St / Woodward house	Delano & Aldrich	1918	•		87
11 East 86th St	Sylvan & Robert L. Bien	1961			87
25 East 86th St (1178-1188 Madison, 20 E. 87 St	Sugarman & Berger	1929			88
49 East 86th St	Pennington & Lewis	1931			88
55 East 86th St	Schwartz & Gross	1924			89
61 East 86th St	Neville & Bagge	1900			89
103 East 86th St	Schwartz & Gross	1914			90
115 East 86th St	George F. Pelham, Jr.	1927			90
123 East 86th St / Citibank	Walker & Gillette	1927			90
151-155 East 86th St	William Whitehall**	1926			91
157 East 86th St	Howells & Stokes**	1903			91
163 East 86th St	E. F. Platt & Bros.	1927			x
173 East 86th St	Charles Stegmayer (?)**	1909			x

Address / Original Owner or Institution	Architect(s)	YEAR COMPLETED	CH HISTORIC DISTRICT	LANDMARKED	PAGE
87TH STREET					
6 East 87th St / Phipps house / Liederkranz Club	Grosvenor Atterbury	1902	•		92
10 East 87th St	F. Augenfeld, J. Pokorny**	1958	•		92
11 East 87th St	Tito di Vincenzo	1953			93
12 East 87th St / The Capitol	George & Edward Blum	1911	•		93
21 East 87th St	Emery Roth	1927			94
47 East 87th St	Leonard Schultze & Assoc.	1947			95
50 East 87th St / Park Avenue Synagogue	Walter S. Schneider**	1926			95
55 East 87th St / The Parc	Schuman & Lichtenstein	1961			96
56 East 87th St	George F. Pelham	1905			96
62 East 87th St	Edward Wenz	1891			97
110 East 87th St	Boak & Paris	1927			97
111 East 87th St / Church of the Advent Hope	Alfred B. Heiser	1956			97
115 East 87th St / 110 East 88th St; Carnegie Towers / R.F. Kennedy School, P.S. 169	Feldman-Misthopoulos	1973			98
120 East 87th St / Park Avenue Court	Skidmore Owings & Merrill	1990			98
125 East 87th St / Sherry House	Sugarman & Berger	1962			99
150 East 87th St	Albert Huttira	1891			99
153 East 87th St / Morgan House	Richard Deeves & Sons	1926			100
154-164 East 87th St / Alan Garage & Franklin Hotel	Frank J. Schefcik	1930			100
159 East 87th St / "13 Hook & Ladder 13"	William Williams (?)	1863*			101
163-167 East 87th St	unknown				x
169 East 87th St	Richard Berger**	1896			102
170 East 87th St / The Gotham	Frank Williams & Partners	1994			102
175 East 87th St / Doyle Galleries	Charles Stegmayer	1909			102

Address / Original Owner or Institution	Architect(s)	YEAR COMPLETED	CH HISTORIC DISTRICT	LANDMARKED	PAGE
115 East 89th St	George F. Pelham	1923			119
120 East 89th St	Irving Margon	1936			119
121 East 89th St	Henry J. Hardenbergh	1888	•		119
141 East 89th St	Herbert Alpert	1960			x
146-156 East 89th St	Hubert, Pirsson & Co.	1887	•		120
157 East 89th St	Barney & Chapman	1905			121
160 East 89th St	Boak & Paris	1938			122
161-163 East 89th St	unknown				x
168-170 East 89th St	unknown				x

90th STREET

Address / Original Owner or Institution	Architect(s)	YEAR COMPLETED	CH HISTORIC DISTRICT	LANDMARKED	PAGE
2 East 90th St / Church of the Heavenly Rest	Hardie Phillip**	1930	•		122
9 East 90th St / McAlpin-Miller house	George Keister	1903	•	•	123
11 East 90th St / MsAlpin-Minot house	Barney & Chapman**	1903	•	•	124
14 East 90th St; 1246-1254 Madison Ave	J.E.R. Carpenter	1929	•		125
15 East 90th St / Emily Trevor house	Mott B. Schmidt	1928	•	•	126
17 East 90th St / Wanamaker Munn / Spence	F. Burrall Hoffman, Jr.	1919	•	•	126
21 East 90th St	George F. Pelham	1927	•		127
51 East 90th St	George F. Pelham	1926	•		127
55 East 90th St / Horace Mann School	Whitfield & King	1904	•		128
57-65 East 90th St	J.C. Cady & Co.**	1887	•		128
112 East 90th St	Eugene Parker	1884			x
113 East 90th St / Allan Stone Gallery	George E. Harney	1878			129
114 East 90th St	Emery Roth	1925			130
115 East 90th St	George F. Pelham	1917			131
120 East 90th St / Trafalgar House	H. I. Feldman	1963			131
121 East 90th St	unknown	1875			131
123-125 East 90th St	Loonie & Parker	1888			131
127-129 East 90th St	Frank Wennemer	1890			132
147 East 90th St	unknown	1885?			x
151 East 90th St	Horace Ginsbern	1937			132
161 East 90th St / Trafalgar Court	Warren & Wetmore	1925			132
162 East 90th St	Bernstein & Bernstein	1901			133
164 & 166 East 90th St	Jacob H. Valentine (?)	1879			133
165 & 167 East 90th St	unknown	1890*			134
168-172 East 90th St	Frank Wennemer	1890			134
169 East 90th St	unknown				x
171-175 East 90th St	A.B. Ogden & Son	1891			135
174 East 90th St	unknown				x
181 East 90th St / The Metropolitan	Philip Johnson**	2004			135

Address / Original Owner or Institution	Architect(s)	YEAR COMPLETED	CH HISTORIC DISTRICT	LANDMARKED	PAGE
168 East 91st St	Charles Stegmayer	1896			157
169 East 91st St	Wechsler, Grasso & Menziuso	1985			158
170 East 91st St	John Hauser	1901			158

92ND STREET

Address / Original Owner or Institution	Architect(s)	YEAR COMPLETED	CH HISTORIC DISTRICT	LANDMARKED	PAGE
1-3, 9, and 15-25 East 92nd St	A.B. Ogden & Son	1891	•		159
5-7 East 92nd St / Garrard Winston house	William J. Creighton	1935	•		160
11 East 92nd St / Untermyer-Clarkson house	Hugo Kafka & Co.**	1885	•		161
6-14 East 92nd St	Thomas Graham	1892	•		161
16-26 East 92nd St / Nightingale-Bamford School	Delano & Aldrich**	1929	•		162
28 & 30 East 92nd St	Henry J. Hardenbergh	1895	•		163
46, 52-56 East 92nd St	William Graul	1888	•		164
48 East 92nd St / John Sloane house	James C. MacKenzie, Jr.	1932	•		164
47 East 92nd St	Keeler & Fernald	1928	•		165
49 & 51 East 92nd St	Frank Wennemer**	1888	•		165
53 & 55 East 92nd St	Louis Entzer, Jr.**	1894	•		166
57-61 East 92nd St	Brandt & Co.**	1886	•		166
58 & 60 East 92nd St	Theodore E. Thompson	1883	•		167
62 East 92nd St / Brick Church Parish House, Sch.	Lawrence F. Peck	1924	•		168
63 & 65 East 92nd St	Brandt & Co.**	1886	•		168
66-70 East 92nd St / Brick Church Parish House	Adams & Woodbridge	1949	•		168
115 East 92nd St	George F. Pelham	1928	•		169
116 East 92nd St	Edward Wenz	1889	•		170
118 East 92nd St	Frank P. Farinella	1976	•		170
120 & 122 East 92nd St	unknown; Albro Howell?	1871	•	•	170
121 & 123 East 92nd St	Jacob H. Valentine	1869	•		171
124 East 92nd St	Weber & Drosser**	1887	•		172
125 East 92nd St	David B. Mann/MR Arch.	2007	•		172
126 & 128 East 92nd St	Weber & Drosser**	1888	•		173
127-135 East 92nd St	C. Abbott French & Co.	1887	•		173
130 & 132 East 92nd St	Weber & Drosser**	1888	•		175
134-138 East 92nd St	Alfred B. Ogden	1881	•		175
140 East 92nd St / The Mildred	Martin V.B. Ferdon	1900	•		175
145 East 92nd St	George F. Pelham	1929			176
151 East 92nd St	John Wells Green (?)	1853*			176
153 East 92nd St	William Hughes	1896			177
155, 159, & 163 East 92nd St	Edward A. Mayers	1906			177
160 East 92nd St	Albro Howell	1853		•	178
162 East 92nd St	Delano & Aldrich	1917			178
166 East 92nd St	Howard Stokes Patterson	1927			179
169 & 171 East 92nd St	unknown				x
170 East 92nd St	Richard Berger	1890			179

Address / Original Owner or Institution	Architect(s)	YEAR COMPLETED	CH HISTORIC DISTRICT	LANDMARKED	PAGE
13 East 94th St	Cleverdon & Putzel**	1893	•		205
10-12 East 94th St / J.H. Choate, Jr. house	George B. de Gersdorff	1920	•		205
14 East 94th St	McCrea & Sharpe	1926	•		206
16 East 94th St	A.B. Ogden & Son**	1892	•		206
15; 21-25 East 94th St	Cleverdon & Putzel**	1894	•		206
17 & 19 East 94th St / Ramakrishna-Vivekananda	Cleverdon & Putzel**	1893	•		208
18-24 East 94th St	Van Vleck & Goldsmith	1899	•		209
40 East 94th St / Carnegie Hill Tower	Edward V. Giannasca	1983			210
64 East 94th St	Jules Lewis	1960			210
71 East 94th St / Hunter College Campus Sch; 1339-1351 Madison Ave / Squadron A Armory	Morris Ketchum, Jr.; John Rochester Thomas	1971 1895			211
121-137 East 94th St	F.S. Barus	1879	•		212
130 East 94th St	George F. Pelham	1924	•		213
138 East 94th St	Neville & Bagge	1902	•		213
139 East 94th St	Boak & Paris	1928	•		214
152 East 94th St	Boak & Paris	1937			214
157-179 East 94th St; 158-180 East 95th St	Thom & Wilson	1880			215
170 East 94th St	George G. Miller	1928			217
178-180 East 94th St	L.C. Weir	1924			x
183 East 94th St	Charles Baxter	1877			217

95TH STREET

Address / Original Owner or Institution	Architect(s)	YEAR COMPLETED	CH HISTORIC DISTRICT	LANDMARKED	PAGE
3 East 95th St / Mrs. Amory Carhart house	Horace Trumbauer**	1921	•	•	218
4 East 95th St	J.E.R. Carpenter	1924	•		219
7 East 95th St / Edith & Ernesto Fabbri house / House of the Redeemer	Egisto Fabbri Grosvenor Atterbury	1917	•	•	220
10-20 East 95th St	Henry Anderson	1890	•		221
17 & 19 East 95th St	Neville & Bagge	1899	•		222
22-28 East 95th St	Thomas Graham	1901	•		222
27 & 29 East 95th St; 1356 Madison Ave The Woodbury and the Elmscourt	Frederick Jacobson	1899	•		223
53, 57 & 61 East 95th St	Rouse & Sloan	1905			224
112 & 114 East 95th St; see 1213-1217 Park Ave					
116-138 East 95th St	C. Abbott French & Co.	1888	•		225
115-127 East 95th St	Louis Entzer, Jr.	1892	•		226
129-143 East 95th St	Frank Wennemer**	1890	•		226
140 East 95th St; 1466-1472 Lexington Ave	Springsteen & Goldhammer	1929	•		227
158-180 East 95th St: see 157-181 East 94th St					

96TH STREET

Address / Original Owner or Institution	Architect(s)	YEAR COMPLETED	CH HISTORIC DISTRICT	LANDMARKED	PAGE
7 East 96th St / Ogden Codman, Jr. house; Manhattan Country School	Ogden Codman, Jr.	1913	•	•	228
8 East 96th St	Rosario Candela	1928	•		229
9 East 96th St	Gronenberg & Leuchtag	1926	•		229

Address / Original Owner or Institution	Architect(s)	YEAR COMPLETED	CH HISTORIC DISTRICT	LANDMARKED	PAGE
12 East 96th St / Livingston house / La Scuola d'Italia Gugliemo Marconi	Ogden Codman, Jr.	1916	•		230
14 East 96th St	Levin Deliso White Songer	1981	•		230
15 East 96th St / Lucy Drexel Dahlgren house	Ogden Codman, Jr.	1915	•	•	230
16-24 East 96th St / The Queenston	Clinton & Russell	1906	•		231
17 East 96th St	Sugarman, Hess & Berger	1924	•		232
21 East 96th St	H.T. O'Hara & Barry Rice	2005			232
49 East 96th St	Thomas W. Lamb	1930			232
50 East 96th St / Woodward Hall	George F. Pelham**	1906			233
53-55, 57-59 East 96th St	George F. Pelham	1906			234
60 East 96th St	Emery Roth	1928			234
65 East 96th St / The Gatsby	George F. Pelham	1924			235
70 East 96th St	Rosario Candela	1929			235
108 East 96th St	SLCE Architects	1994			236
112 East 96th St / 96th Street Library	Babb, Cook & Willard	1905			237
115-117 & 119 East 96th St	Bernstein & Bernstein	1904			237
128-136 East 96th St	Louis Entzer	1892			238
135 East 96th St / St. Francis de Sales Church	O'Connor and Metcalf**	1903			238
138 East 96th St; 1486 Lexington Ave	Frank Wennemer	1890			238
166 East 96th St	Howard Stokes Patterson	1928			239
201 East 96th St / Islamic Cultural Center of NY	Skidmore Owings & Merrill**	1996			240

97TH AND 98TH STREETS

6 East 97th St	Ellis, Aaronson & Heidrich	1928			241
9 East 97th St / Hortense Court	Edward Wenz	1899			241
12 East 97th St	Lafayette Goldstone	1928			242
15 East 97th St / St. Nicholas Orth. Cathedral	John Bergesen	1902		•	242
17 East 97th St / The Mannados	David Stone	1906			244
51 East 97th St	George F. Pelham	1904			244
4 East 98th St / St. Bernard's School	Delano & Aldrich	1915			245
5-17 East 98th St / Mt. Sinai Sch. of Medicine	Robert D. Kohn	1926			246
16 East 98th St	George Keister	1924			247

BIBLIOGRAPHY

The following sources are among those identified by our researchers and writers.

Alpern, Andrew. *The New York Apartment Houses of Rosario Candela and James Carpenter.* New York: Acanthus Press, 2001.

American Architects Dictionary, 1962.

The Art and Architecture of the Brick Presbyterian Church, 2004.

Bedford, Steven McLeod. *John Russell Pope: Architect of Empire.* New York: Rizzoli, 1998.

Carley, Rachel. *The Visual Dictionary of American Domestic Architecture.* New York: Roundtable Press, Inc., 1994.

Ching, Francis D.K. *A Visual Dictionary of Architecture.* New York: John Wiley & Sons, Inc., 1995.

Crosbie, Michael J. *Architecture for the Gods.* Images Publishing Group, 2006

Dictionary of Scottish Architects 1840-1940.

Dolkart, Andrew S. *Touring the Upper East Side: Walks in Five Historic Districts.* New York Landmarks Conservancy, 1995.

Dolkart, Andrew S. and Susan Tunick. *George and Edward Blum: Texture and Design in New York Apartment House Architecture.* New York: The Friends of Terra Cotta Press, 1993.

Folsom, Merrill. *Great American Mansions.* Hastings House, 2000.

Francis, Dennis Steadman. *Architects in Practice in New York City 1900-1940.* New York: Committee for the Preservation of Architectural Records, 1979.

Francis, Dennis Steadman. *Architects in Practice in New York City 1840-1900.* New York: Committee for the Preservation of Architectural Records, 1979.

Goldberger, Paul. *The City Observed: New York A Guide to the Architecture of Manhattan.* Vintage Books, 1979.

Hewitt, Mark Alan and Robert A. Stern. *The Architecture of Mott B. Schmidt.* Rizzoli Staff Edition, 1991.

Kathrens, Michael C. *Great Houses of New York 1880-1930.* New York: Acanthus Press, 2005.

Landmarks Preservation Commission Designation Reports and Architects' Appendices. *Expanded Carnegie Hill Historic District,* New York, 1993; *Hardenbergh/Rhinelander Historic District,* New York, 1998; *Upper East Side Historic District,* New York, 1981; *West End Collegiate and Upper West Side/Central Park West Historic District,* New York, 1990; *Metropolitan Museum Historic District,* New York, 1977

Macmillan Encyclopedia of Architects. New York: Free Press, 1982.

Friends of the Upper East Side Historic Districts. *Modern Architecture on the Upper East Side: Landmarks of the Future.* 2001.

Morrone, Francis. *The Architectural Guide to New York City.* Salt Lake City:
Gibbs Smith, 2002.

Municipal Archives Docket Books.

Pennoyer, Peter and Anne Walker. *The Architecture of Delano & Aldrich.*
New York: W.W. Norton & Company, 2003.

Pennoyer, Peter and Anne Walker. *The Architecture of Warren & Wetmore.*
New York: W.W. Norton & Company, 2006.

Stern, Robert A.M., John M. Massengale, and Gregory Gilmartin.
New York 1900: Metropolitan Architecture and Urbanism 1890-1915. New York:
Rizzoli International Publications, Inc., 1983.

Stern, Robert A.M., Gregory Gilmartin, and Thomas Mellins.
New York 1930: Architecture and Urbanism Between the Two World Wars.
New York: Rizzoli International Publications, Inc., 1987.

Stern, Robert A.M., Thomas Mellins., and David Fishman.
*New York 1960: Architecture and Urbanism Between the Second World War and the
Bicentennial.* New York: Rizzoli International Publications, Inc., 1995.

Trager, James. *Park Avenue: Street of Dreams.* New York: Atheneum 1990

Vlack, Don. *Art Deco Architecture in New York City 1920-1940.* Harper & Row, 1974.

Ward, James. *Architects in Practice in New York City 1900-1940.* New York, 1989.

White, Norval, and Elliot Willensky. *AIA Guide to New York City.* 3rd ed.
New York: Harcourt Brace Jovanovich, 1988.

Withey, Henry F. and Elsie Rathburn Withey. *Biographical Dictionary of
American Architects (Deceased).* Los Angeles: Hennessey & Ingalls, Inc 1970.

Websites:

about.architecture; american-architects; archinform; archiplanet;
arch.columbia; Carter B. Horsley *The Upper East Side Book;* cityrealty;
Dictionary of Scottish Architects; emporis; greatbuildings; New York
Architecture Images; *New York Times* obituaries and archives; nyc-architecture;
NYC Department of Buildings; Office for Metropolitan History
(Christopher Gray); Society of Architectural Historians; propertyshark;
ProQuest; thecityreview; wallfly, wickipedia; plus many architects' websites.

Newspapers and Periodicals:

New York Observer: Articles by Greg Sargent, Gabriel Sherman, others.

New York Sun: Francis Morrone "Abroad in New York," articles by James
Gardner, others.

New York Times: Christopher Gray "Streetscapes," articles by Paula Deitz,
Ralph Gardner, Jr., Grace Glueck, Paul Goldberger, Marc Santora, Peter
Slatin, Wendy Moonan, Robin Pogrebin, others.

Avenue Magazine, Carnegie Hill News, Metropolis, Promenade

COLUMBIA UNIVERSITY LIBRARIES

0045952795